NATIONAL COLLECTIVE IDENTITY

Social Constructs and International Systems

Rodney Bruce Hall

COLUMBIA UNIVERSITY PRESS NEW YORK

Columbia University Press
Publishers Since 1893
New York Chichester, West Sussex

Library of Congress Cataloging-in-Publication Data

Hall, Rodney Bruce, 1960–
National collective identity : social constructs and international systems / Rodney Bruce Hall.
p. cm.
Includes bibliographical references (p.) and index.
ISBN 0-231-11150-9 (CL : acid-free paper). — ISBN 0-231-11151-7 (PA : acid-free paper)
1. International relations and culture. 2. International relations—Philosophy. I. Title.
JZ1251.H35 1999
320.1′2—dc21 98-27127
CIP

Casebound editions of Columbia University Press books are printed on permanent and durable acid-free paper.
Printed in the United States of America
c 10 9 8 7 6 5 4 3 2 1
p 10 9 8 7 6 5 4 3 2 1

For Joan Marie—fellow adventurer.

The reasonable man adapts himself to the world; the unreasonable man persists in trying to adapt the world to himself. Therefore all progress depends on the unreasonable man.

—George Bernard Shaw

Contents

List of Illustrations

Preface and Acknowledgments

This book is a result of my long-term fascination with who we are, why we do what we do, and how we came to be who we are. In the pages to follow I provide an explanation of the consequences of the nationalization of state actors within a systems theory that seeks to explain epochal change in the international systems, and that stems from changes in the social identities of the societies that construct these systems. My preliminary answer is that we do what we do because our ideas about who we are change, and we come to be who we are because these self-understandings change. They impel us to become something new.

I ask that the reader be patient with the elaboration of this explanation in the pages that follow. The elaboration requires both a great deal of conceptual development and a great deal of description. The conceptual development is most fully elaborated in two early, theoretically oriented chapters. Readers unfamiliar with social theory in general and international relations theory in particular may find these to be densely written. I hope their effort will be rewarded with an understanding of how changes in social identities generate epochal change in international systems. Description, developed in the form of analytic narrative, constitutes the rest of the book. I have labored to summarize the theoretical significance of each empirical chapter to assist the reader in understanding the manner in which the empirics support the theory. Some theorists of international relations will judge these chapters to constitute "thick description" and may feel that the theoretical framework could be supported with a more spare examination of empirical cases. I can only reply to colleagues who may provide this criticism by quoting Bismarck, who figures prominently in the text to follow, to the effect that respectfully "I am not of your opinion." To understand a historically unique social order, we must spend some time there. We must characterize it completely enough to understand how it differs both as a domestic and as an international social order from those which proceeded and those which follow it. I cheerfully and consciously surrender parsimony for richer and more nuanced characterization of the societies and systems I wish to study. Social reality is complex. It always has been. Thus we cannot expect to apprehend the evolution of social reality without a serious foray into history. This requires the labor of patient and time-consuming scholarship. My argument is not that we cannot discover social realities that are transhistorically valid, but that we cannot discover them by theorizing in an ahistorical fashion and without digging deeply into the available interdisciplinary scholarship from which we derive our empirics.

Acknowledgments

I have acquired enormous debts, both intellectual and practical, to a number of individuals in the development of this work. I owe multiple debts that I can not repay to Friedrich Kratochwil, now at Geschwister-Scholl Institut für Politische Wissenschaft, Ludwig Maximillians-Universität, in Munich. The basic outlines of my intellectual formation in this discipline were developed under his tutorship as teacher, mentor, and friend. His pioneering work in international relations theory and his notion of "comparative international systems" have provided the major inspiration for this work. He generously offered to see me through completion of an earlier form of this work when he left the University of Pennsylvania for Munich in May of 1995 and was invariably responsive to transatlantic correspondence oriented toward its progress. He averted several false starts by encouraging me to improve the conceptual approach and scope, and patiently provided line-by-line criticism of each chapter as it was written, as well as critical advice regarding revisions of the book manuscript. This work could not have been attempted without his tutelage, encouragement, patience, personal kindness and friendship, or without access to the phenomenal scope of his scholarship.

I owe equivalent debts to Daniel Deudney for sparking my interest in nationalism and for numerous invaluable macro-theoretical discussions that improved the finished product. Dan read an earlier version of the entire manuscript and provided invaluable suggestions for revision. He introduced the issue of nationalism and unwillingness of International Relations theory to engage the issue in a course I took from him as a graduate student, and encouraged me to develop our mutual interest on long-term, historical, social, and political change. Without this stimulus, I would not have thought to develop this work. He was instrumental in helping to limit the project to tractable dimensions early in its conception. His commitment to methodological pluralism has induced me to carefully consider arguments in the development of this work that I might otherwise have missed. His persistent encouragement to emulate his own commitment to methodological pluralism has made this a much better and comprehensible work than it otherwise could have been.

I am grateful to Alexander Wendt of Dartmouth College for introducing me to the concept of the "structure of identity and interests" of actors in the international system and its causal significance for the patterns of politics within the system. He also has my thanks for his valuable comments on several drafts of the work, for useful suggestions for restructuring the final draft, and for many useful discussions.

Thanks also to Martin Heisler of the University of Maryland and to Michael Barnett of the University of Wisconsin at Madison who each read an earlier draft of the complete manuscript and provided valuable criticisms and recommendations for restructuring. Each have raised more issues in engaging my arguments than I can address without writing an entirely different book. Thanks to Hendrik Spruyt of Columbia University for useful discussions and comments about the nature of early modern sovereignty. He provided detailed comments and criticism on the bulk of an earlier draft of the book, challenged me to address several excellent and fascinating questions, and the final product has been improved by corrections made possible by his phenomenal knowledge of European social and diplomatic history. Thanks to Yosef Lapid of New Mexico State University for valuable discussions of the implications of nationalism for international relations theory, for useful epistemological discussions and helpful forays into useful and applicable literature. I am indebted to Richard Mansbach of Iowa State University for useful discussions of nationalism and IR theory, and for the suggestion that I include a more contemporary application of this theoretical framework, which resulted in the concluding treatment of the collapse of the Soviet Union and demise of the cold war. Thanks to Stanley Hoffmann of Harvard University for a providing me with a useful bibliographic introduction to the relevant literature on nationalism, and for brief but kind correspondence on the topic.

I am indebted to Mlada Bukovansky of Dartmouth College and to Ronald Deibert of the University of Toronto for valuable and detailed comments on several crucial chapters, for kind encouragement, and for moral support. Mlada provided particularly valuable criticisms to earlier drafts which led me away from potentially disruptive methodological errors, and many useful discussions. Ron's continuous and thoughtful correspondence has been perpetually valuable, as have been his detailed comments on earlier drafts of the theoretical chapters. Thanks to Mark Zacher of the University of British Columbia and to Yale Ferguson of Rutgers University for valuable criticisms of the core theoretical arguments in the form of a paper that I delivered at a conference in Tokyo in the autumn of 1996. Thanks to Simon Duke, Eric Jones, and Stefano Guzzini for criticisms of a portion of this argument that I delivered in a talk at the Central European University in Budapest in the summer of 1996. Thanks to fellow former-travelers through the University of Pennsylvania graduate program for years of stimulating debate and discussion in which the ideas that led to this work were formed. In this context I am particularly indebted to Reynold Koslowski, now at Rutgers University, to Amir Pasic, now at the Rockefeller Foundation in Washington, and to Sujata Chakrabarti Pasic.

Thanks to Ellen Kennedy and to G. John Ikenberry, both of the University of Pennsylvania, who helped me in numerous ways while an earlier version of this work was in the process of becoming a doctoral dissertation. I am grateful to the staff of the Charles Patterson Van Pelt Library of the University of Pennsylvania for bibliographic assistance and for obtaining for me materials essential to the work but unavailable among its collections.

Thanks to Dominique Arel and David Abramson of the Watson Institute for International Studies for comments and criticisms that helped me to avoid factual errors and misinterpretations of the impact of national collective identity in the demise of the Soviet Union. I am indebted to Peter Dombrowski of Iowa State University and Cecelia Lynch of Northwestern University for suggestions on restructuring of theory chapters in the final revisions. I am grateful to Thomas Biersteker and the overseers of the Thomas J. Watson Jr. Institute for International Studies at Brown University for providing me with a postdoctoral fellowship, superb facilities, access to

Rockefeller Library, and the leisure to complete the final revisions of this book in a stimulating and supportive environment. I am grateful to my parents, James Raymond Hall and Claudine Thompson Hall, who have consistently promoted and encouraged my scholarship throughout my life and supported my life choices to pursue it, and to Letha Helen Hall, who delighted to listen to me talk about this book, but did not live to see it appear between covers.

My greatest debt of gratitude must be reserved for my wife, Joan Marie Hall, for her encouragement, support, and boundless emotional and material sacrifice and patience during long years of study, research and writing that have culminated in the present offering. Special thanks to my children, Joseph, Jacqueline, and Edward James (E.J.). Many an evening or weekend family event, which we might have enjoyed together, were forgone so that this work could take form. My family has permitted me and encouraged me to, sequentially, turn down promotions, reduce my working hours and income, and finally to turn my back entirely on a relatively lucrative career in industry in order to pursue this work and a life of scholarship, irrespective of the significant material sacrifice this has implied for them. My greatest wish is that I can in return give to them, from the knowledge and insight that I have gained in generating this work, something that I hope they will find to be a great deal more valuable than the banal, bourgeois affluence that passes for the good life in America today.

Rodney Bruce Hall
Providence, Rhode Island

March 1998

NATIONAL COLLECTIVE IDENTITY

Part I

Collective Identity and International Relations Theory

1 International Relations Without Nations?

There is no error so monstrous that it will not find defenders among the ablest men. —Lord Acton

The abstraction of the state as such belongs only to modern times, because the abstraction of private life belongs only to modern times. —Karl Marx

To be what we are, and to become what we are capable of becoming, is the only end of life. —Robert Louis Stevenson

Introduction

Nationalist and ethnic conflict, not cold war tensions or "superpower balancing in the periphery" now largely consume the agendas of the United Nations and NATO as well as the foreign policy concerns of powers, great and small. Curiously, these events, and the attention that the great powers would lavish on them, were as unpredicted and unpredictable by our current repertoire of international relations theory as was the end of the cold war. Yet until quite recently, little attention has been given to the issue of nationalism in recent literature in the discipline of international relations theory.

This book will address the issue of the consequences of the "nationalization" of state actors for the composition of the international system and the patterns of politics within it. Part of this endeavor is a clearer conceptualization and delineation of national-sovereign actors from the territorial-state-sovereign actors that had dominated the system prior to the nineteenth century. I will thereby address the question of how the nationalization of state actors results in change in the international system. While some have contended that the international behavior of state actors has been uniform throughout history, I will critically examine this argument. The eighteenth-century system consisted of territorial-sovereign state actors whose regimes relied upon dynastic legitimating principles. By contrast, the late nineteenth and twentieth century systems have increasingly consisted of national-sovereign actors whose regimes have relied upon the "imagined community"[1] of the nation as a legitimating principle. I will develop the consequences of this nationalization of international actors and the resulting behaviors, which cannot be explained with a state-centric theoretical approach.

I will seek to fill a gap in contemporary international relations theory, which fails to account for and explain nationalist phenomena in the international system. The currently dominant theories of international relations are strongly state-centric. They take the state as a fundamental unit of analysis that is unproblemmatically given, fail to inquire into its origins, or to delineate it from the nation. These theories relegate domestic-societal interaction, sources of conflict, or societal cohesiveness (such as ethnic, religious, or other domestic sources) to the status of epiphenomena.[2] The current resurgence of nationalism in the post-cold-war international system, and the potential conflictual consequences of past and present national movements, are therefore opaque to our current repertoire of international relations theory, even though the relative novelty of national collective identity has significant implications for the current practice of modern international relations.

An investigation of the systemic consequences of national collective identity, and its delineation from the consequences of earlier forms that supported a state system, will simultaneously help us to clarify several important issues. These include the origins of the modern nation-state system, historical variations in the institutional forms of collective action, and the distinction between territorial sovereignty and national sovereignty. I seek to uncover the consequences of national collective identity and nation building (as opposed to state building) in the modern era within a framework that results in a useful correction to an existing body of theoretical literature.[3]

The advantage of integrating the literature on nationalism with the literature on international relations is that it may allow for the development of a "systemic" theory that is *action* oriented, and capable of explaining historical change in the international system. We cannot explain nationalism or its causal significance for international politics within a theoretical framework that is committed to a conception of structure that is largely static, or in which structure merely constrains action.

I will begin with the assertion that *changes in the collective identity of societal actors transform the interests of relevant collective actors that constitute the system*. Sovereign state actors may well have autonomous interests that help shape state policy, but the influences, beliefs and prejudices of individuals and sub-state groups within society help to determine how ostensibly objective state interests get translated into state policy.[4] The interests of societal groups are not immutable or objectively determined. Group interests are strongly conditioned by the self-identifications of members of these groups with respect to other groupings within society and with respect to the state.

Thus, to explain the differences in behavior of the late-nineteenth to mid-twentieth-century nation, with that of the eighteenth-century dynastic state, we must assert that "the 'national interest' cannot be the object of a rational determination."[5] We cannot assume that the "interests" of eighteenth-century states and twentieth-century states are equivalent and determinable *ex post facto* by the analyst with recourse to logical inference alone. Nationalism brought with it the abstract notion of "citizenship." The nineteenth-century manifestations of this notion range from full enfranchisement and "universal" suffrage in the United States (among white males) to, at the least, national populism and suffrage, weighted by social class, in constitutional-monarchical Europe. In all but autocratic Russia, the "Revolution of 1848" had injected into European regimes constitutional checks on autocracy, and the conception of the "rule-of-law" that was binding upon the monarch, as well as at least limited participatory, parliamentary institutions. Some conception of "citizenship" was emerging nearly everywhere in Europe and was replacing the more traditional self-identification of being "subject' " to a prince or state. The consequences of these events for the determination of "state-interests" is captured in a trenchant passage in a recent work by Michael Mann.

> As classes and other actors attained civil and political citizenship, the state became 'their' nation-state, an 'imagined' community to which

> they developed loyalties. Its power, honor, humiliations, and even material interests came to be sensed as their own, and such feelings were mobilizable by the statesmen, pressure groups and militaries. Nationalist parties and pressure groups pressed these feelings on statesmen . . . [a] . . . populist, passionate, national tinge..[was given to diplomacy by the] . . . growth of national identities. *But this lacked the precise rationality of interests pursued by classes or particularistic pressure groups and the precise, normatively rooted understandings of insulated old regime statesmen.*[6]

Actor Identities and System Change: Systemic Consequences of Changes in Social Identities

This book advances the argument that actor self-identification is a critical component of a historically changing "structure of identities and interests."[7] Against the "will-to-power" of the state, in realist analysis, as the *ultima ratio* of international political interaction, I will posit the "will-to-manifest-identity" of social collectivities as agents that spawn the social construction of domestic and global social orders. Changes in the prevailing forms of societal self-identification generate changes in this "structure of identity and interests" and result in epochal change in the international system. I will employ the reconstructive theoretical framework developed in the following chapters to identify at least three epochal changes in the international system. The first is the transition from the medieval, heteronomous, feudal-theocratic order to a dynastic-sovereign (Augsburg, 1555) system, the second was the transition from the Augsburg system to the territorial-sovereign (Westphalian, 1648) system that is featured so prominently in realist analysis. The third is the transition to the national-sovereign (the first post-Westphalian) system. Variations in prevailing collective identities, system legitimating principles, institutional forms of collective action, and norms, rules and principles of interaction are the factors that constitute these systems. These generate the "structures of identities and interests" which, in my argument, constitute distinct, historically contingent, empirically identifiable international systems. As the empirical illustration of all of these transitions would be intractable in a single volume, I employ the bulk of the book to illustrate what I refer to as the "territorial-sovereign-to-national-sovereign" transition.

This book addresses, in an integrated theoretical framework, a need for international relations theory to account for and to explain nationalist phenomena and epochal change in the international system. Historical change in the legitimating principles, and of the institutional composition of the international system, are demonstrated to be (in positivist discourse) dependent on the independent variable of changing societal collective identity. The relative modernity of national collective identity is shown to have significant implications for the current structure of modern international relations. Societal self-identification is demonstrated to have had causal significance for the state identities and interests in the transition from what I call "territorial-sovereign" identity that arose at the Westphalian settlement of the Thirty Years War, to the "national-sovereign" identity that had manifested itself in Europe by the late nineteenth century. State interests, institutional forms, and behavior emerge from this analysis as variable products of the evolution of societal collective identity.

The emergence of national-sovereign identity has brought significant changes in the behavior of nineteenth- and twentieth-century national-sovereign nation-states relative to the behavior of the territorial-sovereign states of the eighteenth century. *The behavioral differences are explained as manifestations of the transformation of the historically contingent notions of interest that derive from the distinct sovereign identities that emerge between the two periods.* Historical events to be examined analytically include the Seven Years' War, the Napoleonic Wars, the Concert of Europe, the Revolution of 1848, the Danish-Prussian War, the Austro-Prussian War, the Franco-Prussian War, imperialism before and after 1870, the First World War and, more contemporarily, the collapse of the USSR and demise of the cold war.

I delineate the structure of identities and interests of the territorial-sovereign from that of the national-sovereign. The emergence, in the nineteenth century, of national-sovereign identity and interests problematized territorial-sovereign legitimating principles and subsequently transformed the structure of state interests, practice, and institutions. The emergence of national collective identity in Europe resulted in the replacement of the territorial-sovereign legitimating principle of *raison d'état* with the national-sovereign legitimating principle of national-self-determination. Eighteenth-century dynastic, mercantilist absolutism and easy recourse to war were practices that developed from the norms, rules and principles of an international system legitimated by the territorial-sovereign legitimating principle of *raison d'état*. Territorial-sovereign imperialism was a commercial and strategic venture whose social purpose conformed to the zero-sum nature of dynastic, territorial-sovereign status competition.

The emergence of national-collective identity created problems of secessionism and irredentism, and thus new sources of interstate conflict. It enhanced the resources mobilizable by statesmen. Conflicting class and national identity commitments created tools for statesmen to "divide and rule" domestic society, but radically reduced the insularity of their decisionmaking processes as an enfranchised and nationalized "citizenry" took an interest in the affairs of state with which territorial-sovereign statesmen had not been required to contend. I will demonstrate that national collective identity gave statesmen such as Bismarck the tools to forge a German superstate from the many petty kingdoms and mini-states of German Central Europe. I will demonstrate that national collective identity constrained other statesmen, such as Napoleon III, from "balancing" the creation of a threatening German superstate, and from enjoying the flexibility to form alliances with other powers sufficient to meet the threat of this hostile superstate when the Franco-Prussian War commenced in 1870. These events defy the logic of dominant theories of international relations and cannot be convincingly explained without rigorous analysis of the social identities of the actors.

The emergence of national-collective identity also transformed the practice and social purposes of imperialism. What had been, in the territorial-sovereign system, a territorial and economic venture in the periphery became a crusade to transmit national culture and institutions to the periphery—a process that transformed peripheral societies. The practice and social purposes of imperialism were transformed by changes in the structure of sovereign identities and interests. National collective identity would ultimately not only mobilize entire societies, but also transform national economies for war (national status conflicts). Far from the secret treaties and smoke-filled rooms that characterized the insulated diplomacy of much of the nineteenth century, by the first decade of the twentieth century statesmen were forced to decide questions of foreign policy under the scrutiny of a nationalized press and shrill nationalist pressure groups. In this nationalized environment there is less opportunity for policymakers to make rational decisions. In the course of illustrating and describing these and other consequences of a historically changing structure of actor identities and interests I will demonstrate that transformation in the self-identities and interests of individuals and groups within society, linkage of individual and group interests to the interests of the state,[8] and transformation of the identity and interests of the national-state result from the process of nationalization of state actors.

Several separate historical time frames have been reflected in the cases that I have chosen, in order to trace the changes in the behavior of international actors. They will also provide the basis for interesting comparisons between the predictions of theories of the rational actor, as described by neorealism, and the structural variants of balance of power theories of classical realism. The cases chosen accord with the standards of comparative method. They provide for synchronic and diachronic variation of analytic referents. Synchronic variation is provided by studying the interaction of Westphalian territorial-sovereign actors and national-sovereign actors in well-documented historical events that exhibited a full range of the behaviors traditionally associated with international interaction. These include alliance formation; the initiation, prosecution and negotiated (or forcible) cessation of armed conflict; "internal balancing,"[9] and attempts to establish hegemony in a political[10] or economic[11] context. The cases therefore provide synchronic comparison of the behavioral consequences of the nationalization of state actors. They foster comparative analysis and tests of the presence and consequences of the notion of citizenship, the "eudomonic" relationship between the citizen and the state, mass participation and mobilization, the scope and objectives of foreign policy and armed conflict, the resources that statesmen may mobilize in a crisis, the freedom of policymakers to pursue "objectively rational" policy in the service of "state" interests, and the international transmission of social and political culture through various vehicles.

Diachronic variation of these phenomena is provided in the historical range of like phenomena to be analyzed. The historical scope will range from 1763, when the Seven Years' War ended, to 1918, and the end of World War I, and then jump to the end of the cold war to deal with the demise of the proletarian internationalist identity that emerged in 1917 as a competitor to national collective identity. In testing for the presence of national-states, I use Anthony D. Smith's recent definitions of the characteristics of a nation:[12]

1. the growth of myths and memories of common ancestry and history of the cultural unit of population;
2. the formation of a shared public culture based on an indigenous resource (language, religion, etc.);
3. the delimitation of compact historic territory, or homeland;
4. the unification of local economic units into a single socioeconomic unit based on the single culture and homeland;

5. the growth of common codes and institutions of a single legal order, with common rights and duties for all members.

Even where nationalist phenomenology has been belatedly addressed by mainstream, particularly neorealist IR theory, they have been merely appropriated in a fashion that usually does not disturb or challenge the basic state-centric methodological assumptions of the hard core of the neorealist research program.[13] The preeminence of the concept of the "state" over either the "nation" or sub-state or subnational groupings, as the irreducibly significant social actor in the system, is still unproblematically given in the view of these recent appropriative theorizations.

Recent attempts by some mainstream IR scholars to recognize and account for the resurgence of nationalism as "one of the most explosive forces shaping domestic and global constitutional orders at the end of the twentieth century"[14] have generally constituted simple "theoretical appropriation." In these accounts, nationalist phenomena and variables have been imported in a fashion that suggests that they are derived from more basic elements of neorealist theory. Contributions of this genre suffer from a failure to delineate between the nation and the state as well as a tendency to reaffirm the notion of historical continuity in global politics. This is a tendency to ascribe a systemic reproductive capacity to nationalism, but to deny it any generative or transformative capacity as an agent of systemic change. They also suffer from subsumption of nationalism under the distributional rubric of a power resource, obviating the "constitutive role of nationalism as a global ordering principle."[15]

It is significant that "historically there have been momentous changes in the international system that transcend modifications in the distribution of power among political units."[16] Structural realist theory, however, lacks "transformational logic" that might illuminate these changes; it has only a "reproductive logic" that seeks to account for continuity. Classical realism escapes the static condition of neorealism by introducing a transformational logic that permits systemic change to result from hegemonic agency. However, much of classical realism exhibits a tendency to envisage this transformation largely in terms of positional shifts among the units that result from cycles of hegemonic war, and rotation in the identity of the hegemon, who imposes rules and order on the system.[17] While the system is "generated" in classical realist hegemonic theory, it is still a state-centric view, which demonstrates scant interest in historical changes in the institutional forms of collective action. Nationalist thought and action are among the causes of some of these changes.

When we glance about the post Cold War world, we see the rapid creation of new states and new nationalist self-identifications, in the former Soviet Union, in Eastern Europe, and in the former Yugoslavia, for example. These events are, in no way a consequence of any new "distribution of capabilities." Ukrainian statehood and Polish independence emerged during the peak of Moscow's potency in terms of military capabilities. Rather, I would suggest that the creation of these new states is the product of the replacement of one set of societal collective identities, and the legitimating principles and institutional facts that had resulted from them, with a new set. This has required the construction of new legitimating principles and institutional arrangements, which generate new institutional facts.[18]

I will begin the construction of a theoretical framework in which transformations in the collective identity of international social actors can be demonstrated to be causally significant, not only in helping to structure international outcomes, but also in transforming the international system. I hope to demonstrate that it is possible to construct a theoretical perspective that abandons many of the principal theoretical commitments of the neorealist core research plan without abandoning all of the parsimony of systems theory. I hope to demonstrate that by making a start at a reconstructive, rather than an appropriative theoretical approach to nationalist phenomenology, we can explain nationalist phenomena (e.g. the consequences of nationalization of state actors for behavior within the system), historical transformation in the institutional forms that constitute the "units" of the system, and historical transformation in the principles by which the system is constituted, and reconstituted, with recourse to the same set of analytic referents.

Thus a more coherent theory of international politics must be predicated, in part, on an adequate theory of the nation-state. The theory must permit social agents to demonstrate a systemic generative and transformative capacity, rather than seeing social actors as merely conditioned by a static reproductive logic. Examination of systemic variables alone will not help us to understand the disparate historical paths by which peoples in different parts of the world and in different times have arrived at national consciousness. *Rather, examination of those variables which conclusively generate "potent 'we' feeling" is called for.*[19] Yet it is crucial to my argument that *nationalism is not just a unit level factor, or a "property" of the units* which may be assumed to foster self-seeking of self-interested behavior. National identity is a relatively new form of collective identity *whose development is contingent upon both domestic and international sources*. Nationalism fosters or impels a specific legitimating principle—national self-determination—which has far-reaching consequences for system constitution and transformation. National sovereignty is a form of social institution distinct from that of state sovereignty.

I shall examine factors that conclusively generate strong collective self-identification to avoid the theoretical problems generated by the analyst's imputation of actor identification. Not least among these problems is the problem of correctly designating the relevant social actors whose interaction one wishes to describe and understand.[20] To analyze any system one must designate actors and their interaction. The analytic ontology that results from doing so will very often determine, and limit, the range of phenomena one will be able to analyze. I wish to avoid designating nonexistent actors by projecting contemporary actor designations upon older social systems, as these mis-designations distort our understanding of the present by obscuring its essential differences with the past.

Units and Systems: Actor Designation, Structure, and Interests

It is a major argument of this book that the international system of national-sovereign actors is in many ways, though not in every respect, an essentially different system from the territorial-sovereign system that proceeded it. Why is this the case? A brief dissection of a highly influential passage from Kenneth Waltz's *Theory of International Politics* will provide a useful backdrop for the answer. Waltz argues that:

> A system is composed of a structure and of interacting units. The structure is the system-wide component that makes it possible to think of the system as a whole. The problem . . . is to contrive a definition of structure free of the attributes and the interactions of units. Definitions of structure must leave aside, or abstract from, the characteristics of units, their behavior, and their interactions . . . so that we can distinguish between variables at the level of the units and at the level of the system.[21]

This is the assertion upon which Waltz proceeds to found his definition of political structure, and of political system. Waltz seeks to construct definitions of political structure without any recourse whatever to descriptive categorizations regarding the actors that he regards as behaviorally constrained by this structure. Had he actually done this, then we should feel entirely free to apply this definition of political structure to any range or class of social actor or any range of social phenomena that we can imagine interacting or transpiring within such a structure.[22]

In constructing his system theory, Waltz has underspecified the relevant actors in the system. Designation of actors requires some specification of their attributes in a social context. Social contexts are not, however, static over time. For those of us interested in change in the international system, the Waltzian formulation underspecifies actor designation in two ways. The first means of underspecification is an artifact of structural neorealism's "unitary" hypothesis. Designating a social actor that is comprised of a social aggregate as "unitary" provides theoretical parsimony, but in order to be valid "the actor-elements of the political system examined must be sufficiently cohesive, 'billiard-ball-like', 'monadic', or irreducible so that their further analytic decomposition would not significantly improve the conclusions."[23] Structural neorealism has received more criticism for violation of this injunction of actor designation than can be comprehensively cited.[24]

In this context, Waltz's second form of underspecification of actors lies in his static designation of the character of the "units" of his system as states. The problem with a static actor designation for a system that one wants to analyze diachronically is obvious. Static actor designation may say more about the analyst than it says about the system. Waltz's theoretical framework has been found useful, by many scholars, in the analysis of behavior in a system of Westphalian territorial-sovereign states precisely because he has designated these not as the primary actors in his system but as the *only* actors. In his view, the structure of these actors perpetually reproduces the system. But Waltz does not explain nationalist phenomena as he does not perceive nations as distinct from other forms of state actors. They are exogenized from his system, as are all other historically observed forms of political association that proceeded the Peace of Westphalia, as well as several which have succeeded it.[25] As Frey observes, regarding the impact of actor designation on the resulting *systems*[26], the *structures*,[27] and significantly, on the imputed *interests* of the actors:

> Actor designation often determines issue identification, and vice versa. From the former perspective, *the key process is that actor designation*

> *leads to the imputation of identity and interests which, in turn, leads to issue perception* when there is a perceived interest blockage by other actors.[28]

Thus, in order to more convincingly define political structure in a fashion that renders the concept useful for dynamic rather than static transhistorical analysis, the analyst must take into account the *self-designations* of the actors of the system. Analyst imputation of actor identity, if it is inconsistent with actor self-identification, imputes interests and motivations to the actors that may be strongly inconsistent with actual, self-understood interests and motivations.

Critics argue that Waltz's definition of systemic structure, therefore, actually follows directly from his assumptions regarding the "attributes and interaction of the units." Anarchy, and the absence of functional differentiation, are not, in this view, objectively observable features of the system that may be divorced from imputation of the interests, motivations, and attributes of the units. Helen Milner has searched in vain for "anarchy"[29] and Paul Schroeder argues that he has found a great deal of historical functional differentiation among the units.[30] Anarchy and functional nondifferentiation of the units of the system are not, in this view, structural features of a historically continuous international system. Rather, they are imputed structural features of a system that results from the imputed interests, motivations and attributes of the self-interested, self-regarding, power-maximizing, survival-oriented, Westphalian territorial-sovereign state actors that Waltz has designated in constructing his system theory. Had Waltz designated a different sort of actor, or had he allowed for diachronic variation in the social identities and consequently of the interests of the actors, he might have discovered a different conception of structure, and might have formulated a very different systems theory.

Matters are better, but still unresolved, in earlier influential classical realist theories. A common assumption of both classical realist and neorealist theories of international relations regards the fixity of the "interests" and motivations of state actors in the conduct of social interaction. Hans Morgenthau's formulation of the notion of interest obscures the relationship between interests and power by equating these two very distinct concepts. He asserts boldly, early on in his work, that "[w]e assume that statesmen think and act in terms of *interest defined as power*."[31] Possession of power resources might be variable among states, but the "interest" of statesmen in acquiring them is constant. Morgenthau asserts the "idea of interest is indeed of the essence of politics and is unaffected by the circumstances of time and place." In other words, Morgenthau argues that a state advances its interests in the pursuit of power and failure to pursue power is the failure to act in accordance with one's interests.

Morgenthau's ambiguity on the issue of the consequences of nationalism for international politics provides an interesting means by which to critique his assumptions regarding the notion of interests, upon which the explanatory utility of realist balance of power theory rests. Morgenthau appears to delineate between the causal significance of nationalism (and ideology in general) for elites—who are the ultimate determiners, and executors, of the national interest *qua* power—and the causal significance of nationalism on the interests and motivations of individual citizens who belong to and serve the nation. He regards ideology in general to be a smokescreen behind which statesmen mask their preexisting interests in extending national power, particularly in the context of his evaluation of the foreign policy of the Soviet Union under the rule of Stalin. The general line of the treatment of ideology in Morgenthau's theory is that "ideology functions solely to legitimize or rationalize pre-existing national interests, not create them."[32]

Yet Morgenthau contradicts this starkly in his comparison of the functioning of the prenational "international society" with that of the postnational international system, though he does not designate them consciously as two different systems. Morgenthau waxes nostalgically in relative enthusiasm for the "cosmopolitan aristocratic society" and the "restraining influence of its morality upon foreign policy" before the French Revolution.[33] He credits (or blames) the French Revolution and the nationalization of state actors that its example provided to nineteenth-century Europe with a "decline of the international society and its morality," such that one can scarcely speak of the existence of international society by the end of the nineteenth century.[34] This will appear strange indeed to British readers of Morgenthau, for whom the notion of international society is a central theoretical construct of their discipline.[35] Yet this English-school notion of international society is transhistorically reified in literature of this genre. The transhistorical character of this central theoretical construct disqualifies it as a starting point for my analysis, even though, like classical realism, the English school provides an ontological framework with enough flexibility to allow for a quite interesting analysis of nationalist and other cultural phenomena, as well as an appreciation for the dynamic character of the system.[36]

Morgenthau argues that, bereft of the ethics of international society, national society becomes "morally self-sufficient." This situation has, in Morgenthau's view, "weakened, to the point of ineffectiveness, the universal, supranational moral rules of conduct, which before the age of nationalism had imposed a system . . . of limitations upon the foreign policies of individual nations."[37] These moral rules were "supranational ethics, composed of Christian, cosmopolitan, and humanitarian elements [ostensibly discernible from] the diplomatic language of the time."[38] One can hardly be accused of "deconstructing" Morgenthau in order to easily discern in his writing the "reactionary utopia" Hoffmann suggests that Morgenthau evokes as the ideal climate for the peaceful pursuit of state interests within the precepts of the balance of power.[39]

One problem with this view, aside from its anachronistic elitism, is that it is simply a factual error to suggest that the aristocratic statesmen of the nineteenth century shared this cosmopolitan commitment to the balance of power in accordance with a commitment to supranational ethics and a common vision of international society. This has been adequately illustrated by Kratochwil's discussion of the transformation of the patterns of European politics in this time frame. Morgenthau is quite correct in asserting that the transformation occurred, and that nationalist thought and action were substantive factors in inducing this transformation. Kratochwil, however, illustrates that this transformation could as easily be brought about by a statesman choosing to take Morgenthau's conflation of interests as power quite literally, and "maximize power" irrespective of the ethics (or more properly, the constitutive rules) of international society.[40]

As Kratochwil suggests, the statesman in question was the German aristocrat Otto von Bismarck. Among nineteenth-century European statesmen, it would be difficult to find a more pure, more constant, more regal disdain for democratic norms, democratic institutions, or the notion of popular sovereignty than that which Bismarck displayed. Significantly, though revered as the unifier of Germany, Bismarck was no nationalist. Born a conservative Prussian Junker, he lived and died a confirmed monarchist at a time when only liberals were nationalists and the monarchical principle was philosophically averse to both liberalism and nationalism. His achievement, in his own view, had been that of inducing, through an unrepeatable combination of war and diplomacy, the princes of Germany to hand an imperial German crown to his own King of Prussia.[41]

Bismarck's disdain for the concept of international society was apparent in the way, according to Kratochwil, Bismarck declined to pursue Prussian goals in a manner that recognized Prussian interests were defined with reference to the interests of other actors in international society. As Kratochwil suggests:

> Here Bismarck breaks critically with the accepted tradition. When the Eastern question occupied the European powers in 1876 and Gortschakoff [the Russian Foreign Minister] had argued that the Great Powers had a European responsibility, Bismarck noted on the margin of the dispatch, 'Anyone who speaks of Europe is mistaken,' adding, one line later, 'Who is Europe?.' . . . This is not yet the exclusivity of pure and unadulterated self-interest that emerges later, when social-darwinism makes a cult out of struggle. . . . But it is already a decisive step, from interests defined within a set of conventions to interests conceived of, at best, allowing for *ad hoc* recognition of others through bargaining.[42]

Yet Morgenthau can be lauded for tacitly noting the causal significance of the transformation of European societal collective identities—from territorial sovereignties to national sovereignties—in generating changes in the conduct of European international relations. It is, however, fascinating that a book which begins by declaring interests to be the *ultima ratio* of international politics, and which defines interests in terms of the will-to-power, turns later to "ethics" and "morality" as the arbiters of international conduct. Though he turns to them, these concepts simply have no place in Morgenthau's theoretical schema. Morgenthau may tacitly note the causal significance of nationalist ideology, but it plays no role in his formulation of balance of power theory. In turning to treat the topic of the end of the Concert, Morgenthau simply changes the subject entirely by asserting the superiority of eighteenth-century aristocratic ethics over nationalist ethics. In so doing Morgenthau fails to recognize that one of the principal agents in bringing about the demise of the Concert of Europe was a conservative, Prussian, Junker dynast who had been reared entirely within the normative, aristocratic, ethical discourse that Morgenthau so confidently asserts had held the Concert together.

The larger problem with Morgenthau's analysis of international politics in general, and with his analysis of the causal significance of nationalism for international politics in particular, is that even in acknowledging in a particular case that an ideational factor like nationalism has consequences that must be accounted for, Morgenthau merely asserts that the factor has been appropriated by statesmen and applies the factor as if it had no consequences for his description of state interests in terms of power. His analysis of the behavior of nation-state actors is simply an analysis of the behavior of nationalized "state actors" still ruled by the old power lust. The goals of this will-to-power alone have changed. The new goal, according to Morgenthau, is the transmission of the new, particularistic, national ethics with which these nations have replaced the ethics of his cherished reactionary utopia.

Even when generating insights into nationalist phenomena, Morgenthau must formulate them in the context of these constants of the "power monism"[43] upon which his theory of the balance of power is predicated. It is disingenuous for Morgenthau to suddenly suggest that "relative positions" within a commonly accepted normative framework of understandings and expectations are no longer at issue, only the "ability to impose" one's moral vision on other nations. He is certainly correct in asserting that the normative framework of understandings of the reactionary utopia has been dismantled, with causal significance for the subsequent patterns of national-state interaction. But acquiring the ability to impose one's views on others is certainly a positional issue,[44] and a very extreme positional consequence of what Morgenthau would regard as the failure to successfully balance the power of others. Morgenthau does not intend with this passage to abandon a positional model of international politics; a model that was to taken up at an ever higher level of ontological abstraction later by Waltz's formulation of structural neorealism. He intends to bemoan the demise of the reactionary utopia.

This criticism should not be read as an element of a diatribe against Morgenthau who, unlike Waltz, does recognize and discuss at relative length the consequences of nationalism for international politics. But one wonders why the domestic analogies employed early in Morgenthau's book in order, for example, to invoke a first image cause for the power lust of states cannot be applied here with the salutary effect of recognizing that "goals" of social actors change with changes in their own understandings of their interests. Morgenthau's work is an exemplar of an entire genre of literature on international relations theory that imputes the interests of collective actors from their understanding of the structural effects of human nature. Collective interests are presumed to be a collective representation of the aggregated effects of these morose and intransient aspects of human nature. It is a major argument of this book that these collective interests change with changes in collective self-understandings as social actors, i.e. with changes in collective identity.

Nationalism and the Notion of Citizenship: Civil Society and Self-Determination

At this juncture we are left with the realization that any theory formulated in such a way as to describe the interests of social actors in terms of power, and in unitary terms, is not capable of making an analytic cut into the explanation of nationalist phenomena. This suggests that interests must sometimes be described in a different language, and that their formulation and expression are far from a unitary, or even a merely composite process. The analysis of the interaction of sovereign states will remain forever static if it provides no means by which to analyze transformations in collective identity and especially in sovereign identity. Justin Rosenberg captures the root of the problem succinctly when he argues that:

> what is missing is any sense that the history of the states-system is more than the accumulation of successive power-struggles, any awareness that those competitions between great powers have mediated the continuing evolution, geographical expansion and global consolidation of a world political structure which in many ways is continuous with the changing *domestic* form, legitimacy and power of the state: that the meaning of sovereignty itself is historically specific.[45]

It will not do to simply note that the territorial-sovereign states of modern Europe (and by extension non-European states), having become nationalized, will then suddenly imagine themselves to have become nations, and so proceed to analyze their behavior as if the same norms of sovereignty were applicable to nation-states as they had been for dynastic territorial-sovereigns. As I have demonstrated, Morgenthau does precisely this and attributes the observed differences in the international behavior of nation-states to a shift in the "ethics" statesmen bring to the same old contest. Contrary to Morgenthau's implicit assertion, statesmen in the nationalist era have not spoken with one voice of the same set of prenational ethics and interests. They do not merely articulate a different set of ethics that now simply extend the goals of the state, in relation to those articulated in the pre-nationalist era.

They have spoken in an entirely new voice and have articulated a new set of interests—those of an entirely new social entity. In the nationalist era, statesmen were no longer speaking with the voice of a prince, a dynastic house, or of a kingdom, or empire—the territorial patrimony of the traditional European conception of sovereignty. Nor did they any longer articulate these interests and goals. The statesmen of nation-states began speaking in the voice of a sovereign people, a collective actor possessed of a collective identity and collective interests and goals, in the context of both domestic and international social interaction. This is a very different social actor than was the dynastic-sovereign. The self-understanding, as a social collectivity, of a people who possess sovereign identity in their own name is very different from that of a people who ascribe sovereign identity exclusively to a prince who rules over them in his own name. The novel self-understanding provided them with social agency. One of the most significant consequences of their recognition of this agency is a significant adjustment of their own "interests."

Habermas captures the issue nicely in a recent essay:

> with the French Revolution, the nation even became the source of state sovereignty. . . . Each nation is now supposed to be granted the right to political self-determination. . . . The meaning of the term "nation" thus changed from designating a pre-political entity to something that was supposed to play a constitutive role in defining the political identity of the citizen within a democratic polity.[46]

Of course, as noted above, not all states that developed national collective identity can be characterized in terms of a grant of citizenship within a democratic polity. Peoples with quite limited experience of democratic institutions and marginal exposure to republican ideals nevertheless became quite fervent nationalists in the nineteenth century. Yael Tamir has suggested that there is more than one variant of nationalism, and that identification of nationalism with citizenship in a democratic polity, cited by Habermas, is the liberal variant. There is also a communitarian variant that constitutes a more focused cultural identification and affiliation. These identifications and affiliations are regarded as "a matter of fate rather than choice."[47]

The liberal variant of nationalism, however, has origins that raise serious questions regarding the advisability of modeling international diplomacy and social interaction as a gentleman's game between highly and similarly cultured transnational elites. This is especially the case in societies that did take up the claim of national sovereignty, as opposed to dynastic sovereignty, in the nineteenth century and beyond. The agency of a domestic society cannot be reduced to the international policy of the state. Something critical, and thus far unidentified, underlies this state policy when it is determined neither by dynastic "interests," nor by a unitary societal consensus regarding the societal "interests" that Morgenthau argues are reducible to the extension of state power.[48] This move obscures transsocietal features that illuminate transformations in global social orders.[49] It is crucial to resolve the outlines of this transsocietal structure in order to gain an understanding of both modern international *and domestic* politics.

These observations lead us into a discussion that will more clearly reveal the relationship between the form of the modern state that is successful in international competition and the form that provides a favorable forum for the civil association necessary for the fostering of the concept of citizenship. In the nationalist era in particular, these successful state formations, and citizen-engendering formations, have been largely coterminous. The link between these twin successes has been that states that have been successful in both of these forums have provided favorable forums for capitalist production. Justin Rosenberg observes:

> Under capitalism, the formal subordination in production which accomplishes the extraction of the surplus is not exercised through the state. Formal political inequality is therefore not inscribed in the relations of production . . . [rather] . . . the direct extraction of a surplus is accomplished through 'non-political' relations associated with new forms of social power.[50]

Rosenberg suggests that Marx correctly identifies these new sources of social power, in the first volume of *Capital*, as " 'market forces and the rule of law.' Rosenberg then goes on to help illuminate the link between the "liberal" and "pluralist" elements of a social order that Michael Walzer suggests are crucial to the health of civil society and the notion of citizenship.[51]

> It [capitalism] is a historically specific set of social relations between persons which effects the reproduction of the social order in a deter-

> minate form . . . because incorporation into this association through the labor contract takes the form of a relation of exchange between legal equals, the process of surplus extraction is reconstituted as a private activity of civil society.[52]

The surplus extracted provides both the means of sustaining the material needs of the civil society engaged in generating it, and, through the extractive process of taxation, the material needs for the maintenance of the state, defense of its territorial integrity against international threats, or expansion of the territory administered by the state. More importantly for the evolution of both the notions of citizenship and nationalisms later built on this notion, the surplus extracted also provides the means for the ensurance of the material well-being of the citizen, as the nation-state begins to take an interest in ensuring a minimum level of subsistence for the promotion of the dignity of the citizen. The notion that the state has an obligation to concern itself with the material well-being of the citizen, who often becomes surplus labor in this privately administered system of extraction of economic surpluses, arises early in the nationalist era and is found even as early as the debates of the French National Assembly regarding the obligations of the new republic to rationalize the old regime's system of *bienfaisance*. The nation-state thus acquires the domestic function of utilizing its increasingly rational administrative capacity to ensure that available means were directed at the most critical need.[53]

Rosenberg's analysis demonstrates rather effectively that the modern European international state system did not develop independently of domestic social and economic context. A specific form of the state was privileged, in part by the state-building aspirations of early modern and modern European monarchs. Michael Mann suggests that neo-Marxian arguments such as Rosenberg's are correct, if incomplete. "The modern state did crystallize as capitalist, though not only as capitalist."[54] By a highly complex and historically contingent set of interactions, classes and nations emerged as dominant powerful social actors in the nineteenth century. They emerge "entwined" in the sense that neither developed in the forms observed independently of the other. Upon emerging together, nation-states and classes later slowly squeezed out other relevant social actors and groupings of both a transnational and local or regional nature.[55]

Classical Marxist class analysis, however, is only of marginal utility in unraveling the complex dynamics of the co-constitution of nations and classes in the nineteenth century. This is the case in large measure because classes are neither "pure" constructs with objectively given "interests" that are uniformly grasped and acted upon, nor are they constituted transnationally. Classes as they actually emerged were constituted with "shared norms and passions, inspiring them to recklessness, sacrifice, and cruelty . . . [which helped them to] . . . overcome their diverse economic membership to generate passionate collective behavior. Ideology may be immanent and transcendent among classes."[56] But while capitalism is defined in transnational terms by classical Marxism it "actually emerged within and between the territories of states . . . became sociospatially structured by their domestic and geopolitical relations"[57] giving rise to national as well a transnational forms of capitalist social actors. As capitalism generally emerged within territorial boundaries it thus uniquely formed domestic civil societies in accordance with local peculiarities, prejudices and "interests."

As the dynastic territorial state began to give way to the nation-state, the latter emerged as an institutional form of the agency of classes that are dominated by bourgeois interests and ethics, but by bourgeois interests and ethics that have developed in a specific cultural context. The capitalist class does begin to acquire attributes of a ruling class, and gains broad influence over the policy of the state. But the ethnic and cultural context in which the capitalist class has emerged within a given territory introduces a strong contaminant into the "purity" of class recognition of any "objective" transnational interests.

National and class collective identities contend for dominance in the formation of state policy. Neither nationalist sentiment or its class rival can wholly determine the policy of the nation-state. The state is certainly not simply an accumulation of private interests as the pluralists suggest; neither is it simply the "executive committee of the bourgeoisie" as orthodox Marxism proposes. Neither the state or the nation obtained a solid form without the rise of capitalism and the generation of classes, but the idea of the nation is broader than that of the classes which make the nation possible. At another level, the nation is not possible without the death of traditional forms of the legitimacy of constituted public authority. The idea of the nation arose subsequent to the notion of civic citizenship which had arisen to pluralize the sovereign authority taken on by the principle of popular sovereignty. The notion of citizenship is constructed to house this popular sovereignty. The assertion of the "rights of man" legitimated the pluralistic civil society, built upon the liberal notion of the rational pursuit of self-interest that arose to provide the network of free associations required for the establishment of capitalist production relations.

The notion of citizenship thus legitimates the eclipse of the notion of kingship. Dynastic and bourgeois notions of interest eventually diverge to the point at which the new forms of social power—created in the private extraction of surpluses that constitute capitalist production relations—are exercised to emancipate the bourgeois notion of interest from the unwelcome, grasping extraction of the dynastic state. The idea of the nation further legitimates this arrangement by providing a collective identity transcending the class identity that now largely controls these new levers of social power. *National identity is integrative.* National identity encompasses all of the spaces and spans the specific cultural, ethnic, territorial contexts within which class identities actually arise. Yet I am not making a Marxist argument that national identity merely serves as a figleaf to discreetly clothe an otherwise embarrassingly naked rule of capital within a national context. The idea of the nation has implications for behavior within and between societies every bit as "real" as the equally novel construct of socioeconomic class.

Now it might be fruitful to pause and relate this discussion to the earlier discussion regarding the notion of "interests" in the context of classical realism's conception of the national interest. The development of the notion of citizenship ameliorated the domestic conflict that is latent within the requirement of the state to bow to the interests of capital in the pursuit of the "national interest." The plodding, but inexorable, extension of the franchise to ever-broader circles of domestic European society after 1848, even in the heart of conservative, dynastic, *Mitteleuropa*, slowly introduced and expanded the novelty of domestic legal equality among "citizens" of the nineteenth-century state, and thus had no small part in the creation of a conception of common "interest" of a citizenry equal before the law. Even though their labor had been commoditized, those on the short end of nineteenth-century capitalist production relations had begun to obtain a domestic legal claim, however limited at first, to share in the regulation of the social order within their national context. The emerging civil societies of nineteenth-century Europe had begun to spawn legal freedoms of association, and of contractual relations, in order to provide a favorable legal infrastructure for capitalist accumulation. They thereby provided the context in which the extension of the franchise was proliferated throughout society. The generation of this framework, and the extension of the franchise, created an environment of common enterprise that could not have developed in the traditionally legitimated social order of the *ancien regime*. Even as many of their lives were being "rationalized," in the Weberian sense, to the requirements of this new set of production relations, the common people of nineteenth-century Europe were everywhere, slowly being created "citizens." It should not surprise us that, particularly for those lower "classes" whose economic life had been no better or worse under semi-feudal absolutism, proliferation of the franchise was an effective tool in forging a new collective identity.

Having criticized existing theoretical frameworks for their inadequacies in the analysis of the causal significance of changes in collective identities for international politics I must now suggest what an alternative framework might look like. This is the task that I turn to in the next chapter. I will not provide an overarching "theory of international politics" that competes with existing theories as an autonomous theoretical framework for the analysis of all phenomena of interest to students of international relations. I will not provide a "theory of nationalism." I am agnostic as to whether either of these are attainable. I will provide, in the lexicon of Lapid and Kratochwil, a "reconstructive" theoretical framework in which I will attempt to liken changes in the collective identity of societies and collectivities to what I regard to be observable changes in the nature and functioning of the international system. To the extent that I am successful in this theoretical enterprise, I will hope to have introduced variables of systemic analysis that will enhance the application of systems theory to international phenomena. This will constitute my own first cut at a set of analytic variables I hope will illustrate how systemic structure may be augmented and corrected with a causally significant account of human agency.

2 Social Identities and Social Systems

Dear friend, theory is all gray, and the golden tree of life is green.
—Johann Wolfgang von Goethe

Search men's governing principles, and consider the wise, what they shun and what they cleave to. —Marcus Aurelius Antoninus

A developing body of theory, which argues for recognition of the social construction of political structure, has called attention to the disparate motivational assumptions underlying theories of rational choice, and hermeneutical or phenomenological theories of agents. Theories of rational choice assume that human beings are primarily and causally motivated by an instrumental rationality. Newer approaches argue that they are motivated by complex belief systems, requiring analysts to "empathize with these beliefs before human actions can be comprehended and interpreted."[1]

Alexander Wendt, drawing in part upon the structurationist sociology of Anthony Giddens and the norms-based critical theory of Friedrich Kratochwil and Nicholas Onuf, has proposed a "constructivist" approach to resolve this impasse with the assertion that "social structures are only instantiated by the practices of agents." What interests us most from this discussion is Wendt's derivative insight that *social structures are "inseparable from the reasons and self-understandings that agents bring to their actions."*[2] This insight is essential in forging the link between collective identities and the institutional forms of collective action derived from these identities.

Theories of rational choice attempt to avoid the problem of self-understandings of national agents with the assumption that they are rational actors impelled to action by instrumental rationality and systemic forces. However, many contemporary states view themselves as "national" actors: as communities of shared ethnicity, or language, or history, or belief, or heritage. They regard these linkages as transcending a purely political association which functions, corporately—as might the firm in the competitive market place—to maximize their gains from interaction with other international political units. These self-understandings produce state behaviors that cannot be explained solely by recourse to the prescriptions of rational instrumental action. Rational instrumentalism would, for example, argue for the maintenance and strengthening of multiethnic federation in order to maintain economies of scale, and to maximize bargaining leverage with respect to other international actors. How can we explain the recently observed movements in Eastern Europe, Asia and Africa, and even North America, toward political fragmentation solely by recourse to state-centric rational instrumentalism? The logic of state-centrism alone will not do.

One might argue that Slovenia was sufficiently economically better off than its former Yugoslav partners to rationally seek separation from Yugoslavia, but could a Bosnian Serb republic governed from Pale be economically viable? Quebec and "English Canada" might be economically, even militarily viable as independent entities, but neither could expect to receive better terms of trade or credit with the neighboring United States as independent entities. One recent analyst has gone so far as to suggest that Canada without Quebec might even petition for union with the United States![3] Rational instrumental accounts of the motivations and interests of international actors suggest that instrumental advantage accrues to the creation and maintenance of large states, not smaller, ethnically, linguistically or culturally homogenous states.

Wendt has argued for the assignment of equal ontological[4] status to the state and to the system. His earlier work asserts that one cannot develop a coherent theory of international relations unless both the state and system are problematized. The theory must be capable of explaining the emergence of each and capture the "generative moment" of the system. I argue that the state is just the rational, bureaucratic, institutional manifestation of societal collective identity; of the nation, in the age of nationalism. The state is not coterminous with the nation. Historically the state has both preceded and followed the nation. Significantly, it is the legitimating principles of a given, historical, social order that privilege this rational bureaucratic manifestation of those principles as an institutional artifact of the system.

As the state is privileged at the level of the "system," communities of shared identity construct states to serve their needs as "nations" in the course of systemic interaction. This was so in the past because the Westphalian system, organized under the legitimating principle of *raison d'état*, privileged the sovereign with rights and legitimacy. This is so in the newer era of national sovereignty, organized under the legitimating principle of national self-determination, because the state is still the privileged institutional form, with the provision that it must at least claim to serve as an institutional form of the collective action of a "national" collective identity. Thus I would ascribe equal ontological status to the nation (sovereign), as well as the state (institutional manifestation of sovereignty) and the system.

Collective Identity and International Systems

Nations and the international, national-state system, because they have a "template" to work with, are now a natural feature of the international political landscape.[5] Political entities, because they privilege the rules, or incentive structure, of the contemporary international system, have enormous incentives to mold themselves into this landscape. But this was not always so. We must examine how this "template" was constructed if we are to clearly, conceptually delineate the nation from the state, and apprehend the nature and modes of differentiation of the primary units of a historically developing, rather than an ahistorically continuous international system. A central argument of this work is that change in the international system occurs with changes in the collective identity of crucial social actors who collectively constitute the units from which the system is comprised.

Figure 1 provides my view of how the system changes with changes in collective identity, in tabular form. The table describes the transformation of the European system from a post-Reformation system of largely independent dynasts, segmented by confessional distinctions, to a system of sovereign nation-states. The first column provides the relevant variables, which are subject to change in the historical development of the international system. Changes in these variables are strongly interrelated.

In the discussion to follow, I will provide either a causal or a constitutive linkage between the factors, or variables presented in the first column of figure 1. Historical changes in societal collective identity have causal significance for the principles by which domestic and international social orders are legitimated. Legitimate authority over domestic society, and the perception of the legitimacy of one's rule by other societies and their governments is established by societal recognition that the exercise of this authority is consistent with principles[6] (beliefs about the nature of legitimate authority) which are generally accepted among members of domestic society and by, at least, the elites of other societies.

My argument, expressed succinctly, is that changes in co-constituted individual and collective identity result in changes in the legitimating principles of global and domestic social order, and consequent changes in the institutional forms of collective action, through which that identity is expressed to other societies. The norms, rules and principles of social interaction within, and between, these new institutional forms of collective action are developed by social actors through practice to accommodate the new institutional structure. This new structure manifests the new societal identity and system change.

Figure 1: Systemic Change with Changes in Collective ID

	Dynastic-Sovereign	**Territorial-Sovereign**	**National-Sovereign**
Individual Identity (coconstituted)	Subject of confessional Prince	Subject of Sovereign State	Citizen or Subject of Nation
Collective Identity (coconstituted)	1.Reformed / Unreformed people of Christendom 2. Subjects of Prince "X"	1. Member of social class (aristocrat, *Bürger*, or peasant) 2. Subject of Crown and state "Y"	1. Member of national community by shared ancestry/culture/history 2. National citizen of "Z" - land.
Legitimating Principle	*Cuius regio eius religio* (Dynastic authority)	*Raison d'etat* (Territorial authority)	National self-determination (Popular or national authority)
Institutional Forms of Collective Action	Kingdom and Realm	Territorial-state	Nation-state
Norms, Rules, Principles (socio-political)	Allegiance to Prince / creed. Prince gives the domestic law	Allegiance to Sovereign in service of his/her state. Sovereign gives domestic law. Emergence of civil society.	Allegiance to imagined community of shared ancestry, culture or history. Welfare state gives domestic law with counsel of enfranchised citizenry.
(socio-economic)	Division of labor expands to encompass lay bureaucracy. Limited international trade	Division of labor expands to encompass capitalist production relations. Expansion of international trade	Global Division of labor. Global capitalist economy. International economic interdependence
(inter-societal)	Prince *de facto* emancipated from Papacy. Legal anarchy	State *de jure* emancipated from all sacral legitimacy. Inception of idea of international law	Nation Self-Determination. Limited international law
(security)	Dynastic-Confessional Conflicts	*Raisons d'etat = casus belli* Territory / Resources/ Status Limited wars of Acquisition	Seccessionist/Irridentist Conflict Wars of Unification / Liberation Total Wars of National Conquest
Resulting System	**Augsburg System**	**Westphalian System**	**National-State System**

FIGURE 1 Systemic Change with Changes in Collective ID

The institutional forms of collective action are historically contingent modes of social organization. Historically society has been organized into different institutional forms. Different forms serve, at different times, the needs of different societies which construct them. These forms strongly reflect prevailing concepts of the legitimate relationship of the individual member of society to the prevailing conception of legitimate authority. Lordship was a legitimate form of authority in feudal Europe, thus fiefs were constructed to institutionalize the relationship between lord and vassal. Absolute monarchy, in which the king was thought to hold authority to rule directly from God, was a legitimate form of authority in eighteenth-century Europe, thus the territorial-sovereign state was constructed to institutionalize his unmediated sovereignty over the peoples within the territory he administered. National self-determination of a sovereign people united into a community of shared language, ethnicity, culture, or history has more recently become an accepted form of legitimate authority. Thus the national-state has been constructed to institutionalize these communal affiliations, and to serve them with an institutional form that can manifest to the world the social action that this form of collective identity seeks to express.

Thus the institutional forms of collective action change with prevailing, historically contingent conceptions of societal collective identity. *That which constitutes an appropriate institutional vehicle through which society may take social action is strongly conditioned by what form of polity the society considers itself to be.* A society that rejects lordship as a agency of legitimate authority cannot employ the institution of vassalage to take social action. A society that regards itself as a historically continuous nation, constituted by the ancient common bloodlines of the *Volk*, cannot take the social action it wishes to take, and it cannot express its self-understanding through social action consistent with this understanding, through the institution of a polyglot territorial-sovereign state.

Thus it is no accident, for example, that as German national collective identity developed in the nineteenth century, it turned to relatively ethnically homogeneous Hohenzollern Prussia, and Berlin, rather than the polyglot Hapsburg court in Vienna, for a vehicle by which German national collective identity might receive an institutional form. It is no accident that German national collective identity opted for a *Kleindeutsche* boundary, incorporating only ethnic Germans to the extent possible, rather than a *Grossdeutsche* boundary that would have incorporated the Slavic and Magyar peoples bound up in the Hapsburg Empire.

The norms, rules, and principles of interaction in domestic and international society then develop in practice. They derive from the principles that legitimate the domestic and international social orders. Their development is mediated by the institutions that enshrine and reproduce these principles. To illustrate this assertion, norms of political allegiance develop within domestic society that are consistent with the principles that legitimate the prevailing form of political authority in that domestic society. Domestic institutions reproduce these norms *of* behavior until they become norms *for* behavior, or rules. The individual's allegiance to the institutional manifestation of these principles of legitimate authority is not only expected by norms, but commanded by the rules developed to regulate institutional society in accordance with prevailing (and historically contingent) legitimate notions of sovereignty. Societies with different conceptions of the nature of legitimate authority choose to endow different elements of society with this authority. It is important to note that the choice of element(s) of society in which this sovereignty is lodged emerges as an artifact of societal collective identity. What or whom is regarded as sovereign is strongly conditioned by the self-understandings of members of domestic society with respect to legitimate authority. That which we call sovereign says a lot about who we believe ourselves to be as a polity, whether we are a passive polity (regarding ourselves as objects of authority) or an active polity (regarding ourselves as sources of authority).

Thus, with reference to figure 1, subjects of the dynastic-sovereign state gives their allegiance to the Prince, who rules domestic society, and to his creed. Subjects of the territorial-sovereign state give their allegiance to the sovereign of that state. Citizens of the national-sovereign state give their allegiance to the nation, to the imagined community of shared ancestry, culture, or history to which they believe themselves to be a part. Domestic law is given to domestic society by the prevailing sovereign. The sovereign is that person, institution, or community in which legitimate social authority is lodged in accordance with the legitimating principles of the social order.

The division of labor within and between societies also develops normatively, through practice and subsequent interaction. These arrangements are conditioned by the historically contingent, prevailing legitimating principles of social order as well. The emergence of an educated, literate lay class permitted the development of the rational accounting principles and the techniques of finance necessary for the development of a significant intersocietal trade in the Renaissance period proceeding the dynastic-sovereign era. Important as this division of labor became for the growth of the economy in the private sphere, it also permitted an expansion of the division of labor in the public sphere. Educated lay bureaucrats secularized the "clerisy" of which Gellner has written. This was an enormously important feature in the penetration of the state into the private sphere.[7]

As sovereign identity became segmented more in terms of territorial, rather than confessional or dynastic criteria, the wealth of the territorial-sovereign state became a paramount concern as a resource for use in the defense and expansion of the state. The private economy was encouraged. Surpluses of trade were sought and their proceeds skimmed off by the state to fill war chests for further expansion. Capitalist production relations ensued and the privatization of the extraction of surplus resources from society became a vehicle by which the state could harness activity in the private sphere to advance state capabilities. In the nationalist era, this division of labor expanded globally, as a byproduct of both European economic and cultural imperialism. For the first time, however, the global social order witnessed the emergence of transnational economic interdependence. The colonial periphery became dependent upon western manufactures and cultural products, and the west was in turn dependent on access to raw materials in the periphery for the production of finished luxury goods, and for an outlet for western surplus labor.

Most significantly, the norms, rules, and principles of intersocietal interaction (inter-state and inter-"national" relations) also developed in the practice of interaction. They are very much derived from the principles that legitimate the domestic and international social orders. Their development is mediated by the specific institutions that enshrine and reproduce these principles. In the text to follow, it will hopefully become clear that these institutions enshrine, at different times, a particular form of sovereign-identity, derived from the principles of the prevailing social order that legitimate this form of sovereign identity. The behavior of the institutional forms is strongly conditioned by this identity.

Thus, when in 1555 the German princes were *de facto* emancipated from the heteronomous influence of the late-medieval papacy, juridical anarchy ensued. Dynastic sovereign authority was legitimated no longer through the mediation, or the prop, of the legitimacy of a universal Church, but by the principle of the confessional and dynastic hegemony of the prince. The medieval feudal-theocratic order was transformed into a new system, which I call the dynastic-sovereign system, or Augsburg system. In 1648, when the conflictual results of the Augsburg system were surveyed at the end of the Thirty Years War, confessional hegemony was abandoned as a legitimate organizing principle. Sovereign identity was enhanced by its further emancipation from all sacral notions of legitimacy. Dynastic legitimacy remained valid, but became eclipsed and dominated by the principle of territoriality. The emergence of territoriality as an innovative principle of social closure is of considerable interest and will be treated in chapters 4 and 5. Problems of coordination of common objectives resulted in the development of games of coordination that blossom into the foundations of an embryonic international law. This coordination process matured throughout the territorial-sovereign era.

The emergence of national collective identity transformed sovereign identity within the state. The notion that nations—national communities based upon common language, ethnicity, culture or shared history—are the legitimate wielders of the sword of state sovereignty, has had causal significance for the norms, rules and principles of international as well as domestic society. The notion that the nation, however defined or segmented, is inherently sovereign and self-determining, *has transformed the legitimate social purposes of state action*. The conflict of competing national visions, many of which are housed in national-states bristling with arms, enhanced the urgency of coordination between national-states, providing impetus to the development of a more significant corpus of international law.

The discussion above provides a preliminary illustration of how historical transformations of societal collective identity ultimately result in transformation of the international system. I have made a strong claim here: that an essentially cognitive factor—the self-identification of social aggregates—has causal significance in effecting system change. I regard this to be the case and state the case unambiguously. I do *not*, however, argue that societal collective identity *determines*, of any necessity, the international system. Political structure exists. This structure constrains but does not determine the behavior of social actors and aggregates. Material factors such as geography and technology also have systemic consequences. The present study recognizes these contributors to the constitution of historical international systems both implicitly and explicitly. The purpose of the present theoretical discussion is not to develop a monocausal theory of systems change by replacing material and structural variables with cognitive or ideational variables. The purpose of this discussion is to illustrate that these cognitive factors have causal significance both for constituting the system and for explaining interaction within it. My purpose is to describe and explain a system that is dynamic rather than static. Change in the international system cannot be explained without recourse to the factors developed in these pages. If we do not consider the consequences of actor self-identification, we cannot apprehend either the nature, or the consequences of national-sovereignty or of the national-state.

Having briefly elaborated these ideas regarding systemic change with changes in collective identity, the reader will now hope for fuller elaboration of the interaction between these factors. I will therefore move to develop the concepts of individual and collective identity, legitimating principles, the institutional forms of collective action, and the norms, rules, and principles of interaction in an analysis intended to show how changes in the former result in changes in the latter. I will either constitutively or causally link these "variables" to one another theoretically, then move on to a fuller empirical illustration of their operation in the generation and transformation of empirically observable international systems. The linkage between individual and collective identity emerges as constitutive rather than causal.

Individual Identity

The self-identification of individuals (individual identity) is important inasmuch as it is in part defined in terms of their participation in a collective identity. This collective identity is subject to change by forces and events that are both endogenous and exogenous to domestic society. I might, for example, develop German national collective identity merely because I feel a cultural and linguistic affiliation with my neighbors and subjects of other German-speaking states, even though my culture and language were transmitted to me by my experience of growing up in Prussia, whose borders I may never have left. This is an endogenous source of collective identity. Conversely, I might develop German national collective identity because Napoleon's armies rolled over Saxony and the rest of German-speaking Europe, occupied my home town, raped my mother, and shot my father, and it occurs to me to consider how this might have been prevented by the creation of a single political and military actor from all of the fragmented German-speaking states of early-nineteenth-century Europe. The experience of suffering at the hands of those ethnically and linguistically different from me can affect how I view myself as an individual, and as a member of a social collectivity. This is a societally exogenous source of collective identity. Thus this collective identity locates the individual's identity both with respect to other actors, and to the global order.

Collective and individual identity are co-constituted. My individual identity acquires social significance only with reference to the identities of others, both within domestic society and within international society. If I say that I am, for example, a German-speaking Prussian (in the nineteenth century), I am also saying that I am a subject of the Hohenzollern dynasty, that I regard the crowned scion of that dynasty as sovereign (in possession of legitimate authority) and thus as sources of legitimate domestic law. When I say that I am a German-speaking Prussian, I am also saying that I am not a German-speaking Bavarian. I do not regard King Ludwig as a legitimate source of my domestic law. He does not exercise legitimate authority over myself or my people. On the other hand, if I were to simply say that I am a German, then I am saying something else entirely about whom I believe myself to be, and about what I regard as a legitimate source of authority. If your language and ethnicity is Czech, for example, and not German, I am also saying something about you. I am saying that you are not part of "us." You are "other."

Both Friedrich Kratochwil and William Bloom have illuminated the relationship between individual identity and collective identity in their analyses of the sociology of Durkheim. Kratochwil stresses Durkheim's investigation of the emotive content of social life. In Kratochwil's analysis, which draws here upon Freud, identity is obtained with reference to the structure of relations the individual desires with respect to cherished persons and institutions ("love objects"), and conversely with respect to persons and institutions that become "objects of aggression."[8] In other words, one identifies with those and that which one loves and cherishes, which are familiar and comfortable. We do not develop strong feelings for individuals and things with which we are unfamiliar. That which threatens our objects of affection, or our relationship with them, become objects of our aggression.

Bloom links individual identity to collective identity by invoking Durkheim's notion of "collective consciousness" which, in Durkheim's sociology, creates what he calls "organic solidarity . . . [among] . . . dissimilar individuals."[9] The nonemotive link between personal identity and collective identity in Durkheim is, in other words, provided through the process of the socialization of the individual into the behavioral norms of his or her society. Aided by Erik Erikson's developmental psychology of identity formation,

Bloom recognizes that Durkheim's linkage of personal identity to collective identity through the socialization process may well have enormous emotive content as well. Nevertheless he stresses socialization because "[t]heoretically . . . socialization is the precise point at which the individual meets society, at which psychology meets sociology."[10]

Put differently, socialization is a process by which we become familiar with and habituated to people, places, environments and institutions, and the modes of operation and rules of the latter. Socialization is not, in this context, a remorseless selection mechanism through which successful societal socializers are selected for survival by imitating successful behavior.[11] This discussion of individual identity has, then, led us to three theoretically pertinent observations. (1) Socialization, in the context of identity formation, is a process in which the individual is habituated to his or her society, forms cognitive, and emotive attachments to it, and incorporates its features and norms into his or her identity. (2) The individual's identity is not constituted independently of his or her membership in one or more social collectivities. (3) The individual forms and reforms identity commitments from experiences that result from forces both within, and external to domestic society.

Collective Identity

Through emotive identification (emotional attachment) and the forces of socialization, our individual identity—our ideas about who we regard ourselves to be—are derived in a social context. Individual identity and collective identity are co-constituted. Individuals do possess social agency. Individuals are self-regarding, but constrained by their nature as social organisms to self-identification with social collectivities. In the literature on developmental psychology, this self-identification with respect to others at the earliest stages of the development of the human being and continues much later in life.[12]

Durkheim's intuitive theoretical construct of the "organic solidarity of dissimilar individuals" is given a fuller theoretical form, and receives empirical affirmation, in the literature on social psychology. This is particularly so in the literature on in-group bias.[13] This bias helps center individuals with respect to others in the world. They help individuals to order and organize their understanding of the world, and enhance their self-esteem with by identification with the group. But the question of how this group identification becomes an impetus to social action remains. I have explained why the individual forms identity commitments to social groupings and the processes involved. I have explored the nature of the collective identity that helps to constitute individual identity. I have not, however, addressed the issue of how these collective identities generate social action with respect other groups, or with respect to members of another group. Daniel Druckman, who has addressed this issue in a recent analysis of the literature on in-group biases, suggests that:

> Membership in a clan, religious group, or ethnic group becomes part of the individual's *self identity* and critical to a *sense of self-worth*. The self is threatened by information that calls into question the groups to which one belongs. People learn to react based on their loyalties; they defend those groups that are important to their definition of who they are. Moreover, these loyalties differentiate whom in their environment is appropriate to support and whom to avoid. And such loyalties can foster a *consensus among members* that becomes self-fulfilling and difficult to change. The stronger the loyalty, the more likely members of a group are to *hold similar views and endorse similar strategies. They approach the world in lockstep, perceiving and defining others in the world similarly. There is little, if any, chance for discrepant information to filter through or for reasons to change to be considered.*[14]

This passage nicely captures both the emotive and socialization mechanisms that Kratochwil and Bloom have identified in Durkheim. It also suggests that collective identity and individual identity are not merely co-constituted, but are also mutually reinforcing and therefore likely to become institutionalized and to be reproduced. Collective identity carries with it the means by which it becomes institutionalized. This institutionalization mechanism is the will of the participants in a collective identity that the identity be perpetuated. This will-to-manifest-identity is an expression of the agency of the collective identity and constituted individual identities of those who share it.

It is worth pausing here to reflect upon what I have just argued in the context of the notion of "interests," developed in the previous chapter. What is suggested by my assertion above is that to the extent that collective identity has causal significance for the construction of social collectivities—which become actors in the international political arena—interest may be explained in terms of the aggregated *will-to-manifest-identity* as well as in terms of the will-to-power of the realist tradition. Individual identity is threatened by hazards to those collective identities that are constitutive of individual identity. Therefore individuals perceive that their interest lies squarely in the defense and promotion of this collective identity. The fundamental, even primordial, motive (or "interest") of self-preservation will then ensure that individuals will come fully to the defense of the collective identity that they see as fundamentally constitutive of their selves when they feel that collective identity is threatened.

Significantly, however, it does not necessarily follow that the individuals will invariably promote the aggrandizement of a collective identity that is constitutive of their individual identities under any and all circumstances. This is particularly so when the aggrandizement may threaten the collective identities of those others whom the individual does not perceive as a threat to his or her own (collective or individual) identity. With recourse to the domestic analogy so prolifically employed as an analytic device within realist scholarship, the significance of this assertion is revealed. In this context, individuals in domestic society who will react, and often react violently, when threatened will nevertheless not necessarily exhibit reflexive belligerence to others in the absence of threat. Significantly, some individuals do reflexively behave aggressively, boastfully, deviously, willfully, or violently even in the absence of threat. They must always be "on top." They must always have "the last word." We must be made aware of their accomplishments, and the insignificance of our own in comparison. We regard them as obnoxious at best, sociopathic at worst, and ostracize them from the company of polite society. Their personality disorders are seen as pathologies of inadequate socialization into domestic society. In the international context, when social collectivities exhibit similar behavior, they are regarded as "cultural attributes." In either the domestic or international case, in the absence of threats to constitutive identity, the actor can either behave modestly and cooperatively, or immodestly or belligerently. There is a "will-to-power" in some individuals in the domestic context that is not present in others. So it is in the international context.

All social actors share the will-to-manifest-identity, however, in both international and domestic society. A physical threat of extermination is not required to threaten the will-to-manifest-identity in either domestic or international society. The will-to-manifest-identity may result in a new form of collectivity, a new form of sovereignty, legitimated in a new way. When this occurs, social transformation is in the wind. This can result in transformation of global social orders. When this occurs, the international system, while it may retain features of its previous manifestation, does not escape its own metamorphosis.

Legitimating Principles

Collective identity is closely coupled to the legitimating principles within which it is constituted and interpreted. Social order is predicated on conceptions of legitimate authority, as it is too costly to maintain a social order on the basis of coercion alone. As Kratochwil has explained, the nature of legitimate authority cannot be understood by recourse to Hobbesian analysis and premises alone. The relationship between the "sovereign" and the objects of authority is not one that leaves the sovereign in the state of nature with society. The disinterestedness of the authority cannot be assured under such circumstances; therefore "no 'contract', setting up a governmental authority would ever be possible" under these conditions.[15]

Rather, as Habermas, Kratochwil, and Weber all suggest in somewhat different contexts, the relationship between members of society, and constituted public authority, is mediated by what Weber refers to as the concept of legitimate social order. It is this order to which members of society, the objects of authority, feel a sense of obligation or duty. As Weber intones:

> Action, especially social action which involves social relationships, may be oriented by the actors to a *belief (Vorstellung)* in the existence of a legitimate order. . . . orientation to the validity of an *order (Ordnung)* means more than the mere existence of a uniformity of social action determined by custom or self-interest. . . . such action in addition is determined by . . . [the individual's] . . . subjection to an order, [and] the rules which impose obligations on him, which he is usually careful to fulfill, partly because disobedience would carry disadvantageous consequences to him, but usually also in part because it would be abhorrent to the sense of duty, which, to a greater or lesser extent, is an absolute value to him.[16]

Here Weber's analysis suggests unambiguously that while, from the perspective of instrumental rationality, there are good reasons for the individual to comply with the injunctions that issue forth from legitimate authority, the act of compliance with these injunctions may not be said to have been explained without stricter analysis of motives for compliance. Certainly one good reason to comply with these injunctions is to avoid sanctions for noncompliance. A rational instrumental conception of interests can handily explain compliance with the directives even of illegitimate authority in this context: I must comply or I will be punished. Social actors acquire an interest in compliance with the injunctions and directives of legitimate authority because they value that authority. Their own notions of a moral order, those in which their identities have meaning and their compliance takes on a moral character are at issue.

Similarly, Kratochwil's analysis uncovers Durkheim's distinction between material and moral authority in the context of Durkheim's analysis of "social facts." He discovers that moral authority (legitimacy) helps to establish the notion of obligations, and justifies the threat of physical sanctions for noncompliance.

> Durkheim maintains that certain social phenomena are best investigated by tracing their origin to a collective experience and that there are significant analogies between the sacred and the moral. This last claim allows for a clearer conceptualization of obligation. . . . Sanctions are then no longer simply the penalties attached to certain actions by the Hobbesian sovereign, who thereby changes the utility calculations of the individual. As Durkheim emphasizes again and again, the term 'moral authority' is 'opposed to material authority or physical supremacy.' . . . moral facts expressed in rules of conduct are valid not because of threatened deprivations, but because of their duty-imposing character, which is in turn the precondition for the legitimacy of physical sanctions.[17]

Thus Kratochwil reminds us that physical (material) sanctions, and the material authority whose agency they manifest in a social context, are legitimated not solely by their role in mitigating anarchy by enforcing order, but also by the belief that compliance with them is a moral act, the fulfillment of an obligation to a moral (legitimate) social order. People comply because they wish to comply to fulfill an obligation to the order they value as legitimate. The threat of physical sanctions is extended to the minority who have not apprehended this duty. No social order would be possible if the threat of physical sanctions alone stood in the way of noncompliance. It is not the existence of law, or of institutions dedicated to their enforcement alone that ensures compliance with the strictures of the social order. As Helen Milner recently reminds us regarding the questions of compliance with international law, and the strictures of its institutions:

> It seems not to be their existence that matters, but their capacity for commanding obedience. This capacity depends much on their perceived legitimacy, as it does for domestic institutions. These institutions will have little influence internationally or domestically if they lack legitimacy. . . . A sense of legitimacy is essential to the maintenance of any order.[18]

But notions of moral or legitimate social order are not static. They change over time. The analysis above helps us to understand how legitimate social order is upheld and reproduced, even in the absence of material or physical sanctions, or even the threat of them. It is not so helpful in explaining how notions of legitimate social order decay, become transformed, and are replaced. We need a framework of analysis that addresses the dynamic nature of societal notions of the legitimacy of social ordering principles.[19] Why do notions of the legitimacy of the social order change? How do changes in collective identity transform the legitimating principles of social order, and thus generate a new order? I turn to the work of Habermas to establish further the link between specifically *collective* identity and the legitimating principles of social orders.

Significantly, Bloom observes that Habermas comes at the notion of identity from the epistemological perspective of philosophy rather than psychology (or sociology). For Habermas, the unraveling of the mysteries of identity and identification is a major task of philosophy. He argues that it is through the "self-reflective symbolism of identity" that both the individual and society attempt meaningfully to locate themselves in both their profane (immanent) and cosmic (transcendent) environment.[20] Habermas proposes that this is accomplished by the individual or collective social actor with recourse to an "identity-securing interpretive system" (a system of beliefs about self-identity, collective identity, and social function in a legitimate social order). If this identity-securing interpretive system generally conforms to the experience of the social actor of the "realities of social existence," the social order is legitimated. But "if there is not an appropriate symbolic mediation . . . between the individual or the group and the social structure, the anxious need for a secure and meaningful identification will manifest itself in either the change of the interpretive system [a new ideology of legitimate social order] or a demand for change in the social structure. If the interests inherent in identification are not met, then the system is not legitimated."[21]

This is the "legitimation crisis" upon which, in the view of Habermas, social orders rise and founder. Crucially important to my argument is Habermas's assertion that threats to social identity bring about these legitimation crises. In my own view, these threats result in the transformation of the legitimating principles upon which social orders rest. As Habermas observes:

> Only when members of a society experience structural alterations as critical for continued existence and feel their social identity threatened can we speak of a crisis. . . . Crisis states assume the form of a disintegration of social institutions.
>
> Social systems too have identities and can lose them; historians are capable of differentiating between revolutionary changes of a state or the downfall of an empire, and mere structural alterations. In doing so, they refer to the interpretations that members of a system use in identifying one another as belonging to the same group, and *through this group identity assert their own self-identity*. In historiography, *a rupture in tradition, through which the interpretive systems that guarantee identity lose their social integrative power, serves as an indicator of the collapse of social systems*. From this perspective *a social system has lost its identity as soon as later generations no longer recognize themselves within the once-constitutive tradition.*[22]

International relations theorists should be as capable as historians of differentiating between these different macro-level social phenomena. Habermas's discussion above provides a plausible linkage between the ideologies that legitimate a social belief system and the principles of social action by which members of a society are socialized into that system. The belief system, or "interpretive system" links individual identity and a collective identity in a context in which meaning is provided to individual identity through its ideological subsumption in a collective. This provides the individual with a "transcendent" identity inasmuch as the collective will transcend the individual. *The principles that legitimate the collective identity are the principles* that *legitimate the social order that provides an intersubjective social meaning to collective identity*. These principles are institutionally reproduced and transmitted to the individual through his or her socialization into the society that is generated and regulated by this system of beliefs.

As Habermas observes, "ruptures" in this institutionally transmitted tradition occur when the interpretive system (ideology of identity) which legitimates social order, and gives meaning to collective identity, is challenged. The challenge deprives the interpretive system of its utility in locating individual identity in the social milieu. It does so by challenging the validity or legitimacy of the collective identity that is constitutive of individual identity. This challenge can arise from sources that are either endogenous or exogenous to domestic society. This challenge often involves the creation of what Kratochwil refers to as new "institutional facts."[23]

It can also result from various discontinuities with tradition, specifically discontinuities in "community," in "society," and in "authority," particularly if these occur rapidly so as to induce the discomfort of disorientation in the individual and in society.[24] Discontinuities in community, society and authority can involve urbanization and industrialization, war and/or economic deprivation, and collapse of political regime, respectively. All of these social discontinuities can, however, have sources that are exogenous to domestic society. All can result in transformation in the orientation of a polity with respect to international society.

Most important, however, is the observation that the social order's survival is crucially dependent upon the consent given to its legitimating principles by social actors. The social order must continue to provide an institutional framework for social action that is consistent with the dominant forms of societal collective identity. *Neither legitimating principles or social orders can survive change in the other without being transformed*. Thus the agency of collective actors is found in their tendency to express their collective identity through institutional forms that are consistent with that identity. These institutional forms must also be amenable to the social action that is characteristic of a particular form of collective identity. These institutional forms enshrine the principles that legitimate these identities. Agents of the societies whose principles these institutional forms represent take social action that is impelled by "interests" that are defined in terms of the *will-to-power* only to the extent that this social action promotes the *will-to-manifest-identity* that is enshrined in the legitimating principles and institutions of the new social order.

Institutional Forms of Collective Action

The next set of variables in the first column of figure 1, the institutional forms of collective action (Kingdom / realm, state, nation, etc.), are the institutional artifacts of the societal relations and authority patterns. I have suggested above that this authority is constructed from the prevailing collective self-identifications and self-understandings, and from the principles that legitimate these. Importantly, these institutional forms are constituted with, and by, prevailing conceptions of legitimate collective identity. *These institutional forms are not fundamental. They are not theoretically or ontologically primitive. They are not enduring. These forms change with the prevailing conceptions of legitimate social order and with the collective identities consistent with this order.* This observation calls into serious question the utility of state-centric theories precisely because the state is merely one of many possible and historically observed institutional forms of collective action.

It is not by accident that social revolutions within domestic society result in immediate transformation of domestic political institutions that are deemed constitutive of the despised regime that has been supplanted. The destruction of the institutions of the *ancien regime* in this context is a willful and public act of nullification of the principles which legitimated the social order that spawned these institutions. The first act of the French National Assembly, upon learning of the plans of Louis XVI to restore absolutist rule in France with the assistance of foreign armed force, was to radically assert the collective identity of the sovereign people of France by destroying the institution of the monarchy. In this case this was most effectively accomplished by the physical destruction of the incarnation of that institution, Louis. The American Revolution replaced a parliament with a congress, a king with a president, an aristocracy with a bureaucracy. The Bolshevik revolution similarly replaced a monarch with a politburo, a Duma with soviets, the Okhrana with the Chekists.[25] When the Soviet Union gave up the ghost the entire political structure studied for decades by western scholars and intelligence analysts ("Kremlinologists"), diplomats, and journalists came down in an instant, like a bulldozed segment of the Berlin wall.

The fact that these institutions have been variously replaced by institutions modeled on those of liberal western states, or very often by nothing at all, reflects the ambiguity with which the successor states of the Soviet Union have addressed the task of defining and articulation the principles of the new social order, especially in Russia. But this does not attenuate the force of the reality of the destruction of the old institutions that had been identified with the old regime. Two of the most discredited of these institutions, the KGB and Red Army, have suffered the most. The former was almost entirely demolished, particularly with regard to its domestic surveillance function. The latter has been allowed to starve for lack of resources to the point of evident ineffectiveness.[26] This outcome is as inexplicable within the confines of neorealist analysis as was the collapse of the Soviet state and its Eastern European compatriots.[27] When we realize how closely that these institutions of state security are associated with the *ancien regime* in Russia, the rationale behind their neglect and demise becomes not only clear, but familiar, in spite of the loss of the security functions that they provided.

Significantly, Theda Skocpol, in her influential treatment of social revolution, *defines* social revolutions as "rapid, basic transformations of a society's state [institutional] *and class* structures."[28] I will pause here to briefly analyze Skocpol's notion of social revolution in order to illuminate the distinction between this concept and my conception of transformation in a social order. First of all, Skocpol analyzes what is really a very much more circumscribed phenomena than transformation of a global social order. She analyzes social revolution in a domestic context while the social orders that interest us transcend state boundaries. Yet importantly she delineates between social revolutions and political revolutions in the domestic context and we should do no less in a broader context. While political revolutions can simply result in a change of personnel within a constant institutional context, or even can go so far as a change in personnel and institutional transformation, social revolutions are accompanied by "transformations of class relations."[29]

> In contrast, rebellions, even when successful, may involve the revolt of subordinate classes—but they do not eventuate in structural change. Political revolutions transform state structures but not social structures, and they are not necessarily accomplished through class conflict. . . . What is unique to social revolution is that basic changes in social structure and in political structure occur together in mutually reinforcing fashion. And these changes occur through intense sociopolitical conflicts in which class struggles play a key role.[30]

Skocpol's structural Marxian heritage appears to predispose her to talk about "structures" in favor of agency. Yet her distinction between social and political revolution in the domestic context is useful because it demonstrates that social transformations that involve the ascendancy of one socioeconomic class over and in place of another, coupled with transformation of political institutions, are more fundamental than mere institutional transformation. This distinction is essential in understanding the radical distinction between the institutional forms of the territorial state, and the national-state. Not only was the territorial state constructed from institutions such as monarchy that the nation-state has dispensed with, but it also represented the interests of a different coalition of class actors than does the contemporary nation-state. The territorial-sovereign and national-sovereign states are legitimated by different principles, and these principles articulate a distinctly different structure of class interests as well as a very different range of prevailing societal identity commitments.

Norms, Rules, and Principles

The norms, rules, and principles for intrasocietal and intersocietal relations are developed, in practice by newly constituted social actors within and between societies. These norms, rules, and principles take forms that foster interaction among the prevailing institutional forms of collective action. They are distinct from, but derived from, the legitimating principles of these collective self-understandings. As they develop in practice I will defer further discussion of them to the following chapters, where their development and causal significance for the patterns of politics between the "units" of the three historical systems depicted in figure 1 will be developed in the course of empirical analysis of these systems.

In the preceding pages, I have outlined the principles by which the units are constituted and interact, and that the result is a "system." This system is not static. Definition of its "structure" alone does not serve to tell us how the units interact, nor does this say much about the probable outcomes of interaction.[31] The system may be transformed as well as reproduced. The system's "structural form" is mediated as much by the interests of relevant social actors defined in terms of the *will-to-manifest-identity* as it is defined in terms of the *will-to-power*.

Figure 1 outlines the manner in which I regard changes in these variables in Western European history as having resulted in change from the Augsburg system that effectively sprung from the Reformation, and effectively ended the medieval feudal-theocratic order, to the Westphalian system that legally ended the wars that were one long-term result of the Reformation, to the present nation-state system that followed the age of nationalism. Systems *reproduce* themselves so long as the institutional forms of collective action are capable of providing modalities of social action for the prevailing expression of societal collective identity. Systems are *transformed* when they become structural impediments to the social action and self-conceptions of both domestic and international social actors, and the principles that legitimate these self understandings. The norms, rules, and principles by which the system functions are transformed, through subsequent practice, to regulate social action in accordance with the new legitimating principles of the new social order.

Thus these new norms, rules, and principles develop in practice to provide reasons for new forms of social action. Note that I delineate between causes and reasons here following Kratochwil's observation that norms and rules should not be seen as "causal" in the sense that their prescriptive force causes a social actor to take a given action. Rather, they "provide 'reasons' which decisionmakers will find persuasive, and to which they will therefore defer . . . [such that] . . . all rules and norms are problem-solving devices for dealing with the recurrent issues of social life: conflict and cooperation."[32]

Sequencing: Agents and Objects of Systemic Transformation

One topic of theoretical relevance that I have so far left untreated is the question of sequencing of the changes in the factors of variables of systemic transformation that I have linked causally in the preceding discussion. Must collective identity change within a given society, or all societies before the system changes? Can the converse be true? Can the system change and thus force changes in societal collective identity upon some members of international society? Do changes in collective identity at the level of domestic society result in changes in the rules of the international system, or is the converse the case? The answer, I believe, is actor specific. It depends upon whether a given international actor is a agent of systemic transformation or an object of systemic transformation, constrained to respond to the agency of others.

I believe that evidence may be presented that the causal sequencing of the variables I have sketched out in the matrix in figure 1 may work both ways, under specific conditions. As I suggested earlier, it does *not* appear to be the case that changes in collective identity *must precede* changes in the legitimating principles of the social order within which the collective identities have meaning. It is not clearly necessary for collective identities and legitimating principles to change first, in order to evoke changes in the institutional forms of collective action. It appears to be the case that the reverse sequencing can easily occur, under certain conditions. It is important to stress, however, that a given form of societal collective identity, a given legitimating principle for a global social order, and a given institutional form (which manifests that collective identity to other societies), must be prevailing and held in common by the recognized actors in the system for a system to be constituted, or to be transformed from a prior configuration of these variables. The legitimating principles of a social order privilege some institutional forms, and not others.

Once constituted, a given system can provide, as neorealist scholarship suggests in more Darwinian terms,[33] enormous incentives for a given society to reconstitute itself in conformity with the privileged institutional forms, and to mold their identities and societal legitimating principles into collective identities and legitimating principles that are similarly privileged by these forms. Thus in the age of nationalism, for example, societies organized along traditional, tribal, or otherwise distinctly nonnational forms, may be impelled by the norms, rules, and principles of the national-sovereign state system, not only to construct states to provide rational bureaucratic agencies of their collective identity as an actor in the system, but also to construct nationalist movements and myths to legitimate their participation.[34]

Thus many societies that have suffered from the experience of European colonialism have set upon nation-building projects in order to construct national collective identities that will legitimate the institutional forms of collective action they have acquired as a colonial legacy.[35] These nation-building projects in the postcolonial third world have been taken on precisely because the self-identifications of former colonial peoples have been rather rudely transformed by the colonial experience. They have learned that colonial occupation and exploitation were the consequences of failure to construct the rational bureaucratic organizational structures (states) that serve to manifest collective identity to other societies and ensure the maintenance of these identities (societal security). Having acquired states as institutional artifacts of the colonial experience, in the age of nationalism they have endeavored to construct the collective identities that are required to legitimate, in both domestic and international society, the institutional forms of collective action that are privileged in the national-sovereign system.

The development of national collective identity has both international and domestic (systemic and unit level, in neorealist parlance) sources. National collective identity can develop from a very large number of domestic sources of that identity, and then provide a new legitimating principle for a domestic social order. The new legitimating principles then require a new institutional form—leading to a new global social order and "system" when aggregated with those of societies which have achieved a similar collective identity by their own path. Conversely, national collective identity can develop in response to what might amount to a structural condition. This condition entails the privileging of a specific institutional form of collective action, and therefore, of specific legitimating principles of that institutional form. In shorthand:

Sequence 1:

{Δcollective identity → Δlegitimating principles → Δinstitutions → Δdomestic & international norms/rules/principles → Δsystem}

or, conversely, under different conditions,

Sequence 2:

{Δsystem → Δdomestic & international norms/rules/principles → Δinstitutions → Δlegitimating principles → Δcollective identity}.

The sequencing of this transformational logic, for a given society that is in route to a change in collective identity, depends strongly upon whether that society is experiencing transformations in domestic social relations (irrespective of whether the source of this transformation is exogenous to that society) and whether that society is in a position to make its agency felt throughout international society. This second of these criteria is, of course, fertile ground for bringing the structural variables of classical- and neo-realism into the analysis (such as the distribution of capabilities across the system) with the caveat that we must expand what counts as a capability to include, at a minimum, cultural resources.

Societies that experience rapid and/or far reaching transformations in domestic relations, and who are well positioned to exert influence on other societies, tend to follow Sequence 1. They constitute *agents* of systemic transformation. One example would be the advanced, industrialized, imperialist national-states of the late nineteenth century. Societies that are domestically socially conservative or stagnant tend to reproduce their social structure and institutions domestically and—to the extent that they are in a position to exert influence on other societies—to reproduce international systemic structure as well. If these domestically socially conservative societies are poorly positioned to exert influence on other societies, they tend to follow Sequence 2. They become *objects* of systemic transformation. One example would be the peripheral peoples of late-nineteenth-century Africa and Asia. The agency of those who follow Sequence 1 creates a systemic transformation, whose influential norms and rules the subject society cannot avoid.

To the extent that the norms and rules of the international system privilege an institutional form that is at variance with the institutional form of collective action of the target society, the latter experiences powerful incentives to replicate the privileged institutional forms, their legitimating principles and associated collective identities. These traditional societies find themselves under siege by the agency of the system transforming societies, irrespective of the form these traditions take. This is so precisely because the legitimating principles of the traditional social orders are challenged when their institutional forms cannot replicate the success (the agency, felt throughout the system) of the system transforming societies. In both of these sequences societies encounter the transience of institutional facts. In the first sequence societies are impelled to create new institutions. In the second sequence they are required to adapt to new institutional facts. The forms that these adaptations take encompass, but are not exhausted by, the structural neorealist concept of socialization of these actors by the structure *qua* agency of the international system.[36] These sequences will be revisited and better illustrated in chapter 8 when I turn to the analysis of late-nineteenth and early-twentieth-century western imperialism.

3 Identities and Social Orders: International Systems in Modern History

Tempora mutantur, nos et mutamur in.
(The times change and we change with them.)
—Lothair I (795–855)

All great changes are irksome to the human mind,especially those which are attended with great dangers and uncertain effect.
—John Adams

This chapter will provide an empirical illustration of how change in societal collective identity helped to produce three historically distinct international systems. The rest of the book, beginning with the following chapter will provide an empirical elaboration of the consequences of transformation of societal collective identity and attendant system change for relations between states and nation-states.

Collective Identity and Early-modern Dynastic Sovereignty

Recall the assertion that individual self-identification with respect to constituted public authority is conditioned by the emotive and socialization mechanisms outlined by Durkheim. In the early modern era a strongly dynastic principle of authority legitimated the early modern state. Early modern dynastic authority also carried with it the ideational (for Durkheim, sacral) baggage of the medieval-feudal theocratic order. Monarchs and lesser nobility were strongly identified in terms of religious confessional status from the onset of the Protestant Reformation in the early sixteenth century on through the end of the Thirty Years' War in the mid-seventeenth century. They were Catholic or Protestant princes, and their subjects were decidedly expected to conform to the confessional status of their prince. No sixteenth century European prince could tolerate the chronic unrest that tended to result when the people became reform-minded much faster than did he.[1]

Given the passing of a generation for the reproduction of reformed ecclesiastical institutions, and allowing for regional variations in the level of penetration of a given early modern state into the daily life of society, individuals would generally not fail to identify themselves as the subject of either the "most Catholic" or "most Christian" prince "X." If state penetration of society was particularly significant, as it sometimes was, particularly in Germany, the subjection of the post-Reformation European to a prince with a specific confessional status was likely to be an attribute that was constitutive of his or her individual self-identification.[2] Little prodding would be required to evoke this self-identification in any event. In a period defined by religious conflict, a primary source of personal identity for most mature and reflective early-modern Europeans would be a religious, and specifically confessional Christian self-identification. This status was strongly constitutive of their self-identification and their collective identity as either reformed or unreformed people of Christendom, and the collective status of subjects of their Protestant or Catholic prince was largely an extension of this individual identity (see figure 1, in chapter 2).

This is not intended to imply that Christian factional or confessional status was the only component of early modern collective identity. Certainly, as has been the case in all eras, Europeans of the time identified themselves with an ethnicity or a linguistic community, but because of fragmented topography and difficulties of travel and communications, these were fragmented into many subdivisions of dialect. Hobsbawm has noted, in addition, that linguistic historians share a general consensus that it is only recently that linguistic distinctions have become means by which "friends" and "foes" are identified. Moreover, linguistic nationalism is the "construction of nationalist intellectuals, of whom Herder is the prophet"[3] and is not any sort of element constitutive of self-identity early in the modern era.

Of course, it is not difficult to find references to "nations" in the historiography of the European early modern period in general, and of the Reformation period in particular.[4] Even before the maelstrom of the Lutheran Reformation Maximilian I had commissioned the Alsatian publicist Jacob Wimpheling to draft a memorandum of complaint to the Roman Church that could be read as an articulation of national principles, as could an earlier letter written by the chancellor to the Archbishop of Mainz, Martin Mair, to Cardinal Enea of Siena in 1457. "National" grievances against Rome began their articulation as early as the 1417 Council of Constance, according to Gerald Strauss.[5] Together, these *Gravamina Nationis Germanicae*—grievances of the German "nation"—constitute the grievances of various German princes and Holy Roman Emperors, but are hardly a key to a collective identity of peoples, even though the princes sometimes spoke in their name. If they did so, they did so as a rhetorical device. Various Roman responses to these documents of grievance suggest that Rome suspected that these princes most often spoke in their own names, which the legitimating principles of the Augsburg system gave them the perfect right to do. For precisely this reason it is nonsensical to speak of sixteenth-century nations or nationalism.

This legitimating principle identified the prince as sovereign, emancipating the prince, at least in Protestant states, from the tutelage of the Roman Church. E. H. Carr appears to uncritically accept sixteenth-century usage of the term "nation" as an operationally viable progenitor of contemporary nationalism, and refers to what I call the Augsburg system as "the first period" of nationalism. We should note that in the view of the best and most recent scholarship on nationalism, it is simply a factual error to equate a limited consciousness of cultural, ethnic, and linguistic distinctions among societal elites with the nationalism that Anderson, Smith, Gellner, Greenfeld, and Hobsbawm have so rigorously analyzed. Irrespective of these shortcomings, Carr does provide an insightful passage that illustrates the legitimating principle of the Augsburg system, though the applicability of this principle should be dated from the 1555 Peace of Augsburg to the 1648 Treaty of Westphalia, not from Augsburg to the French Revolution, as Carr's "first period of nationalism" conception would have it.

> In the new national [*sic*] unit it was normally the secular arm which, relying on the principle *cuius regio, eius religio*, emerged predominant; but there was nothing anomalous in a bishop or prince of the church

> exercising territorial sovereignty. The essential characteristic of the period was the identification of the nation [*sic*] with the person of the sovereign. Luther regarded 'the bishops and princes' as constituting the German nation.[6]

What was primarily constitutive of the collective identities and legitimating principles of the social order that grew up around the Augsburg system was the fundamental orientation of each toward the person of the prince, and particularly toward his confessional status within the Christian faith. New domestic sociopolitical principles had developed from the transformation of collective identities. Individuals had previously regarded themselves as generic subjects of Christendom, subject to both the secular, temporal authority of a lord and a king, and the spiritual authority of the Church and the papacy. They now acquired a more particularistic, factional collective identity developed during the Reformation.[7] Where ties to Rome had been cut, the spiritual authority of the papacy had been thoroughly supplanted by that of a "national" Church that professed one of the rapidly proliferating variants of the reformed faith.

In the economic sphere, the rise of the lay bureaucracy had slowly ended the medieval Church's monopoly of literacy, and literate laymen began to populate the courts of princes and kings for the first time. This had the salutary effect of providing European princes with the option of entrusting those matters of "state" which required literacy to men who were not invariably the scion of the medieval Church.[8] This expanded the longstanding feudal, trifunctional division of labor[9] to include a class of lay-bureaucrats, and involved laymen in the extraction of societal resources to the benefit of the princes of the lesser nobility, and of the crown. This lay literacy also accelerated the development of the manufactures of artisans and permitted the expanded operations of the merchants who traded across the borders of the realms of the day, as this expansion required rational bookkeeping systems that permitted merchant and artisan to tally their accounts.[10] Significantly, it had also permitted the laymen to receive religious ideas at variance with those promulgated by the Church, study and ponder them at their leisure, and discuss among themselves what they had read in the privacy of their homes. Thus literacy had in no small measure helped to provide society with a tool for economic expansion that helped sustain an extractive crown which required these resources for its state-building proclivities. The expanded societal division of labor made possible by lay literacy also helped to induce the Reformation, which made the Augsburg system possible.[11]

Most importantly the Reformation and its adaptation by many European princes had created the intersocietal norm of dynastic sovereignty in the principalities and free states that adopted Protestantism. Rome could be freely and willfully ignored without fear of domestic retribution, or even domestic sullenness, in these newly created Protestant states. The prince could take any action that pleased him with respect to other states and princes without fear of excommunication, the interdict, or the ban—or at least without fear of any serious consequences of these papal penalties, which he was likely to already have suffered in any case. And often this had involved no suffering at all in the domestic political arena, as a Protestant prince in the German states in particular had as likely as not adopted Protestantism because his people had done so in the heady and raucous years of the 1520s. Under such circumstances, a papal sanction might even enhance the domestic standing of such a prince. An intersocietal norm of what we might call "dynastic self-determination" then developed, at least among the Protestant princes.

In the immediate aftermath of the Reformation, nontoleration of religious difference appears to have emerged as a norm. Disastrous wars of religion were fought among Catholic and Protestant princes of the Holy Roman Empire. The introduction, by way of Geneva, of Calvinism in the French "Huguenot crescent" had resulted in the conversion of up to ten percent of the population of sixteenth-century France to Protestantism. From Hapsburg Austria and Germany to Valois France, the initial reaction of Catholic monarchs ruling regions where the reformed faith had been introduced was invariably to repress these religious identities.[12] These wars ran on for decades, exhausting both sides, their length and their viciousness persuading Catholic dynasts reluctant to accept this result that Protestant collective identity could not be put down by force of arms. Concerned for the integrity, and anxious for the pacification of their states, the Hapsburg Holy Roman Emperor and the last Valois and early Bourbon dynasts converted the norms of intolerance to principles of toleration of religious confessional distinctions of the principalities within their realms. Significantly what began as toleration was later, in the seventeenth century, to take on the characteristics of a positive right.[13]

The internecine French Wars of Religion ended with just such a toleration edict, the 1598 Edict of Nantes. But in Germany, the 1555 Peace of

Augsburg had left a tenuous political consensus for mutual toleration of neighboring principalities populated by people of another faith. This consensus did not develop into a principle of mutual toleration of religious difference between societies, or within many societies. We must avoid generalizing from the French case. Religious identity continued to be highly, and aggressively, constitutive of societal collective identity. We should pause here to note that the sequence of events described above cannot be understood within the conceptual framework of structural realist theory.

By the dawn of the seventeenth century, a fifty-year-old peace of convenience had proved to be an inadequate institutional prop to a highly underdeveloped principle of toleration between Protestant and Catholic German principalities. In order to ensure and protect their Protestant collective identity, and dynastic interests, the Protestant princes of Germany and the *Freistaaten* (Free States, independent of the control of the Emperor) formed a military alliance called the "Union" in 1608. Catholic princes countered with the "League" the next year and tensions between these two political and military alliances escalated into hostilities by 1618, inaugurating the Thirty Years War. Emboldened by support from his relative, the Hapsburg King of Spain, the Catholic Hapsburg Holy Roman Emperor pressed his claims of rights over the Protestant princes and *Freistaaten* and in 1629 directly threatened Protestant collective identity with the Edict of Restitution, decreeing much of Protestant Germany Catholic, and threatening to make good the decree by force of arms. Protestant monarchs in Denmark and Sweden now joined the fray in defense of Protestant collective identity.

Catholic France behaved anomalously, supporting the Protestant cause in hopes of weakening the Hapsburgs, whom they chronically faced as foes in Spain, Germany, and Austria.[14] Here, significantly, France behaved as Morgenthau's balance of power theory would predict, but it is worth noting that at the time that the Union and the League were allying themselves against one another, the first Bourbon king, Henri de Navarre (Henry IV), still sat on the French throne. During the French civil Wars of Religion Henry had fought as a leader of the Calvinist faction. He had only begun taking instruction in Catholic doctrine, and converted to Catholicism as an expedient, and had displayed an ambivalence toward his religious confessional status throughout his life. Henry died in May 1610 at the hand of an assassin, Ravaillac, who was connected with the extreme Catholic *politiques* in the French politics of the day.[15] This incident discredited the domestic faction of the "League" in France for years to come, and the influence of

French Catholic *politiques* with Henry's successor was bound to have suffered enormously. Moreover, France had endured more than forty years of religious civil war in the sixteenth century, ending much later than the 1555 pacification of Augsburg. War exhaustion, a new, religiously pragmatic Bourbon dynasty, the death of the first Bourbon King of France at the hands of an agent of the French Catholic faction, and the threat of Hapsburg powers on nearly all land borders goes a long way toward explaining the anomalous behavior of a still overwhelmingly Catholic French nation during the Thirty Years War.

Here appears what looks like a significant, if temporary, wrinkle in the fabric of France's collective identity as a Catholic nation. Certainly four decades of religious civil warfare had resulted in a "legitimation crisis" of the French regime as a Catholic social order. It is interesting to ponder what the future of France might have been without the installation of a *de facto* Calvinist, *de jure* Catholic, but in every way religiously pragmatic prince on the French throne as the century waned. The extreme Catholic faction of the sixteenth-century French body politic had been so averse to accepting the religious toleration that characterized French domestic policy with the accession of Henry that it began to agitate for a pro-Spanish policy and alliance with Catholic Hapsburg Spain, which posed as a chronic challenger to France. Le Roy Ladurie notes this "clear and explicit preference for religion over nation [sic]" with the consequence that:

> the intelligentsia of Henry of Navarre's reign went so far as to cut the nation [*sic*], in its own interests, from its Catholic roots. France began gradually to acquire the shape familiar today, divorced from heaven-sent notions of sacrality and sometimes even away from royal descent. The nation [*sic*] strove to achieve its own unique identity, even if, from this point of view, it was a long way off in *c.* 1600.[16]

Significantly, as France wandered in to its own protracted involvement in the Thirty Years War on the side *opposing* France's co-religionists, this passage from Ladurie indicates that Catholicism was no longer hegemonically constitutive of French collective identity. It is doubtful that this can be said of the Hapsburgs, or other Catholic belligerents. Certainly, the formation of the "Union" is an event that in itself suggests that Protestantism was sufficiently strongly constitutive of the collective identity of the states and principalities comprising it to serve as an impetus to a collective security arrangement. This suggests that France had passed through, and had spent more time being tempered in, the cauldron of Christian factional warfare earlier and more thoroughly than its fellow belligerents in the Thirty Years War. As France had excised religious identity, at least to this extent, from its collective identity in this cauldron, France emerged into the thoroughly modern era a bit earlier than the rest of Europe, as indicated by the earlier decoupling of religious identity from French foreign policy.[17] Only a religious conflagration roughly equivalent to France's four decades of religious civil war permitted the rest of Europe to emerge from the crucible of the Thirty Years War in a similar form.

Collective Identity and Westphalian Territorial Sovereignty

In the modern, Westphalian era the confessional status of the prince continued to have constitutive consequences for individual self-identification. The reproduction of ecclesial institutions, be they reformed or unreformed, had continued apace from the time of the Reformation. The general European exhaustion at the end of the wars of religion, and the secular Westphalian settlement, had dissipated religious identity and confessional status as primary sources of interstate conflict.

In domestic society religious identity continued to be constitutive of individual self-identification. In an international context religious identity now lacked the highly emotive quality required to so thoroughly demonize those abroad who possessed a different religious identity. It appears that decoupling of the religious complexion of a foreign power from the issue of its status as a sovereign power was an innovation formulated by societal elites, and then slowly adopted by their subjects. The monarch, Catholic or Protestant, had acquired a sovereign status that was in no way conditioned by his or her confessional status. While all members of society might now still be the subjects of a sovereign whose confessional status they shared, that status was now largely relevant only in a domestic context. In post-Westphalian international conflict, the enemy of the subject's Protestant prince and state might be Catholic, but his Catholicism was incidental to his belligerence, rather than responsible for it. To the extent that the individual experienced a filial loyalty to the prince, and a cultural affinity to the prince's lands and peoples, the individual would identify with the prince and his state, and defend him and it in the absence of a confessional motivation.

The prince's legitimacy, and the state's sovereignty, were now emancipated from the issue of confessional status. The individual's self-identification now coalesced with a collective identity and institution that was no longer hegemonically dependent upon confessional status. This development had causal significance for future *casus belli* in conflict with other societies.

The Westphalian peace settled the great religious issues that had stirred up the vehemence of the European masses for three or four generations. Protestant and Catholic states, it had been determined, after war exhaustion and military stalemate, would live side by side, so that all could live. With the disastrous war behind them, seventeenth-century European states for the most part settled down to resume their state-building projects within their own borders. For the next century and a half, from the Westphalian settlement to the French Revolution, the agency of the European masses, which had been so evident in their mobilization to religious causes from 1525 to 1648, would be supplanted by the agency of the burgeoning state.

In the Reformation period, particularly in the case of the German Reformation, princes had followed their people[18] as often or as significantly as the converse had been the case, particularly in the urban areas, which had been hotbeds of social unrest and religious reform. Popular sentiment had brought on the Reformation (with the notable exception of the English Reformation).[19] Popular sentiment in the Netherlands and the *Freistaaten* had resulted in the formation of military alliances along the religious cleavages between the "Union" and the "League." Popular sentiment had exacerbated the viciousness of the Thirty Years War. Popular religious ardor had now finally collapsed in war exhaustion and the states that had emerged juridically autonomous and equal from the Westphalian settlement now resumed their penetration of their societies without the distraction of general and protracted continental warfare.

This is not to suggest that the century following Westphalia was wholly devoid of conflict. Kalevi Holsti has documented up to twenty-two European conflicts between 1648 and the close of the broader War of Spanish Succession ending in 1713. One or two of these conflicts involved as many as five European states.[20] Holsti observes, however, that of the fifty-one issues that he identifies as contributing to the initiation of hostilities in these twenty-two conflicts, only three of the fifty-one issues involved the protection of co-religionists and, according to Holsti's reckoning, the issue was primary in none of these conflicts.[21]

Osiander has argued persuasively that the most novel and important principles of international interaction inaugurated by the Westphalian settlement were those of *autonomy* (each state would be recognized as an autonomous actor in its foreign and domestic relations) and *equality* (each state and its prince or representatives would be treated as equivalent actors in their rights and obligations in their relations with one another).[22] As Osiander suggests:

> Equality was the unavoidable corollary of autonomy. . . . In the European system at large, rejection of the universal authority formerly vested in the Emperor and pope logically implied complete equality for all the actors that recognized each other as such. In a system where the autonomy principle was accepted fully, the question could no longer be that of where in the system actors ranked, but merely whether or not they legitimately (that is consensually) belonged to the system.[23]

Having created the principles of international autonomy and sovereign equality among states and princes, the international system began to operate on principles that were quite inconsistent with the equation of the state with the faith of the prince. With religious identity subsumed within a sovereign identity of an expanding state, societal collective identity began to coalesce around that state. Popular passions, lacking religious fervor to give them impetus, lost their significance in affairs that were external to domestic society. The belief system of the common people again became less significant to intersocietal interaction than the belief systems of the sovereign, and political and societal elites, specifically "the nobility, the military leaders, churchmen, members of parliament (where parliaments existed)."[24] International conflict rarely involved any conflict of faiths in the Westphalian system.

Evan Luard suggests that international policy was determined by the uniquely secular Westphalian legitimating principle "the interest of the state: *raison d'état*."[25] The justifications of the policies and actions of the Westphalian state were inevitably provided in terms of this interest of the state, particularly the justifications for going to war. Luard stipulates these justifications with recourse to the empirical support of the justificatory utterances of belligerent monarchs between 1648 and 1789. Territorial-sovereigns went to war (1) to defend the "honor" of the state; (2) to enhance the "glory" of the state and its "standing" in Europe; (3) to "anticipate" or "pre-empt" war by another state; (4) to protect the "interests of subjects" of the state, particularly their trade and commercial interests whose surpluses often provided the financial life's blood of the crown.[26]

Significantly, more than any other system, the interests of the state justified most expedients in the Westphalian, territorial sovereign system, and "war was thus widely seen as a legitimate instrument for promoting national interests. Rulers themselves were frank in declaring that view."[27] Just as significantly, interests were not invariably defined in terms of the will-to-power even in frank admissions that the interests of the state justify recourse to war for their attainment. The defense of "honor" and pursuit of "glory" suggest a significant congruence of the prestige of noblemen and dynasties with the "interests" of the territorial-sovereign state. The great confessional issues had been settled. The system had evolved into a system governed by the principles of autonomy and equality among princes, segmented according to another constitutive principle of the system, that of *territoriality*. John Gerard Ruggie suggests that this issue dominated international politics straight from the Peace of Westphalia through the Seven Years' War. The latter conflict will constitute the first case to be studied in the empirical chapters of this work, to serve as an illustration of international behavior in the non-nationalized system.

> This first [Westphalian] phase was followed by warfare in which the nature of the units [territorial-sovereign states] was accepted but their territorial configuration remained contested. We might call these 'configurative' wars. The Wars of Succession of the early eighteenth century—Spanish, Polish, and Austrian—and the Seven Years' War (1756–63) illustrate this form. Among other factors, these conflicts revolved around the principle of territorial contiguity versus transterritorial dynastic claims as the basis for a viable balance of power. In the end, territorial contiguity won out, at least in the European core.[28]

Ruggie goes on to assert that "[h]aving established territorially fixed state formation, having insisted that these territorial domains were disjoint and mutually exclusive, and having accepted these conditions as the constitutive bases of international society" the territorial sovereigns of the late-seventeenth through eighteenth century reduced all problems of international interaction to a territorial solution.

As the territorial-sovereign state continued to increase its penetration in domestic society, particularly where various forms of absolutist rule developed, significant innovations in the composition of armed forces were developed. Even without the ideologically mobilizing power of nationalism, eighteenth-century states had developed the technical administrative capacity to ensure a significant amount of continuous revenue would flow to the crown. One of the most significant consequences of this enhanced extractive capacity of the state was the development of professional standing armies. Monarchs were no longer content to have access to small armed forces, only in time of war, which they were constrained to lease on an ad hoc basis from private military contractors, as they had done throughout the Thirty Years War. This had tended to require the raising of large sums of money quickly, and at high rates of interest. The increasing capacity of the state to extract surpluses from domestic society had permitted the provisioning and payment of relatively large armed forces in peacetime, and eighteenth-century monarchs generally availed themselves of the opportunity to create these forces. One illustration of the effects of this extractive capacity is the case of Prussia, which was able to field and maintain 6,000 men at arms in 1660, 30,000 by 1688, 83,000 by 1740, and 200,000 by 1786.[29]

No "national" collective identity could be found among these eighteenth-century European societies, and the citizen-army of later Revolutionary France was nowhere in sight. Due to the rigors and miseries of military life in this period recruitment was a chronic pressing need. This need was alleviated in part by mass infusions of the alien exiles who obtained opportunities for advancement in these absolutist armed forces that would otherwise be unavailable to them. The officer corps provided an outlet for the energies of the scion of the domestic nobility. Some foreign mercenaries could be obtained, but much of the rank and file had to be recruited or otherwise pressed into service from among the dregs of domestic society.[30] While the crown could assemble quite sizable standing forces from such an ensemble, the mere recounting of the disparate social origins of its constituents leads one to question its cohesiveness as a military unit.

In this sense, as societal collective identity had solidified around the state, however entwined this state might be with a dynasty, it permitted the growth and societal penetration of the state to increase dramatically the state's extractive capacity to furnish the state with the ornament or tool (depending upon circumstances) of powerful standing armed forces. This territorial-sovereign collective identity had not yet, however, provided the capacity to mobilize the society's emotive connection to the state such that life and limb would be offered willingly by those who served. The societal emotive response to the "sacrality" of legitimate authority that Durkheim investigated manifested itself in allegiance to the crown. Yet the vast majority within domestic society were pleased to pursue profit with their own peaceful professions, and more than pleased to see the crown fight its wars with the aid of foreign mercenaries, alien exiles, haughty domestic nobles, and ne'er-do-well adventurers. This was particularly the case inasmuch as military obligations, and access to a military career, was the perquisite of the aristocracy in absolutist Europe.

While societal collective identity might cohere at the intersocietal level around a dynasty and a state identified with the dynasty—as exemplified by the Bourbons, Hapsburgs, Hohenzollerns, and Romanovs—societal collective identity at the level of domestic society was still largely fragmented by *de facto* legal inequality among members of prenational European society. Under conditions of legal inequality, as exemplified by the estates system in France, the emerging urban and rural bourgeoisie would pay their taxes to crown and state, but would not yet do the fighting themselves.[31] The urban and rural poor, encompassing large segments of prenational European society, could not be induced to believe that they had any stake whatever in society, or to the regime that ruled over it. Absolutist eighteenth-century European regimes thus tended to view the non-noble segments of their societies as compliant suppliers of resources for the maintenance of the state. Of course this provided a significant advantage in international competition for those states—larger states with larger populations—which tended to have more resources to extract for the procurement of larger armed forces.

Significantly, however, Hendrik Spruyt has recently pointed out that the size of a territorial state, and its population, are imperfect predictors of the military effectiveness of a state. It is the resources that the state can mobilize that are key to its military success. Yet he argues further that success in war was "not the dramatic decisive selection mechanism"[32] ensuring that the form of the territorial-sovereign state, juridically recognized in the Peace of Westphalia, would yet rule as the constitutive "unit" in the modern international system. The territorial-sovereign state was competitively privileged, in Spruyt's view, as it provided the institutional structure that a political authority needed to gain a competitive advantage in military and economic competition. Yet selection:

> also advanced . . . by the process of mutual empowerment. Sovereign actors only recognized particular types of actors as legitimate players

> in the international system. Because the Hanseatic system of rule proved to be incompatible with that of territorially defined states, and because it was less able to credibly commit itself to international treaties, it was not considered to be a legitimate player in international relations . . . it was barely recognized in the Peace of Westphalia. Yet very small entities, which were organizationally compatible with sovereign states, were considered to be legitimate. The miniature states of Germany and Italy continued in the international system until their respective unifications.[33]

One significant consequence of this process of mutual empowerment was the emergence of the conception, however limited, of international law. Of course the influence of this conception on the policies and behaviors of territorial-sovereign states and their monarchs was quite limited. Luard notes, for example, that Charles XII of Sweden was tutored by Pufendorf, whose international legal conceptions seem not to have stemmed Charles's bellicosity on the throne.[34]

Yet the effectiveness of international legal thinking is not circumscribed by its presumed effectiveness or ineffectiveness in inducing pacification among states. Neither is its utility circumscribed by presumed rates of compliance with its prescriptions, particularly so early in the conceptualization and institutionalization of international legal thinking. This is best illustrated with recourse to Kratochwil's arguments regarding the international legal status of the highly contemporary phenomena of international regimes.[35] In Kratochwil's analysis, the analogy of domestic legal jurisprudence is wholly applicable to the question of the status of international legal reasoning, as the accumulating corpus of prior authoritative decisions functions in a similar capacity to the function of precedent, and case law, in domestic legal jurisprudence.

Kratochwil argues that human actions require interpretation. As this is the case, instances of noncompliance with regime norms and rules must be interpreted and adjudicated with reference to the "reasons" offered to mitigate the charge of noncompliance. It is inherent in the properties of Kratochwil's description of norms that they are counterfactually valid. An instance of violation of a norm does not render it invalid. Norms are not generalized universal propositions that can be invalidated by the demonstration of a single counterfactual instance, as is the case with the universal propositions positivist inquiry so diligently seeks to uncover. Kratochwil argues that an admission of noncompliance by an international regime participant can even strengthen the regime for the future, if sufficient reasons for the stipulated instances of noncompliance are provided. The adjudication of the subject instance of noncompliance can add to the corpus of authoritative decisions against which future compliance issues are to be decided, providing a significant additional guidance for adjudication of these cases.[36] This reasoning appears to be as valid when applied to general international legal norms as it is to specific twentieth-century international regime norms. However, little "case law" was available as bases for adjudication by authoritative decisions, even by small ensembles of powerful dynasts, in eighteenth-century Europe.

Yet even at this time, as Luard relates, the principles of *raison d'état* did not forestall the development of international norms that exhibited a constraining effect on belligerent conduct, and one may observe in the historical record the evolution of an eighteenth-century discourse on the legitimate uses of force. Monarchs invariably took pains to depict their wars as "just." Further, they began to define the rights of neutrals, particularly circumscribing action that might be directed toward neutral shipping and commerce, and to issue codes of conduct for their armies operating abroad.[37]

Another significant consequence of the mutual empowerment of states which Spruyt suggests resulted from mutual recognition after Westphalia, is what Paul Schroeder calls the "fact of functional differentiation."[38] As Schroeder recounts, Waltz argues that an imperative for success in domestic competition is specialization, while in international competition the state must look after its own interests and replicate all of the functions of all other successful states in the system. While most states did replicate the institutional structures and domestic "functions" of other successful states in the system, Schroeder recounts that as a matter of historical, empirical fact:

> throughout the Westphalian era states both great and small, aware of their vulnerability and threats, sought survival in the international arena not only by means of strategies other than balancing (by bandwagoning, hiding, and transcending) but also, precisely by specializing. They claimed, that is, an ability to perform certain important international functions or fill particular vital roles within the system that no other unit could do or do as well, and expected other powers

> to recognize these functions . . . failure to specialize in the international system could equally well be punished.[39]

The Westphalian autonomy and equality principles identified in the Westphalian consensus agenda by Osiander appear to have been flexible enough to mitigate "anarchy" to the extent that specialization became a feature of the Westphalian territorial-sovereign system. Osiander further suggests that in the face of a French grab for European hegemony in the War of Spanish Succession, the preservation of the territorial-sovereign system, and the principle of "subordination of 'private' [state] to 'public' [system] interest" became a new intersocietal consensus principle upon which the Treaty of Utrecht was founded.[40] This public / private distinction indicates, to Osiander, Europe's "self-awareness" as a system, the notion of a "public" interest of the system, and the illegitimacy of the subordination of this public interest to the "private" interests of a state, house or dynasty. *Thus interest defined in terms of the will-to-power of realism, was subordinated by an intersocietal consensus principle that legitimated the system wide social order.* State interest, defined in terms of the will-to-power, was juridically subordinated to the interest of a "system" *qua* international social order that was defined in terms of the *will-to-manifest-identity* of a system of states free of the hegemony of any other state, and embodied in the equality principle.

Thus while the structure of identities and interests of the prenational territorial-sovereign state system conforms on many levels to a notion of state interests that is consistent with that of classical realism, interests can not be so neatly defined in terms of the will-to-power as Morgenthau's account suggests. If Osiander's account is correct, *the balance-of-power principle emerged as an intersocietal legitimating principle of the territorial-sovereign states system for the first time at Utrecht, in reaction to an unprecedented Westphalian grab for European hegemony by France.* If this is the case, then interest defined in terms of the will-to-power is in large measure a contingent artifact of the French attempt to violate the existing interest defined in terms of the will-to-manifest-identity of a self-aware system of states.

This is a useful illustration of the statement that arose in the context of my earlier theoretical development of the significance of collective identity in the transformation of the international system. Once reconstituted by transformations in collective identity—and by the related variables developed earlier in this chapter—the norms, rules, and principles of intersocietal interaction develop through practice. *Practice admits historically contingent phenomena, such as attempts at hegemony, to influence the generation and subsequent evolution of these structures.* At the level of domestic society, collective identity, in the Westphalian system, delegated social agency entirely to state elites, who developed these intersocietal principles without consulting domestic society. Elite mediation of collective identity does nothing, however, to defeat the significance of territorial-sovereign identity for the understanding of state behavior, and the patterns of politics within that system. On the contrary, I will shortly develop the notion of national-sovereign collective identity to illustrate precisely the significance of these transformations in collective identity on the norms, rules, and principles of intersocietal interaction in a system where less political authority in international interaction is delegated to societal elites.

Collective Identity and National Sovereignty

It is difficult to argue that religious or confessional identity was strongly constitutive of *individual* identity, let alone collective identity, at the dawn of the age of nationalism in the late nineteenth century. The ideas of the Scottish and French Enlightenments had fostered a radical secularization both in European society and in the colonial periphery. Many of the fathers of the American Revolution, for example, had supplanted increasingly deinstitutionalized forms of Christianity with an optimistic deism in their personal religious confessions. Their correspondence rarely refers directly to a deity, but is merely spotted with diffuse references to "divine providence."[41] The secularism of leading lights of the French Enlightenment, particularly of D'Alembert, Diderot, Condorcet, Voltaire, Rousseau, Mably, and Marat has been well studied and scarcely requires reference.[42]

In the nationalist era religious identity and national identity are generally decoupled. Religious identity in the liberal west is thoroughly relegated to the status of a cultural attribute within domestic society, a matter of personal preference no more significant in the civic order than is the individual's tastes in music, food, clothing, or any consumer commodity. Religious identity emerged (in the context of the civil societies that emerged from the associational framework that founded the capitalist state) as a cathectic choice. This is particularly true in the liberal, citizen-based variant of nationalist thought. The more culturally based, Hegelian, communitarian form of nationalist thought, in particular, views society as an organic entity. In this variant of national identity, of course, individual identity constituted in such a context is less likely to ascribe a purely incidental, cathectic signification to religious identity or other cultural attributes. This fact does not defeat the assertion that religious issues were largely domesticated in the nationalist era, in what had become a radically secularized world.

Yael Tamir has illustrated the importance of more secular cultural attributes of individual identity for the formation of national collective identity. She has done so in the context of a comparative analysis of liberal and national thought. Both the liberal and communal schools of nationalist thought contain a theory of human agency. Though she makes no reference to him, she develops her analysis in a fashion that elaborates on the utility of Durkheim's notions of "collective consciousness" and "organic solidarity" in a discussion linking individual identity and collective identity. She observes that;

> . . . both schools of thought can agree on characteristics of individuals as agents who look to society to lend context to their personal thoughts, namely as agents who acknowledge that their ends are meaningful only within a social context . . . [but conflict between them] . . . concerns the process whereby individuals acquire membership in particular social groups, *the links between these memberships and personal identity.*[43]

Tamir argues that liberals and nationalists agree that "affections, loyalties, and social ties are constitutive factors of individual identity" but liberalism views these as matters of personal choice. Communitarian nationalists see these "affiliations as inherent, as a matter of fate rather than choice."[44] Still, the thesis of Tamir's book is that one can be a liberal and a nationalist at the same time. This was and still is certainly true of American nationalism. The distinction between liberal-nationalist and communitarian-nationalist self-identification will become important later on when the book addresses the consequences of nationalism for international behaviors, particularly in the context of explaining variations in western versus central European nationalist behavior.

Yet the twin development of the ideologies of liberalism and nationalism is highly germane to the development of the notion of national-sovereign states. It is difficult to see how national-sovereign identity could have been constructed without the assistance of the liberal pluralism that is so essential for the unimpaired functioning of capitalism. Recall the discussion in chapter 2 regarding the importance of capitalist production relations for the development of the notion of citizenship. I argued that the freedoms of association and freedoms to strike private contracts—and a structure of property rights conducive to capitalist accumulation[45]—were essential positive rights in the legal structures of states where capitalist production relations were successfully established. The extraction of societal surpluses through the private modality of capitalist production relations had accelerated from as early as 1750 to as late as 1830 and had continued through the nineteenth century in a great industrial revolution. The effects of this economic revolution were so varied and profound for European and American society that even a significant stipulation of them would fall far outside the scope of the present study. One of the most important of these effects, however, is that particularly "between 1848 and the early 1870s . . . the world became capitalist and a significant minority of 'developed' countries became industrial economies."[46]

The years coincident with the operation of the vaunted Concert of Europe—particularly those between 1832 and 1880—saw the "triumph of old regime liberalism" in which increasing societal liberalism was passed into domestic law by states governed by the notables of the *ancien regime*,[47] who permitted this expansion of liberal ideology and law to flourish. They did so in reaction to the French Revolution, in hopes of avoiding what they perceived to be the unenviable wages of absolutism; in reaction to the threatening cataclysm of challenges of Revolutionary France, under various guises from Jacobinism to Thermidor to Directory to Empire; and in reaction to the demands of their burgeoning domestic petty bourgeoisie, whose aspirations had been heightened by a newly found property stake in society.

National-sovereign collective identity had been recently forged in the American and French Revolutions. Both uprisings were undertaken against more or less virulent forms of autocratic decisionmaking that were so characteristic of territorial-sovereign identity. Both had emerged to replace notions of the individual-as-subject with notions of the individual-as-citizen. The roots of this notion of citizenship in both the French and Scottish Enlightenments are easily discernible. The liberalism and pluralism latent within these traditions, and the revolutionary ideologies of "citizenship" founded upon them, made these revolutions against monarchy susceptible to consolidation by the bourgeois elements of society, which sooner or benefited from these struggles. This occurred sooner in the American case. The American Revolution was led entirely by property owners, men who had a significant stake in society. The federal constitution that emerged from the convention which had been convened to replace the failed Articles of Confederation had firmly entrenched property rights in the fundamental law of the land.[48] Bourgeois consolidation occurred later in the French case as the revolutionary status of citizenship, and the principle of popular sovereignty, was created largely by aristocratic rather than bourgeois reaction to French absolutism, and coopted by the bourgeoisie.[49]

Certainly the French Revolution was a "bourgeois revolution" in the sense that it did not occur "in a backward, or in a late or uneven developing country," a fallacious component of Skocpol's argument, according to Mann.[50] A major crisis of legitimacy of the old regime in France had resulted from the prolonged and increasingly serious financial crisis that resulted from France's loss to Britain in the Seven Years' War. "Britain acquired a global empire [in the war]; France acquired debts."[51] Subsequent to this loss, in virtue of this debt, the French Monarchy not only suffered challenges to its legitimacy from having alienated the aristocracy on account of its persistent autocracy, but now suffered from a "crisis of confidence" of the French financiers and bourgeoisie on account of the insupportable war debt.[52] It certainly constituted a significant "legitimation crisis," in the Habermassian sense, for the old regime in France.

Whatever the intellectual origins of national collective identity in its early American and French manifestations, the notion of citizenship and of sovereignty lodged in the people, rather than in the monarch, and the right of these people to determine their own affairs, became legitimating principles for a new social order struggling to emerge from civil society. This civil society might have been created-to-order for the benefit of the full flowering of capitalist production relations. As capitalism flowered through the nineteenth century, a conception of economic class was experienced by domestic society, but contrary to the expectations of Marx, the political organization of nineteenth-century domestic society did not emerge directly from the relations of production. Certainly the notion of economic class could have never developed without the triumph of capitalist production relations. The Marxist notion of economic class is an artifact of the fact that Marxism emerged as a critique of liberalism and would otherwise be incoherent. Political organization by economic class was mediated, however, through societal reaction against one institutional artifact of the territorial-sovereign state that was in crisis by the nineteenth century: its militarism.[53] The twin burdens of high taxes, and conscription to support the inefficiency and militarism of the old regime state, resulted in a legitimation crisis for the social order upon which this particular institutional form of collective action was founded.

In turn, the bourgeoisie and then the petty bourgeoisie and workers and peasants now "claimed civil citizenship [in order] to freely protest political economy, and when protest was ineffective they demanded political citizenship."[54] This protest ultimately brought on the "failed" revolution of 1848. The state found that it had to expand participation in order to hold at bay this new legitimation crisis and progressively extended the franchise to ever broader circles of domestic society throughout the nineteenth century. Class, as previously observed, was an attribute of individual identity, but an attribute that always developed in a specific cultural, domestic context. As the expansion of the franchise continued throughout this "long nineteenth century," the struggle for it was shared across classes. The simultaneous expansion of literacy, with the franchise, to ever more humble, less propertied segments of society enhanced the cultural affinity within domestic society, and its significance.[55] The privileges of the old regime served as a common source of grievance that transcended the class-identities of the non-noble classes. There then developed a "cross-class-self-consciousness" that expanded into national collective identity.[56]

It is interesting, in the context of this discussion of the importance of the struggle for enfranchisement in the development of national collective identity, to consider the manner in which the enfranchisement of the citizen *qua* co-national implies closure against non-nationals and creates noncitizens, and thus disenfranchises others. Note that eventually citizenship was everywhere acquired either by ascription (birth) or by naturalization.[57] In the context of Ruggie's discussion of territoriality in the international system we might note that the territorial-sovereign state was also a method of territorial closure to individuals and interests pertaining to another sovereign. Territorial sovereignty permitted closure against them through the physical control of a contiguous territory, and of its borders, by a centralized political administration. In the territorial-sovereign system European powers typically administered individuals within their borders in the capacity of subjects, not citizens. In the national-sovereign system, the regulation of citizenship provides the nation with an expanded capacity of closure against noncitizens.

This capacity becomes extremely important as the territorial-state gives way to the nation-state *qua* eudomonic state, which is by now concerned with the material well-being of its citizens. The notion of enfranchised citizenship, the citizen as an individual with a material stake in the well-being of the nation and a voice in the regulation of its affairs, in many ways constitutes a fundamental legitimating principle of the national-sovereign system. The difficulties that autocratic territorial-sovereign dynasts experienced in meeting these expectations accounts, in many ways, for the legitimation crisis of the old regime as it blinked into the glare of the nationalist era. This is well expressed in the following passage by a recent work of Rogers Brubaker.

> Domestic closure against noncitizens rests on this understanding and self-understanding of modern states as bound nation-states—states whose *telos* it is to express the will and further the interests of distinctive and bounded nations, and whose legitimacy depends on their doing so, or at least seeming to do so. The routine exclusion of noncitizens from modern systems of "universal" suffrage is exemplary in this respect. Suffrage has always and everywhere been closed, but the post-French Revolution nationalization of politics occasioned a gradual shift in the axis and rationale of closure. . . . That the exclusion of noncitizens from the franchise for national elections has nowhere been seriously challenged, even in the many European states with sizable populations of long-term resident noncitizens, testifies to the force—indeed the axiomatic status—of nationalism in modern states.[58]

Conclusion

The literature on the causes of nationalism is vast. This book is predominantly concerned with the consequences of nationalization of territorial-sovereign actors, not the causes of nationalism. The book has not yet been written that can coherently delineate among the competing explanations, none of which are, in any case, likely to be wholly applicable for any particular case or state. What is undeniable, for those familiar with the literature on the causes of nationalism, is that many of these "causes" are endogenous to the societies which spawn these nationalisms. They invariably include what structural neorealism dismisses as "unit level causes." This is no doubt in large measure the reason that the word "nationalism" can not be found in the index of Waltz's 1979 formulation of structural neorealist theory.

What I have hoped to emphasize with the reconstructive theory and the brief empirical illustration developed in the proceeding pages is that any system theory that hopes to account for and explain phenomena which accompany transformation in the international system must comprehend the self-identifications of collective actors in the system. This perforce entails an examination of the "units" as it is within the units (and their cultural, linguistic, and shared historical contexts), as well as the system, that these self-understandings arise. The self-understandings, or collective identities of collective actors, do have causal significance for the interaction of the "units" and thus must be included as an element of structure.[59]

These self-understandings have, historically, strongly influenced which states have allied with other states and for which purposes. Societal self-understandings have helped to determine the norms, rules, and principles of interaction between societies, privileging some modes of interaction and constraining others. Contrary to the assumptions of systemic theories featuring the billiard-ball model of the state, the character of the units has historically affected their behavior quite substantively. The institutional forms of collective action have evolved to reflect changing notions of legitimate domestic and global social order with significant and empirically observable impact on the norms and rules of interaction between the units. The structure of the notion of interests of the units that motivates their behavior is strongly influenced by the structure of identities that mediates their self-identifications and self-understandings with respect to legitimate social authority.

I will now move, in Part II of this work, to describe and analyze the structure of identities and interests that constituted a system comprised of actors possessing territorial-sovereign identity. I would ask the reader to pay special attention to the notion of state interests that emerges from this structure of sovereign identity.

Part II

Territorial-Sovereign Identity

4 Raison d'Etat and Territorial Sovereignty: Mercantilist Absolutism and Eighteenth-Century Imperialism

We are king and master and we do as we please.
—Friedrich Wilhelm of Prussia

No one reasons, everyone executes! —Friedrich the Great

Power or weakness does not in this respect produce any difference. A dwarf is as much a man as a giant. —Vattel

In the eighteenth century state-building projects and international rivalries in many ways developed in tandem. They were both aspects of the development of the fundamental legitimating principle of the territorial-sovereign international system. This is the doctrine of *raison d'état*; the notion of the primacy of the interests of the state, which could only with great difficulty be delineated from the interests of the dynasts who ruled most eighteenth-century states. State sovereignty and the personal sovereignty of a dynast went hand-in-glove in the Hapsburg and Russian Empires, in France, Prussia, and elsewhere. The sovereignty of the state was an extension of the sovereignty of its lord. Throughout the early modern period, as political theory slowly emancipated itself from political theology, political theorists from Machiavelli to Bodin to Hobbes had developed the notion of sovereignty as a justification of, and prop to, the development of state power. Thus eighteenth-century sovereignty had both internal and external dimensions, and domestic and international consequences. I will explore these dimensions in turn.

Internal Dimensions of Territorial Sovereignty: The Eighteenth-Century Domestic Social Order

The religious conflict had abated, but its memory gave credence to the notions of these theorists of sovereignty. The sovereign emerged as judge and legislator, granted the authority to settle religious differences and to resolve the problem of religious minorities within his territories. According to this doctrine the sovereign had been granted absolute power, which vastly exceeded the kingly power of medieval monarchs who had relied so heavily on the advice and consent of lesser nobles in their realm. The monarchy was now winning the domestic struggle for power with the lesser nobility. The sovereign had the power of life and death over all who were "subject" to his sovereignty, which was now purported to derive directly from God, so Friedrich Wilhelm could claim "[w]e are king and master and we do as we please."[1]

While the eighteenth-century monarchs had to contend with limits on their power and freedom of action as a result of continued, though diminished, privileges and pressures of the domestic aristocracy, it is certain that their sovereignty entitled them to so substantial a measure of authority over the state that it necessarily blurred the distinction between the state and the dynasty. The state-building projects of monarchs had left them with "supreme legitimate power over the people residing within their borders" as well a monopoly of coercion (the legal disposition of armed force), taxation (collection and expenditure), administration (control of public life through a rational bureaucracy that served at the pleasure of the Crown), and lawmaking (setting of public policy and enactment of laws governing civil society).[2]

The process of transition from feudal norms of heteronomy and diffusion of political power among the nobility had proceeded speedily in the west of Europe, and more slowly in the east. In central and eastern Europe and particularly Russia, the nobility, accompanied by the church and the Crown, had retained a legal monopoly on land ownership throughout the most of the eighteenth century. There existed "no land without a lord." Ancient norms of personal servitude ensured the rural nobility of a ready availability of peasant labor. The rural nobility retained vast discretion in the administration of their lands and the governance and discipline of the peasantry within them. The rural peasantry was strapped with significant obligations to provide labor services to work the land attached to the *demesne*. Peasants were bound to the land by the tie of serfdom, lacking freedom to leave or change their occupation or even to travel without the permission of the noble. Peasants were required to lease out their own plots and land from the lord for payments in money or in kind. While ostensibly entitled to tenure of their land by longstanding norms, this tenure could in practice be forfeited for serious offenses, with the lord determining what a serious offense was.

All of these arrangements of serfdom, with their feudal residues, were more or less odious regarding the status of the peasantry. They were perhaps less odious in the German states (with the significant exception of Prussia) and Hapsburg Empire and more odious in Poland and Russia where the peasantry was subject to routine and vigorous corporal punishment, as a disciplinary measure, at the discretion of the lord. The peasantry was effectively reduced by legal measures to the status of chattel.[3] Significantly, the stronger feudal residues of the central and eastern European states limited the penetration of the Crown and its state into vast tracts of rural society in the countries where its strength held. The administrative power of the nobility in these realms served as a buffer between the state and the peasantry which constituted the bulk of the population of eighteenth-century Europe. Rural peasants in such circumstances were much more likely to identify themselves as stewards and servants of their local noble and lord than as subjects of the Crown. The particulars of such a peasant's personal circumstances, the quantity of labor he performed, the dues and taxes he paid, which woman he was permitted to marry, the rents he paid on his lands, the materials from which he was permitted to construct his meager shelter, and the number of stripes he bore upon his back, were determined entirely as a consequence of his relationship with his local lord, not his sovereign.

Peasants were tied to the land and to the commune, even in western Europe where a mixed system of land-ownership that ran the gamut from noble landlords to urban landowners to free peasant proprietors to peasant tenants and, at the bottom, landless laborers, prevailed. Even here the feudal residues survived in the eighteenth century, though generally the labor services still owed to the rural nobility in the east were replaced by a system of seigniorial dues and fees.[4] In addition to these, in France, for example, the weight of the taxes levied by the Crown in the forms of the *taille* (the royal land tax), the *capitation* (the head tax), and the *gabelle* (salt tax) were all ultimately payable by the peasantry.[5] Thus even where eighteenth-century European peasants were legally of free status they remained for practical purposes bound to land and condition by heavy taxes and seigniorial dues and debt. In France the taxes and obligations alone typically skimmed off about half of the proceeds of the gross harvest, and the peasant family was required to set aside seeds for the next planting, meet rents and debt obligations, and maintain themselves on what remained, ensuring an insecure and marginal existence on a deficient diet and under often quite squalid conditions.[6]

The heavy labor and grinding poverty of such conditions year-to-year and generation-to-generation had infested the peasantry with the attitude of traditionalism. The aspirations of the bulk of the peasantry were of necessity quite modest, generally limited to the assurance of subsistence of the family. Submissiveness to authority and acceptance of lowly station became peasant communal norms. With eyes fixed so firmly on the ground, the primary sources of peasant self-identification tended to derive rather firmly from the manor (or *chateaux*), the parish, the local village or commune, and the family. The "interests" of the peasant lay in the maintenance of subsistence for the family, avoiding the wrath of the *seigneur*, and the maintenance of a ragged respectability in social intercourse with peers.

At higher levels of domestic society a spectrum of noble elites vied for distinction and patronage. The eighteenth century saw little if any of the social mobility that was to characterize the nineteenth. Noble birth continued to confer a distinction upon the beneficiary that was quite independent of the merits of the individual. Generally the landed aristocracy sat at the summit of the social pyramid in largely agricultural eighteenth-century Europe, followed by the wealthy urban nobility and clerics. An increasingly vulnerable group of nobles with titles and no wealth clung to the trappings of aristocracy throughout the century as well.[7]

The aristocratic class cultivated its own system of values that was quite distinct from either the merchant and emerging bourgeois classes, and even further from the dogged and resigned traditionalism of the peasantry. The continental nobility, and especially the French nobility, cultivated a regal disdain for what they considered to be the "money-grubbing activities" of the "vulgar rich" who came in for such poor treatment in the appraisals of St. Simon. Assured of income and credit as a result of their landed estates and attendant seigniorial rights to rents and dues accruing from this proprietorship, they were a profligate class of conspicuous consumers. They despised the bourgeois virtue of frugality that had aided the accumulation of the fortunes of the "commercial nobility," who in their eyes offered them insult in the ludicrous pretense of seeking social acceptability among them. In counterpoint to the pretensions of this "commercial nobility" of the "vulgar rich" they prided themselves as a "military nobility" of ancient lineage in the service of the Crown and "state," belonging to a race apart.[8]

The urban nobility prospered in the twenty odd cities on the continent with populations exceeding 100,000. While the landed aristocracy held their titles from their ancient lineage and their lands from ancient feudal norms, the urban nobility, who generally lacked landed estates, relied more directly on the patronage of the Crown for the maintenance of their wealth and position. The Crown's sovereignty had a very real and immanent meaning in both their political and economic systems of accounting. Their extravagant and opulent lifestyles, their large expenditures and prodigal, wasteful, and lavish social engagements were often financed by short-term debts and regarded as "short-term investments" in their futures. The system of royal patronage that they relied upon demanded that they obtain the highest level of visibility. The more visible one was, the more "sinecures, pensions, and favorable marriage alliances for one's children" would likely be forthcoming.[9]

In France in particular, the aristocracy had squandered their resistance to the absolutist state for the trappings of power and preeminence, and for lifestyles of idle and rather purposeless opulence. The Bourbons had stripped the French nobility of real, political power, except for a residual role as judges and magistrates, and had fed the nobility on patronage and pageantry in its stead.[10] This is particularly in evidence when one examines the fate of the court nobles, who served a purely ornamental function for the Bourbon monarchy, enhancing the status of the Bourbon kings by their presence, by their attendance to the king's whims, and by the exchange of their ancient power and authority for this "unproductive, even dissipated existence."[11] A trenchant passage by Liah Greenfeld describes the dilemma of the court noble.

> The great and proud nobles were indeed reduced to the position of children. Denied all independence and treated without respect, they were expending their pent-up energies in intriguing against each other

> and for the attentions of the ruler whose supreme power over them they no longer dared to contest, and in fear of displeasing him. Their exaggerated concern over formal dignities coexisted with pathetically, pitifully undignified behavior vis-a-vis the king. . . . Court life was not conducive to proud bearing. A manual for courtiers . . . advised utter self-effacement and submission to the will of the sovereign. Among the qualities most necessary for a courtier, it recommended "patience, politeness, and no will at all; listen to everything, and tell nothing. Always appear to be content. Have a lot of friends and very few confidants."[12]

A significant result of the humiliation of the French aristocracy was their alienation from the regime. The government of France emanated from the Crown to the *intendants* who administered the thirty-six *generalités* and the Crown's advisers at court. These latter were not the pathetic court nobles consigned to preening in the presence of the sovereign. The *intendants* and real advisers were the king's men. The primary self-identification of the bulk of the French nobility, however, under such humiliating circumstances was with their class, rather than with the *roi* or the *patrie*, and Greenfeld has argued that this was to have dire circumstances for the French regime later in the century. These issues will be treated in chapter 7.

The personal sovereignty of the Prussian kings over domestic matters was similarly unconstrained. Friedrich the Great (who ruled 1740–86) was the consummate Prussian autocrat, and exercised an intensely personal rule over the Prussian state, a style of rule that he had inherited from his father, Friedrich Wilhelm I.

> He directed the state in person, all threads came together in his hand, and the only center of unity was his own mind. Order, in Prussia, had not come from free discussion and collaboration. As Friedrich the Great once observed, if Newton had to consult with Descartes and Leibnitz, he would never have created his philosophical system.[13]

The Prussian kings invariably held a highly pessimistic view of the potentialities of the common classes, whose limited capabilities required their firm supervision by the Prussian nobility in the eyes of the Hohenzollerns. A significant consequence of this outlook was the strictest preservation of the privilege of military command in the hands of the Prussian nobility. No social mobility whatever was available for the Prussian of low birth throughout the century. Autocracy limited the posts available to them in the civil service as well, and over time even this limited platform of authority became a preserve of the nobility.[14]

Significantly, however, the Prussian kings resolved the problem faced by every eighteenth-century dynast—namely "how to subdue the nobility without earning their enmity and without creating severe social instability"[15]—with the singular solution of setting them apart as a military class *de facto* as well as *de jure*. There would be no Prussian sales of military titles to wealthy bourgeoisie as in France. As a consequence the Prussian army was intensely professional, competent, and efficient, and consequently extremely effective, whereas the French army under the old regime was topheavy, and bloated with amateurs and dilettantes, and consequently significantly less effective. In this manner Friedrich consistently managed to instill an identification of the Prussian aristocracy with the Prussian state, by making them the guardians of the state in fact as well as in name, and in bolstering and providing opportunities for attainment of the fundamental motivating factors of their class, especially their "honor, class-consciousness, glory, or ambition."[16]

Though he valued patriotism, Friedrich certainly did not expect it from the common classes. From these obedience alone was both prized and expected, whether they were soldiers or civilians. The self-identifications and self-understandings of the masses of common people were of no consequence to the absolutist dynasts who ruled them, so long as they produced and obeyed.

> Between populations and their governments little feeling existed. The tie between the sovereign and subject was bureaucratic, administrative and fiscal, an external mechanical connection of ruler and ruled, strongly in contrast to the principle brought in by the Revolution, which . . . effected an almost religious fusion of the government and the governed. A good government of the Old Regime was one that demanded little of its subjects, which regarded them as useful, worthy, and productive assets to the state, and which in wartime interfered as little as possible with civilian life. A 'good people' was one which obeyed the laws, and paid its taxes, and was loyal to the reigning house; *it need have no sense of its own identity as a people, or unity as a nation, or responsibility for public affairs, or obligation to put forth a supreme effort in war.*[17]

For the subject of an eighteenth-century state who lacked the badge of nobility, the pursuit of preferment within the humble boundaries allotted them by a highly stratified society dominated their daily life. Wealthy merchants might pursue social recognition and material comfort, or even promotion into the nobility. They were not entirely without influence with monarchs who understood the benefits to the domestic economy, and thus to the state's revenues, promoted by their trade. This was particularly the case, as we shall see, for merchants engaged with colonial pursuits and trading companies engaged in international trade.

The peasantry, as we have seen, was overwhelmingly preoccupied with the pursuit of subsistence. The lower bourgeoisie found solace in the pursuit of mastership as artisans and master craftsmen. The best journeymen might set themselves up as a master. This was a cherished badge of citizenship, denoting honorable social status and considerable economic privileges to guilded masters. The attainment of mastership entitled its possessor to a modicum of moral respectability, and as the century progressed, as masters increasingly became capitalists and proprietors, hope of much more.[18] This hope of enfranchisement with expanded political rights, however, was to be realized only in France, and then quite late in the century.

Journeyman artisans lacking proprietorship over their means of production increasingly acquired the status of proletarians as their masters simply salaried them. A significant indicator of the extent to which the eighteenth-century state discounted the sentiment of vast majority of its working subjects is how it dealt with labor unrest. These regimes prized social control above all other domestic concerns. Labor unrest was regarded simply as a threat to public order, and was brutally dealt with as such. The social conservatism and stratification inherent in the domestic social order demanded the unquestioned subordination of workers to employers and government actively abetted this process by forbidding strikes or labor demonstration, and even requiring that a journeyman's master provide a certificate indicating that all their affairs had been settled before the journeyman or worker could lawfully leave his employment.[19] The nonpropertied classes had even less incentive to identify with the Crown than did their employers in such circumstances, and it is not difficult to see how legitimation crises continued to erupt for absolutist regimes as capitalism developed and increasingly privatized the function of the extraction of resources from domestic society.[20]

A significant exception to this absolutist form of sovereignty had developed in England, however, where "Whiggism" had triumphed in the "Glorious Revolution" to ensure the demise there of Stuart theories of the divine right of kings.[21] A constitutional monarchy had been restored with the Protestant Hanoverian succession. While the power of the English monarch was circumscribed by a power-sharing arrangement with parliament, this was no figurehead Crown. The Crown employed patronage and sinecures, dispensed by its government ministers to ensure working majorities for its policies in parliament. The Duke of Newcastle became the quintessential master of patronage dispensation for George II, and such arrangements enabled the recruitment of highly talented non-nobles, such as William Pitt the Elder (1708–78)—later Lord Chatham—into the service of the government.[22]

But while absolutism in England had been held at bay, English suffrage still strongly resembled a corporate, or group privilege rather than a universal franchise, "almost a form of property, whose exercise was expected to bring some direct benefit."[23] Most Commons seats available early in the century represented corporate boroughs. It was the privilege of the leading family in the area to nominate a candidate for parliament, with the result that many seats "seemed almost hereditary with sons replacing their fathers as the generations passed" such that on the eve of the Seven Years' War, three quarters of the 1761 Parliament consisted of men whose ancestors had served in the House.[24] The government of England during the reigns of George I and George II therefore bore a strong likeness to a form of one-party government dominated by Protestant Whig Peers in the House of Lords and their non-noble counterparts in the House of Commons. The rest of parliament was populated by a hundred or so Tories who were systematically excluded from participation in ministries and regarded as covert subversives or Jacobites waiting for an opportunity to restore the ousted Stuarts by force.[25] Party labels had limited meaning, however, and the parliament more nearly represented a "loose network of interests and 'connections' based on individual ties and individual ambitions."[26]

The Whig ascendancy, which dominated English politics in the eighteenth century, opposed the Tory demands for a more democratic political order. Whiggism held that a democratic form of government, in which political equality was granted to all, independent of birth and particularly property, was inherently unstable. The Whigs feared that such a system would undermine both the notion of limited monarchy and the responsibilities of the aristocracy. They explicitly rejected natural law arguments regarding the inalienable rights of all men to a voice in their government. They therefore rejected Tory theories of popular sovereignty as rigorously as they rejected absolute monarchy and favored a program that ensured a constitutional monarchy, Protestant succession, the rule of law, and most particularly the defense of property against encroachments by the Crown or the Commons.[27]

Thus England's government appears, more than any other eighteenth-century arrangement, to bear a strong resemblance to Marx's "executive committee of the bourgeoisie" with the exception that it was most prominently led by a small landed aristocracy. Unless one was a noble or a wealthy merchant or other form of bourgeois one's franchise was extremely limited. Yet the self-definition of England as a Protestant nation, since at least the end of the sixteenth century,[28] had created a vehicle for social mobility for commoners that had been unknown on the continent (with the exception of the United Provinces). A sense of national feeling extended at least to those well enough educated to benefit from this "nobility." Thus it may fairly be argued that identification with the regime of some form extended further down into the common reaches of English society than it did elsewhere. The notion of the people as sovereign, however narrowly the "people" might be in practice defined, had deep roots and enjoyed significant credence among the common people in the England of the eighteenth century.[29] As will be seen later, this was to have significant consequences for the early emergence of national collective identity in England in relation to the continental absolutist states, and for England's behavior as an eighteenth-century territorial-sovereign power.

External Dimensions of Territorial Sovereignty: The Eighteenth-Century International System

The employment of the notion of personal sovereignty to buttress traditional divine right doctrine as a legitimating principle for domestic rule entailed also accepting the legitimacy of the rule of other sovereigns, including one's enemy. One might challenge the right of one's adversary to rule over a particular bit of territory, but not his right to rule *qua* sovereign. Significantly, after his downfall, Napoleon was granted "sovereignty" over the island of Elba and was fashioned "emperor" of Elba by his conquerors.[30] This illustrates the extent to which even the deposed and despised were recognized as sovereign entities in their persons by other sovereigns, and also served the purpose of emphasizing the sovereign legitimacy of the dynastic victors. As Ruggie has argued:

> The issue here was not who had how much power, but who could be designated *as* a power. Such a designation inherently is a collective

> act. It involved the mutual recognition of the new constitutive principle of sovereignty. . . . Reciprocal sovereignty thus became the basis of the new international order.[31]

Externally sovereignty defined power and rights in relation to other states. A sovereign power's rights with respect to other states included, at a minimum, the right to sovereign independence from all external power, the right to enter into diplomatic relations with other states under the principle of *pacta sunt servanda*,[32] and the right to make war if required to defend the interests of the state. The doctrine of *raison d'état* alone was to govern the conduct of the statesman of a sovereign power in the eighteenth century. Most if not all eighteenth-century monarch's likely subscribed to the following words of Friedrich Meinecke:

> *Raison d'état* is the fundamental principle of national conduct, the State's first Law of Motion. It tells the statesman what he must do to preserve the health and strength of the State . . . an organic structure whose full power can only be maintained by allowing it in some way to continue growing; and *raison d'état* indicates both the path and the goal for such a growth.[33]

Louis XIV had referred to this doctrine as "the first of all laws by common consent," and Friedrich the Great, alluding to the inapplicability of private morality to interstate relations implied by the doctrine, had written that the "fundamental rule of government for all states . . . is the principle of extending their territories."[34] Neither does it appear that the amoral doctrine failed to take hold of many seventeenth and eighteenth-century European monarchs regarding their personal affairs. Peter the Great allowed his son to be tortured to death for an offense against the state. Friedrich Wilhelm of Prussia sentenced the young friend of his son to death for a minor offense and forced his son and heir to witness the execution. Elizabeth of Russia usurped the throne and imprisoned her son, Ivan, and Catherine II colluded in the overthrow and eventual murder of her husband Peter III in usurping his throne.[35] Dissimulation, deliberate breaches of treaty obligations, betrayal of allies, "cheerful justification of aggressive war," acquiescence in brutality in the conduct of war, general unconcern about the human costs of war—

all of these dismal characteristics and practices were justified by the doctrine of *raison d'état*.[36]

Significantly, a problem for both the seventeenth- and eighteenth-century international systems was the absence of agreement regarding what the principle of sovereignty implied in a system where the principle of *raison d'état* could be employed to legitimate almost any action that a territorial-sovereign state might take while invoking it. Luard has documented numerous violations of the sovereignty of the smaller states in the system which did not necessarily entail the smaller state becoming a simple victim of territorial aggrandizement of a larger one, though the latter was hardly an uncommon occurrence. It is worth examining these issues briefly in order to avoid overstating the extent to which the post-Westphalian principle of sovereignty had actually exiled feudal heteronomy. The system remained transitional, even on through the eighteenth century, in that "the more powerful states were able to treat some territories in ways wholly inconsistent with the normal rules of sovereignty."[37]

Examples of this transitional phenomenology abound. The stubborn refusal of the papacy and Holy Roman Emperor to accede to the banishment of their influence from the system, as "non-sovereign entities," was not least among these. The smaller German states would often be excluded from the perquisites due to sovereign states—even the exchange of ambassadors and routinized diplomatic relations—for fear of angering the Holy Roman Emperor who still claimed feudal rights over many of them. As John Herz has observed:

> But there remained the chief problem: how to define the status of those rulers who, because of their membership in the Empire, were subjects of the emperor. Could one be "sovereign" and "subject" at the same time? . . . If so, what did their subjection to the emperor amount to?[38]

In other cases, the sovereign right of a ruler to a monopoly of force in his own territory was denied by other powers, either as an artifact of an atavistic feudal relationship or occasionally merely imposed on a nominally sovereign state. Unauthorized transit by foreign armed forces in a military exigency was not uncommon. The right of protection of religious minorities in another territory was sometimes sought and sometimes even granted. The right of a state to determine its own constitution was sometimes limited by external powers, and veto over a constitutional change was sometimes demanded by a neighbor. The right to determine succession to the throne of a deceased monarch was often contended by other states, to which the wars of Spanish, Polish, Bavarian, and Austrian succession attest. Intervention in the affairs of a foreign power to assist a revolutionary movement was the most frequent violation of sovereignty, and thus the most frequently prohibited in seventeenth- and eighteenth-century treaties.[39]

Yet it is not abnormal today for states to seek influence in the affairs of others. Violations of the principle of sovereignty do not obviate the viability of the principle. The normativity of system legitimating principles ensures their counterfactual validity. The issue here is definitional, and regards an absence of the development of consensual knowledge[40] regarding the contemporary definition of sovereignty, which "provided no exact measure of the degree or type of independence that a state could expect to enjoy."[41]

Problems of consensual knowledge regarding these definitional issues tended to see progress in the conference diplomacy following major wars involving most or all of the major powers in the system. Osiander has suggested, for example, that the principles of autonomy of states, equality among them, balance of power among states, and guarantees of the security of states emerged from the Peace of Utrecht as the "consensus principles" upon which the European system of international relations was founded at the end of the War of Spanish Succession.[42] Postcontinental war conference diplomacy was, however, a rather costly means of establishing consensus for system principles and the norms of international behavior, and elementary rules began to develop in the absence of the impetus of major conflagrations.

As Ruggie has argued, the "paradox of absolute individuation" implied by territorial sovereignty required the inviolability of embassies and foreign diplomatic personnel.[43] Thus the ambassador became immune to prosecution even for serious crimes, was exempted from liability to civil suits for injuries, could not be taxed or held accountable for payment of debts, nor could his goods be seized for payment of debts or his religious practice in his private chapel be interfered with. Neither could his mail be opened. Safe conduct was guaranteed for diplomatic personnel even of governments with whom hostilities had commenced.[44] Significantly, these solutions were fostered by the implications of the principle of territorial sovereignty. It is difficult to suggest here that purely rational instrumental reasons for action can account for the eighteenth-century rules governing the diplomatic relations. The Ottoman Turks were also possessed of instrumental rationality, also experienced the need to exchange ambassadors and conduct diplomatic relations, yet felt no compulsion to adhere to these rules. Occasionally they violated them rather dramatically.

The century saw the development of a system of rules that was incorporated into a developing corpus of limited international law in the areas that most seriously challenged the consensual knowledge of territorial sovereigns. Rules governing the effectivity of treaties, the limits to sovereign jurisdiction on the high seas, trade, the rights of neutrals during war, maritime rules governing use of the sea all saw progress in the eighteenth century.[45] This did not mean that as the century waned, all problems of consensual knowledge in these areas were resolved, particularly in the area of maritime neutral rights.[46] British insistence on the right of blockade during war, their broad definition of contraband, which could be seized under the prize law they had adopted, was a major point of contention for neutral maritime trading powers like the Dutch, and later the Americans, who relied upon maritime commerce and argued for a "free ships, free goods" principle to be applied to them by belligerents.[47]

While Luard points out that these controversies reflect "deep differences of interest" among eighteenth-century, territorial-sovereign states, he also demonstrates how territorial sovereignty as a system-legitimating principle lent itself to demands for the mitigation of many of its effects through the development of interstate rules that slowly became codified into a system of international law. The controversies:

> also clearly demonstrated the determination of the majority to establish principles of international behavior which would protect them from arbitrary and high-handed action at the hands of one or two dominant naval powers . . . [significantly] . . . the rules which the majority demanded eventually came to be accepted as representing the "public law" of the continent.[48]

Nonetheless, there was certainly no prohibition of war or any serious question of the legitimacy of war attending the principle of territorial-sovereignty. War was deemed legitimate in order to obtain reparation for losses, for breach of a legal pact, for self-defense, for maintenance of a state or dynastic right, to prevent intended or threatened injury, to punish offense (however broadly defined), to anticipate the designs of another state, to prevent reoccurrence of attacks, to assist an ally under treaty obligation, to assist the uprising of the "unjustly oppressed" in another state, to maintain the balance of power, or merely to uphold the "honor" of the state.[49]

Dynastic Status, Mercantilism and the Notion of Interest in the Absolutist State

Having established the absolutist character of rule in the majority of eighteenth-century European states we certainly might be led to characterize the "interests" of the state in this period in Morgenthau's terms of the will-to-power. It would appear that the will-to-power in the hands of an absolutist dynast, however, was an implement by which he or she expressed his or her will-to-manifest-identity. The whims and wills of absolute monarchs in the eighteenth century tended to be sized to the scale of the power that they wielded. They wished to be grand, admired, feared, immortalized, and deferred to in higher proportions than were their peers. They willed-to-manifest-identity as conquerors, emperors, and hegemons. They strove to become the composers and fiddlers of the tune to which the rest of Europe, even the rest of the world, would dance. Aggression was a natural impulse for such a powerful *enfant terrible*. As Schumpeter has argued:

> War was a part of their settled order of life, so to speak—an element of sovereign splendor, almost a fashion. Hence they waged war whenever the occasion was offered, not so much from considerations of advantage as from personal whim. To look for deep-laid plans, broad perspectives, consistent trends is to miss the whole point.[50]

The principle of *raison d'état* provided eighteenth-century absolutists with an ideal justification to exercise their caprice in international competition. Absolutism itself, however, blurred the distinction between the dynast and the state and it is clear that the assertion of Louis XIV at the beginning of the century, that *L'Etat c'est moi* was roughly equally applicable in Hohenzollern Prussia, in Russia, and in the Hapsburg Empires of Austria and Spain. That the absolutists themselves regarded the interests, reasons, and status of the state to be quite nearly conterminous with their personal and dynastic interests and fortunes is exemplified by the energy they expended in jealously ensuring their status relative to other monarchs and states. Yet this absolutist "status anxiety" lacked the provincial character of the pettier status conflicts of earlier centuries when the only concern was to win status for the ruler's person and house. Now the "central concern was with the positions occupied by the states with which the rulers increasingly identified themselves."[51] The principle of *raison d'état* legitimated the practice of seeking personal and dynastic glory under the rubric of seeking glory for the state.

The status competition among dynastic states was manifested in many edifices and institutions that survive to the present day. Not the least of these were the splendid and ostentatious palaces and public buildings built by nearly all European monarchs—even those who controlled territories of minuscule dimensions. Similarly, while they were institutions necessitated by the conflictual nature of eighteenth-century international relations, and made possible by the consolidation of state-building projects and nascent capitalist activity, the standing armies that were everywhere created in this period were status symbols of the first magnitude. They were ornamental as well as functional, and in the case of very small states served more of the former than the latter purpose. The pretension of this activity had impelled Friedrich the Great of Prussia to quip caustically that "there is no prince . . . who does not imagine himself to be Louis XIV: he builds his Versailles, has his mistress, and maintains an army."[52] Consider in this context the rather amusing pretense of the "Elector of Palatine, [who], though by no means wealthy, at one time possessed 30 regiments, of which a quarter of the manpower consisted of officers; and, though without a seaboard, boasted a Grand Admiral commanding a few small craft which he sailed up and down the Rhine."[53]

Eighteenth-century European monarchs demonstrated what today appears to be a singularly neurotic fetish regarding issues of precedence in what might otherwise be regarded as trivial circumstances. We might refer to this as protocol fetishism. The relative honors shown to their ambassadors at formal diplomatic functions, courtesies shown to each, order of their placement at the dinner table, were intensely scrutinized and bitterly contended. Rather minor breaches of diplomatic protocol involving issues of precedence could have the most bizarre and serious consequences, not infrequently resulting in violent incidents, so that ambassadors found excuses not to attend functions where these issues were likely to arise.[54]

Similarly contended were "first salutes" on the high seas as monarchs would insist that foreign ships dip their flags in salute before allowing their flags to be dipped. Enormous importance was attached to hierarchy of titles: The Marquises wished titular promotion to Dukes, who in turn craved the superior title of Elector, who fashioned themselves Kings, who styled themselves Emperors. Significantly, one could not unilaterally assume a higher title in order to achieve this desired importance. The recognition of one's higher status by others was essential. In withholding this recognition, individual status-anxious aristocrats and rulers could stoop to absurdity, as might have been the case with the Holy Roman Emperor who emphasized his superior titular precedence over mere kings by refusing to refer to them as "majesty," and offering instead the title "*serenitas*."[55]

It is worthwhile to ponder this anecdotal evidence of what appears to contemporary eyes as neurotic status-anxiety of a magnitude that might, if isolated in an individual or small group, be attributed to some form of clinically interesting mental pathology. As it was rather a concern shared by each of the rulers of the various states that comprised Europe, we should rather take it as a concern with relative position in a status-conscious age. What is unclear is whether the concern with relative position which characterized the international politics of the entire century was a concern for the relative position of monarchs or of states. Breaches of diplomatic protocol are still negatively sanctioned. This occurred as recently as 1995 when Britain's Queen Elizabeth II chose to schedule a vacation, forcing a delay of President Clinton's planned state visit to the U.K. to confer with Prime Minister Major. This snub was reportedly offered as Elizabeth had been annoyed that Clinton had chosen to accept the Russian invitation to attend ceremonies marking the fiftieth anniversary of the capitulation of Germany in World War II, without attending London's celebration. The consequences of this pique were, however, confined to a rescheduling of the American-British summit meeting. Louis XIV had, by contrast, sent a French squadron to Genoese waters to demand a first salute from the port, and had ordered the city bombarded when this was refused.[56] It was the inseparability of the territorial sovereign and absolutist state, the impossibility of slighting one without slighting the other, that renders these piquant displays of status-anxious protocol fetishism explicable.

Territorial-Sovereign Identity and Mercantilist Theory and Practice

One of the most significant consequences of the Westphalian settlement and the close of the era of the Wars of Religion had been a shift in both the rationales and character of the system of continental alliances that had structured European international relations between the sixteenth and seventeenth centuries. With the delegitimation of religious ideas and affiliations, and the rise of the principle of *raison d'état*, the continent fell away from the familiar pattern of conflict between the Austro-Spanish Hapsburg axis and the coalition of Protestant powers aided by a France encircled by Hapsburg territories. Consequently the continental system became much more multipolar, and increasingly characterized by a loose system of very short term alliances.[57]

The creation of standing armies and their regular employment in the acquisition of new territory, whether to buttress state or dynastic status, and to compensate for increasing uncertainty in alliance politics due to the delegitimation of religious-military affiliations, created a pressing need for steady flows of revenues for their maintenance. Continental struggles became wars of shifting, short term coalitions. Financing them was a challenge for an era characterized by the scarcity of coin and the continued flow of funds to armies of professional soldiers, many of whom were mercenaries recruited from foreign lands and distinctly unmotivated by more than the desire to earn money and to survive. Thus finance was of paramount importance for monarchs who wished to sustain a successful campaign.

An artifact of the segmentation of the political world according to the principle of territoriality[58] was an economic closure corresponding to the political closure segmented by territory. As state-building and territorial consolidation crystallized the state as an institutional form, Europe witnessed the emergence of economies whose boundaries roughly coincided with those of the state.[59] As European monarchs continued to discover the extent to which success in their martial status-contests relied upon their ability to mobilize the "industrial, commercial, financial, military and naval resources"[60] of their territories, they increasingly viewed these resources as interchangeably fungible, globally scarce, and fundamentally limited. The absolutist regarded the wealth of the state as his or her personal war chest. The scarcity of coin and precious metals, and the rudimentary nature of early-eighteenth-century credit vehicles and banking systems had led to bullionism—the view that all wealth resides in the possession of precious metals, that money had to be secured either by plunder or trade.[61] The Crown could tax trade and sell monopolies to individual merchants or trading companies. These revenues made up a crucially significant share of the revenues of the Crown, which was almost universally anxious to see such economic activity expanded.

The overseas traders and merchants were increasingly seen as the real growth engines of the global economy that began to develop during the eighteenth-century colonization process, and they were responsible for generating much of the wealth of Europe during the century. The state actively supported the establishment and operations of maritime trading companies that were engaged in competition with the trading firms of other states for commercial domination in the periphery. Trade in the West Indies was particularly lucrative for the British and French Empires. This chain of small tropical islands provided imports of tobacco, coffee, cotton, dye indigo, and sugar for manufacture into finished products in the mother country, which could then be re-exported to other European states for specie.[62]

The establishment of colonies in large measure resulted directly from the desire to increase the flow of limited tradable commodities. Colonies were, unlike continental territory, coveted not from a desire for conquest, honor, or glory but for the products they could supply and the taxable wealth they could generate. This motivation is fundamentally distinct, as we shall see in chapter 8, from the imperial impulses that were to impel the territorial segmentation of the globe in the late nineteenth century, during the nationalist era. In the eighteenth century:

> Europeans did not settle in the remote foreign regions out of a desire for conquest, but to secure access to particular commodities which could be profitably traded in Europe. . . . Except in the Americas, permanent settlement was usually not intended, still less the detailed administrations of local populations.[63]

Trade with one's colonies was an enormously important contribution to the balance of trade. France's colonial trade grew from 25 million livres in 1716 to 263 million livres in 1789, which constituted growth from 20 percent to 50 percent of France's total foreign trade.[64] Similarly, North American colonial trade alone constituted 20 percent of her total foreign trade in 1750 and 34 percent by 1785.[65] Figures for trade with British India are not available, but recognition that France's colonies on the subcontinent were forfeit in the 1763 settlement of the Seven Years' War leads us to suspect that these figures would be much higher with the inclusion of the Indian contribution.

The territorial-sovereign state had a powerful incentive to establish colonies, particularly in regions where valuable commodities, unavailable in

Europe, could be extracted or grown. Colonies were seen not as strategic liabilities but as economic assets, particularly where they were established by trading companies that maintained their own armed forces, which many did. At one time the army of the British East India Company numbered 150,000 and the state-sponsored firm employed its own navy as well.[66] Similarly, the Virginia Company of London had governed in accordance with martial law in the establishment of the Virginia colony, and had maintained a strict military form of governance there for many years.[67]

But the major incentive to establish colonies for eighteenth-century mercantilist regimes lay in the extension of the sovereignty of the state (and its monarch) to the remote colony, not for purposes of accruing status to either, but for the capability, unavailable on the continent, to leverage the terms of trade to the advantage of the mother country and to shield it from competition. Colonial trade was "directed," or "managed" trade. It was reserved to the home country alone and as such constituted "a pure monopoly."[68] Moreover, such managed arrangements could be designed to ensure not only a captive market for the manufactures of the mother country, and a supplier of rare and valuable commodities for those manufactures, but a perpetually captive market as well. Residing under the sovereignty of the mother country, colonists could be obstructed from developing manufacturing industries, and generally were, as manufacturing industries at home needed markets and abhorred competition.[69] Consider the case of the British Navigation Acts, which specified the terms of trade for Britain's American colonies. These acts ensured that a precious stream of coin continued to flow into British coffers. According to one economic historian "The basic elements of the system . . . tended to drain specie from America to Britain. There is no need to quote colonial witnesses concerning the distress which results from lack of ready cash [in America]."[70]

Yet mercantilist theory and practice routinely subordinated private economic interests to the perceived interests of the state, and *raison d'état* justified and legitimated this view and practice inasmuch as wealth and power were so closely coupled in the thought of the day. Edward Earle captures the issues succinctly in a rather extreme formulation.

> In modern terminology, we would say that the predominant purpose of mercantilist regulations was to develop the military potential, or war potential. To this end exports and imports were rigidly controlled;

> stocks of precious metals were built up and conserved; military and naval stores were produced or imported under a system of premiums and bounties; shipping and the fisheries were fostered as a source of naval power; colonies were settled and protected (as well as strictly regulated) as a complement to the wealth and self-sufficiency of the mother country; population growth was encouraged for the purpose of increasing military man power. These and other measures were designed with the major, if not the single, purpose of adding to the unity and strength of the nation [*sic*].[71]

Of course mercantilist assumptions are highly suspect, and the critiques of the classical economists of the Scottish Enlightenment, specifically that of Smith, began to appear later in the decade.[72] These critiques became influential and began to guide even British economic policy in the nineteenth century, but certainly not in the eighteenth. What is important to the present study is not whether or not wealth and military power are fungible, or whether they are mutually interdependent. The last is a question that is still a point of much contention in international relations theory.[73] What is important is that eighteenth-century governments believed that they *were* valid, and predicated their economic policies on their perceived economic, military, and strategic needs, acting on assumptions very similar to those of classical realist and neorealist theories of international relations. As I will demonstrate later in the work, national sovereigns were by no means invariably strident economic nationalists unless they were simultaneously imperialists, as was the case with Nazi Germany's employment of the Hjalmar Schacht's "influence effect" trading strategy.[74]

Critical links between extreme nationalist economic nationalism and mercantilism are the assumptions regarding the political order in which economic activity is conducted. Mercantilism "envisages 'a world not of markets but of states.' "[75] Colonies were seen as extensions of the state, and as such sources of raw materials for home industries, of strategic materials and naval goods such as hemp, flax, copper, pitch, and tar. There were seen as provenders of precious metals, as sources of a positive balance of trade, a means of import saving, sources of cheap slave labor,[76] markets for manufactures of the mother country, distress goods markets for mitigating the effects of protectionist tariffs elsewhere, as well as outlets for surplus production and surplus capital for the mother country. They were generally prized for helping to reduce dependency on other states for commodities and markets.[77]

Comparative Institutionalization of Dynastic-Sovereign and Territorial-Sovereign Authority

Thus an important element motivating eighteenth-century colonialism was that it was integral to the state-building exercise, but unlike the situation on the continent, competition for colonial territory in the periphery was oriented toward building up the wealth, and consequently, it was thought, the power of the continental state. A real distinction between dynastic interests of earlier centuries, and the state interests that developed significantly in the eighteenth century, regarded the desire to render the sovereignty lodged in the monarch and in the state "impermeable" by shielding it in impermeable territory.[78] Dynasts of earlier centuries desired the loyalty or allegiance of their subjects in the lands they ruled. They cared little for direct control, and expended little effort toward creating unified administrations for this purpose. Each territory "acquired" might continue on its own path with its customs and institutions undisturbed, and might even extract a pledge from its new ruler to speak the language of the acquired territory.[79] The acquisition of the territory had added honor to the name and revenues to the coffers of the dynastic sovereign's house. It was yet in this house that the dynast's primary self-identification and legitimation was lodged, rather than in the institutional structure of a state.

The territorial sovereign, however, "is sovereign because he has the power to constrain *his* subjects, while not being so constrainable by a superior power. The decisive criterion thus is actual control of one's 'estates' by one's military power."[80] As the legitimacy of the territorial sovereign's rule was now predicated on his administrative sovereignty, recognized by his peers, over his lands, and not his dynastic rights by feudal custom or residue, he now required an institutional structure to "house" that legitimacy, and to reproduce it for his scion. While it is generally accepted that the Westphalian settlement resolved the legitimation crisis created by the segmentation of European international politics along confessional lines, an unintended consequence of the settlement was the creation a crisis of dynastic legitimacy by enshrining territorial rule as the legitimating principle of European government. This dynastic legitimation crisis was simultaneously a dynastic "identity crisis," thus in no small measure an impetus to the state-building projects of territorial sovereigns. This was so precisely because it was the institution of the modern state that replaced the dynastic house as sanctuary for the continued legitimacy of dynastic rule.

This territorial sovereign was, however, now vulnerable to the caprice of his peers in a way in which his dynastic house never had been. Dynastic claims to territory based upon custom or ancient privilege no longer held the sway they once had. As these claims could now be contended, territory was desired "to create readily defensible and powerful states" with rounded frontiers "to create more self sufficient units" of sovereignty.[81] Territorial sovereigns had thus developed a passion for contiguous, defensible territories, and many conflicts were fought in order to unite divided dynastic holdings. Thus the principle of territoriality was the only means of social and political closure available to resolve the legitimation crisis created by the Westphalian settlement.

On the continent, any and all means were employed in the acquisition of state-buttressing territory. War, as we have seen, was considered not only a legitimate means, but the most decisive means, and most wars had clear territorial objectives when they were launched. Negotiation was generally effective only when one had territory in hand to bargain with. Purchase was not uncommon (and is, significantly, quite difficult to imagine in the nationalist era). Matrimony still could serve to acquire territory, but now in a manner limited by the "balancing" concerns of others. The loss of territory was inevitably bitterly resented and could result in prolonged "wars of recovery."[82] As we shall see, Austria's preoccupation with recovering Silesia, lost to Friedrich the Great of Prussia, served to align the Hapsburg monarchy with its ancient nemesis France during the Seven Years' War, with disastrous consequences for both.

Most significantly, the land-grabbing proclivity that accompanied the state-building of the period, and that was even more pronounced in military struggles for territory in the colonial periphery, was in large measure a direct consequence of this dynastic legitimation crisis. The absence of logical frontiers had not been such a significant impetus to international violence when dynastic-feudal claims had held sway. Now these claims although largely defunct, had not been replaced by any clear linguistic, ethnic, or cultural alignments within contiguous territories ruled by the emerging, centralized administrative apparatus of the absolutist state. As Luard suggests, "one state had as good a reason to claim a particular territory as another."[83] With the diminution of the legitimacy of dynastic claims to territory, armed conflict often proved the only means by which competing claims to territory could be adjudicated. Certainly this was doubly so in the periphery, where commercial quasi-military enterprises and the settlers that followed on their heels pushed aside, enslaved, and in most conceivable fashions exploited the indigenous peoples they encountered there, as well as the resources of the lands these peoples had previously regarded as their homes.[84]

Neither had the conquest of Central and South America by the Spanish and Portuguese Empires been concerned with the participation or allegiance of the people who settled in these areas; their allegiance to the mother country was taken for granted. The participation and allegiance of the peoples subjected to this imperialism had not even been a topic of debate after the middle of the sixteenth century. Their participation as slave labor was adequate for their Spanish masters. Rosenberg argues that "the Spanish theory of empire' was indeed the IR theory of its day, the language with which privileged groups within an imperial formation figured to themselves the superior rights of their ascendancy, and fought out the fate of subject peoples."[85] He cites data to demonstrate that this theory of empire resulted in the decline of the native population of Mexico from 25 million to 1.5 million, and of Peru from 5 million to less than 300,000 between the sixteenth and seventeenth centuries.[86]

More significantly for my argument, however, Rosenberg helps to illuminate the importance of the extension of the sovereignty of the mother country to the territory of the periphery in his description of the legitimation of territorial-sovereign colonialism and imperialism as part and parcel of the legitimation of the larger social order.

> The Spanish Empire, for its part, was literally an extension of Castilian society. Because . . . political relations traveled with the commodities, the lines of social power effecting the relaying of surpluses are clearly visible: *they take the form of an extension of the political jurisdiction of the metropole*. Thus the Iberian empires, like nearly all precapitalist structures of geopolitical power, can be visualized as geographical entities. . . . This unseparateness of politics and economies (the perception of "economies" as social orders) is harder to visualize today. Indeed the contemporary international system could hardly look more different. Lines of political jurisdiction halt at fixed national borders,

> while those of economic activity speed on through a myriad of international exchanges without undermining the ramparts of formal sovereignty above. . . . But once the wealth-creating properties of a free market were understood, *the state conceived an interest* in allowing the latter to regulate itself, and increasingly restricted its own activity to the more properly political functions of government.[87]

Without criticizing Rosenberg's strongly Marxist perspective, I would argue that more than "economies" were perceived as social orders in the precapitalist era. I do not dispute the validity of Rosenberg's observations regarding the companionship of political relations with commodities, or their importance in the constitution of social power. I argue only that these economic relations did not, *in themselves*, legitimate this exercise of social power, or the ideology of empire.

The extension of the sovereignty of the mother country was also the extension of a well-developed system of hierarchical social relations that followed from the extension of the residual, personal, dynastic sovereignty of the crowned European heads to the territories subject to it, both on the continent and in the periphery. The identity commitments of the purveyors and ideologists of the territorial-sovereign empire were derived from their self-identification within what they perceived as a legitimate system of social relations. The extension to the periphery was deemed a natural, legitimate, even essential consequence of the broader social order. This social order constituted even a far more "hegemonic construct" than is illuminated in Gramsci's account of the co-optation of Italian society during the Risorgimento.[88] Jesuit, Franciscan and Dominican priests, *conquistadores*, *ecomenderos*, and *corregidores* in turn converted, conquered, occupied, and exploited these colonial holdings as agents of a social order whose legitimacy they did not question, and whose extension to the periphery they viewed as a natural extension of the sovereign who personified that order. Their motivations varied from the other-worldly religious fervor of the Catholic orders, to the extremely worldly fortune seekers who supervised the exploitation of the continent. Their self-identification as agents of the extension of the sovereignty of the contemporary social order not only justified, but for many even sanctified, their endeavor in their own eyes. Atavistic ideologies and social forms had not entirely fallen with the Westphalian settlement on the Catholic Iberian peninsula. As Michael Doyle argues, perhaps too strongly:

> Christendom is also the proper perspective from which to view the religious drive behind the Spanish justification for empire. Colonization, in effect, was an entrepreneurial venture of Christendom, organized on a private basis by soldiers and merchants and priests, sanctioned by the pope, and coordinated by the competitive monarchs of Spain and Portugal.[89]

Rosenberg's assertion that the state "conceived an interest" in relinquishing its jurisdiction over the domestic economy as it gained awareness of the benefits of skimming the profits of the privatization of production relations is fortuitous in demonstrating the co-constitution of identities and interests in the context of the maturation of the territorial-sovereign state. This realization was still blunted by mercantilist theory and practice on the eve of the Seven Years' War, or "The Great War for Empire," as it was contemporarily known. Yet even through the mercantilist blinders, the territorial-sovereign state began to perceive the outlines of benefits of the privatization of societal resource extraction in the field of finance, where the emerging capital was most mobile and liquid. It is to the strategic significance of this realization in Europe to which I turn in the next chapter.

Conclusions and Theoretical Reprise

The chapter was dedicated to illustrating the territorial-sovereign structure of identities and interests and explaining its causal significance for structuring territorial-sovereign institutional forms (internal dimensions of territorial-sovereignty) and patterns of politics among similarly legitimated institutional forms (external dimensions). State interests emerged as an extension of dynastic interests. Bereft of purely dynastic means of legitimating rule over specific territory after Westphalia, territoriality came to dominate the notion of state interests and state-building projects and rivalries emerged as a consequence of a new, territorial-sovereign legitimating principle of *raison d'état*.

Internally, territorial-sovereign absolutism institutionalized this principle in the domestic social order by granting monopolies of coercion, taxation, administration through a dependent nobility, and legislation to the sovereign, in whom all legitimate authority was lodged. Social privilege conferred by birth articulated domestic social identities. Co-constituted peasant self-identity and collective identities were attached to the manor, parish, commune, and family and were subject to such rigorous social control under conditions of social immobility that their allegiances were taken for granted by the Crown. Co-constituted aristocratic self identity and collective identity varied among territorial-sovereign states in accordance with variations in the requirements of territorial-sovereign absolutists to subdue the nobility. As the French Crown allotted them no substantial role within the state, their primary identity commitments became attached to their class as they experienced increasing alienation from the state. As the Prussian Crown employed the nobility as a true military aristocracy, their identity commitments became attached to the state as well as their class. As the English Crown ruled at the behest of a Protestant Whig oligarchy, the English nobility identified themselves more completely with the state and the period saw no English absolutism whatever, which contributed to a socially broader and earlier development of national collective identity in England.

Externally, territorial-sovereign absolutism institutionalized the system-legitimating principle of *raison d'état* in numerous ways with significant consequences for the subsequent patterns of politics among territorial-sovereign states. Adherence to the principle entailed the reciprocal recognition of various territorial-sovereign rights including the right to autonomy, or independence from external control, the right to enter into autonomous diplomatic relations with other states, and the right to make war for *raisons d'état* which proliferated. In practice, these principles legitimated territorial expansion at the expense of other states. An explicitly *territorial* sovereignty resulted in legitimate balancing behavior unique to that form of sovereignty, which was characterized by a rapidly changing system of short-term alliances, frequent conflict, fought largely with mercenaries with limited self-identification with the state and characterized by short-term wars of shifting coalitions, and financed in a fashion that tended to employ the collective wealth of the state as the personal war chest of the sovereign, and augmented by colonial fetishism in the periphery.

A uniquely territorial-sovereign mercantilist, absolutist structure of state identities and interests emerged that was largely coterminous with the interests of a dynastic sovereign. This structure of identities and interests legitimated and engendered a quasi-dynastic status competition on the continent and in the periphery, as well as status-anxious protocol fetishism with occasionally deadly consequences. It also engendered a colonial fetishism in the periphery to assure captive markets and a supply of strategic goods as a benefit of extension of territorial-sovereignty to the periphery. The conflictual nature of the resulting territorial-sovereign system impelled the development of a limited international legal structure to fill a developing need for consensual knowledge regarding maritime and neutral rights, the effectivities of treaties and the treatment of diplomatic personnel.

In the pre-Westphalian, dynastic-sovereign system, the collective allegiances and legitimating principles of rulership were lodged in a dynastic house rather than with the state. This had obviated a pressing requirement for contiguous territory to securely house sovereign authority. Dynastic territory could not be *legitimately* challenged and war could not be *legitimately* employed merely as a means of territorial expansion, in the absence of a different cause or pretext. In the Westphalian, territorial-sovereign system, the collective allegiances and legitimating principles of rulership were lodged with the state, though that state was often incarnate in the person of a sovereign. Ancient dynastic claim to territory could no longer ensure against its legitimate appropriation by a competing territorial-sovereign. Wars of territorial conquest were legitimated by the invocation of *raisons d'état* in prolific manifestations as wholly legitimate *casus belli*.

5 Territorial-Sovereign Identity and the Seven Years' War

War is diplomacy by other means. —Clausewitz

America has been conquered in Germany.
—William Pitt the Elder

The Financial Revolution and Strategic Consequences

It is less than clear whether the eighteenth-century explosion of financial vehicles owed more to the requirements of nascent merchant capital, to compensate for the scarcity of coin, or to the requirements of the state for the finance of war materiel. It is quite clear, however, from a quick look at some good data available on Britain[1] during the period that both capital and the state were placing rapidly growing demands on the available specie to finance emerging industrial production, and export promotion and growth, and to finance frequent conflicts with other territorial sovereigns.

The scarcity of coin was particularly troublesome to merchants, who had to keep "money in motion" in order to glean profits. In the absence of plentiful specie, their needs for ready capital to finance entrepreneurial trading ventures resulted in expanded use of bills of exchange and notes of credit, and the expansion of somewhat rudimentary banking practices. There is no doubt that these requirements and innovations had a highly salutary effect in the development of a structure of international credit.[2]

The data presented in figure 2, for example, indicate that at the dawn of the eighteenth century Britain exported only 3.8 million worth, or 20.6 percent of its gross industrial output of 18.5 million. By 1755, on the eve of the Seven Years' War, British exports of manufactured products had nearly trebled, to 9.2, or 30.1 percent of a gross industrial output that had grown to 30.4 million. This strongly suggests that Britain was experiencing a booming period of export-led industrial growth and that the demands for financial vehicles to accommodate it would have been intense, even without competition from the increasingly extractive demands of the flourishing and powerful state.

The data presented in figure 3 suggest that the financial demands of the belligerent, eighteenth-century British state on the available pool of capital

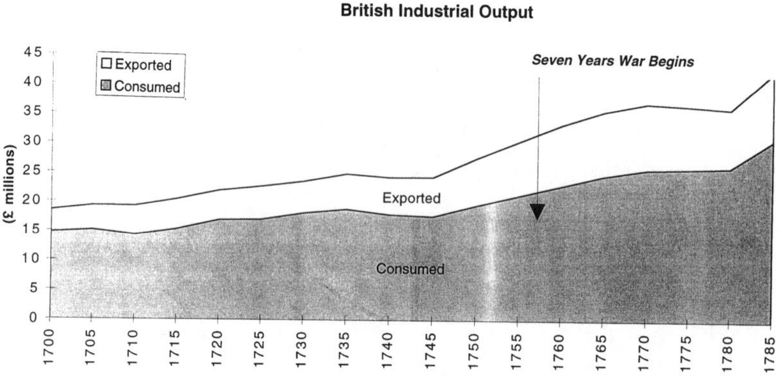

FIGURE 2 Growth of British Exports as Proportion of Industrial Output[3]

FIGURE 3 Growth of Eighteenth-century British War Expenditures[4]

were similarly intense. British annual expenditures to finance its efforts in the War of Spanish Succession had averaged only around 7 million, rising to almost 9 million annually during the War of Jenkin's Ear, and the War of Austrian Succession, but had climbed to an impressive 18 million per annum during the Seven Years' War. Paul Kennedy argues that the standing armies (composed almost entirely of mercenary and foreign troops in the anomalous case of Britain) and large navies "increased the government's need to nurture the economy and to create financial institutions which could raise and manage the moneys concerned." Wars were now "struggles of [financial] endurance" and the country that could best maintain its credit to keep the supply of fresh troops and *materiel* flowing generally won.[5]

Good government credit in the financial markets entitled its bearer to more ready credit at lower rates of interest than an adversary with poorer credit. Raising credit to finance military operations was relatively easy in the United Provinces, where merchants were a significant part of the government. In fact, Dutch surplus capital was available to any and all with good credit, and a great deal of eighteenth-century war debt ended up being financed in Amsterdam. The eighteenth-century Dutch masters had begun earning the title of the "nation of shop keepers" that Napoleon was to so contemptuously fling at them early in the next century. For the Dutch, good credit, not religion, ideology or nationality, was the criterion of evaluation in assessing the benefits of providing loans to foreign governments.[6]

Kennedy argues that the fates of Britain and France in the emerging contest over colonial possessions in North America, the Caribbean, and the Indian subcontinent provide the "best example of this critical relationship between financial strength and power politics."[7] Although British industry and technology were not advancing appreciably more rapidly than that of the French during this period, and the French system of taxation was "even less regressive" than that of the British in some ways, Britain had developed some advantages in the realm of finance over, for example, France, which Kennedy asserts enhanced her power in wartime and buttressed political stability, and thus economic growth, in peacetime.[8]

There were, for example, no British "tax farmers" to skim off profits from the collection of taxes. The inefficiency of the French tax farming system was a two-fold curse for France. James Riley's exhaustive study of French finances around the time of the Seven Years' War indicates that fully 38 percent of taxes collected ended up in private hands without even being recorded as revenues accruing to the Crown. In addition the arrangement was a source of great resentment to the French people, and this resentment made the collection of revenues even more difficult than might have been the case if the people felt that their taxes were fairly assessed and efficiently administered. According to Riley his data:

> provide a figure for all the revenues extracted from the populace under the authority of the king: 424.8 million l.t. According to this source, the taxpayers paid 162.4 million in 1752 that did not reach the king. Even the aggregate tax figure was considerably below what many people believed, for '*l'opinion vulgaire*' held that the taxes totaled 600 million (and therefore that some 338 million did not reach the king).[9]

To add to these difficulties, the French state had developed no system of national accounting, and the Bourbon monarchy, in its profligate absolutist disdain for frugality, had ignored chronic and severe deficits for decades. It had levied heavy taxes on commerce quite "inequitably" and "arbitrarily" and the sale of offices had no doubt diverted capital from private commerce, while the commercial monopolies granted by the Crown for revenues had erected severe disincentives to entrepreneurial enterprise.[10] As a result of its spending patterns and poor repayment record, the French government had acquired a quite poor credit rating in the Amsterdam credit markets relative to Britain, and thus paid much higher rates of interest than did Britain to secure foreign loans. Kennedy asserts that the French paid roughly double the rates that the British had to pay, and thus accrued roughly double Britain's interest payments on an equivalent debt.[11] Riley notes that in 1759, as the war continued, "subscriptions on royal loans had slowed, which is to say that lenders had stopped advancing money at the yields offered."[12] Thus in the midst of its great war with Britain the French government was forced to offer higher yields with the result of "a rise of 40 percent in the cost to the government of financing loans."[13]

Britain, on the other hand, had avoided not only the inefficiencies of tax farming, but also an oppressive French system of internal tolls and other disincentives to commerce. Britain also enjoyed the institutional advantage of having created a central bank, the Bank of England, which had been around since the late seventeenth century and permitted the control of the money supply, which it could increase throughout the banking system to meet the rising needs of commerce and government for specie, and issue paper money to further obviate shortages of coin. Even more important, British obligations were guaranteed by the power of Parliament to raise additional revenues. The security implicit in these arrangements resulted in better British credit, and lower rates of interest to the government as secure British obligations were increasingly attractive to nervous foreign investors.[14]

Another advantage Britain held in holding down high interest debt relative to France was that the British aristocracy (and oligarchy) allowed itself to be taxed, unlike its French and Prussian counterparts. Woloch notes that "[t]he English land tax was levied on the chief source of a gentleman's income: the rent he collected on his land. In wartime it rose temporarily to four shillings per pound of assessed valuation" such that "the English landed [and ruling] class probably paid the heaviest taxes in Europe."[15] One obvious result was that the British had an incentive to avoid running up high interest debt while the French aristocracy, and particularly the French monarchy, did not. This is interesting as a study in the variation in territorial-sovereign identity. Both the French Bourbon monarchy and the British Whig Oligarchy had good reasons, stemming from the particulars of the internal dimensions of their territorial sovereignty, to regard the wealth of their countries as their own wealth.

The exemption of the French aristocracy from the burdens of both taxation and decisionmaking and the absolutist stature of the Bourbon monarchy, however, encouraged the latter to view the resources of the country as both its own and as essentially limitless. The British Whig Oligarchy, however, had paid some of the taxes that they levied from their own pockets, and had thus acquired very personal experience that relieved them of such naïveté. Thus, as a detailed study of the British policy of subsidizing the armed forces of French enemies on the continent during the Seven Years' War demonstrates, the British Parliament rigorously scrutinized and hotly debated every proposal for every subsidy and other expenditure throughout the war. Neither did the government carry every proposal.[16] Each man voting on each spending proposal did so with the understanding that some of the money that he was allocating would have to be paid from his own pockets, and that this burden would be proportional to the expenditures he approved. The extension of territorial-sovereign identity in the British case to an active oligarchy liable to a share in the costs of empire—an identity that I argue had, conversely, not been internalized by the passive sycophants arranged ornamentally and impotently in the Bourbon court—had instilled in the British ruling class a conception that their personal interests and finances were bound up with those of the state. The Bourbon monarchy had experienced state finance only as a beneficiary. It lived in profligacy and encouraged the dependent aristocracy to do likewise. If money became scarce, it could be borrowed. The interest would be paid by the peasantry.

The eighteenth-century financial revolution, and the British mastery of it relative to adversaries, was to have enormous strategic consequences for British military success in the coming contest for empire. The French inability to mobilize financial resources as efficiently as could Britain was to strongly contribute to her losses of her North American and Indian colonial possessions and, as we shall also see, to the crisis and instability that was to topple the monarchy and assist in the transition from French territorial-sovereign identity to French national-sovereign identity by the end of the century. Significantly, variations of the institutional manifestations of the internal dimensions of territorial-sovereign identity that Britain and France had shared throughout most of the eighteenth century had been mirrored in a variation in the notion of interest among British and French elites. An important result of these variations were the aforementioned consequences for their respective abilities to leverage the financial revolution for the mobilization of strategic resources.

The Seven Years' War

The question of the sources of the Seven Years' War has been and remains a topic of debate among historians. It is well outside the scope of this book to join that debate. The purpose of Part II of this book has been to outline the causal significance of territorial-sovereign identity for the patterns of eighteenth-century European international politics adequately to foster a useful comparison with the patterns consistent with the later development of national-sovereign identity. This section will attempt to hold to that purpose, yet I will not avoid offering an explanation for the origins of the war as they pertain to my theses. My explanation is, in short, that the war's origins, scope, terms of engagement, and terms of disengagement were in large measure artifacts of the unintended consequences of the territorial-sovereign structure of identities and interests of the belligerents. I am hopeful that the meaning of this assertion will become clearer as I develop the following analysis.

North American Colonial Pressures for War

Certainly the major proximate cause of the war was the conflicting imperial ambitions of Great Britain and France in North America. As the conflict began, Britain controlled the lion's share of the North American eastern seaboard from its Acadian border at the southern end of the Bay of Fundy in the north, to Georgia's colonial border with Spanish Florida in the south. British colonial penetration into the continent had extended north to encompass the source of the St. John River, west to Lake Champlain in New York, west to the Allegheny River in Pennsylvania, and west of the Allegheny Mountains in Virginia and the Carolinas. French colonial penetration had spread both east and west of the great St. Lawrence and resulted, as one traveled southwest along it, in the settlements of Quebec and Montreal, on to Ft. Frontenac at its joining with Lake Ontario, south from the St. Lawrence to Crown Point and Ticonderoga on the west shore of Lake Champlain (with British expansion halted at the east shore).

From Lake Erie the French had accessed a tributary of the Allegheny from whence they had traveled to establish upon it Ft. Duquesne which threatened to halt the westward expansion of the British Pennsylvania colony. Worse from the British perspective, was that from their modest foothold on the Mississippi delta at New Orleans, the French had traveled hundreds of miles north up the Mississippi to establish Ft. de Chartres, and Ft. François on the banks of the Ohio, which lay due west of Virginia. Ft. Miamis near the south bank of Lake Michigan, and Ft. St. Marie at the junctions of Lake Superior and Lake Huron completed what clearly appeared to British eyes as a French attempt to subdivide the continent at the expense of further British westward expansion.[17]

The 1753 establishment of Ft. Duquesne, and the subsequent aggressive French behavior in attempting to clear British settlers and traders from the headwaters of the Ohio, was particularly incendiary in escalating the colonial competition to military competition in the North American periphery. Commercial and mercantilist, not just geographic or peripheral strategic considerations, were brought into play by this French action against these British traders, particularly because, as Julian Corbett reminds us:

> these same traders were mostly agents of the English Ohio Company, which was engaged in opening up a trade route to the great lakes, and its principal shareholders were the magnates of Virginia and Maryland, who had a concession of the Indian trade from the Crown.[18]

This resulted in the famous expedition of the Virginia militia to attempt to expel the French, led by Lieutenant-Colonel George Washington, which met disaster at Ft. Necessity. Corbett marks the start of the Seven Years' War with Newcastle's appraisal of the failure of Washington's expedition.[19] This is likely not the best date from which to mark the start of the war, which was as yet undeclared, particularly as Corbett himself points out that Washington's mission was little more than a peripheral reprisal, involving few or no regular British troops, and was far from being regarded as a act of war in either London or Paris. As Corbett himself suggests, just a few pages later in his narrative:

> the practice of reprisal was not yet obsolete. It still formed a debatable march-land within which the frontier between peace and war existed, but could never be traced. There were innocent forms of reprisal which were clearly distinguishable from war.... Such were the seizure of vessels illegally fishing, or the seizure of vessels carrying contraband or breaking a blockade. . . . But we have lost what in the middle of the eighteenth century was still recognized. Between such innocent forms of reprisal as those mentioned and actual war there were still other forms rising in intensity up to a state of general reprisal which was scarcely if at all distinguishable from full hostility. It was therefore natural for a statesman of the eighteenth century to draw no hard and fast line between diplomacy and strategy. For him every turn of hostilities presented itself diplomatically, and every diplomatic move as an aspect of strategy.[20]

Corbett's analysis reminds us of the extent to which eighteenth-century diplomacy and strategy were the games of elite professionals, wholly inaccessible to society at large. The insulated manner in which they were conducted was a characteristic, practical manifestation of territorial-sovereign identity. We can see Morgenthau's "reactionary utopia" as territorial-sovereign identity-in-action. If Clausewitz could blithely assert, with regard to war on the continent, that it was simply "diplomacy by other means," with what concern would the eighteenth-century statesman view war in the periphery? The sovereignty of the mother country had, to be certain, been extended to the periphery through colonial occupation. But as I have suggested, following Luard, this extension of British sovereignty over the North American periphery was instrumental for the mother country, a means of assuring monopolies of trade and flows of coin and credit to the mother country.

This extension of British sovereignty over the North American periphery *was not* constitutive of British territorial-sovereign identity, at least in the eyes of the mother country. The collective identity of Great Britain in 1754, in the eyes of its European subjects, encompassed the union of England, Wales, and Scotland (and later Ireland, through simple annexation, at the turn of the nineteenth century).[21] It did not encompass the North American colonies.

It is important to discern that the British extension of British sovereignty with regard to these colonies was, so far as the British Crown and government were concerned, an extension of sovereignty *over*, not an extension of sovereignty *to* the territory of these colonies. Thus British colonial "citizenship" was, proportionally, very much a "second class" citizenship. The realization of this curtailed franchise among many of the inhabitants of these colonies later in the eighteenth century was manifested to them with particular force by the Crown's consistent assertion of its right to tax them as subjects of the British Empire while consistently refusing to allow them representation in the *British* parliament. Both Hans Kohn and, in a similar account, Liah Greenfeld, suggest that this treatment undermined the self-identification of the British colonials with the British state, and fostered the creation of a uniquely American collective identity.[22] The consequences of this differential exercise of eighteenth-century British territorial-sovereignty, and the belligerent colonial reaction to it upon the construction of an American national identity, are still celebrated in the United States on the fourth day of every July.

The European "Diplomatic Revolution" and Unsettled Scores

As Europe prepared for the Seven Years' War it was still fully in the hands of European territorial sovereigns. As I suggested in chapter 4, the Bourbon–Hapsburg rivalry which had dominated European international relations from the Westphalian settlement through the close of the War of Spanish Succession had begun to give way to a more multipolar arrangement. The issues surrounding the realignment about to occur in Europe were led by the Franco-British competition in the periphery, and the Austrian vendetta against Prussia over the loss of Silesia in 1740. This action by Friedrich the Great had roughly doubled the territory of Prussia, created a "Great Power" to upset Austrian hegemony over the German states, and enraged the Hapsburg dynasty. The Prussian acquisition had also upset Russia's ambitions in central Europe. We should also consider the importance of the personal caprice of territorial-sovereign monarchs in the equation. The Russian Czarina, Elizabeth, clearly despised Friedrich II of Prussia as an individual, which provided venom to the potion of dynastic ambition and more than soured the relationship between Berlin and St. Petersburg.[23]

As Britain and France squared off over control of territory in the colonial periphery Britain had begun to cast about the continent in search of allies there. Dutch fear of a French neighbor, which had clearly recovered its strength so many years after the Treaty of Utrecht had formalized the demise of the last French bid for continental hegemony, had placed the previous British arrangements with the Dutch in question. Prussia had been hostile to Britain since 1753 due to an unresolved maritime dispute. Moreover, the existing British defensive alliance with Russia was due to expire in 1757. Apprehending the dangerous isolation to which these problems threatened to consign them as they contemplated war with France, the British monarch and government instituted a frenetically active diplomacy in 1755 in order to correct this isolation.

The Hanoverian succession of 1714 had dealt Britain another misfortune. As war with France for empire in America loomed, the reigning British monarch, George II, was simultaneously Elector of Hanover on the continent. In the event of continental hostilities, little Hanover was vulnerable to being overrun either by France from the west, or by Prussia from the east. So long as George was attached to his electorate, royal pressure for the provision of the defense of Hanover was to be a factor in every decision taken by Newcastle, and later by Pitt, in the conduct of British foreign policy. Unfortunately for Newcastle and for Pitt, George was very much attached to Hanover, as his sovereignty over it provided him with a great deal of personal income and enhanced his status as a player in the politics of Central Europe and the flagging Holy Roman Empire. Of course this dual-sovereignty of a monarch over, in this case, both English- and German-speaking territories separated by geography, language, culture, and history is no longer possible in the national-sovereign era, for reasons that will be treated at length later in this work. Yet such an arrangement was quite unremarkable in the eighteenth-century territorial-sovereign system, and, I will argue, had causal significance not only for the conduct of British diplomacy, but also for the British conduct of the war. The causal significance of such an institutional fact is beyond the notice of realist and structural neorealist systems theoretical explanations which would generally emphasize arguments like this one:

> The Seven Years' War—whatever its immediate causes—represents a deeper structural crisis within the global political system, generated by the need to readjust relations among the "core states" in the system in line with intervening changes in power distributions and in a more general sense, to resolve prewar ambiguities in the order and status hierarchy of the system itself.[24]

It is never made clear in such arguments why these "immediate causes" are of no interest or significance. Neither is it ever really made clear what these "system needs" are, or at what point they become dire. Schweizer cites, as his inspiration for this analysis, the "power transition theories" of Organski and Kugler, and the "cycles of hegemonic war" thesis of Robert Gilpin that I have referenced earlier in this work, among other theorists such as George Modelski and Immanuel Wallerstein.[25] It is not my purpose, nor do I have time or space in this chapter, to critique at length the myriad functional-to-structural, liberal realist-to-Marxist theories of the causes of war with reference to this single eighteenth-century case. Neither is it clear what might be gained by such an endeavor. My purpose with this section is merely to identify the significance of territorial-sovereign identity for the origins, conduct, and terms of termination of the Seven Years' War for later comparison with these behaviors and patterns of politics in the national-sovereign era. It is worth pausing to note, however, that it is puzzling to see a historian acquire the structural realist passion for the reification of functional-structural teleology in this context, and to generate an assertion in which the designation of actors is abandoned in place of the agency of a disembodied "system" that is in "crisis." Social systems are transformed and replaced when they cease to be reproduced by social actors, but they are intentionally transformed by the agency of these actors. Similarly, alliance systems do break down, but in response to specific decisions taken by specific social actors.

The passage quoted above is a very strange argument when the prose is disaggregated, as I have just done, in order to clarify what is being said. I have by contrast been careful to point out that *France* and especially *Britain*, not "the system," needed to adjust relations among core states. Britain needed to do so because France was challenging her in the periphery and threatening to isolate her on the continent. Britain and France "needed" to fight the Seven Years' War because they were, respectively, eighteenth-century territorial-sovereign mercantilist oligarchies and autocracies, and they were playing the game that they had been created to play. Elizabeth of Russia, and Maria Theresa of Austria needed "to resolve prewar ambiguities in the order and status hierarchy" because Friedrich had played the game well at their expense and they consequently despised and resented him. The "system needed" the legitimate functioning of mercantilist, oligarchic, and autocratic territorial-sovereigns in order to continue to exist in its eighteenth-century form. It ceased to exist when these did. Failure to recognize that the functioning of a system is dependent on the variable "needs," motivations, interests, and agency of social actors, which must be designated in the ontological construction of a system theory, is the greatest error of structural realist teleologies of this form.

Let us return to the European theater of the war for further illustration. The discussion to come will deepen my critique of structural realist system theory by demonstrating that without correction it cannot adequately explain the notion of interest that informs the practice even of territorial-sovereign alliance formation. I will demonstrate that commitments to particular territories cannot be explained by structural realist theories without incorporating a more rigorous analysis of the prevailing, historically contingent, structure of sovereign identities and interests.

The Defense of Hanover and Issues of Territorial Sovereignty

The devastating seventeenth-century English Civil War that had toppled the Stuarts and created the monarchical vacancy that the Hanoverian succession was designed to fill had also resulted in a distrust of a large standing army that had remained to the eve of the Seven Years' War. It was a measure of the value Britain placed in further westward expansion in North America, at the expense of France, when Parliament voted 1,000,000 on March 22, 1755 to enhance the army and navy.[26] It was generally felt in Britain that her forces were adequate to deal with the French on the North American continent, and on the seas approaching and surrounding it, as the British had established "a clear working superiority"[27] over the French in naval forces. The relatively diminutive size of Britain's standing army, and the lack of enthusiasm for strongly enhancing it, however, suggested to the British that they would need to fight the French on the continent with the forces of others. This could be accomplished only by alliance diplomacy, or by the payment of subsidies, or with a combination of these strategies.[28]

The payment of subsidies implied either subsidizing the armed forces of allies engaged in hostilities for their own *casus belli*, or payment of cash to the sovereign of troops who would serve under British colors and direction for a period of time specified by treaty. Such an arrangement was essentially a contract for mercenary troops, whatever the arrangement might be called. In significant contrast with the national-sovereign era, there were, during the period of the Seven Years' War, a large number of states who seemed to specialize in these services, and whose sovereigns relied upon the revenues from such contracts to make ends meet. This arrangement was entirely consistent with a mercantilist, territorial-sovereign structure of identities and interests, in which military and economic resources could be fungibly and interchangeably applied through the logic of the principles of *raison d'état*. When these principles were later replaced by those deriving from a national-sovereign structure of identities and interests, then mercenary armies attached to states and procurable through the payment of subsidies to their "sovereign" disappeared. This arrangement was to become unsustainable in a system legitimated by the principle of national-self-determination.

Eldon's 1938 study of the British policy of subsidies to the continent during the Seven Years' War provides an appendix that details the annual British subsidies to no less than ten such states. According to this data, Britain provided subsidies to, or contracted troops from Mentz, Brunswick-Wolfenbüttel, Bavaria, Saxony, Hesse-Cassel, Hanover, Prussia, Brunswick, and Portugal.[29] Britain also subsidized Russia for a time early in the war. Among these states, Russia and Prussia, at least, were belligerents in their own right, and should not be seen merely as provenders of mercenaries in order to glean state revenues. Russia, of course, fought on the side of France. Eldon demonstrates that the diplomatic record provides evidence that Saxony and Bavaria, however, were highly dependent upon subsidy money to maintain themselves as states.[30] Both of these states approached Britain for such arrangements. Saxony was initially engaged for the defense of Hanover (to quell the fears of George) with the understanding that Britain would defend Saxony if attacked, presumably by Prussia.[31]

Clearly Saxony's armed forces did not exist solely for the purpose of defending Saxon territory, a finding somewhat at odds with the assumptions of the structural realist position, which assures us that the system is an anarchic, self-help affair, and that states maintain military capabilities primarily to ensure their own survival. Clearly the territorial-sovereign system was at least somewhat tolerant of functional differentiation among the units.[32] Bavaria was not to be so engaged by Britain during the war as the Bavarian Elector demurred on renewal of an existing subsidy arrangement with Britain until he could ascertain the sentiments of Austria,[33] whose immanent presence and preponderance of force no doubt weighed heavily on his mind.

Parliamentary debate on the issue of the defense of Hanover had come about indirectly through debate on a measure to provide a subsidy to Hanover to pay and provision 8,000 Hanoverian troops for its defense. That this measure would be advanced by the government, men who were appointed by and beholden to the king, could not have been a surprise for the Whig oligarchy assembled in parliament. Such a measure allowed George II to ensure the defense of his Electorate with troops, paid with British money, and to ensure his own revenues in the bargain. Pitt, then still in opposition, included in his arguments against the measure the fascinating dilemma that the government's emphasis of the defense of Hanover *demonstrated that treaties made with other powers for the defense of Hanover had been made in the interests of the Electorate of Hanover, namely George II, not in the interest of Britain.* Many felt that the interests of *Britain* would be best served by surrendering Hanover until the end of the war, and demanding it back as a condition of peace.[34]

Eldon has captured the gist of the debate on the pros and cons of a British subsidy policy on the continent in his study of the pamphlets circulating in Britain in the summer and fall of 1755 that debated the issue. They are worth pausing to discuss, not only as they recount an important debate whose outcome would strongly influence further British conduct of the war, but also because they provide a fascinating glimpse at the *notion of interest* of the eighteenth-century mercantilist oligarchy of Britain.

Those opposed to the subsidies argued that Britain could never gain enough on the continent to compensate for the cost of the subsidies. They argued that the European costs would starve British military forces in America. They asked why Britain should hire German princes to defend their own lands. They argued that France would not, in any case, overrun those countries on the continent with which Britain was engaged in active trade, and thus saw no benefit to the trade of the country whatever from a continental war. They argued that continental wars had always impoverished Britain in the past. This was just a play into French hands and that mercenary troops were, in any case, untrustworthy.[35]

Also gleaned from the pamphlets are the arguments of those favoring the subsidy arrangements. The pro-subsidy forces argued that subsidies were the best and cheapest way of diverting France, and conversely the most expensive for France. They argued that the Russian subsidy would prevent Prussian aggression, by cowing Prussia and thus neutralizing Friedrich. They argued that German subsidies would permit their continental fight to take the offensive, and would allow Britain to focus on the destruction of the French navy and commercial shipping, and thus to defend the colonies. They argued that it was better to pay in British money than in British lives, and that the destruction of French shipping alone could not destroy French trade due to the inevitable persistence of land routes and neutral carriers. They argued that there could be no markets for re-exports from British colonies if France overran Europe, and that the maintenance of an English army on the continent would be much more expensive than the provision of mercenary troops. They also argued that an English militia would draw men from economic pursuits, that Britain's real wealth lay in the pursuits of industry, trade and commerce, and thus that it would be wasteful to turn productive workers into soldiers.[36]

The fact that these points were debated, and hotly debated, is highly suggestive in itself, even though many of these arguments are highly problematic upon further examination. Lacking the mercantilist blinders of these eighteenth-century oligarchs, we might find, from our national-sovereign perspective, serious flaws with the premises of most of these arguments. What is particularly noteworthy is that nearly all of them, both pro and con, are *predicated on the assumptions and notions of state interest that were consistent with the legitimating principles of mercantilist, oligarchic, or absolutist, eighteenth-century territorial-sovereign identity*. In this *Weltanschauung*, as we have seen, international economic competition is a zero-sum game. What helps you must hurt your opponent. Men, money, commodities, trade, armed force are all fungibly interchangeable.[37] Colonies are valuable as they promote trade and gain wealth. More of this is better, thus more colonial lands are war objectives. Continental allies with whom one trades minimally are expendable. British subjects are too valuable for the commodity value of their labor to risk losing to French cannonade.

These people thought like capitalists, not like patriots, let alone nationalists. This is not to suggest that there was no "love of country" in eighteenth-century Britain or France, but that this sentiment did not appear to significantly influence either decisions to go to war, or war objectives, or the conduct of war, or even who would do the fighting. These decisions, at least in the British case, appear to have been more strongly influenced by love of profit than of country. Here is, in many dimensions, the model of the state-as-firm in the competitive marketplace that inspires many theories of rational choice in the literature on international relations. Debates such as these certainly give advocates of these theories something to hang their hats on. But these theories fail to mention the extent to which the character and issues of such debates change when the notion of state (or later, national) interest changes. Such a transformation was to begin, before the end of the eighteenth century, in the British notion of state interest with the humiliating loss of the North American colonies that provided much of the impetus for the commencement of hostilities, and with the delegitimation of mercantilist thought that followed the development of liberal economic theory of the later Scottish Enlightenment. Then, mercantilism might have been abandoned in favor of liberalism, but a territorial-sovereign oligarchic structure of identities and interests had remained. But during the opening gambits of the Seven Years' War, the debate was settled when Parliament voted 301 to 105 in December of 1755 to retain the pledge of assistance to Hanover with the lame assertion that British "honor" was at stake in Hanover. George had his way. Russian and Hessian subsidy treaties were also approved that month.[38]

An active British diplomacy had also turned toward Berlin and Vienna in the hope that if defensive alliances could be arranged with both of these, France would wisely eschew continental hostilities and be forced to confine these to the sea and North America, where Britain had a strong advantage in forces deployed and deployable. Prussia had not been a natural British ally, but Friedrich's seizure of Silesia from Austria in 1740 had transformed Prussia into a considerable continental power, and Friedrich was still anxious merely to maintain and consolidate Prussian control over it by 1755. Neither is it inconceivable that dynastic loyalties played some role in this British-Prussian diplomacy when we realize that George II was Friedrich's uncle.[39] By the end of November 1755 Britain had promised to renew its guarantee of Prussian control of Silesia and to settle Prussia's grievance of the ships Britain had seized from Prussia in the previous war if only Prussia would guarantee Hanover's neutrality in any future conflict. The result of this diplomacy was the Convention of Westminster, signed January 16, 1756, in which each party pledged peace and friendship.[40] This alliance poisoned British diplomacy with Austria, however, and the Austrian Empress, intent on recovering Silesia from Friedrich, "refused point-blank to subscribe to a treaty in which Prussia was a party."[41]

The Convention of Westminster, concluded in large measure to secure Prussian defense of George's Hanover, triggered the rest of the European realignment that has become known as the "diplomatic revolution." The hasty arrangement of the convention, and the fact that it was concluded without consultation with other interested parties, namely France, Russia, and Austria, strongly irritated these and set in motion the diplomacy that led to their own alliance. It was not lost on the court in St. Petersburg that the British subsidy arrangement with Russia that had just been signed in December was starkly contradicted by the Convention as it "provided for Russians coming into Germany [*sic*], the former for keeping them out."[42] The Austrian vendetta regarding Prussian control of Silesia assured that the Hapsburgs had at last found a common cause with the Bourbons, in their capacities as territorial sovereigns, that their common Catholicism had never been able to foster when, in their capacities as purely dynastic sovereigns, Catholic Hapsburgs had squared off against the Catholic Valois and Bourbon kings of France in centuries past.[43]

This *rapprochement* was cemented in a Franco-Austrian alliance with the signing of the First Treaty of Versailles on May 1, 1756. Britain declared war against France two weeks later, Russia promised assistance to Austria in the event the latter was attacked by Prussia, and Franco-Russian *rapprochement* strengthened with an exchange of ministers in May. By June, Friedrich's strategic-political position was quite precarious. Certain of the imminence of hostilities he decided on a preemptive move to strengthen his strategic-military position and invaded Saxony against British wishes and advice to the contrary. Russia mobilized in response and promised assistance to France and Austria. Newcastle then suspended British subsidy payments to Russia lest they be used to fight Friedrich.[44]

This series of events suggests that it is less illuminating than it would appear to suggest that "whatever its immediate causes . . . [the war] . . . represents a deeper structural crisis in the global political system."[45] The British requirement to provide for the defense of Hanover resulted directly and solely from the dual sovereignty of George II over Britain and Hanover. The Prussian alliance was clearly designed primarily to assure Prussian defense of Hanover. France was to be belligerent in any case. Since neither Russia nor Austria were situated geographically to provide a credible guarantee of Hanover's security, they were not approached in this regard. Only Prussia possessed the geographic proximity and military capability to either defend Hanover as a British ally from a powerful and belligerent France, or to seize it as an enemy of Britain. In the absence of the requirement to defend Hanover, and the Prussian alliance that predominantly secured this defense, British diplomacy would have been free to pursue, and much more likely to secure, Austrian and Russian alliances that might well have prevented any French action on the continent.

It is therefore quite reasonable to argue that one of the major "immediate" causes of the continental theater of the war was the unique character of George II's dual territorial sovereignty over Britain and Hanover. It is not at all clear from the diplomatic record that either Britain or France perceived any structural crisis they needed to resolve on the European continent or that hostilities initiated in the North American periphery would have migrated to a European theater at all without the British anxiety over the status of Hanover.

The European alliance realignment that we now call the "diplomatic revolution" occurred only after the signing of the Convention of Westminster, and in reaction to it. The realignment was due not to any parsimonious, disembodied, structural determinism latent within the "system," but to Austria's having an axe to grind with Prussia, and to Russia's ambitions in central Europe—ambitions that could be much more easily achieved after the demise of Prussia. The European theater of the Seven Years' War was thus engaged largely because the whims and caprice of eighteenth-century territorial sovereigns led to decisions (George's insistence on the defense of Hanover at all costs, Maria Theresa's insistence on the recovery of Silesia at all costs, Friedrich's anxiety to leave a Prussia augmented by Silesia to his heir, Czarina Elizabeth's loathing of Friedrich) that had unintended consequences. Opposition to the will of the king in Hanoverian England could have cost the average ambitious Whig Oligarch dearly in patronage and position,[46] and the whims and words of Maria Theresa, Friedrich, and Elizabeth were law in their lands.

In the conduct of the War the defense of Hanover appeared to take precedence over many other objectives as well, including sound military and political strategy. With William Pitt the Elder, the earlier opponent of continental subsidies, in charge of the government in 1758, George II again displayed the division of his loyalties between Britain and Hanover. Friedrich was now receiving British subsidies to the tune of £670,000 sterling per year. After the Prussian defeat at the Battle of Kolin in June of 1758, and the subsequent Prussian evacuation of Bohemia (in which much of Friedrich's mercenary army had disappeared in mass desertions), Friedrich had gathered his strength and prepared to resume the offensive. Pitt wanted to send Friedrich a strong letter of British support of this intention, but George wanted the forces under Friedrich's command in Hanover excluded from the campaign under the lame pretense that this would be impossible "due to his [George's] obligation to accept an Austrian agreement regarding Hanover's neutrality."[47] After leaving George's presence Pitt expressed the opinion that a separate peace for Hanover would be an intolerable breach of faith with Friedrich and ordered Newcastle "to give Prussia the strongest assurance of support" counter to George's wishes. It was a rare act of courage in an eighteenth-century statesman to issue an order directly in contravention of the wishes of the monarch, but it was not rare in Pitt, who "did not find it easy to co-operate with others . . . [and for whom] . . . politics was a matter of absolutes."[48]

George had evidently moved privately to obtain a separate peace for Hanover in any case, perhaps leery of a direct clash on the matter with the formidable Pitt, whom he needed as Britain grappled with war on two continents. In any event, later in the year, George's son, the Duke of Cumberland, concluded the Convention of Closterseven and a separate peace for Hanover, acting on the full powers of his father. The temerity of George when confronted with this breach of faith was remarkable. As Eldon recounts it: "The king [George] insisted falsely that the convention had been signed contrary to his orders."[49] Not even the equally audacious Pitt had a stomach for questioning the king's veracity, but Pitt, in his capacity as head of the government, insisted upon the abrogation of the treaty in vehement terms, and refused to allow the exchequer to send any more funds to Hanover until the troops there were again in motion against France.[50] Later, in the summer of 1759, George declared that *his* Hanoverian revenues were only sufficient to pay *his* 42,000 Hanoverian troops, and that consequently Britain would have to pay all other expenses associated with the defense of Hanover. An angry Pitt refused and instead spoke of terminating all continental operations.[51]

Conquering America in Germany?

In reading such accounts, it is both fascinating and terrible for those of us reared in the era of national sovereignty to watch an eighteenth-century statesman be required to negotiate with, and to outmaneuver his monarch in order to ensure that the latter conducts foreign policy in a manner consistent with the "interests" and security of the state whose throne he has mounted. A conflict in the "interests" of the sovereign *qua* king of Britain and the empire, and the interests of the sovereign *qua* Elector of Hanover, could be acknowledge and debated, as Pitt had done while still in opposition. Ultimately, however, precisely because the interests of the king *qua* dynast and the interests of the king *qua* territorial sovereign could not be decoupled, the "interests" of George in both capacities had to be accommodated, and reconciled with those of the British Empire, as Pitt had done when he left the opposition and agreed to lead George's government. The same William Pitt the Elder who had so vehemently opposed the defense of Hanover, and the expense of the system of continental subsidies designed to ensure it, was now called upon to defend the subsidy policy as expenses mounted with the progress of the war. As Schweizer himself suggests, though he does not grasp that the assertion damages his structural realist explanation of the origins of the war:

> Although Englishmen often resented the union of Hanover and Britain, abandoning Hanover was strategically [?] and politically [much more to the point] unfeasible. . . . the impossibility of severing the connection insured that Hanover's interests would be considered by British administrations, and, on occasion, would predominate. It also meant that Britain was obliged to make provisions for Hanover's defense and thus for continental war, by subsidies to allies, through a British expeditionary force or both.[52]

It is difficult to argue, in the face of this realization, that British "sovereignty" was so firmly lodged with the people or with the Parliament as Britons then and now might wish to believe. George may have had a Parliament and the wishes and interests of British oligarchs to contend with, but his arrangement of the defense of Hanover throughout the war, in the teeth of voices and evidence that suggested this policy could not be easily reconciled with the seemingly objective political and strategic interests of the British Empire, demonstrates that George II was an eighteenth-century territorial sovereign in his own right. Even though it would appear he acted to protect personal and dynastic interests, the principle of *raison d'état* still legitimated his actions to the extent that he successfully extended his sovereignty over, and *to*, German Hanover. When it became clear that he insisted upon this extension, the British notion of "state interest" adjusted to incorporate the necessity of the defense of Hanover. As this is the case, and as this example serves to help illustrate, it becomes quite problematic to speak of the "objective interests" of the state in a trans-historical or an ahistorical fashion.[53] It is difficult to see how any rational-choice model, let alone structural neorealism, can account for this. One suggestion that emerges from this discussion is that the interests of whatever institutional form of collective action which forms the units that populate a given historical system are not static, not "an object of rational determination,"[54] or objectively given even within the time span of a single military conflict, let alone across the time frame in which that "system" is dominant, or across "systems" that I argue are constituted and reconstituted by transformations in the prevailing forms of collective identity.

This British conduct, and especially Pitt's conduct to the end of the war, illustrate that British war objectives had certainly expanded from colonial territorial aggrandizement in the periphery at least to encompass extracting Britain from the European theater of the conflict without surrendering or endangering Hanover, and without undue cost in lives or money. Money may have won out over lives near the end when, as British finances became strained, Pitt acceded to the introduction of British troops to the "German war" by May 1760, upon learning the huge cost in money that Friedrich demanded in exchange for allowing Britain to conclude a separate peace with France.[55] Further, by the close of 1759, in the North American periphery, the strategic points of Niagara, Ticonderoga, Crown Point, and Quebec had all fallen to British forces and Pitt had begun to realize, contrary to his earlier opinion, the real benefits that the British free hand in the North American theater, occasioned by the continental subsidy policy, had gained for Britain at the expense of France.

Other British war objectives and "interests" had remained constant. As Montreal fell in September of 1760, the British conquest of North America was moving to mopping-up operations and Pitt and Newcastle had determined to continue the war only to obtain the most favorable (and lucrative) settlement from France. Pitt was now kept quite busy defending the "German war" before the restless Parliament that was the first to convene with a new king, George III, on the throne. Prussia's price in money for a separate British peace with France remained too high, however, and Russian diplomacy under Elizabeth insisted on Russian acquisition of Prussian territory in return for a Russian cessation of hostilities.[56] At this point Pitt provided the final demonstration of his extreme mercantilist proclivities as head of the British government when Spain, hoping to bolster its own colonial empire, concluded an alliance with France in mid-August of 1761. Spain's miscalculation was enormous and its timing disastrous. Pitt was anxious to use the alliance as a pretext to declare war on Spain to allow the British navy to capture Spanish treasure fleets.[57] Spanish gold from America would alleviate severely strained British finances and defray the long-term expenses of the unexpectedly expensive war for Britain. Outvoted on this measure, he resigned October 5, 1761, and consigned himself to defending, as a private member of Parliament, the continental war "for having diverted the energies of France. " 'America,' he said, "has been conquered in Germany.' "[58]

Irrespective of the merits of this claim, Parliament was not consoled by the fact that America had been conquered so long as the war raged on in Europe at a ruinous cost, principally in British money. Fortunately for British coffers, for Prussian territorial integrity, and for Pitt's reputation the irascible Russian Czarina Elizabeth died in January of the following year, "when Frederick II's military fortunes were at their lowest point." She was succeeded by the Pro-Prussian Peter III, who offered Prussia peace on terms so favorable that Austria and France, in recognition that they could now hope only for a return to the *status quo ante bellum* at best, were forced to sue for peace.[59] The 1763 Peace of Paris left Great Britain in control of the North American continent east of the Mississippi River, the Indian subcontinent, and a number of strategic islands.[60]

Thus this eighteenth-century, transcontinental war ended with Britain overwhelmingly the big winner.[61] Had America been conquered in "Germany"? Pitt has long been lionized by historians as the visionary who saw that the strategic division of French energies between two continents and an ocean, made possible by the system of subsidies to the continent, had left British forces free to ride herd over the Atlantic and Caribbean and the North American continent, in spite of the evidence that he clearly held the opposite opinion while in opposition and vacillated while in office.[62] Pitt may well have been, and probably was, convinced of the efficacy of this policy at some point, most likely in the *annus mirabilis* of 1759, when French colonies fell to British forces around the globe. More important than the answer to this question, in my view, is the uniquely territorial-sovereign notion of state interest that animated the subsidy policy. To illuminate this notion I will conclude this chapter, appropriately, with a citation from the last paragraph of Eldon's study of the subsidy policy.

> Whether we take the word of the [British] pamphleteer who wrote: "if you take your people from their work, and make soldiers of militia men . . . you will certainly be the cause of its (money) going abroad, never to return again," or whether we quote the ministerial doctrine that "we must be merchants while we are soldiers," . . . we can see operating even in war time the belief that it is better to work for one's country than to die for it.[63]

These sentiments, particularly the notion that it is better to work and produce for your country than to die for it, are quintessential tenants of the notion of interest that animated the eighteenth-century, mercantilist, territorial-sovereign state system. This last sentiment, as we shall see, was to become quintessentially alien to the national-sovereign collective identity that was soon to break upon America and Western Europe, and from there to Central and Eastern Europe and the globe.

Conclusions and Theoretical Reprise

The Seven Years' War provides a highly effective illustration of the causal significance of the territorial-sovereign structure of identities and interests for the security conduct of territorial-sovereign states. First, variations in the institutional manifestations of territorial-sovereign identity strongly influenced the manner in which France and Britain engaged in strategic financing of their respective military efforts. French absolutist tax-farming put France at a significant disadvantage relative to British oligarchic arrangements which proved more fiscally efficient and rewarded Britain with more favorable terms of credit. Variations in territorial-sovereign identity were also mirrored in the respective notions of interests of French and British state elites, encouraging thrift on the part of British elites who were, in part, spending their own resources to conduct the war. French defeat was attended by a financial crisis resulting from its crushing war debt. This debt was to play no small role, when compounded with the debt acquired by France to assist the American provincials in detaching themselves from Britain, in bringing down the French absolutist regime within thirty years of the close of the war.

I have argued that that scope, conduct, terms of engagement, and terms of disengagement of belligerents during the Seven Years' War are inexplicable without recourse to analysis of the manner in which the interests of the belligerents were structured by their territorial-sovereign social identities. Analysis of George's dual territorial sovereignty over Britain and Hanover is required to explain the *scope* of the war and the diplomatic revolution that demolished a classical European system of alliances which had stood for centuries as more consistent with the balancing requirements of European actors. The choice of alliance partners and the theaters of conflict are otherwise inexplicable. They are equally inexplicable without analysis of the consequences for alliance formation of the whims and caprices of the territorial-sovereign monarchs who were to become belligerents. No argument predicated on assumptions of rational instrumental decisionmaking on the part of belligerents can explain why a continental European theater of the war should have been opened, unless the interests of actors are properly understood to be structured by historically contingent territorial-sovereign social identities.

Similar analysis is required to apprehend the *terms of engagement* of the war. On the part of the British, the peripheral war was fought primarily with the British navy and provincial troops *over* whom the British Crown had extended sovereignty, but *to* whom the Crown had not awarded full citizenship. The British oligarchy reasoned like capitalists, not like patriots, evincing evidence of their love of profit rather than love of country in decisionmaking regarding whether or not to conduct the war, for what objectives, and with whom. The state-as-firm model is quite nearly reified in this portrait of mercantilist, oligarchic, territorial-sovereign decisionmaking. But the notion of state interests that emerges from this portrait is a construction of a very specific structure of social identities and theories that exogenize this notion of interests by assumption to all actors in quite different systems consequently severely limit their potential explanatory utility.

I have argued that similar analysis is required to apprehend the *conduct* of the war. On the British side, the primacy of the defense of Hanover was continuously elevated over other, more likely genuinely strategic priorities, in decisionmaking regarding the application of strategic resources—namely troops and subsidy funds for more troops. In the person of one territorial-sovereign individual and his system-legitimated proprietary sovereign interests, we are witnesses to the spectacle of a conflict of interests between the sovereign and the rational, objective, strategic and pecuniary interests of the nation. This dichotomy was to become an impossible contradiction in terms in the national-sovereign system that followed. In the system structured by territorial-sovereign identities and interests, however, the division had to be accommodated and reconciled. The British notion of state interests had to adjust to accommodate the proprietary and quite territorial interests of the sovereign's second territorial-sovereignty. Thus we observe that it is ineffectual to theorize about the objective interests of state or nation in a transhistorical or ahistorical fashion—a fashion in which socially constructed and empirically verifiable notions of state or national interests are disregarded in some accounts in favor of *a priori* assumptions.

Lastly, I have argued that similar analysis is required to apprehend the *terms of disengagement* from the war. It is certainly true that France had suffered serious military defeats in the periphery and might well have been financially exhausted in the last year of the war. It is also certainly true that the death of Elizabeth and the accession of a capriciously pro-Prussian Peter to the Russian throne had left France bereft of continental allies with the resources to effectively assist France in a successful conclusion of the continental theater of the war.

Part III

National-Sovereign Identity

6 The Emergence of National-Sovereign Identity: Revolutionary Nationalism and Reaction

> The bane of stable international systems is their nearly total inability to envision mortal challenge. The blind spot of revolutionaries is their conviction that they can combine all the benefits of their goals with the best of what they are overthrowing. —Henry Kissinger

> All French persons are placed in permanent requisition for the service of the armies. Young men will go off to battle; married men will forge arms and transport provisions; women will make tents and clothing and serve in the hospitals.
> —Declaration of the Montagnard Convention (1793)

> We pieced our thoughts into philosophy
> And planned to bring the world under a rule
> Who are but weasels fighting in a hole.
> —William Butler Yeats

The first crises of legitimacy of the old (territorial-sovereign) regime were to come before the end of the eighteenth century. It was to begin in the periphery with a colonial challenge to the claims of territorial sovereignty with the 1776 declaration of the sovereignty and independence of Britain's North American colonials. It was to continue on the continent with the crisis of the old regime in France, and much of the rest of Europe to the middle of the nineteenth century. This chapter will therefore be predominantly concerned with the events between 1789 and 1848, which Hobsbawm has appropriately termed the "age of revolution."[1]

The French Dual Legitimation Crises: *Ressentiment* and National-Sovereign Identity

Recall that in chapter 4 we saw that the rampant absolutism of the French monarchy had deprived the French nobility of their ancient class identity as quasi-feudal legislators and rulers of the French nation. Absolutism had instead reduced them, in some cases, to the status of royal patrons, and in other cases to a purely ornamental status, as courtiers and royal sycophants, highly dependent upon royal patronage. Their class identity and solidarity did not dissolve in the face of their increasing irrelevance in the governance of the French nation, however. They saw the Crown's penchant for ennobling the wealthy bourgeois as a more direct threat to the status and legitimacy conferred upon them by their ancient bloodlines. This affront served as an adequate grievance to redirect their class identification with the French Crown and state into a primary allegiance to other members of their class. In order to meet the twin threats of the absolutist tendencies of the Crown, and the incursions of the wealthy bourgeois class into its ranks to its identity and status, the French nobility had begun to redefine and reorganize itself to construct a new, firmer basis for its identity and status.[2]

If the "virtue" of nobility based upon blood lineage would no longer be recognized, the French aristocracy would apply their wealth and leisure to the creation of a new barrier against bourgeois incursions into their ranks. Thus, as Greenfeld argues:

> In the eighteenth century the [French] aristocracy appropriated education as a quality peculiar to it. It redefined itself as a cultural elite . . . schooling became a necessary condition for success in high society . . . the importance of the Court decreased proportionately. . . . Talent became a ground for ennoblement. Middle-class intellectuals mixed with *grands seigneurs* in salons and academies. They enjoyed comfortable incomes and could marry into respectable circles. They were pampered by generous pensions and "cultivated" by noble admirers: 30 percent of Rousseau's correspondents, 50 percent of Voltaire's,

> came from the nobility. . . . Authors, it was said, acquired "a kind of nobility." The definition of intellectuals as an aristocracy was not entirely new . . . Against another intruder, however, the nobility stood firm. While it came to recognize culture as ennobling, it would not yield to money. Money could buy nobility, but it could not buy social acceptance.[3]

Thus the newly educated aristocracy of birth became augmented with an "aristocracy of merit," and intellectuals who were "cultivated" by their aristocratic patrons formed an affinity with their patrons. Greenfeld points out that even Rousseau, who has come down in the annals of political philosophy as the great democrat, had himself formed such an affinity. It was Rousseau who had said " 'The best possible government . . . is an aristocracy.' " But in an aristocracy of merit " . . . the wisest should govern the many.' "[4] These flights into the utopia of the philosopher-king were, however, overshadowed in the work of Rousseau by the legitimacy of the true seat of post-dynastic, post-territorial sovereignty. This is the general will.[5]

But it is not the Rousseauian vision of the sovereignty of the state, lodged in the general will, that alone provided the ideological basis of an emerging French nationalism in the French aristocracy. Nor was it elite or mass alienation from the atomizing capitalism of the vulgar rich, or their use of the profits of this mode of economic organization to arrogate unto themselves the noble titles that had been the birthright of the French aristocracy. *The sources of French nationalism, as it emerged in infantile form in the middle of the eighteenth century, were by no means purely endogenous to French domestic society*, and it is here that Greenfeld provides her greatest contribution to our understanding French nationalism.

As the eighteenth century progressed, the "Anglophilia" of the French intellectual elite that had been evident in the admiration of the English constitution, articulated in Montesquieu's *L'Esprit des Lois*, "gradually gave way to Angolophobia."[6] The gradual decline of French stature and fortune on the international stage after the death of Louis XIV, the humiliating defeat at the hands of the British in the Seven Years' War, and loss of vast colonial possessions at its conclusion, had contributed to a fierce *ressentiment* of Britain among the French elite. Greenfeld attributes the term *ressentiment* to Nietzsche, and later development and definition of the concept to Max Scheler. She suggests that "*ressentiment* refers to a psychological state resulting from suppressed feelings of envy and hatred (existential envy) and the impossibility of satisfying these feelings."[7] It is an essential concept in her explanation of the development of, respectively, English, French, Russian, German, and American nationalisms.

It is worthwhile to pause here to unpackage this concept a bit further, with Greenfeld's assistance, and to situate this concept in the context of my theoretical framework, elaborated in chapter 2. I have earlier argued, with Habermas, that a "legitimation crisis" results in a society when powerful societal members "feel their social identity threatened." In response they revise their "interpretive system" to revise their group identity and "through this group identity assert their own self-identity."[8] Greenfeld's application of the concept of *ressentiment* to the legitimation crisis that Habermas develops is particularly useful in understanding the cognitive origins of national collective identity. Though she does not invoke Habermas, her argument strongly reflects his.

> The adoption of a new, national identity is precipitated by a regrouping within or change in the position of influential social groups—a crisis of identity, structurally expressed as "*anomie*"—which creates among them an incentive to search for and, given the availability, adopt a new identity. The crisis of identity as such does not explain why the identity which is adopted is *national*, but only why there is a predisposition to opt for some new identity.[9]

Quite. So why does this new identity crystallize as national identity?

> The fact that the identity is *national* is explained . . . by the availability at the time of a certain type of ideas, in the first case a result of invention, and in the rest of an importation . . . *national* identity is adopted because of its ability to solve the crisis . . . where the emergence of national identity is accompanied by *ressentiment*, the latter leads to the emphasis on the elements of indigenous traditions—or the construction of a new system of values—hostile to the principles of the original [in the case to follow, English] nationalism.[10]

As French intellectuals and nobility looked about them at the close of the eighteenth century they saw much to fear and loathe in Britain. They had been mortified by the results of the Seven Years' War, and pined for vengeance against the British. As Greenfeld suggests, the educated classes in France were enthusiastic supporters of the French efforts in support of the American War of Independence. Lafayette was greeted as a conquering hero upon his first return to France in February of 1779. Primary source material abounds to illustrate both the contemporary French enthusiasm for humiliating Britain, and their cognitive dissociation of the British nation with the principles of liberalism and progress, which they saw as engendered by the American Revolution.[11] Moreover, the loathing of the French intellectuals, noble or not, of the *bourgeoisie vulgaire* had led them, with the assistance of the work of Mably, to despise Britain as "[a] capitalist society, a nation that was unjust, avaricious, venal, corrupt, and dominated by commercial interests . . . [thus] . . . no fit model for France."[12]

Thus the thrust of Greenfeld's argument is that the revolution would never have been possible without the disaffection of the nobility, their move toward reconstituting themselves as a cultural elite in the face of their political irrelevance on the absolutist state, and without the ideology of national collective identity, which sprang from the resulting French Enlightenment, and from *ressentiment* of Great Britain, the principle rival of France. The ideology of nationalism had sprung from the French nobility and the intellectual elite, not from the bourgeoisie, who later appropriated the revolution. Greenfeld makes it clear that she regards the French bourgeoisie as scarcely being in a position to conceptualize, let alone create and effect, a social revolution. Again, for Greenfeld the French bourgeoisie "consisted of a middling sort of people, smart enough to recognize a good opportunity. The elite forged and armed the middle classes with weapons it had not much use for itself."[13]

The force of Greenfeld 's argument is, however, predicated on her assertion that the relative decline of the international status of France vis-à-vis Britain "was at best of secondary importance for the middle-class nationalism, and it was much less fueled by wounded pride and a desire to get even [than that of the aristocracy]."[14] This argument is certainly plausible, given the evidence she has presented that the aristocracy and intellectuals had their own reasons to despise capitalist Britain. But she goes on to immediately admit that unlike the elites who developed and articulated the concept of national-sovereign identity, lodged in the people, that "bourgeois who remained bourgeois rarely articulated their views, we know much less about what they really thought."[15] One potential pitfall of accepting this argument without comment is that we really have very little historical or documentary insight into how the French bourgeoisie felt about the Revolution as it was being prepared, as the written records that they have left to us most often are limited to the balancing of sums of money in their ledgers.

It is not my intention in this discussion to advocate the adoption of Greenfeld's explanation of the development of the notion of national-sovereign identity in France over competing explanations. Greenfeld clearly takes pains to refute the contentions of theorists as diverse as the Marxist Barrington Moore to the French aristocrat Tocqueville that the French Revolution was a bourgeois revolution.[16] Skocpol, conversely, has argued that the fiscal crisis resulting from the disastrous French war debts ushered in the revolution, and that any contribution resulting from French class struggle (which implies the existence of a French bourgeois class identity) was a product of this crisis.[17] Yet, as Greenfeld points out, there is little documentary evidence of this from the pens of the contemporary French bourgeoisie. Michael Mann's recent persuasive explanation contains elements of all of these explanations, in his neo-Weberian, multicausal IEMP model.[18]

> Classes were not "pure" but also were defined by ideological, military, and political forces. The Revolution *became* bourgeois and national, less from the logic of development from feudal to capitalist modes of production than from state militarism (generating fiscal difficulties), from its failure to institutionalize relations between warring elites and parties, and from the expansion of discursive ideological infrastructures carrying principled alternatives.[19]

What I should like the reader to take away from this brief development of the Revolution and the national-sovereign identity that resulted from it is an understanding that (1) the legitimation crisis that spawned the Revolution had sources that were both internal and external to French society. (2) The sources of this legitimation crisis were cognitive and material, ideational (agential) and structural. (3) Those who argue that the crisis of legitimacy of the *ancien regime* might be explained largely with recourse to sources internal to French domestic society must contend with the fact that the development of the specifically national-sovereign identity of the new regime can not be explained without reference to factors external to domestic society, such as competition with England. Finally, (4) the power of the

French bourgeoisie and the idea of the French nation arose simultaneously. This last observation is a pattern that will become familiar.

It is, however, far too simplistic to suggest that French nationalism arose as a response to English nationalism, or that the French nation was constructed to place France on par with the British nation which had so wounded the Frenchman's self-esteem within his collective self-identification. French nationalism and French nationhood did not arise as a necessary consequence of a remorseless "socialization" mechanism, weeding out dysfunctional modes of state organization with the obdurate purpose of an automaton. France did not shed absolutism to defeat Great Britain, or to become America. France developed national-sovereign identity because the territorial-sovereign identity of the absolutist Bourbon monarchy had become, through external defeat, internal fiscal crisis, and domestic exclusivity, too shabby an overcoat to clothe the talent, energy, and ambition of the self-aware people of all classes that the territorial-sovereign state had misused.

Yet it is not at all clear that the idea of the French nation had been internalized by all, or even the majority, of Frenchmen as Louis and his queen mounted the scaffold on a cold January's day in 1793. National-sovereign identity had surely existed in France, by Greenfeld's account, by the middle of the eighteenth century among the educated elite. Yet it is not difficult to envision an alternative demise of the Bourbon monarchy without it. I will give Douglas Johnson the last word regarding the causes of the Revolution.

> There should be no problem in understanding the Revolution. Towards the end of the eighteenth century the government of France ceased to function. There was no revolutionary party; there was no revolutionary opposition; there was no revolutionary situation; there was no accumulation of crises which exploded. There were many features which made government more difficult. Some of these were in the realm of ideas, which undermined the traditional authority of an anointed king. Some were in the nature of hard facts, such as inflation and rising expenditure. Some were in the nature of accident, such as bad harvests. Some were in the nature of circumstances, such as the presence of a young and well-intentioned king who drew attention to problems and ills which he was unable to solve. And some were to be found in the fact of innovation, when Frenchmen found themselves,

> for the first time, englobed in a parliamentary assembly and involved in a situation that created confrontation, dispute, attitudinization and division. And out of all these features, the French nation emerged.[20]

Yet it was a specifically national-sovereign identity that emerged. Johnson's observations capture the dynamic and unpredictable interplay of social and political agency and structure required to delegitimate and topple a political regime, and in this case, a social order as well. National-sovereign collective identity may not have been the cause of the Revolution, but it was clearly a consequence of the Revolution, and of the subsequent reaction of the crowned heads of Europe to the more than figurative decapitation of one of their own.

Territorial-Sovereign Reaction to the New Regime: The Conflict of Territorial-Sovereign and National-Sovereign Principles

So much has been written about the events surrounding the French Revolution that I will radically minimize further narrative description of the event itself. What will interest us are the enormous consequences for French society and domestic institutions and particularly for European international relations, of the passing of sovereignty from Louis XVI to the French *nation* in 1789.

The social and political institutions of the French state were completely and continuously transformed by the new legitimating principles of the French nation. The post-Revolutionary French civil order and government were to undergo several well-studied transitions between the formation of the National Assembly from the Estates General in 1789 to the declaration of the Second Republic in the Concert period. The Revolution produced a series of regimes. The French state was governed as a constitutional monarchy from 1789 through 1792, until Louis's execution. A Jacobin dictatorship ruled for the following two years as the Terror decimated leading lights of the French Enlightenment, such as Condorcet, those who had worked to overthrow the Girondists, such as Marat, and finally leaders of the Committee of Public Safety such as Danton and Robespierre. This was followed in turn by the thermidorian reaction, the Directory, the Consulate, the Empire, and finally the Bourbon Restoration in 1815, which followed the defeat of Napoleon.

Whatever might be said about the imperfect state of the French nation-building project at the time of the First Republic, the immediate and repeated transformation of French civil institutions indicates that the cognitive and political negation of the old regime in France was completed quite early in the life of the new French civic order.[21] The National Assembly, while Louis still drew breath, was predominantly concerned with struggling for power with him in a domestic context, and with attacking the principles that legitimated his reign. Foreign concerns were initially quite low on the Revolutionary agenda, and thus French national-sovereign identity lacked an external focus for a time. As Paul Schroeder suggests in his recent and monumental study of the period between the close of the Seven Years' War and the Revolution of 1848; "Only from about mid-1791 did the spirit of nationalism, aroused and mobilized by the revolution, become clearly visible, initially more in domestic affairs."[22]

Lacking a direct threat, the National Assembly initially made no moves to threaten other European states with republican revolution by force of French arms. Neither did the vast majority of Louis's brother monarch's expend much effort to assist him, frustrating an effort by the Swedish king Gustavus III to organize his rescue. The French national sovereigns of the National Assembly, and the territorial sovereigns in the rest of Europe, appeared to gaze upon one another without serious concern for a time. Yet Schroeder provides us with a passage that provides the link between the domestic and international consequences of the creation of national-sovereign identity in a system dominated by territorial sovereigns.

> Just as the Revolution fundamentally changed domestic politics, so it changed the nature and rules of the international game. Its new revolutionary political language and culture, in defining the state as the highest incorporation of the popular will . . . dramatically raised the stakes of domestic politics, making the central issue that of who truly represented the people's will and had the right to govern by its name and authority. Those who fought and lost in this contest for representing the popular will . . . were by implication . . . not part of the people but its enemies, traitors to the Revolution and the fatherland [read nation] . . . In a similar way, the Revolution presented a chal-

> lenge to the whole legal and conceptual basis of international politics. Instead of international claims and transactions being argued and fought out on the basis of treaties and legal rights, the popular will was now to be the decisive factor. This vastly increased the potential for international conflict, magnified uncertainties, and elevated quarrels over concrete interests into struggles over fundamental principles and world views.[23]

Thus the same principles of national-sovereign identity that legitimated the transformation of the French domestic civil order, which Isser Woloch has analyzed so rigorously, presented an *intrinsic challenge to the legitimacy of the international order dominated by states which possessed territorial-sovereign identity*. This illustrates my assertion, implicit in Figure 1, chapter 2) that *the transformation of collective identity from territorial-sovereign to national-sovereign identity resulted not only in a necessary change in the institutional forms of collective action, but also in a challenge to the legitimating principles of the territorial-sovereign international system*. Yet clearly France had not yet succeeded in transforming these system legitimating principles. The question of whether national-sovereign or territorial-sovereign principles would prevail would be contended for decades to come. This contention was to begin immediately upon the French National Assembly's articulation of national-sovereign principles of international conduct in the Assembly's assertion of French national sovereignty over Alsace-Lorraine.

The rights of the Bishops of Speyer and Trier, conferred by their positions as *Herrschaften* of the Holy Roman Empire, came into direct conflict with French claims that "their rights base upon popular sovereignty transcended those based upon treaties."[24] This challenge was monumental and potentially lethal to the small German princes and clerics without resources to oppose the French national Leviathan. Again Schroeder captures the issue in language sufficiently trenchant to quote at length.

> The French concept of an exclusive sovereign authority exercised by a single government over a clearly defined territory clashed directly with their life-principle, that of *Landeshoheit* (territorial supremacy rather than sovereignty). . . . Sweeping away feudalism might be the way to consolidate revolutionary France; it would destroy Germany, and could undermine much of the rest of Europe. . . . quarrels with

> greater powers were bound to arise, for France's new principles gave it new powerful weapons of territorial expansion. Louis XIV had had to find or invent legal justifications for his annexations; France now could claim any territory where the people, or any group it chose to regard as the people, proclaimed its allegiance.[25]

This passage emphasizes my earlier suggestion *that it matters a great deal to what or whom people in a polity give their allegiance. That which they regard as a legitimate source of domestic and international political authority defines them as a polity.* Schroeder's analysis suggests that the principles of national-sovereign identity create as many or more problems as they solved for the international system. National collective identity problematizes, at a minimum, the issues of minorities, territory, migration, and state integrity and security. Unhappy ethnic, linguistic, religious, or otherwise delineated minorities are tempted toward secessionism in the hope that a powerful nation will assist them in separating from the state to which they are attached. National-sovereign identity problematizes the issue of title to land as dynastic and territorial-sovereign legal claims are delegitimated. Ethnic and minority migration is encouraged in such an environment, creating the problem of refugees. The integrity, identity, and security of polyglot states is problematized when the legitimating principles of such a state face a national-sovereign challenge. Easy and peaceful means by which to resolve these problems are difficult to identify.[26]

What Schroeder identifies here, in his discussion of the manner in which French national-sovereign principles challenged territorial-sovereign principles and patterns of international conduct, is the kernel of what would become, in the reign of Napoleon III, the "principle of nationality." This would ultimately be more fully articulated by Woodrow Wilson as the principle of "national self-determination." Charles Tilly has recently generated a very short but valuable analysis of the principle for its use "as justification for political action."[27] Consider his elaboration of these principles as justifications for political action in the context of Kratochwil's observation that norms, rules, and principles, provide, not "causes" but "reasons for action."[28] Tilly suggests that the principle operates as follows.

> 1. Each distinct, homogenous people has a right to political autonomy, even to a state of its own.

2. If such a people controls a state of its own, it has the collective right to exclude or subordinate members of other populations with respect to the territory and benefits under control of that state.
3. In that case, furthermore, even small or weak states have the right to formulate domestic and international policies without interference from other states.
4. If, however, such a people lacks a state, or at least substantial political autonomy, it has the right to struggle for independence or autonomy by extraordinary means.
5. Outside peoples and their states have the right and obligation to forward such struggles.[29]

Schroeder argues that the conventional account of the origins of France's revolutionary wars, in which France's doctrines spurred fearful neighboring countries to counter-revolution, is far too simplistic because many of these states were too small and divided to decide together on such a course of action. The great, conservative, monarchic powers were, in any case, making their own incursions in violation of accepted, traditional legal props to the legitimacy of revolutionary France's smaller neighbors. Yet Schroeder reminds us that:

> Still, the fact remains that by its doctrines the French Revolution challenged every state in Europe whose existence rested less on power than on the old traditional legal order, most of whom (the Low Countries, Germany, Switzerland, and Italy) were France's neighbors.[30]

Yet France had not moved to generate external subversion or made any threatening moves toward its neighbors in 1791. Problems began to emerge when it was learned that Louis and Marie Antoinette, virtual prisoners of the National Assembly, had been agitating through their private channels for a war of restoration in which Austria and other outside powers would intervene, invade, and restore the Bourbon monarchy to the throne by force of arms. A member of the Girondin party was in charge of the foreign ministry at the time, and the Girondins began courting war with Austria as a means to utterly overthrow the monarchy by laying bare the fact that Louis was plotting with foreign powers against the French nation.[31] Schroeder recounts how revolutionary France and the dynastic regimes to the east finally blundered into hostilities owing to an inept and agitated French diplomacy. The blunder was compounded by Austrian insensitivity to the anticlericalism and principles of national sovereignty now prevailing in France with the Austrian "demand that France return Avignon and Venaissin to the Pope" and "demands for assurances about the royal family and a monarchic constitution"[32]. In the hyper-charged atmosphere of French revolutionary struggle, and to a National Assembly which had already wrested sovereign authority from the captive Bourbon monarchy, "Austria's proposal waved a red flag before the Gallic bull."[33] The National Assembly declared war on the Austrian Emperor on April 20, 1792 and nearly a quarter century of uninterrupted European general warfare began. Five months to the day after the French declaration of war the artillery of a French national army halted an Austro-Prussian advance into northeastern France at Valmy.

It is worth pausing to mention here that Stephen Walt has recently provided a rather sophisticated and nuanced, multivariate realist account of the causes of the French war of 1792 in which he describes the conflict as a result of the dynastic ambitions of other powers, a struggle for power within France and a series of miscalculations by both sides.[34] Walt provides ample and persuasive evidence that, just as Schroeder suggests, the revolutionary and republican character of the new French regime did not in itself immediately impel the conservative dynasts of Europe to launch a war of restoration to strangle the new regime in its cradle. He also provides quite valuable analysis of the reasons that both revolutionary and old regime states misperceive one another's strengths and weaknesses, enhancing the potential for armed conflict through misperception of both intentionality and capabilities. But he ultimately shies away from attributing any direct causal significance to revolutionary ideology as a cause of war for either the revolutionary regime or for the *ancien regime* foe. He focuses his analysis on "misperceptions" that are "reinforced by ideology"[35] Thus revolutionary ideology, and the novel social identities that they articulate, are relegated to the status of unintentional causes of conflict in Walt's analysis. If these ideologies are so difficult to identify as causes of conflict, it appears strange that they generate such tangible strategic consequences when conflict comes.

Early Strategic Consequences of National-Sovereign Identity

The Battle of Valmy was unspectacular as a military engagement in itself. It was a set piece artillery dual, involved at most 70,000 troops on both sides and resulted in at most 500 casualties on both sides. More men had died of dysentery in the two weeks leading up the battle. Yet Goethe, who witnessed the battle, summarized its significance with the pronouncement that "Here and now a new epoch in world history has begun and you can say that you were there."[36] Goethe's utterance was recalled by him years after the event, and may well be a case of prophesy *ex post facto*. If so, we might forgive him for imagining he had said this at the time, because the events immediately succeeding the Battle of Valmy accomplished all that Goethe allegedly claimed that the battle would. Upon halting the Austro-Prussian advance at Valmy, a French force to the south crossed the Imperial frontier ten days later.

> The day after Valmy, the newly elected National Convention abolished the monarchy; two days later, Year 1 of the new republican age began. Over the next few weeks, decrees flowed from Paris promising aid to the cause of liberation everywhere. In the first months of 1793, following the trial and execution of Louis XVI, France went to war with most of Europe.[37]

The French forces Goethe had watched fought a professional combined Austro-Prussian army to a halt, and which were so soon to charge through the frontiers of the German states allied with the Hapsburg Empire, were already armed forces of a new kind. While the French National Assembly had left their eviscerated monarchy in titular command of the French armed forces, it had abolished the purchase of commissions in the army by the nobility and wealthy bourgeoisie in order to curb the "adjuncts of feudalism." Promotion in the army was now predicated on "talent (demonstrated aptitude on examination or in performance) and merit."[38] As a result of the subsequent rapid rate of resignation and/or emigration of royalist officers, remaining junior officers were promoted rapidly, and noncommissioned officers received commissions. Woloch relates that between 1791 and 1792 more than 70,000 new rank-and-file soldiers had enlisted. In comparison with the old royal army, he argues that the ranks of the new revolutionary army were comprised of soldiers who were "younger . . . less experienced . . . [but] . . . more socially heterogeneous more attuned to the new patriotism. Many of the regulars . . . understood that they too were citizens."[39]

This identification of the rank-and-file soldiers with the regime for which they fought, and the self-identification of the soldier as citizen—endowed with rights under the law wholly equivalent to those of his officers—had significant consequences for the motivational attributes of the troops. It permitted an expansion of the tactics and conduct of warfare that were possible relative to the tactics and maneuvers that might be practiced with the mongrel, largely mercenary forces of territorial-sovereign states.

In a similar fashion, Barry Posen has recently argued that the French mobilization of an engaged, motivated, citizen-soldier resulted in a transformation in the conduct of warfare between 1792 and 1815. The involvement of the French people was crucial, and for the first time the armies of France were comprised mainly of Frenchmen. The absence of the requirement to pay high wages to professional warriors allowed France to field larger armies than were possible under the old regime, and to replace battle casualties with levies on the French populace. The motivated French troops were capable of longer maneuvers at greater speeds, and the troops could live off the land without fear that forage parties would inevitably desert.[40]

Michael Mann has recently argued that Napoleon was able to harness French national sentiment to a military hegemonic project.

> He exploited the revolutionary national ideals of citizen-officers in France and in client "sister-republics," giving them careers, autonomy and initiative. . . . Bonaparte harnessed ideological to military power, enhancing the "immanent morale" of citizen soldiers, especially among lower officers and noncommissioned officers. This further alienated his old regime enemies. . . . Not merely an external realist enemy, he [Napoleon] also appeared to incite class and national subversion in their realms. This war brought ideologies and the specter of a new social order. . . . He mobilized militarily the economic power conferred by Europe's agricultural revolution, linking it to officer morale. . . . He linked officer morale, agrarian surpluses, and divisional tactics and mobility into a distinctive campaign strategy.[41]

Posen notes that the establishment of literacy as a criterion for promotion had obvious salutary effects on the quality of the French officer corps. He also asserts that there is good evidence that officially disseminated political propaganda contributed to the élan of the troops as well as "a rise in the self and group-imposed standards of performance and sacrifice"[42] among the troops. In light of these observations Posen argues, quite correctly I believe, that "nationalism increases the intensity of warfare, and specifically the ability of states to mobilize the creative energies and the spirit of self-sacrifice of millions of soldiers."[43]

It is much more difficult to argue, however, that "it [nationalism] is purveyed by states for the express purpose of improving their military capabilities."[44] It is problematic to reduce the dissemination of national identity to the status of a state-sponsored prop to the function of state security. Posen does cite Greenfeld's argument that *ressentiment* against Britain was a factor in the development of French nationalism after France's defeat in the Seven Year's War, and that it was also a factor in the development of German nationalism after the Prussian defeat by the forces of Napoleonic France at Jena.[45] To his credit, Posen is quick to limit his claims with the assertion that "[t]he purpose of my argument is not to deny the influence of other political, social, and economic phenomena on the development of nationalism"[46] but it is problematic to suggest that "nationalism can be expected to persist wherever the military security of states depends on mass mobilization."[47] This argument tends to reduce nationalism and its dissemination to an artifact of the structural neorealist notion of systemic socialization. This is the observation that the units of the system are socialized by the political structure of the system to replicate the behavior of the successful units.[48] We can credit this observation without reducing the transmission of nationalism throughout the international system to a consequence of socialization.

I will return to criticism of what Lapid and Kratochwil have described as this "appropriative" neorealist endeavor in chapter 7 when I develop the birth of the German Empire in the aftermath of the Franco-Prussian War. For the moment, let me counter Posen's assertion with the observation that with the exception of Britain, no nationalized "units" or states were to be found among the members of the Fourth Coalition, which finally defeated France in 1815. Napoleonic France finally fell not to mass mobilization armies that replicated the nationally motivated forces of revolutionary or Imperial France, but as a consequence of two factors resulting from sustained warfare. The first of these is the political unity of the largely still territorial-sovereign members of the Fourth Coalition, who had finally achieved a political consensus regarding how the peace would be established and preserved.[49] The second factor was Napoleon's insensitivity to the limits of his nation's capacity to sustain conscription at the rates he required to reverse the misfortunes that befell him on the battlefield in 1813. This insensitivity caused Napoleon to miscalculate his mobilization capacity in light of the favorable reports he was receiving regarding the extent to which the French people had been finally habituated to conscription, as the result of an all out assault on *insoumission* (draft evasion) that had begun in 1810. He therefore snubbed coalition overtures for a peace. As Woloch's analysis reveals:

> Confident of replenishing his man power, Napoleon rebuffed the coalition's peace overtures and resumed the struggle while ordering new levies of unprecedented size on the class of 1814 and on prior classes. By grotesquely overtaxing the remarkable conscription machine that his administration had created, the emperor shattered it completely in the course of 1813. . . . Accelerated, expanded and repeated levies everywhere jolted the accustomed patterns of life, which had already adjusted themselves to the rhythms and routines of the regime's normal conscription demands.[50]

Thus Woloch argues that had Napoleon sought seriously to negotiate a peace at Dresden or Prague in 1813 he would have most likely at the least remained "master in his own house." Instead he made impossible demands on his conscription apparatus and lost all.[51]

Let us return briefly to Posen's argument that the Fourth Coalition had to develop mass mobilization armies to defeat those of Napoleonic France. While Prussia, for example, did make belated attempts to organize patriotic resistance to defeat Napoleonic France beginning in 1813, the *Landwehr* militia that was created from the Prussian citizenry was nevertheless a "pale imitation of the French citizen army."[52] It is also true that though the *Landwehr* acquitted itself well in the final campaigns between 1813 and 1815, the Prussian state reacted against the notion of citizens in arms after the peace in an attitude captured by the suggestion of the Prussian minister of police that "[t]o arm a nation means to organize and facilitate rebellion and sedition."[53] Mann does argue, in mild support of Posen's argument, that owing to pressure from professional officers, the *Landwehr* was indeed retained as a reserve force in the Prussian order of battle. Subsequently, however, according to Mann, "[t]here developed a Lutheran Prussian-German national identity, linking religious and national sentiments to loyalty to a strong state."[54] What Posen's analysis does not capture is the fact that in relatively religiously and ethnically homogeneous Prussia, all of the elements of a uniquely Prussian national identity—Lutheranism, German language and ethnicity, the strong state, not to mention *ressentiment* against a belligerent France—were already present before the Prussian Crown acceded to a limited arming of the citizenry.

It is not at all clear that limited moves toward a Prussian citizen-soldier contributed to the development of a German, or even parochial Prussian nationalism as much as this move implicitly recognized the pre-existence of these sentiments among the populace. Historian James Sheehan has recently argued that:

> If Prussian troops were more effective in 1813 than they had been in 1806, it was because they were better trained, better equipped, and better led, not because they had been suddenly infused with national passions. . . . Prussia in 1813, like Austria in 1808, did try to harness patriotic passions behind its military efforts . . . But, while Frederick William's proclamations of February and March 1813 had evoked the folk and fatherland as values around which Prussians should now rally, the king made clear that he was speaking to and about "my folk," the patriotic subjects of the Prussian Crown, not the cultural community of Germans so important to Arndt, Jahn and others. . . . The *Volk's* role in its own "liberation" was at best a minor one. Napoleon was defeated by regular armies, not patriotic poets and quaintly attired gymnasts.[55]

Moreover, if the Prussian state is really thought to have cultivated national sentiment for security purposes to the extent that Posen suggests, it is difficult to understand why Friedrich Wilhelm IV spurned the German Imperial Crown that was offered him by the German people after the upheaval of 1848. One might expect that he would prefer to rule an imperial superstate and a huge tract of German Central Europe, and command the combined armed forces of this territory, than remain the sovereign of Prussia alone, if the "imitate-or-die" socialization mechanism of neorealist theory is really the *ultima ratio* even of state security behavior in this context. Yet Friedrich Wilhelm disdained to receive either sovereignty or purview over these territories and their "capabilities" precisely because he did not believe that there existed, or should exist, a German "nation" with authority to offer any of this to him. In April 1849, once again in command of Prussia after the anxious upheaval of 1848, he rejected the German Imperial Crown offered to him by a delegation of the Paulskirche Parliament as a " 'hoop of mud and clay hung about with 'the carrion stench of revolution.' "[56] Shulze mentions, to be sure, that Friedrich Wilhelm might have also been concerned that Austria might not have stood for such a move. Hapsburg imperial claims to suzerainty over many German states still had not been withdrawn. Though neither had they been withdrawn in 1870 when Austria did acquiesce to the formation of a German Empire under the leadership of Prussia. But in 1849 territorial sovereignty yet prevailed in Prussia. Rather than grasping the opportunity to employ an emerging pan-German national collective identity to found a pan-German Empire, a king of Prussia offered studied insults to these national aspirations in a manner calculated to explicitly deny the legitimacy of anything resembling national-sovereign identity.

Structural realists might argue that Friedrich Wilhelm's action was in part a consequence of fear of war with Austria. It is difficult, however, to argue this was a major rationale in light of the observation that Friedrich Wilhelm knew that he could have relied upon his ability to draw military resources for such a war from a larger ensemble of German states than he later actually employed to defeat Austria less than twenty years later, in the Austro-Prussian war of 1866. Moreover, such an assertion requires the analyst to ignore all of the abundant evidence resulting from Bismarck's interaction and correspondence with Friedrich Wilhelm, that the notion of Germany meant nothing whatever to the latter even upon the founding of the German Empire twenty-one years after the King of Prussia first spurned the Crown of an Imperial Germany. In light of these observations, Posen's recent analysis may well accomplish its modest stated objective of convincing us that his argument that seeks to explain the transmission of nationalism with recourse to the neorealist socialization mechanism alone is "plausible," given the security requirements of nineteenth-century states for mass mobilization armies. Nevertheless, in view of fuller accounts and unexamined variables, his analysis does not persuade.

Concert: A Territorial-Sovereign Interlude

With the close of the Napoleonic Wars and the peace resulting from the Congress of Vienna the victorious governments of Europe settled down to take stock of the upheaval they had suffered for more than two decades. All students of international politics recognize that the resulting Concert and Metternich's construction of the "Vienna system," in which regularized problem-solving meetings of the victorious monarchs addressed threats to the peace of Europe, gave the continent an extended peace lasting more than forty years after the Vienna peace of 1815. Robert Jervis, in seeking to answer the question of how such cooperation was possible "under anarchy" from a rational choice, game-theoretic perspective, argues that:

> the concert was characterized by an unusually high and self-conscious level of cooperation among the major European powers. The states did not play the game as hard as they could; they did not take advantage of others' short-run vulnerabilities. In repeated plays of the Prisoners' Dilemma, then, each state cooperated in the expectation that others would do the same. Multilateral and self-restrained methods of handling their problems were preferred to the more common unilateral and less restrained methods.[57]

Kissinger has recently observed that subsequent to the founding of the Vienna system Europe enjoyed a period of unprecedented and uninterrupted peacefulness that lasted until the Crimean War, forty years later. There would be no general war for an even longer period. Unlike his intellectual progenitor, Morgenthau, however, Kissinger does not attribute the success of the Concert, or the founding of the Holy Alliance of 1815, to the "institutionalization" of allegedly moral principles that Morgenthau saw as underlying the notion of the balance of power.[58] Kissinger evokes Morgenthau's reactionary utopia in the sense that he argues that the Concert period was so peaceful, indeed because: "the continental countries were knit together by a sense of shared values. There was not only a physical equilibrium, but a moral one. . . . The balance of power reduces the opportunities for using force; a shared sense of justice reduces the desire to use force."[59]

Unlike Morgenthau, however, Kissinger also points to reasons for this success that help us to perceive that it was the post-Napoleonic domestic institutional structure of Europe that enabled this sense of shared values to manifest itself in effective diplomacy and cooperative policy. Kissinger argues:

> But *how a people perceives the fairness of a particular world order is determined* as much *by its domestic institutions* as by judgments on

> tactical foreign policy issues . . . For nations simply do not define their purpose as cogs in a security system. *Security makes their existence possible; it is never their sole or even principal purpose.*[60]

Thus for the duration of the Concert period, it appears that the will-to-power was subordinated to the domestic security requirements of territorial sovereigns to be secure from the domestic upheaval and Jacobin revolutionary threats that most of the surviving monarchs of Europe laid squarely at the feet of the national-sovereign doctrines of a now defeated French foe. The best way to maintain security was to fall back on and defend the territorial-sovereign identity of the old order in Europe and the "principle of legitimacy" that sustained that order. Osiander makes it apparent that the statesmen who labored to construct the peace at the Congress of Vienna clearly understood that they could no longer take for granted the compliant assent of the European masses to their public actions, in a continent whose lowly had been awakened and sensitized by the emergence of national collective identity in France.

> As a result, despite all the endless festivities celebrating the post-Napoleonic restoration, the peacemakers were in a precarious position. Napoleon was gone, but "the revolution" had only gone underground. Dance as they might, the political order that the plenipotentiaries represented was under mortal threat from current and ultimately unstoppable social developments. The genie of populism was out of the bottle and nothing could put it back in. All of the main negotiators sensed this.[61]

As a consequence, the Congress negotiators put together a settlement that played to domestic opinion at home, while taking advantage of the proclivity of war-weary European masses to blame Jacobin democracy for two decades of war and suffering in establishing the new consensus principles of the postwar European domestic as well as international social orders. Few of the statesmen who pulled together the peace at the Congress of Vienna had a smaller wish to see a resurgence of republican government or ideology in France, or anywhere else in Europe, than the French representative, Talleyrand. It was he who suggested the principle of dynastic legitimacy as a postwar legitimating principle for a domestic social order that would be capable of defending itself against future and resurgent assaults by Jacobin ideologues. Metternich, representing the court at Vienna, and Castlereagh, representing Britain, quickly acceded to Talleyrand's suggestion and helped him to defend it throughout the negotiations.

> Because the fixation with dynasticism was so much based on wishful thinking, the underlying fallacy went unchallenged. Talleyrand believed, or wanted to believe, that dynastic legitimacy was an essential safeguard for stability. In his view, stability could only be ensured in the long run if, in each state, power was transferred from one individual to the next in a manner that did not give rise to internal quarrels.[62]

Kissinger suggests that Metternich, similarly, identified peace with "legitimate rule" after the Napoleonic War. He "sought to institutionalize the values he considered ancient"[63] and took advantage of the religious, dynastic passions of the Russian Czar Alexander to forge in turn the Holy alliance among Prussia, Russia, and Austria and the Quadruple alliance, which added Great Britain to the mix of the defenders of the old order. Actually, at this time, the ideas of liberalism and republicanism had gained so much currency throughout Europe that a return to simple dynastic legitimacy as a legitimating principle of European social order was no longer possible. In recognition of this it was modified, argues Osiander.

> A different, simpler concept soon prevailed, namely that only monarchical rule was legitimate. This came to be called the "monarchical principle." With it went a concomitant rule of monarchical solidarity—meaning that, if kingship was in danger anywhere, all rulers had a duty to intervene to uphold it. . . . This new reactionary conception was one that all the great powers rallied to.[64]

Metternich's maneuver of channeling Alexander's religious vision of a Holy Alliance of anointed monarchs into formal political and military alliances, predicated on monarchical legitimacy, reinforces Osiander's observation.

While they were anxious to re-establish European social order and political legitimacy on a monarchical basis, the statesmen negotiating this new order with Alexander were more than slightly bemused by the religious and dynastic anachronisms that Alexander proposed as the legitimating principles of the postwar European order. Castlereagh, for example, had mirthfully referred to the Holy Alliance as a " 'piece of sublime mysticism and nonsense.' "[65] Metternich, however, sought to avoid crisis in the future by moral consensus predicated by the assertion "that the ideological danger posed by the revolution outweighed their strategic opportunities"[66] and indulged the Czar in order to cement alliances between rulers committed to "legitimate rule." These monarchs agreed in solemn treaty language to act only in concert with one another. Thus the domestic imperative of territorial-sovereign identity reasserted itself and the wagons were circled to hold at bay the liberal and republican "barbarians at the gate."

> The vested interest which they [Concert territorial-sovereigns] developed in the survival of their domestic institutions caused the continental countries to avoid conflicts which they would have pursued as a matter of course in the previous century . . . [for example] . . . Had Prussia sought [earlier] to exploit German nationalism, it could have challenged Austrian pre-eminence in Germany a generation before Bismarck . . . [but the Prussians] . . . refrained from pushing their advantage because it ran counter to the dominant principle of maintaining the status quo. Austria, seemingly on its death bed after Napoleon's onslaught, was given a new lease on life by the Metternich system, which enabled it to survive for another hundred years.[67]

But while the "principle of legitimacy," in Kissinger's lexicon, or the "monarchical principle," in Osiander's lexicon, emerged from the Vienna congress and animated the actions of the Concert, I am certainly not arguing that this principle constituted a return to the dynastic-sovereign, or Augsburg system that had even pre-existed Westphalian territorial sovereignty. This is not at all the case. Rather than constituting a return to Augsburg, the Concert of Europe constituted a return to Westphalian territorial-sovereign identity and practice in self-consciously dynastic clothing. This clothing was donned to cover a rather embarrassingly naked rule by the forces of reaction, now triumphant over the prostrate republican ragamuffins. Yet for many reasons that the next section of this chapter will uncover, the Vienna weavers of the gown of "dynastic legitimacy" were, irrespective of their intentions, industrious tailors to a naked emperor. At this date, as Osiander reminds us:

> the concept of dynastic legitimacy is best described as a rather impressive red herring. Talleyrand was fooling himself (but he was not the only one). Dynastic legitimacy could not be a factor of stability [at this date]. The premise was wrong: it was not because there were dynasties that the pre-revolutionary order had been stable, it was the existence of a stable, hierarchical social order, in which political authority presupposed high rank owed to birth, that encouraged the development of the dynasties.[68]

Osiander's objection nicely illustrates one of the major theoretical premises of this book. Institutional forms of collective action (dynasties in this case) result from the legitimating principles of social orders (political authority as a birthright). Construction of institutions, however, will not guarantee their legitimacy. Declaring something to be so will not make it so. Extreme insularity of decisionmaking by societal elites is required for this to be the case. Decisionmaking by elites in the Concert period was extraordinarily insular by the standards of today's national-sovereign perspective. Decisionmaking was sufficiently insular to permit the "conspiracy of princes" from which the Concert was constituted to function—admittedly to the benefit of the peace of Europe—for nearly half a century after the Congress of Vienna. It was not, as we shall soon see, sufficiently insular to reestablish the unchallenged "dynastic" or monarchical "territorial" sovereignty that had pervaded European notions of legitimate social order from the early sixteenth century. Too many chinks had appeared in this armor. By 1870, the chinks would be opened widely enough for the sharp instrument of national-sovereign collective identity, reforged in the intervening decades, to administer a mortal blow to the Concert and its pretense that it constituted a Holy Alliance of Christian princes.

State Penetration and Economic Transformation: The Road to 1848

The period between the Congress of Vienna and the Revolution of 1848 was a time of rapid social and economic change throughout much of Europe, and not least in what was to become Germany. All of this rapid change portended a new legitimation crisis of the old regime which had been reconstituted and propped up with the brace of monarchical legitimacy. Society moved rapidly into new patterns of socioeconomic relations which existing institutional arrangements could only obstruct. Social identities were of ancient classes and stations of life were being rapidly destroyed and reconstructed and, as my theoretical developments suggest, institutional forms of collective action and governance were increasingly incapable of manifesting the newly emerging social identities of broad tracts of the European populace.

The period saw rapid growth in population. The population in Prussia alone increased 87 percent between 1816 and 1865 and was attended by massive migration from the country to the cities, and between rural areas as well.[69] In 1816 less than two percent of the Prussian population resided in Berlin, and no more than four percent in the eleven Prussian cities with populations from 20,000 to 100,000 inhabitants. This had doubled by 1849, and more than a quarter of Prussia's population was to be found in towns with populations greater than 2,000 inhabitants by this date.[70] These patterns were repeated throughout the German-speaking states of Central Europe in this period.

As the cities were experiencing rapid population growth and the incursions of market forces into the familiar patterns of ancient guild privilege, the state began to increasingly take an interest in municipal affairs, and urban autonomy was rapidly eroded by both state and economic forces. The cities now became mere administrative units of the state. The guilds also steadily lost power to the state's regulatory power and the Prussian guilds were soon mere "economic associations rather than expressions of corporate identity and instruments of social control."[71] Proprietorship began to replace residence or guild or corporate privilege as the means of acquiring citizenship in a municipality. As Sheehan argues: "By making property the sole criterion for active citizenship, the Prussian law cut away the special rights, privileges, and liberties with which cities had once determined who could belong and who could not."[72] The combined influences of state and market penetration of urban society had significant implications for urban identity commitments. Both of these forces were integrative in the sense that they reduced the insularity of municipalities and demolished the particularistic attributes of their local power structures. They were also constitutive of new forms of identity inasmuch as they attended a redefinition of citizenship as a commodity acquired with the acquisition of capital. Coupled with advances in technology and communication, such as the escalation of steel production and the development of railroads, they also created the "basis of a German common market . . . [though] not [yet] a German national economy" as the market coupled with the state constructed the *Zollverein* customs union to expand transregional trading arrangements.[73] And as one analyst has suggested, this arrangement cannot be explained by the classical rational-choice theoretic assertion that Prussian hegemony was being exercised to provide a stable trading regime.[74]

Rural social relations were no less transitional in this period. Land reform in Central Europe proceeded at a pace negotiated between noble resistance and the inexorable state penetration into traditional rural life. Peasant emancipation developed sufficiently to slowly evince a change from the ancient "personal *Herrschaft* to state authority" in the countryside.[75] Noble resistance was intense in Central Europe and the state was forced to compromise continuously at the expense of the peasantry. When Prussian land reform finally came, the elimination of personal servitude of the peasantry came with it, but noble claims to compensation resulted in the conversion of these services to cash payments. Now while the peasants had the legal right to purchase land, very few could afford to do it. Landowners quickly converted to hired labor and the short-term result was roughly equivalent to the result of mass migration from the rural areas to the cities, namely a "growing population of landless agricultural laborers, who were now totally at the mercy of the market."[76]

One permanent and quite progressive change had occurred in this process, however. While the landed nobility retained enormous wealth, power, and privilege, the social basis of this power had changed. The power and prestige of the Central European "German" nobility no longer "flowed from their pedigree and person, but few could doubt that their power and privilege depended on the state." They were thus "transformed from an autonomous *Stand* into a regional elite" and as a result "the *Standesherren* struggled to define a position between sovereignty and citizenship . . . nobility was [now] seen as a temporary inhibition to economic progress and social emancipation, the doomed residue of a declining order."[77]

Noble class identity remained intact in Central Europe during this period nonetheless. Sheehan notes that the *Herren* survived the demise of the *Herrschaft* so well that an 1833 visitor to Prussia wrote home that society was well divided into "the vons and the non-vons," and this was so precisely because of the relationship of the "vons" to the monarch who remained "the state's symbolic center and ultimate source of authority."[78] *The status of the German nobility was increasingly mediated through the authority of the state.* The status of the German nobility was now a claim, and no longer an institutional fact that recalled only longstanding tradition to substantiate it. This status now had to be defended. It was no longer constitutive of the social order. As Sheehan reminds us of this period, their "status became what Weber would call an effective claim . . . [which] . . . is not a condition of a possession or a fact of life; a claim must be made, it requires action and can be granted or ignored."[79]

Under the new conditions of social and economic life, in which the function of the extraction of societal resources was increasingly privatized, and one's political standing was increasingly juridically predicated on effective proprietorship, the claim of the nobility to social status was likely to be ignored if the claimant lacked wealth and property, and to be granted if the claimant possessed these. In the absence of property, office (another commodity now mediated through the state) helped buttress effective claims to social status of many of the less well-to-do among the German nobility.

In the German states the army was the traditional place for claimants to social status to make their claims effective. The vaunted reforms of the Prussian army of which Posen has recently written—in making his case that nationalism was cultivated by states to enhance the effectiveness of their armed forces—had not taken hold in Prussian society.[80] While in the initial enthusiasm for reform at the conclusion of the Napoleonic Wars nobles had constituted a "bare majority" of officers in the Prussian army in 1818, only fourteen percent of Prussian officers above the rank of colonel lacked a "von" in their name by 1860.[81] Posen acknowledges a period of "reaction" that made itself felt in the Prussian armed forced between 1815 and 1870. Yet he argues that "*Landwehr* officers were chosen from the local elite and included many members of the middle class."[82] How many? Either Posen overstates this case, or more likely the *Landwehr* was so small a component of the armed forces that Prussia actually relied upon for its defense that the bourgeois component of the *Landwehr* officer corps dissolved into insignificance when these forces were aggregated with the regular army. If Sheehan's statistics are reliable, there were very few non-noble officers in the Prussian army at mid-century.

What is most important for our purposes is that the new social landscape, molded increasingly by the forces of capital and of the state, had great causal significance for the reconstitution of social identities within European society. In the German case, state penetration and the increasing reliance of the nobility upon office rather than noble title to buttress a claim to social status, had slowly transformed this class identity into corporate identity. The titled soldier was "likely to be an officer first and an aristocrat second. . . . both the army and the bureaucracy [another noble preserve] developed their own ethos and corporate identities."[83] While this may be taken as evidence of the "uneven" nature of German modernization, inasmuch as noble elites helped the Crown to preserve traditional values and institutions, it is also clearly the case that power, wealth, and status no longer coincided as they had in the past. A noble title certainly enhanced the prospects and chances of an aspirant to these social tools, but the nobleman was no longer excused from the burden of competing with "non-vons" for what had once been his birthright. In this sense, the nineteenth-century German nobility "were a product of their age, not a residue of pre-modern times."[84] The "empire of civil society" was claiming what had been the legacy of (even the German) nobility as one of its first trophies in the struggle to remold the social order into its own likeness.

The British were well ahead of Central Europe in this process. In spite of the serious economic deprivation felt in the country in the aftermath of the war and the violent and repressive measures taken to suppress reaction to it, the British people had been alienated by the Jacobin terror, and associated extreme democratic views with the regime of the erstwhile French enemy. This tendency insulated British political institutions from serious revolutionary threats during this period. Michael Mann refers to the period from 1815 to 1832 in Britain as a period of "reform, not revolution."[85] While governments of the German-speaking states on the continent were accommodating the rising urban bourgeoisie with citizenship based on proprietorship, and penetrating rural society by accommodating the peasantry with legal emancipation and subordinating the rural nobility to the state, the British state was making a series of accommodating moves of its own.

One of these moves was in recognition of the loyalty with which British Catholic subjects had served in the wars, and in recognition of the problems that juridical discrimination against Catholics was creating in the governance of an increasingly rebellious Ireland. With the passage of Catholic emancipation in 1829, "[t]he old regime abandoned its Protestant soul as well as potent segmental controls over the souls of its subjects."[86] The other major concession involved the move to enfranchise small-property owners to buttress their loyalty to the regime and remove from them any source of temptation to ally themselves with the occasionally rebellious masses. Mann argues that "[h]aving abandoned absolutism, the particularism in major government departments [Whiggism], then a hieratic church, the [British] regime had no principles left." Significantly, it no longer felt that it needed any principles other than to enfranchise and thus co-opt and remove from opposition any significant component of the forces of capital. What came next was a coup which constructed, in Britain, the edifice of the emerging "empire of civil society."

> It [the British regime] also recognized the contributions of the petite bourgeoisie to Britain's rising prosperity. Britain could now dominate the world through free trade backed by economic government. The petite bourgeoisie had a property stake in the nation. It should no longer be excluded—provided it broke with the "populace." So . . . the rulers looked to detach the petite bourgeoisie from the mob. . . . Property—whatever its source, lineage, or patronage—was to rule the nation. . . . the state had changed from particularism and segmentalism, centered on the king in Parliament, to universalism, centered on a capitalist class-nation.[87]

This pattern of slowly but inexorably enfranchising increasingly more humble and less substantial possessors of capital as a means to ensure domestic stability occurred more slowly on the continent, but may be seen as a pattern characteristic of the century. Most often these maneuvers were not intentional nation-building projects, but tactical concessions designed to permit a ruling class still committed to a territorial-sovereign structure of identity and interests to hold on to power. When these tactical concessions did not come quickly enough for the peoples that state penetration—and the civil associational networks required for the development of capitalist production relations—had imbued with a nascent "national" collective identity, troubles came and upheaval followed.

And so trouble came to Central Europe by mid-century. The trouble was the culmination of what Mann suggests were the four great "crystallizations" of society resulting in capitalism, militarism, liberalism, and nationalism which had all been institutionalized in the half century between approximately 1770 and 1820. And thus Mann is at pains to point out that "classes and nations rose together, structured by all four sources of social power."[88] Militarism had dominated the life of Europe for more than two decades and the wreckage left in its wake had made such an impression on all Europeans that we might expect that the experience of the war alone could well have induced the average European to take an interest in public affairs in the ensuing peace. But early-nineteenth-century Europeans were not dealing with the consequences of the militarism of the past alone. The had also seen the "growing involvement of the state in social life—as tax collector and policy-maker, educator and employer, regulator and patron."[89] Thus the steady increase of popular interest in public affairs in the ensuing decades is not surprising. The period witnessed the growth of civil society. The state-as-educator had enhanced discursive literacy and created a demand for more political news in the press. As a logical consequence of increasing state penetration into society, people developed an increasing self-identification with the state, and with the political process. "Slowly . . . Germans created the intellectual systems and associational networks upon which participatory politics could be based. As a result, the character of public life was fundamentally altered."[90]

The Revolution of 1848: The Questions of Citizenship and Sovereignty

But in German Central Europe, the conservative social residue that attended the nobility's retention of social status, through the acquisition of state office, had attenuated the move toward nearly unlimited social mobility through the acquisition of capital, as had occurred in Britain, where peerages were readily created for those with the price of entry. The Hanoverian rulers of Britain had acceded to a constitutional rule of a capitalist nation and prized above all other qualities in the men they recruited to head their governments the capacity to balance the ledgers of the government. The dynastic rulers of Prussia and Austria had not come to their thrones with the understanding that they would subordinate their sovereignty to a constitution. They might buy off the peasantry at the expense of their nobility, and increase noble dependence on the Crown for the status left to them in the bargain, but they would not accede to the limitations of their sovereignty and power by any constitutional device without dire exigency. This attitude had lent German society a conservative cast residual of the old order, and it pervaded social and institutional domestic life.

Thus as capitalism transformed economic life and created a German bourgeoisie, this bourgeoisie lacked both the courage of its convictions required for the advancement of bold claims of its own, and the fear of lower orders required to encourage it to advance claims on behalf of these orders to fuller participation in civil and political life. The German bourgeoisie was a very ideologically and politically timid class relative to, for example, its British counterpart. Here we have some evidence with which to credit the claim that Mann has recently made that, contrary to what Marx believed and argued, class organization does not emerge directly from the relations of production. The bourgeoisie are "more likely to choose segmental than class organization. . . . Political organization by classes also has specifically political causes involving the institutional particularities of states."[91] Thus when the consequences of militarism and emerging capitalism raised the ire of the petty bourgeoisie and laboring masses "[these masses] claimed civil citizenship to freely protest political economy, and when protest was ineffective, they demanded political citizenship."[92] But unlike the British case, the protesting classes found no allies in the German bourgeoisie. Not yet in any case. German liberalism during this period was limited-franchise liberalism. Many German liberals, who were themselves in a minority position in their countries, did not wish to extend the franchise to wage laborers, apprentices, small farmers, or shopkeepers, let alone women or servants. German bourgeois liberalism was very insecure indeed. No Rousseauian vision of the general will pervaded it, therefore no governmental responsibility to accede to the wishes of the general will was implied.[93] In order to rectify this situation, the common people were required to voice their protest in much more emphatic terms than had been required for these classes to gain civil and political citizenship in Britain. Their voice may be heard in the events attending the Revolution of 1848.

At the very time that the growth of the participatory impulses of the peoples of Central Europe were escalating, changes in their leadership were yielding disappointing results. In Austria the death of the Emperor had brought an idiot to the throne in 1835. At the time that Metternich was dealing with Austrian reaction to the fall of the Bourbon monarchy in 1830 that had been restored by the Congress of Vienna a scant fifteen years previously, he suffered the emboldenment of the Austrian political opposition with the accession of the highly "mentally deficient" Ferdinand who "could do no more than sign his name."[94] In Bavaria, King Ludwig had made it quite clear that he was far more interested in the arts than politics and had left the day-to-day administration of the affairs of the Bavarian state in the hands of the reactionary von Abel, who was hardly the man for the times, and proceeded to systematically alienate progressive opinion in Bavaria.[95] The accession of Friedrich Wilhelm IV in Prussia in June of 1840 lead to initial hopes that the new reign would be progressive. These hopes were quickly dashed and discontent was seen in Prussia as well.

Radical liberal opinion demanded universal suffrage, an armed domestic militia, the equalization of educational opportunity, reform of the tax system, the abolition of residual social privilege, and structural transformation of the civil service to enhance the possibilities of its service as a vehicle of upward mobility. The steady and stubborn refusal of governments to move on this agenda swelled the ranks of the opposition in the climate of insecurity engendered by rapid economic change during the period. By the 1840s the opposition included, according to one sympathetic contemporary, "everyone with talent, all free and independent spirits, in short, the entire third estate."[96] Yet these disaffected persons constituted only a small minority of the populace, until economic recession deepened the crisis. According to Hagan Schulze:

> This multiform national opposition received its explosive charge from the growing impoverishment of the society and economy. Pauperism in all its misery, essentially due to the Malthusian consequences of overpopulation, had come to the fore. . . . The frequently horrendous poverty was exacerbated by the changing social structure, shifting from an artisan to an industrial base. Whole sectors of artisan production, in particular domestic manufacturing, were unable to meet competition from cheap factory products—inhuman hours of work, child labor, starvation wages and scarcely imaginable living conditions were the result.[97]

But while economic distress is easy enough to identify as an impulse to social protest, upheaval, and even revolution, why did the 1848 revolution manifest itself as a nationalist movement and result in nationalist demands? Why did the Prussian peoples press an imperial German Crown upon Friedrich Wilhelm in the immediate aftermath of the upheaval, and call together with other Germans the all-German Frankfurt Parliament with the task of drafting an all-German constitution? One reason was that the intellectual energy behind the 1848 revolution was, unlike the French Revolution, in large measure provided by the German bourgeoisie. 1848 came at a time when "nationalism was an expression of *bürgerlich* emancipation . . . an ideology of modernization."[98] The creation of an all-German state was desired, among other reasons, because the national state was seen at this time as an essential precondition for economic modernization and competitiveness by the bourgeois classes.

The deepening economic crisis and fatuous inactivity on the part of German, Central European governments in response to it, coupled with news from abroad that Louis Philippe had fled Paris in the face of the proclamation of the Second Republic, radicalized peoples whose expectations had, by this time, been disappointed long enough. Still the upheavals of 1848 began in a manner which did not threaten the recalcitrant absolutists of Central Europe in any way. The early demonstrations were led by moderate liberals and were characterized by "[d]ignified processions, carefully drafted petitions, respectful audiences with the ruler."[99] But the volume of protest quickly escalated.

A massive protest in Vienna on March 13 demonstrated to Metternich how anachronistic had become the insular decisionmaking he had for decades accustomed himself to, and upon which the Concert system he had helped found in 1815 depended. One of the demands of the belligerent mob that had gathered outside the *Landhaus* that day in Vienna was Metternich's resignation. Within twenty-four hours he had drafted his resignation and fled Vienna with his wife and with money borrowed from the Rothschilds.[100] On the 15th the Austrian Emperor abolished censorship and promised to convene a constitutional assembly in hopes of placating the crowd. On the 17th Friedrich Wilhelm promised to abolish censorship of the Prussian press, to reconvene a united Prussian *Landtag*, to reform the German Confederation, and to accept a constitution for Prussia. Unfortunately Prussian troops fired on demonstrators on the 18th and the barricades went up in Berlin. Unrest had become insurrection. The most economically threatened professions, journeyman artisans and craftsmen, manned the barricades with the most zeal. Friedrich Wilhelm responded to the demands of *Militär zurück* by the end of the day and ordered the withdrawal of the troops from the capital. On the 19th the proud King of Prussia was forced to stand in respectful silence as the bloody bodies of the victims of the revolution were carried by in solemn procession.[101] For a moment in the middle of the nineteenth century, proud territorial sovereignty bowed in solemn and fearful acknowledgment of the civic citizenship upon which the liberal variant of national-sovereign identity is constructed. As Mann reminds us, this civic expression took on an even more national character in 1848 in the polyglot Hapsburg Empire.

> The Revolution of 1848 was a Europe-wide movement for civil and political citizenship led by whichever social classes lay just below the existing political citizenship line. . . . But in more confederal regimes this came packaged with "national" issues, as we saw in Germany. As revolution spread to more confederal Austria, it acquired more territorial, provincial, and "national" organization—which led to easily the most serious fighting of 1848. More than 100,000 persons were killed in the Austrian revolutions.[102]

It was precisely the confederal character of Austria that forced German nationalists to abandon the *Grossdeutsche* model of a future German nation, in which the incorporation into the German nation of necessity required incorporation of its non-German elements, in favor of the *Kleindeutsche* model under Prussian leadership. The ethnic and "national" passions released in Hapsburg Austria by the events of 1848 went a long way toward deciding the issue of the borders of a future all-German state for the German nationalists who participated in the revolution in Prussia, Bavaria, Saxony, and elsewhere. The construction of such a state was a clear goal of the men who had extracted so many concessions from German princes, and who had gained a commitment to allow organized discussion of a united German Empire from an intimidated Friedrich Wilhelm in Prussia.

Almost as soon as the revolution had been "won," however, cracks in the edifice of the German "nation" that was to result from it could be readily discerned. One problem was that the economic depression continued, and no pronouncement of a suddenly pliable prince could alleviate the suffering that had helped to spark the upheaval. In essence: "People wanted *Fressfreiheit* not *Pressfreiheit* [*sic*], 'freedom to feed,' not 'freedom to read.' . . . The lower orders' persistent restlessness [after March 1848] frightened and infuriated the moderate [liberal] opposition. "[103]

The continued popular unrest may have "infuriated" the moderate opposition, it also intimidated the *Bürgertum*, or bourgeoisie, as a whole. They wanted "law and order" restored, and an end to the unrest, almost at any cost. In this they had developed a common cause with the monarchy.

They were pleased to have extracted participatory citizenship for themselves from the Crown, but were not willing to extend it to the lower orders whose restless and violent proclivities in the continuing economic difficulties threatened their own safety and property. Thus the moderate and radical opposition began falling out with one another, and gave great cheer to the momentarily intimidated conservative elements of society, not the least the monarchy, in the process. Thus *though the crisis of legitimacy of the old order had come and gone, the revolution had difficulties in consolidating, in new institutional forms, the gains it had won through spirited political action* because:

> Once the initial victory over the old order had been won, the victors started to fight among themselves about whose vision of the future should triumph . . . Popular violence could still disrupt local institutions, force concessions, and create disorder, but it could not provide the basis for a new social or political order.[104]

The reason it could not do so was because victorious liberals of various stripes could not resolve the question of the identity of the new "sovereign." Political citizenship had been won. National-sovereign identity of a sort had been forged, but two crucial questions remained unresolved that left the specific features of this identity hazy, and consequently, for the moment, inoperable as a form of sovereignty which could be effectively institutionalized, and in whose name effective political action could be exercised.

All victorious participants in the 1848 revolution recognized that the nature of sovereign identity was changing, and that the territorial-sovereign "they" were becoming a national-sovereign "we." The question of precisely who "we" referred to in the pan-German "national" context was still contended and clouded by pre-existing territorial, institutional, and social class divisions. Sovereignty predicated on tradition and privilege was giving way to sovereignty predicated on citizenship, but who had become a citizen was still unresolved. Moderate liberal Prussian property owners might be prepared to accord this citizenship, in the hoped for all-German state, to moderate liberal Saxon or Bavarian property owners, but not to Prussian shopkeepers or artisans. The second question was less and issue of class identity than of ethno-linguistic and institutional identity. Others might be willing to enfranchise the petty bourgeoisie, but could not resolve the territorial segmental issue of who was to be included in the German nation. What institutional form could properly manifest this newly emergent, pan-German national collective identity? The Prussian state appeared to be the only vehicle to receive the national-sovereign identity that was being generated, but once Friedrich Wilhelm refused to accept the Imperial German Crown from the hands of those whose heads bore no Crown, this new, half-formed national-sovereign identity could not be readily institutionalized without better definition. It would be provided with better definition within a quarter of a century and the ultimate architect of German national-sovereign identity would be the arch-conservative Prussian Junker Otto von Bismarck. Such an irony as this is difficult to contrive for the purpose of constructing fictional entertainment, and appears to be possible only within the consistently bizarre chronicles of factual history.

Conclusions and Theoretical Reprise

The chapter has assisted in illustrating a number of my earlier theoretical suggestions. It has shown how the legitimation crisis of the old regime in France emerged from the transformation of elite social identities and ultimately resulted in the emergence of national collective identity in France, quickly followed by a transformation of the institutional form of French collective action from a territorial-sovereign to a national-sovereign form. With reference to the work of Liah Greenfeld, I have illustrated how the social identities of the French nobility had been threatened by the rigorous absolutism of the French Crown, inducing the French nobility to adopt a new social identity. In response, they redefined themselves as a cultural elite and abetted in the development of an anti-regime ideology that delegitimated the aristocracy of birth upon which the territorial-sovereign, absolutist social order was founded, instead legitimating an aristocracy of merit upon which notions of popular sovereignty were founded. These popular-sovereign ideas, joined with *ressentiment* against Britain, ensured the new legitimating principles of the new regime would be national-sovereign principles.

The legitimation crisis which set off this territorial-sovereign to national-sovereign system transition, beginning on the continent with France, had both domestic and international sources and consequences. The sources of the legitimation crisis were both cognitive and material, both agential and structural. French national collective identity may well have emerged in tandem with an incipient French bourgeois class identity, but the ideological formation and legitimation of the popular and national-sovereign element of these identities was largely provided by disaffected elites. The causally significant transnational dynamic that solidified a specifically national collective identity was what Greenfeld calls *ressentiment* against Britain, not a systemic socialization mechanism compelling France to emulate Britain. The social identities of the French people had transcended and thus consequently dispensed with the territorial-sovereign, absolutist state. Their will-to-manifest national-sovereign identity was reflected in their subsequent demolition of the territorial-sovereign, absolutist institutions and reconstruction of a prolific number of domestic social institutions which reflected popular and national-sovereign principles.

While French national-sovereignty was initially quite quiescent internationally, the old regime statesmen of Europe had soon discovered that French national-sovereignty constituted an intrinsic challenge to the legitimacy of the monarchical, territorial-sovereign domestic and international order. The contended issue of whether national-sovereign or territorial-sovereign principles would prevail proved a source of decades of violent conflict in Europe and the periphery. The emergence of French national-sovereignty altered the rules of international engagement in asserting that the popular will overturned territorial sovereign legal rights, treaties, and juridical bases for international claims. This increased uncertainties, elevated disputes over interests into disputes over principles, and enhanced the potential for international conflict. Significantly, almost ironically, the new national-sovereign legitimating principles provided their promulgators with new bases for territorial expansion.

The emergence of national-sovereign collective identity created a number of new sources of potential conflict in the international system. Extraterritorial expressions of allegiance to a people with shared language, culture, or history—or simply a shared vision of social and political organization—became potential bases for the advancement of irridentist territorial claims, or conflictual secessionist movements. National-sovereign identity problematized ethnic, linguistic and cultural minorities, territorial integrity and security, migration, titular claims to dynastic lands, and the integrity and identity of polyglot states. Territorial-sovereign legal claims were delegitimated and peaceful resolution of disputes became more difficult in the absence of consensual knowledge regarding systemic legitimating principles. Norms developed from national-sovereign legitimating principles would later acquire the characteristics of assertions of positive rights which could be employed to legitimate political action. Tilly has stipulated these rights regarding domestic and international political autonomy, territorial states for distinct, homogenous peoples, exclusion of "others" from benefits and membership, struggle for autonomy by extraordinary means, and external, consensual assistance of these struggles.

Immediate strategic consequences of national-sovereign collective identity emerged at Valmy and were executed by contemporarily novel mass-mobilization armies. These were larger in size, more heterogeneous in social composition, superior in motivation and tactical innovation, and lower in cost than the elitist and mercenary forces of their territorial-sovereign monarchical adversaries. Nationalist fervor could now be harnessed to military operations and could exploit class and ethnic divisions within opposing forces and states. But it does not follow that mass mobilization and the national collective identity that engendered them were transmitted throughout the old regime, territorial-sovereign states of Europe to compete with the novel French force. National collective identity and its strategic consequences are not reducible to an artifact of a posited structural realist socialization mechanism in the international system. The behavior of the Prussian Crown was widely at variance with that predicted by structural realist socialization mechanisms. The Prussian monarchy disdainfully declined the pan-German Imperial Crown (and consequently, potentially declined to lead a quite instrumentally useful German superstate) offered by the Paulskirche Parliament in 1849. The Prussian monarchy later brought the country to constitutional crisis rather than accept an expansion of the citizen militia with a term of service less than required to eradicate their liberal and civilian impulses.

During the territorial-sovereign interlude between the defeat of Napoleonic France and the Revolution of 1848 my analysis suggests that reconstruction of institutions predicated on old regime principles will not guarantee their continued legitimacy. The Vienna attempt to reconstruct domestic and international social order with old regime legitimating principles had a number of theoretically relevant consequences. First the concert was held together not only to ensure a balance of power but, in Kissinger's words, the "shared values" of the old regime statesmen. Thus maintenance of the domestic and international social order obviated opportunities to engage in territorial-sovereign status competition. In order to extend the life of the territorial-sovereign social order, old regime statesmen were required to reconstruct the territorial-sovereign structure of identities and interests. To stabilize it they had to pacify it and expunge from it the norms of war that had earlier developed naturally from the systemic legitimating principle *of raison d'état*. Thus insularity of decisionmaking during the concert period might have been sufficient for the formulation of a "conspiracy of princes," but was clearly insufficient to continue to permit state behavior consistent with an unchallenged exercise of absolutist territorial-sovereign will.

A new legitimation crisis of the social order was brewing throughout territorial-sovereign Europe during the concert period as well in response to the forces of state and market penetration of traditional society. These forces rapidly reconstructed individual and collective social identities and their relationships to the state. In the urban centers these forces were integrative for social identities, demolishing the social bases of urban particularism and fostering a redefinition of citizenship as a commodity to be gained or lost with the transfer of capital. In the rural areas these forces slowly eroded the authority of the *Herrschaft* and transferred peasant allegiance to collective identification with the state. Noble status was increasingly no longer constitutive of the social order but had to be defended.

First in Britain, and later nearly everywhere, the territorial-sovereign state became increasingly anxious to enfranchise and co-opt increasingly lower strata property owners to ensure their participation in the projects of the state, and uncoerced access to their capital. Thus, as Mann argues, classes and nations rose together. As state penetration into social life increased, and increasingly lower socioeconomic strata of society were enfranchised, so increased the self-identification with the state of the newly created citizenry, radically altering the character of public life, and ultimately demolishing the insularity of old regime decisionmaking.

But this franchise was to be granted only in the third, or as late as the fourth quarter of the nineteenth century for the vast majority of the denizens of central Europe as the absolutists who reigned there were induced to subordinate their territorial-sovereign wills to a constitution only after the threat to their regimes posed by the Revolution of 1848. This will be developed more fully in the next chapter. The revolution had emerged as a nationalist movement with nationalist demands as it was intellectually the product of the German bourgeoisie who regarded their pan-German nationalism to be an expression of bourgeois emancipation. While Britain had already acceded to the constitutional rule of the capitalist nation, central European monarchs responded minimally with limited-franchise liberalism. The timidity of the

German bourgeoisie—their fear of enfranchising bourgeois of less exalted status than themselves—abetted this anemic monarchical response. Thus the life of the territorial-sovereign institutional form in central Europe was extended by the inability of the central European bourgeoisie to consolidate a new institutional form to house its expressed will to manifest its social identity. This was so even while the legitimation crisis of territorial-sovereign legitimating principles had come and gone. This was so even in the midst of the emergence of national collective identity and the expression of the principles of national sovereignty connoted by the convening of the Frankfurt Parliament. The victorious liberals allowed their revolution to remain unconsolidated by a new institutional form as debate over this form brought to the surface a lack of consensus among themselves regarding the identity of the new sovereign.

7 Use and Misuse of the Principle of Nationality: The Demise of the Second Empire and the Birth of the Second Reich

The great questions of the time are not decided by speeches and majority decisions—that was the error of 1848 and 1849—but by iron and blood.

—Otto von Bismarck

Of the moral powers in the world he [Bismarck] has not the slightest notion.

—Heinrich von Treitschke

It is not a rare event in history that treaties are broken. But that a treaty is broken *anticipando,* [beforehand], that was an innovation reserved to the genius of Bismarck.

—Friedrich Ferdinand von Beust

I stand or fall with my own Sovereign, even if in my opinion he ruins himself stupidly, but for me France will remain France whether it is governed by Napoleon or by St. Louis and Austria is for me a foreign country. . . . I know that you will reply that fact and right can not be separated, that a properly conceived Prussian policy requires chastity in foreign affairs even from the point of view of utility. I am prepared to discuss the point of utility with you; but if you pose antinomies between right and revolution; Christianity and infidelity; God and the devil; I can argue no longer and can merely say, "I am not of your opinion and you judge in me what is not yours to judge."

—Otto von Bismarck

The timidity of the German bourgeoisie kept the Frankfurt Parliament floundering about with self-doubt. The 1848 revolution had left them with a pan-German parliament that was ostensibly empowered to forge a constitution for a German national entity of some form. This was a move toward what they wanted. Thirty-eight German states had been combined in the *Deutscher Bund* (German Confederation). But this "was only a *Staaten-Bund* (a federation of states). What the German Liberals wanted was a *Bundes-Staat* (a federated state)."[1] But the Frankfurt parliament delegates were both deeply divided in terms of what they wished to do, and burdened with an abiding ambiguity regarding precisely what they had been empowered to do, by whom, and in whose name they were authorized to speak.

Identity vs. Institutions: The Problems of the Frankfurt Parliament

While it was clear to all that "[p]olitical legitimacy [now] required more than the traditional support of the aristocracy or state"[2] it was just as clear that the Frankfurt delegates "were uncertain if they could or should speak for the *Volk*."[3] This was so precisely because the German monarchs who had sent them to Frankfurt with their ostensible blessings had sent them there with a necessarily ambiguous status. While the Frankfurt delegates were supposed to represent the disparate elements of the German "nation," the power to administer daily public life remained in the hands of the German states. An immediate question arose in light of this dilemma, of what, precisely, the "sovereignty of the nation" meant in practice. The members of the Frankfurt parliament were not able to resolve this question. A major impediment for them in resolving it is that they lacked any practical institutional capacity that would permit them to act upon and manifest their prospective sovereignty. Any decision taken by the executive of the Frankfurt parliament would have to be effectively ratified by the monarchical administrations of the various states from which it was comprised, because only these state administrations could, in practice, carry out the Frankfurt parliament's "decisions." As Sheehan describes it, their dilemma was that: "Had they a state to serve, the Frankfurt executive would have served it well; but while the parliament could claim to represent the German nation, its executive could hardly pretend to be a state."[4]

It was for this reason that the Frankfurt parliament was dissolved so easily and peacefully when, after having finally settled upon a *Kleindeutsche* solution to the question of Germany's borders, its major decision—to offer an Imperial German crown to the King of Prussia—was spurned by the Prussian King. In dismissing the decision of the representatives of the "German nation," Friedrich Wilhelm effectively denied the *existence* of the German nation, at least the existence of the German nation as an entity that possessed a sovereignty which either mirrored or rivaled his own. As the Frankfurt parliament had determined that the German nation could become a German national-state only with the agreement of the Prussian state, the decision of the head of the Prussian state to remain precisely that robbed the German nation of an institutional form. For the time being, the German nation would have to live on in the *Volksgeist* in ethereal, incorporeal, insubstantiality—as an idea, a wish, a feeling. The German nation simply could not exist except under the rule of a German prince who held in his hands the reins of a state which could institutionalize the collective identity that the Frankfurt parliament embodied and expressed. Unfortunately for the devotees of the German nation, in 1849, this German prince regarded it as a contradiction in terms that he had been, or could be, "elected" the Emperor of a united German empire. Ironically, at this time, no man in Prussia had been more pleased at Friedrich Wilhelm's refusal of the imperial crown than Otto von Bismarck, then a member of the Prussian Second Chamber. His speeches to the chamber in April of 1849 resonated with "bitter and sarcastic criticism of the Frankfurt constitution. Bismarck had stigmatized this constitution as 'organized anarchy' because it gave universal suffrage to the German people."[5]

Thus the aspirations of the German-speaking peoples for the revolution of 1848 were, by the close of 1849, fairly well defeated by the combination of bourgeois timidity in the face of the continuing unrest among the laboring classes, and the naive faith of German liberals in the power of novel political institutions like the Frankfurt parliament—a body unable to envision a nonmonarchical form of collective action to manifest pan-German national collective identity. Friedrich Wilhelm was a confirmed territorial sovereign and would not (and likely could not) subsume pan-German national-sovereign identity under the paternal wing of his quasi-dynastic territorial sovereignty. He rejected the aspirations and claims of the advocates of pan-Germanism outright.

Friedrich Wilhelm had effectively taken back nearly all that he had offered when the victims of the 1848 revolution in Prussia had been trundled past him on the streets of Berlin. He had, however, softened the blow of his haughty refusal of an imperial German crown by offering his own constitution to the Prussian people as a grant from the Crown. Friedrich Wilhelm's constitution eschewed the threatening innovation of universal suffrage that the Frankfurt constitution had sought, replacing it with a very limited *Drei-Klassen-Wahlrecht* (three class suffrage) in which the weight and effect of the vote was apportioned in accordance with the taxes paid to the state.[6] This move had the desired effect. It effectively "split the opposition, isolate[d] the radical left, and consolidate[d] monarchical authority."[7] Yet the Prussian constitution, and the emancipation of the Austrian peasantry, remained as lasting legacies of the 1848 revolution. While the forces of reaction appeared to have triumphed for the moment, their victory was accompanied by none of the reactionary triumphalism that had followed the defeat of Napoleon.

> The conservatives seemed to have won, but most of them believed they would have to fight again. Their victory in 1849 was not . . . attended by those inflated hopes and bold ambitions that had been so apparent in 1815. After this revolution, there was no "Holy Alliance," no Gothic posturing or talk of restoration. "The old times are gone and can not return," declared the Prussian minister Manteuffel in 1849. "To return to the decaying conditions of the past is like scooping water with a sieve."[8]

The Second Republic and the Second Empire: Consequences for Alliance Formation with Territorial Sovereigns

The revolution of 1848 had resulted in a second republic in France, and the great nephew of Napoleon Bonaparte had been elected President of the Second Republic shortly after the French King Louis Philippe was forced to flee Paris. While the German states were watching their princes withdraw many of the gains that they had thought they had won in the 1848 revolution, the French Second Republic was proving itself to be the stillborn child of the Parisian radicalism of 1848. "President" Bonaparte seized power in a bloody coup in 1851 and offered the politically fickle French a new and glorious empire in place of the Second Republic in a plebiscite. Weary of republicanism, Bourbons, and Orleanists (constitutional monarchists) the French people acceded to a Second Empire by a vote of 8,000,000 in favor to a mere 250,000 opposed. Bonaparte was proclaimed the Emperor, Napoleon III, on December 2, 1852.[9]

Napoleon III's reign was not to be conducted with the carefree, unselfconscious, pseudo-autocratic authority that Friedrich Wilhelm managed to carry off in Prussia, in spite of the parliamentary window-dressing that the latter had been required to give to his government from 1848. Napoleon III wished to reign as had his grand-uncle, but he found it unexpectedly difficult to carry off the trappings of absolutism. The violence with which he had established his empire rankled Great Britain and all republicans. The plebescitory manner in which he had formally acquired his title left serious questions regarding his legitimacy as a monarch in the eyes of his continental peers. In any event his dynasty was distressingly young and quixotically *nouveau royale* from the perspective of the courts of Vienna, St. Petersburg, Berlin, and Madrid. None of these princes thought that Napoleon's Second Empire would last. There was nothing attending the history of the government of France between 1789 and Napoleon's coronation in 1852 to suggest that it would.[10] Consequently they had been very hesitant to grant him the full, official recognition that was due to a brother monarch, and they addressed him in their official correspondence, throughout his reign and to his considerable irritation, as *notre très cher ami* [our very dear friend] rather than *Sire mon frère* [Majesty my brother]."[11] Thus, as Kissinger argues, Napoleon III was somewhat obsessed by his lack of legitimate credentials in the eyes of his peers. He "yearned to be accepted by the legitimate kings."[12] This recognition was to be continuously denied him and Kissinger regards this fact as "one of the psychological roots of Napoleon's reckless and relentless assault on European diplomacy"[13] during his reign.

Whatever the state of Napoleon's psychology, I will certainly argue that the absence of a long, historically continuous line of blue-blooded and titled ancestors left the second Emperor Napoleon with the problem of legitimating his rule. It was not possible to legitimate the Second Empire with recourse to the dynastic, divine right that the other monarchies of mid-nineteenth-century Europe still so resolutely relied upon. Whether by design or by default, faced with the absence of traditional legitimacy, but bearing the name of Bonaparte, Napoleon III inherited the nationalist credentials of his uncle. France had chosen the Second Empire in lieu of the Second Republic in her craving for a return to the national glory of the first Empire.[14] A Bonaparte served this purpose. He professed a belief in the power of the development of "completed nation-states" as a progressive, organizing, and modernizing force of history and was soon to play the champion of the principle of nationality in the conduct of his foreign policy. Posturing as a defender of national self-determination, Napoleon "attacked the Vienna system"[15] which defended the order of the traditionally legitimated monarchs of Europe. Kissinger argues that Napoleon "was driven to dependence on public opinion [to maintain his legitimacy], and his policy fluctuated with his assessment of what was needed to sustain his [domestic] popularity."[16] He was consistently popular only when that policy consistently defended the principle of nationality.

By 1854 Napoleon had entered the Crimean War on the side of England to check Russian expansion into the collapsing Ottoman Empire. This move was quite popular at home precisely because it avenged France against Russia's role in the defeat of the first empire. Later in the decade he was to bring French troops into the fray of a War of Italian liberation against Austria. These hostilities posed a conflict of state and "national" interests that became a classical pattern for the hybrid international system of the nineteenth century: a mixed system of the competing territorial-sovereign and national-sovereign entities. The Austrian "interest" in engaging the Italian campaign was the maintenance of "social order, political legitimacy and religious faith..[against] . . . Bonapartism, nationalist passions and secularization."[17]

Having already made an enemy of Russia, Napoleon's Italian campaigns now earned him the permanent enmity of Hapsburg Austria, at whose expense the Italian unification had come. Significantly it also earned him the mistrust of Francophobe Great Britain, which was by no means pleased to witness new "Napoleonic" military activity such a short time after the Battle of Waterloo was supposed to have ended it once and for all. Nor had his Italian campaigns earned Napoleon the good will of the Pope. The advancing unification of Italy presented an obvious threat to the Papal States, and Napoleon had been forced back in 1848 when still President of the Second Republic to send a substantial French garrison to Rome in order to protect Pius IX from Garibaldi and the Roman Republic. Pius had issued his continued defense of his temporal authority in the forms of the encyclical *Quanta cura* and the December 1864 *Syllabus errorum*, thus as Prussian aggression and German unification loomed on Napoleon's eastern horizon, he could not yet remove the garrison without inflaming devout French Catholic opinion.[18] Unfortunately for Napoleon, French domestic opinion might have adored the principle of nationality, but not at the expense of the papacy. French identity might have been national, but it was also overwhelmingly Catholic. The papacy might be defied, as it had been during the First Empire, for the sake of the expression of French national identity,[19] but not for the sake of Italian national identity.

Worst of all, his actions in Italy had not even earned him the unequivocal gratitude of Italian patriots who were upset that Napoleon had not freed all of northern Italy, as he had promised, and were no more pleased that the French garrison in Rome prevented the eternal city from becoming the capital city of the united Italy that the Risorgimento insisted it must become.[20] This was later to cost him the potential for an alliance even with Italy when Napoleon was to cast about in vain for help against the threat of a war with Prussia. Even though Napoleon had wed his cousin, Prince Jerome Napoleon (who was known in France, quite irreverently, as "Plon-Plon") to Clotilde, daughter to the Italian King Victor Emanuel II, Italy would not ally with France while French troops still protected the temporal power of the papacy.[21] This was so precisely because the papacy had for so long been so effective in sustaining political fragmentation on the Italian peninsula.

It is worthwhile to pause here and observe the extent to which the insularity of decisionmaking for statesmen, which had been quite complete a century before the reign of Napoleon III, had become so badly eroded by this time that Napoleon could not make the move required to lock up an alliance with an emerging nation that he had helped to create. When the British nation had required continental allies in preparation for squaring off against France in the Seven Years' War (chapter 5), they could not solidify an alliance with the logical and historical counterbalance to France—Austria—because their "constitutional" monarch, George II, insisted that he held personal sovereignty over Hanover. Thus the continental sovereignty and property interests of a British monarch, who was ostensibly subject to the rule of constitutional law, required that the interests of the British nation had to be subordinated to the his personal "dynastic" interests. Clearly the decision-making freedom of Pitt's administration had been impaired only by the countervailing interests of the Whig oligarchy in the British parliament.

A century later Napoleon III, ruling France without the constraints of a constitution (until months before the end of his reign), found himself unable to make a decision to abandon a militarily helpless papacy to Italian nationalists in order to maximize his opportunity to gain a military ally that otherwise had been given every reason to support him. He could not do so precisely because such a decision would so badly inflame domestic opinion that his regime likely would not have survived its domestic aftershocks. Napoleon could make no decision regarding foreign or domestic policy that could not be soundly excoriated in the *corps légeslatif* or in the press. Contrary to the situation of Hanoverian Britain a century before, every decision that Napoleon III took would be subjected to the comment and criticism of a constituency much more socially heterogeneous than the Whig oligarchy and Tory fringe with which George had been required to contend. Each major decision that Napoleon III had taken had resulted in an unofficial plebiscite in France regarding the question of whether his rule and his "dynasty" would continue to be tolerated.

Napoleon would soon further aggravate his strained relations with Russia by playing the champion of the cause of the long-suffering nationalists of partitioned Poland when they revolted against Alexander II in 1863. This policy played well to the appreciative Parisians, but gained the lasting enmity of Alexander. According to Aronson:

> Nor had a recent state visit [by Alexander] to Paris done anything to endear the Russian Emperor to Napoleon III's regime. His [Alexander's] arrival had been greeted by shouts of "Long live Poland!" and, on driving back one day with Napoleon from Longchamps, he had been shot at by a young Polish patriot. Napoleon's tactful observation that as the two of them had been under fire together they were now "brothers-in-arms" was frigidly received by the outraged Tsar. He returned to Russia in a very bad humor.[22]

Neither had Napoleon's ill-advised policy that seemed to clearly veer away from the support of national self-determination abroad (in addition to protecting the papacy against Italian nationalists) endeared him to the court in Madrid. Napoleon had acceded to the encouragement of his Empress of Spanish birth, Eugenie, to install Maximilian, the brother of the Hapsburg Austrian Emperor, as a Catholic puppet Emperor in republican Mexico.[23] This feat, and the subordinate relationship of Maximilian's "Empire" to the French Empire, made France appear glorious in the eyes of domestic French nationalists of all political opinions. The glory this move bestowed on France allowed most Frenchmen to ignore the fact that Maximilian had essentially imposed a Catholic Hapsburg imperial government on a national republican Mexico. The Spanish, who saw Mexico as part of their diminishing Empire in America, did not forget. Yet Spanish resentment was to cost Napoleon little in the end. A new problem of Spanish succession, as we shall see, was to cost him a great deal more.

Thus we may see that Napoleon III was constrained in his choice of alliance partners by his reliance upon a foreign policy designed to appeal to popular nationalist domestic sentiment. In spite of his "imperial" pretense, his decisionmaking was lacking the insularity of his old-regime counterparts. He had to rush about Europe as a champion of national sovereignty to maintain his domestic legitimacy, and completely isolated France in the process. Emperor or no, the national-sovereign agency of the French polity had manifest itself in Louis Napoleon's foreign policy as an implicit condition of his continued rule.

National Identity as a Tool of Statesmen: Bismarck Engineers the Danish and Austro-Prussian Wars

While French foreign policy had veered off into alternatively nationalist and reactionary adventures throughout Europe and the New World, Prussian energy had been directed toward a developing constitutional struggle at home. Wilhelm, finally turning to Bismarck to guide Prussia through the crisis, appointed him Prussian Prime Minister and Minister for Foreign Affairs on September 22, 1862. Bismarck had emerged as the only man who would defy the Prussian parliament and appeared to be the man who was least likely to allow constitutional scruples to frustrate his policy in the service of the Crown.

The events surrounding the emergence of this constitutional crisis in Prussia serve to further undermine the structural realist account of the emergence of Prussian nationalism through military reform. If this account were adequate, we would expect to see the Prussian King and his military advisers enthusiastically advancing the development of the Prussian *Landwehr* in order to ensure the conscription of tens of thousands of enthusiastic, patriotic Prussian troops in the service of the Crown. But as Eyck relates to us in his history of the development of the German Empire under the leadership of Bismarck, it was the more liberal factions of the Prussian parliament, not the Prussian Crown or the Junker aristocracy, that supported expansion of the *Landwehr* as a constituent element of the Prussian army. Yet a constitutional crisis between the Prussian parliament and the Crown developed over the issue of the length of service that the *Landwehr* soldier was to serve. Eyck notes that the Prussian King Wilhelm I wanted the term increased from two to three years, not for reasons of specifically military exigency, "but still more in order to destroy their [the conscripts'] civilian outlook . . . [h]is reasons were of a political as much as a military nature.'[24]

Wilhelm and his generals seriously mistrusted the *Landwehr* precisely because it was "a creation of the War of Liberation . . . the citizens in arms."[25]

> [General Leopold von] Gerlach called . . . [it] . . . the one really liberal institution in the country. But what endeared the *Landwehr* to the people made it suspicious to the King and [Albrecht von] Roon. They disliked the *Landwehr-Mann* as too intimately connected with civilian life. The *Landwehr* man of today was the voter of yesterday and of tomorrow. When in the year 1849 Prussian troops were sent against the South Germans who had risen to fight for the German constitution of the Frankfurt Assembly, some *Landwehr* men had clearly shown their discontent. The King wanted to avoid a repetition of similar signs of political independence. His plan of reorganization aimed at a weakening of the *Landwehr*.[26]

Thus far from demonstrating his anxiety to create a mass mobilization army to compete with the army of Napoleon III's France, for example, Wilhelm had decidedly demonstrated his fear of it. He so mistrusted the liberal, democratic ethos exemplified in the man of the mass army that he set out to reorganize away the offending characteristic quite irrespective of any concern for the subsequent effectiveness of the product as a fighting force. This starkly contradicts the expectations of structural realism, which anticipates that states will internally balance external threats through arms racing and/or force modernization. If the mass mobilization army of the first Napoleon was viewed as a highly effective modern military innovation, the impulse of old regime states to emulate it should, in the structural realist view, have been irresistible. Yet it does not appear that the men responsible for optimizing the army's fighting effectiveness felt any pressing need for an army full of motivated *Landwehr* men in any case as Eyck relates that "[t]he King acted on the advice of his military advisers,"[27] von Manteuffel and von Roon. The issue here was, of course, that as much as Wilhelm might appreciate a nationally motivated fighting force to serve as guardian of the Prussian state, it was a Prussian state, not a German superstate, that he wished them to guard. In Wilhelm's world view the Prussian state was still coterminous with the Prussian Crown. He wanted the Prussian soldiery to be king's men, or he would not have them in arms at all. The parliament would not vote for the army bill without provision of funds for the *Landwehr*, so Wilhelm, in essence, insisted upon, at a minimum, a three-year term of service to allow his officers time to beat the last civilian and liberal impulse out of each individual *Landwehr* conscript, to ensure that they became the king's men.

For Wilhelm and the Prussian conservatives, the Prussian army was an instrument of both foreign and domestic policy. "To defend the state from its enemies abroad, the army had to be a mass force based on conscription, but to defend the social order from domestic unrest it had to remain a politically reliable servant of the king."[28]

Therefore Wilhelm had opted for a very limited change in the composition of the Prussian army and because "[l]ike many of his brother officers Roon doubted the militia's [*Landwehr's*] effectiveness and questioned its loyalty"[29], Wilhelm preferred to staff his soldiery with reliable if uninspired mercenaries. His mercenary, professional soldiers may not have possessed a passion for charging into enemy fire for the fatherland (most were not Prussian), heedless of life and limb, but were clearly beholden specifically to the *King* of Prussia. The liberals in the Prussian parliament, however, were unhappy about both the expense of a mercenary army, and the fact that it was officered by Prussian noblemen who had "contempt for the rest of the nation."[30] Thus for Prussian liberals, the militia was part of their dream of "national liberation."

The aristocratic, territorial-sovereign structure of identities of the Prussian king and his officer corps structured their interests such that they regarded the expansion of a Prussian citizenry in arms as inimical to the interests of their class and those of a monarchical, territorial-sovereign Prussian state. They deemed an army composed of the king's men, dominated by his loyal nobility, to be constitutive of the territorial-sovereign Prussian state. The increasingly popular, national-sovereign structure of identities of the bourgeois liberal component of the Prussian parliament structured their interests such that they regarded the expansion of a Prussian citizenry in arms to be constitutive of any institutional form of collective action that would be minimally capable of manifesting their emerging national-sovereign identity abroad. In consequence: "The conflict over the army reforms, therefore, was more than a conflict between the military and civilians, or between throne and parliament, it was also a *conflict between two visions of Prussia's identity.*"[31]

This was the atmosphere in which Bismarck was recalled to Berlin from his post as Ambassador to Paris to lead Wilhelm's government. It is important to pause and note that 100 years earlier Bismarck's irridentist claims to be acting on behalf of the welfare and interests of ethnic Germans would have been completely unacceptable as a pretext for intervention in the matter, let alone *casus belli*. From the inception of his administration Bismarck consistently steered Prussian policy on a unilateral course oriented toward Prussian aggrandizement. Bismarck indeed sought the unification of the German states, but he sought this unification only as he envisioned it—under Prussian rule. He was to masterfully employ popular pan-German nationalist sentiment as a tool toward the attainment of this goal. To that end Prussian policy under Bismarck, from 1863, set out to destroy the "legitimate structure of Europe" that had been codified in the 1815 Vienna treaties.[32] Like Napoleon III, Bismarck's policy was entirely subversive of the legitimating principles, and the agenda of Metternich's Vienna system, which had assumed a common Austrian and Prussian interest in the maintenance of conservative institutions as a bulwark against the forces of liberalism and democracy in the domestic opposition of each.[33]

Unfortunately for Austria, Bismarck did not feel that he required this bulwark to maintain order and conservative monarchical rule within Prussia. His domestic political policies were consistently designed to exacerbate the split between the Protestant, Prussian liberal opposition of the *Bürgertum*, and the Catholic and working-class liberals, not to mention the socialists. After the defeat of France in 1870, Bismarck would execute the most elaborate machinations to ensure this split, particularly as he launched his *Kulturkampf* (cultural struggle) campaign against the Catholic *Zentrum* (center) who had been emboldened in their opposition by the ultramontane results of the first Vatican Council.[34]

Austria, then as always, was much more dynastic than territorial in outlook. Due to its polyglot ethnic and linguistic composition, cemented by a coextensive division of ethnicity with geography, the Austrian state had never been and could never become a "national" state. In deference to their imperial subjects' traditions, the Hapsburgs had traditionally taken separate coronation oaths for the regions that they ruled. "Hapsburgs swore to defend each province and to respect its traditional customs, laws, privileges, and religion."[35] In doing so the Austrian Hapsburgs attempted to govern a fairly conventional Empire along the lines of the Roman model of antiquity, as it existed after what Michael Doyle has described as the Augustan revolution of imperial administration.[36] The Austrian Hapsburg Empire was at this time, at the most, what Michael Mann calls a "confederal state" subjected to a dynastic, monarchical, absolutist rule softened only by the mitigating parameters of Hapsburg respect for cultural and linguistic particularism.[37] It became increasingly difficult for confederal Austria to simply maintain what it held in an age when the idea of the nation was making its rounds in Europe, and while Russia was frustrating Austria's hopes of expansion into the soft areas of southeastern Europe created by the quickening Ottoman collapse. The very last thing that Austria wanted to do at this time was to struggle with Prussia for regional hegemony of the German lands of Central Europe.[38] Equally unfortunate for Austria, Prussia felt it had to struggle with Austria to gather up these lands. Austrian Hapsburg princes had been continuously elected Holy Roman Emperors by the German Electors from 1438 until the last Holy Roman Emperor had resigned and done away with the office in the first decade of the nineteenth century. While the office was gone, the allegiance to Hapsburg Austria among the many remaining German princes had not receded. This was so particularly in the Catholic south of German Central Europe. Bismarck was to eventually determine that he must remove the sparkle from the imperial Hapsburg diadem in order to bring the German states under the rule of Prussia. He was soon to provide such a drubbing of Austrian prestige.

But Austria was not to be the first victim of Prussian aggression in the developing Bismarckian scheme to unite the German lands under Prussian rule. That misfortune was to befall a non-German state, specifically Denmark. Significantly, Denmark attracted Bismarck's quite negative attention in this regard precisely because it was a non-German power. Even before, and especially after an 1848 insurrection by the German-speaking inhabitants of the Danish-ruled Duchies of Schleswig and Holstein, tangled disputes had emerged regarding to whom the titles to the Duchies would revert upon the death of the Danish King Friedrich VII. Schleswig-Holstein was a region of mixed Danish-German ethnicity. Friedrich had held title to both while he lived. The dispute had been an essentially legal, titular dispute of the sort common in the eighteenth century. It had been an issue of contended "dynastic" succession and essentially a question of a nature that was to become very uncommon in the more recent era of national-sovereign identity—which prince would own and rule the territory upon the death of their present sovereign. It was a dispute so complex in the legal reasoning required to resolve it that Britain's Lord Palmerston had once jested that "Only three men have ever understood it. One was Prince Albert, who is dead. The second was a German professor who became mad. I am the third and I have forgotten all about it."[39]

Upon the death of the Danish sovereign in 1863, Bismarck moved quickly to reduce the issue essentially to a German national irredentist claim to recover separate ethnic Germans. Of course, Bismarck had never viewed the Schleswig-Holstein affair from the perspective of a German nationalist and was unlikely to have given a fig for whether or not the ethnic Germans had been mistreated by their Danish rulers. Yet claims that such mistreatment had occurred had been advanced and German nationalists throughout the German-speaking states of Central Europe had expressed enthusiasm for the separation of the Duchies from Danish rule. Bismarck was interested in annexing the Duchies to Prussia. When the Danish king died without issue, Bismarck became anxious to take advantage of the controversy regarding the right of succession over these Duchies in the name of the German nationalist cause, not because he had any sympathy for it but because "Prussia did not have, either in law or in history, the smallest title to the Duchies."[40] He had earlier written, to Manteuffel, "I have not the smallest doubt that the whole Danish business can be settled in a way desirable for us only by war. The occasion for such a war can be found at any moment we consider favorable for waging it."[41] The death of the Danish king provided that moment.

Bismarck was able to take advantage of German nationalist sentiment in this context in large measure because Friedrich VII had, somewhat foolishly and autocratically, attempted to "impose a new constitutional order on Schleswig without the promised consultation" back in March of 1863.[42] Upon Friedrich's death, rival claims by Prince Christian of Glücksburg (to both Schleswig-Holstein and the Danish Crown) and Prince Augustenburg (a "progressive" candidate supported by most German liberals) were evaluated by the Diet of the German Confederation in late November. The Diet was effectively powerless except as a negotiating forum for delegations of the German princes of the loose Confederation formed at the end of the Napoleonic Wars, but among its delegates were many German liberal nationalists. In the event a consensus in support of Augustenburg's candidacy emerged.[43] This was the combined result of inflamed and nascent German nationalist passion over the alleged mistreatment of the German minority in the Duchies, the attempt by a Danish prince to impose a constitutional order on them without consultation with the estates, and the prospect of the continuation of this alleged state of affairs under a new Danish sovereign.

The specific events leading up to the joint Austro-Prussian military operations that were launched early in 1864 to wrest Schleswig-Holstein from Danish control are complicated. What is essential for our purposes here is the difference in Austrian and Prussian motivation, stemming from variations in their respective structures of identities and interests, in cooperating in the joint conquest of Schleswig-Holstein, and the insights that analysis of this difference provides in understanding the growing cleavage in the Austrian and Prussian notions of their state identities and interests. This rift was critical in nullifying the Vienna system, and ending the prolonged period of peace among conservative dynasts that had for so long characterized the functioning of the Concert of Europe. As Sheehan describes the situation, Bismarck and the Austrian Foreign Minister, Count Johann Bernhard von Rechberg, had very different sets of assumptions regarding the significance of their cooperation in operations against Denmark for the future of Austro-Prussian relations. These differing assumptions stem directly from differing Austrian and Prussian understandings of their respective state interests, which in turn stemmed from differing conceptions of sovereign identities. The difference is hardly surprising given Austria's reliance upon the continuation of Metternich's Vienna system to avoid conflict with Prussia, while nationalist and secessionist trouble was appearing in its multiethnic empire. It is less surprising still when we consider the character of Rechberg, who "called himself a Conservative statesman and a pupil of Metternich."[44]

> Rechberg saw the Schleswig-Holstein problem as the occasion for creating the constellation of forces that he had always wanted: a Confederation dominated by an Austro-Prussian condominium directed against liberal nationalism and in favor of the status quo. His interest in Schleswig-Holstein *per se* was minimal; his principal aim was to lay the basis for a broad and lasting set of agreements with Berlin. This was not Bismarck's intention. Although he did not reveal his goals to

> anyone for another year, he was attracted to the idea of annexing the Duchies to Prussia. Moreover, his agreement to work with Vienna in support of the treaties of 1852 [with the Confederation, which Denmark had violated] was purely tactical, a way to keep the game going while he waited to see what would develop.[45]

In his dedication to conservative principles of government, the leading place of the ancient aristocracy in the leadership of domestic society, and to monarchical rule, Bismarck was every bit Rechberg's match. Unlike Rechberg, however, and unlike many of his Prussian peers such as Gerlach, Bismarck did not regard adherence to the Vienna system as in any way essential to the maintenance of dynastic rule in Prussia. This led him to reject the premises, advice, and wishes of Prussian conservatives. As Kissinger has recently argued, Bismarck "challenged the conventional wisdom which identified nationalism with liberalism."[46] Thus Bismarck did not see any inherent liberal threat to the Prussian monarchy or social order in a pan-German policy that excluded Hapsburg Austria. As a consequence, Bismarck rejected the suggestion that an Austrian alliance was essential to the maintenance of conservative monarchical rule in Prussia. Instead he believed "the illusion of the need for an Austrian alliance served above all to inhibit Prussia from pursuing its ultimate goal of unifying Germany"[47] under the Prussian Crown. But in rejecting the necessary identification of nationalism with liberalism, a linkage that was almost axiomatic to the adherents to Metternich's doctrine when he constructed the Vienna system in 1815, Bismarck also rejected the proposition that liberal institutions were required to achieve the unification of Germany. This was a proposition that had been equally axiomatic among the German liberals who had gathered in Frankfurt after the 1848 revolution to construct an all-German constitution. Bismarck felt that the legitimacy of the Prussian monarchy and the strength of the Prussian state was of an order that rendered it impervious to the threat of this logic. Thus he could flirt with the Prussian left, the liberals, and the Prussian, German nationalists when it suited him; and he could employ what he regarded as their delusional, pan-German, national enthusiasms for his own purposes. As Bismarck had himself written in this context:

> The sense of security that the King remains master in his country even if the whole army is abroad is not shared with Prussia by any other

> continental state and above all by no other German power. It provides the opportunity to accept a development of public affairs much more in conformity with present requirements. . . . The royal authority in Prussia is so firmly based that the government can without risk encourage a much more lively parliamentary activity and thereby exert pressure on conditions in Germany.[48]

I shall shortly describe the manner in which Bismarck was able to play to not only the Prussian liberals, but also the liberals and nationalists throughout the German Confederation, to gain sympathy for Prussia in the struggle he planned to stage later with Austria. Meanwhile he had, on the basis of Rechberg's delusions regarding Bismarck's intentions, in January 1864 engineered the joint invasion of Schleswig by Austrian and Prussian forces. They crossed the frontier on February 1.[49] With annexation of the Duchies as his aim, Bismarck carefully avoided all overtures for a peaceful settlement throughout the ensuing conflict; Denmark was forced to sue for peace by August, and to cede the Duchies to the joint control of Austria and Prussia. Schleswig-Holstein were to be administered by an Austro-Prussian "condominium" of the very sort Rechberg had favored, even though this arrangement favored Prussia, which was geographically situated to exercise an authority over the area that Austria could not.[50]

Bismarck wished, of course, to annex both Duchies directly to Prussia, but could not employ such a demand as a legitimate basis for war with Austria, a war he desired in order to humble Austria in the eyes of the Confederation as well as to complete the Prussian conquest of Schleswig-Holstein. Neither his sovereign, the Crown Prince of Prussia, nor the opinion of the smaller German states he wished to woo under the sovereignty of the Prussian Crown would tolerate such a selfish act of aggression.[51] The Prussian sovereign and his son would not tolerate it as it would have been a blatant breach of faith with a brother-monarch. The smaller German states would not tolerate it as it would have been a blatant breach of faith with a brother-German. Significantly, *Bismarck had been required to play by territorial-sovereign and national-sovereign rules simultaneously*, which he did quite successfully. He could advance a national-sovereign cause of war—his irridentist claim to defend the rights of ethnic Germans—but yet be required to employ this national-sovereign cause of war to control the region in faithful condominium with territorial-sovereign Hapsburg Austria. The best that

Bismarck could therefore manage to advance his design, for a time, was to engineer the Convention of Gastein, which ended the condominium arrangement by dividing the Duchies between them, awarding Schleswig, in the north, to Prussia and Holstein, in the south, to Austria. The convention was completed on August 14, 1865.[52] This division was extremely unpopular throughout the Confederation.

But unfortunately for Austria, the Convention of Gastein was signed in the nature of a provisional, not a permanent settlement. This provided Bismarck with the opportunity to manufacture "grievances" against conduct of the Austrian administration of Holstein, and continuously badger the Austrian Ambassador and court with a series of hostile notes until Austria was provoked to send a very sharp note to Bismarck in response.[53] This note upset the Prussian king and was now allowed to serve as a pretext for the creation of a rift in Prussian relations with Austria, particularly in light of the growing realization in Berlin that a military conflict with Austria might provide a means of suspending the escalating constitutional crisis between the Prussian parliament and the Prussian Crown.

Bismarck had met with Wilhelm on February 21 to consider how to deal with the crisis and had convinced Wilhelm "that only three alternatives were now open to him: a liberal ministry, a *coup d'état* against the constitution, or war."[54] The first two options were unacceptable to Wilhelm, as he was repelled by the idea of a liberal ministry and did not wish to renounce the constitution his father had drafted. Thus when Wilhelm called a Crown Council on February 28, 1866 to formulate future Prussian policy he was persuaded without difficulty to grant Bismarck permission to begin negotiations with Italy for a military alliance against Austria. This was concluded by April 8. The following day Bismarck instructed the Prussian Minister in Frankfurt to introduce to the Diet of the German Confederation a proposal to convene a German parliament elected on the basis of universal suffrage![55] This was precisely the franchise that the Frankfurt Parliament that had convened in the aftermath of the Revolution of 1848 had sought, and had been denied them when the Prussian King had refused to accept the imperial German Crown and to vitalize that franchise.

The move was carefully and cynically calculated to gain sympathy for the Prussian government as an administration of progressive design which supported liberal, pan-German national unity in comparison with the creaking, dynastic, particularistic Hapsburg court in Vienna. The move served its purpose admirably. It was a singular success for Bismarck when we realize that the move helped to convince the peoples of the German Confederation that Prussia was demonstrating itself to be not only liberal, but also German nationalist in outlook at the very same time that Prussia had in essence demolished the German Confederation by concluding an alliance with Italy against another German member of the Confederation. Bismarck admitted as much when he confided to Benedetti, the French Foreign Minister:

> I have induced a King of Prussia to break off the intimate relations of his House with the House of Hapsburg, to conclude an alliance with revolutionary Italy, possibly to accept arrangements with Imperial France, and to propose in Frankfurt the reform of the Confederation and a popular parliament. That is a success of which I am proud.[56]

Bismarck's reference to "arrangements with Imperial France" refer to the ultimately unsuccessful negotiations that he had been conducting with Napoleon III. Bismarck had hoped to bring Napoleon into the war against Austria, or at the least to ensure Napoleon's benevolent neutrality, by suggesting to Napoleon that if France wished to incorporate all French-speaking regions of Europe (clearly alluding to Belgium) into the Empire, in accordance with the Emperor's devotion to the principal of nationality, that Prussia would take no notice. These overtures to Napoleon III had scandalized Gerlach, Bismarck's mentor and Wilhelm's military adjutant. Gerlach regarded Napoleon as an illegitimate upstart, as had been his great uncle before him, and counseled rapprochement between Vienna and Berlin to isolate illegitimate and chronically revolutionary France. In the margin of a letter from Gerlach protesting to Bismarck that "Napoleon is our natural enemy" Bismarck had scrawled "What of it?"[57] For most conservatives, even so late in the nineteenth century, the legitimacy of the principles of the Vienna system was ironclad. Men like Gerlach regarded the mechanized hum of Bismarck's radical, *realpolitik* move away from Metternich's creation with incomprehension and incredulity. Yet Bismarck appears to have realized that in order for Prussia to unambiguously wrest leadership of German Central Europe from Hapsburg Austria, Prussia would have to exploit pan-German national sentiment and was qualified to do so in a fashion that Austria was not. As Kissinger has recently argued:

> Had Prussia sought [earlier] to exploit German nationalism, it could have challenged Austrian pre-eminence in Germany a generation be-

> fore Bismarck . . . [but] . . . refrained from pursuing their advantage because it ran counter to the dominant principle of maintaining the status quo. Austria, seemingly on its death bed after Napoleon's [I] onslaught was given a new lease on life by the Metternich system, which enabled it to survive for another hundred years.[58]

In a similar sense, Bismarck's move to bring a motion for universal suffrage before the Diet of the German Confederation was astonishing. Universal suffrage certainly existed nowhere in the German states at that time. In a masterstroke, Bismarck made the severe, autocratic, and parochial Prussian government appear to be simultaneously democratic and pan-German nationalist; actually it was neither. Bismarck had calculated that his motion to grant universal suffrage for confederal elections would take the wind out of the sails of his domestic parliamentary adversaries; especially the liberal, bourgeois, Progressive party, in the upcoming elections. He particularly expected that this would assist him in ending the constitutional crisis by making him appear to be, though quite suddenly, more liberal than the liberals. The move made him appear to support German unification as well—inasmuch as nationalism and liberalism were such cognitively linked concepts in the minds of Prussian and other German liberals—as well as in the minds of their conservative adversaries. Bismarck had no doubts that he would succeed in his aims in these moves, as he had seen this accomplished before, in France. As Eyck argues persuasively:

> His [Bismarck's] practical model was Napoleon III, whose government was sustained by the masses and opposed by a portion of the educated upper middle class; Napoleon had introduced universal suffrage to get rid of the Second Republic [in 1852] and had been successful in that. Bismarck was confident that he would be able to achieve the same success.[59]

Bismarck did achieve the same success, and more. War between Austria and Prussia finally came and Prussia prevailed quickly and spectacularly even though the Prussian army had been universally thought to be no match for the Austrian forces. Prussian artillery was still of the light, muzzle-loading variety in 1866— inferior to the Austrian guns—and the Austrian cavalry forces were vastly superior. But the Austrian forces took much longer than Prussia's to mobilize, and Austrian tactical doctrine had not evolved, in spite of the lessons they might have observed at the sides of the Prussians in the Danish War, to adjust to the Prussian advantage in infantry. Aside from the Prussian capacity to mobilize its infantry more quickly and to move it into strategic position more rapidly with rail transport, the Prussian infantry was equipped with breech-loading weapons with rifled bores. These had decimated the Austrian infantry, which had lined up in disciplined rank and file to provide accommodating targets for the Prussian riflemen. The Austrian infantry was encumbered with muzzle-loading weapons that were both less accurate and capable of a lower rate of fire than the Prussian rifles.[60] As a result, the Austrian forces were defeated decisively at Sadowa a mere three weeks after Prussian troops had crossed the Saxon frontier.[61] The armistice was concluded on July 26 in Nikolsburg.

The terms of the armistice were extraordinarily moderate for Austria. Bismarck had wished to humble the Hapsburgs to turn the eyes of the Confederation squarely to Prussia for future leadership of a united German Empire. He had not wished to make of Austria a permanent and implacable enemy. He had been required to argue at great length, and at significant personal cost, with an obsessively triumphant and momentarily vindictive Wilhelm, that no Austrian lands should be annexed to Prussia as part of the settlement.[62] Prussia was not to be so moderate in its terms for the northern German states who had supported Austria in the war. Hanover, Hesse-Cassel, Nassau, and the Free City of Frankfurt were annexed to the Prussian Crown,[63] their monarchs were deposed, and they ceased to exist as independent actors in the international arena. Saxony, which had also favored Austria, was spared this fate only by vociferous Austrian opposition, although it was required under the terms of the peace to enter the new confederation that would be formed under the leadership of Prussia.

National Identity as a Constraint for Statesmen: The Second Empire's Failure to Balance

Quite contrary to Bismarck's expectations, his subordinate, Goltz, had induced Napoleon III to accept this annexation of vast tracts of northern Germany, along with its three to four million inhabitants, into the Prussian state. The fact that Napoleon did not oppose this annexation, although it created a much more powerful, and therefore more dangerous, German state on his western border, is also quite contrary to the expectations of realist balance of power theories of international relations, quite irrespective of whether they are of the classical realist or the neorealist variant.[64]

The neorealist variant argues that a state can balance internally, by an arms race, as easily as externally, by alliance formation. Waltz has argued that "[b]alance-of-power politics prevail wherever two, and only two, requirements are met: that the order be anarchic and that it be populated by units wishing to survive."[65] Waltz constructs this argument in order to argue that bipolar superpower competition in the twentieth century was not inconsistent with the classical realist notion of the balance of power as an explanation of state behavior. Certainly the notion should have therefore been just as applicable in the late nineteenth century, in a clearly multipolar European system which featured, at a minimum, Austria, Britain, France, Prussia, and Russia as Great Powers. Clearly any variant of balance of power theory would argue that it was explicitly inimical to French state interests to sit idly by and watch large tracts of Central Europe and up to four million people, and their goods and wealth, become annexed to an already powerful Prussian neighbor to the East. Yet this is precisely what Napoleon III did, however much hand-wringing might have accompanied his inactivity. How might this behavior be explained?

The major component of the explanation appears to lie in the manner in which Napoleon III's regime had been legitimated. Throughout his reign Napoleon had consistently posed as the defender of "national self determination" and had attacked the Vienna system coterie of traditionally legitimated, conservative monarchs on this basis.[66] His nationalist rhetoric and campaigns had been inspired in no small measure by a store of personal conviction that the future belonged to national states and not dynastic states. Kissinger has argued that Napoleon III in fact "dreaded German unification but was sympathetic to German nationalism and dithered about solving that insoluble dilemma."[67] Moreover, a great deal of his popularity and legitimacy within France derived from his role as a symbol of the progressive future of national states. Irrespective of its acceptance of a Second Empire, France still regarded itself to be one of these. France may have chosen an imperial form of government with the 1852 plebiscite that resulted in Napoleon's installation as Emperor, but it was a national-imperial state that had enthusiastically supported Napoleon's nationalist campaigns throughout the continental periphery in the intervening years between the proclamation of the Second Empire in 1852 and the Austrian debacle at Sadowa in 1866. A major difficulty of the Emperor Napoleon III, was that over the years he had been "driven to dependence on public opinion, and his policy fluctuated with his assessment of what was needed to sustain his [domestic] popularity."[68]

Napoleon's seeming inability to play the balance-of-power game when it would bring his policy into conflict with the principle of nationality—which had served so admirably to legitimate his regime—indicates that his decisionmaking procedures could not be conducted with the insularity of more traditionally legitimated statesmen. Just as he had been unable to abandon the papacy for fear of inflaming domestic Catholic opinion, neither could he oppose the operation of the principle of nationality in Central Europe without inflaming radical domestic nationalist opinion. To oppose the principle of nationality, which had long served to legitimate his foreign policy, and in some sense his domestic rule, would simultaneously risk exposing himself as an aspiring traditional autocrat. A Second Empire which represented and glorified the French nation was popular when successful and at least tolerated when not. A Second Empire which represented the Bonaparte family and dynasty, and nothing else, would be unpopular even when successful and deposed when not. The legitimating principles of the Second Empire were the those of nationality and the belief that the imperial institutional form of collective action was best suited to glorify the French nation and thus manifest the agency of the French nation abroad.

Bismarck was, of course, not immune to the pressure of domestic opinion in the formulation and conduct of his policy, but he had several crucial advantages over Napoleon. First, Bismarck served a Prussian monarch whose legitimacy to rule in that capacity was unquestioned by the broad mass of Prussian society. The only elements of Prussian society that conceivably questioned the legitimacy of Wilhelm's reign were the radical liberals and socialists. Both of these elements were marginalized fringe groups in the context of the prevailing Prussian political discourse of the 1860s. Second, Wilhelm's legitimacy was enhanced by his emergence as a rallying point for pan-German nationalist sentiment. Bismarck's skillful maneuvers in the Diet of the German Confederation had created the illusion of a liberalizing, German-nationalist Prussian monarchy.

The illusion was enhanced by a number of institutional facts.[69] One of these had emerged with the failure of the decisions of the Frankfurt Parliament to be implemented by the Prussian Crown. Pan-German nationalist sentiment could only realize its ambitions to become institutionalized in a German nation by attaching itself to, or becoming adopted by, an existing German prince or state to acquire an institutional form. The Hapsburg Austrian state was both unsuitable for this purpose by virtue of its polyglot demography, and disinclined to serve this role by virtue of the dynastic, Hapsburg conception of Austrian state interests. Thus Bismarck could play the nationality card to his domestic audience, and to a broader Central European audience, as a German nationalist leader. He could annex the defeated German powers, which had sided with Austria in the Austro-Prussian War, into a *Norddeutscher Bund*, as part and parcel of a legitimate irredentist claim[70] to gather up German-speaking lands of Central Europe into a greater German Reich.

In order to oppose this move, Napoleon would have been required to repudiate the legitimating principle of his own regime and its historical foreign policy in its entirety. As Kissinger has recently argued, Napoleon effectively had two options. First, he could adhere to the tried and true strategy of Richelieu and strive to keep Central Europe fragmented. Adopting this policy would, however, have cost him his credentials as a nationalist with all the attendant potential consequences that I have just outlined above. Otherwise, he could strive for the leadership of Europe by placing himself and his Empire at the head of a nationalist crusade, as had his uncle before him.[71] Instead, "[u]nfortunately for France, Napoleon pursued both strategies simultaneously."[72]

It is also likely the case that Napoleon was badly outmaneuvered by Bismarck, who had earlier pandered to Napoleon's nationalist and revolutionary penchants, as well as to his avarice, by "encouraging the emperor's appetite for territorial expansion on the Rhine [at the expense of Luxembourg and Belgium] without committing himself on how this appetite might be satisfied."[73] It also appears that Napoleon had deluded himself into believing that Austria would defeat Prussia in the conflict without difficulty, but curiously "he [Napoleon] never seemed to have asked himself why Bismarck was so determined on war if Prussia was so likely to be defeated."[74] Napoleon at this time and from this time on, was seriously ill with a large stone in his bladder, and this infirmity can not have failed to contribute to his irresolution.[75] His health alone provided him with significant impediments to rational decisionmaking. He had refused, in this state, to accede to the pleas of Metternich[76]—and of his Empress, Eugenie—that he mobilize at least a part of his armed forces, as a warning to Prussia.[77] He was convinced that the war would be a long one, and that he could intervene if he chose so.[78] Additionally, "Bismarck threw Napoleon the sop of letting him mediate the peace,"[79] though this attempt at intervention also failed and was ultimately exercised only after Austria had been defeated.

Napoleon believed that he could not ask for anything for France so long as he was in the process of mediating the Austro-Prussian peace, but when this task was completed he sent Benedetti to Bismarck on July 23 to ascertain Bismarck's attitude to a French proposal of a secret convention between France and Prussia that would award France with its 1814 frontiers, and Luxembourg as well.[80] It would appear, then, that Napoleon was suffering from the illusion—which Bismarck had taken no small pains to encourage—that he had achieved an understanding with Prussia, based on the principle of nationality. Prussia would be allowed to gather up German states in Central Europe, and would in return wink at French annexation of Belgium and Luxembourg. Yet it is a tribute to the growing strength of national sentiment in what was soon to become Germany that Bismarck found it completely impossible to yield Luxembourg to France.[81] Nevertheless, we should not delude ourselves that this was Napoleon's intent before the Austro-Prussian war began. This does not salvage either classical or neorealist understandings of the balance of power. Napoleon did not intend to balance Prussian gains in Central Europe with acquisitions of the significant French-speaking territories that lay between France's northeastern frontier and the Rhine. At least he did not intend to do so before the Austrian defeat at Sadowa.

Kissinger argues persuasively that Napoleon had not expected Austria to be defeated, let alone so soundly and quickly defeated. Prior to the onset of the war Napoleon had not seriously entertained Prussian allusions to their support of French acquisitions in Belgium or in Luxembourg, which Britain would have been opposed in any case. But "since he expected Prussia to lose; his moves were designed more to keep Prussia on its course to war than to bargain for benefits . . . Prussia was expected to offer France compensation in the West for extrication from its defeat."[82] But this did not occur; rather the converse. In his shock at this outcome, Napoleon attempted to retrieve the situation by calling a European congress. While his call was ignored, Bismarck allowed him to mediate the peace in bilateral negotiations between the belligerent parties. Napoleon faintly hoped to intervene sufficiently with his mediation efforts to avoid the "complete reversal of the European balance of power"[83] that was developing from the results of the war. Bismarck, however, had procrastinated in these "diplomatic efforts" to terminate hostilities, while simultaneously hinting broadly that Napoleon should make an ultimatum to the Belgian King that Belgian integration into the Second Empire would be essential to offset Prussian political and territorial gains as a result of the Austrian war.[84]

Austria's rapid military collapse, coupled with Bismarck's hints that France could be compensated for its neutrality in a manner consistent with French devotion to the principle of nationality, especially in Belgium, appears to have secured that neutrality. Upon the attainment of a peace, however, Bismarck had lost interest in the question of French irredentist interests in Belgium and Luxembourg. Napoleon pursued this issue in order to obtain compensations subsequent to the Prussian territorial gains and the humiliation of Austria. French balancing was, after all, quite tardy. It was a forlorn hope, *ex post facto* of the Prussian *fait accompli*. The French failure to balance Prussian aggrandizement prior to the Prussian victory had effectively and permanently ended the French hegemony in Central and Western Europe that France had enjoyed since the reign of Louis XIV.

Note that the difficulties Louis Napoleon experienced in proceeding diplomatically around the machinations of Bismarck do not simply demonstrate that he was outmaneuvered by superior statesmanship or superior intelligence on the part of Bismarck, irrespective of whether we believe that Bismarck might have had the upper hand in each. These difficulties more nearly reflect the problems that Louis Napoleon, as head of a regime that was a hybrid variant of the territorial-sovereign and national-sovereign institutional forms, experienced in operating within a mixed system of territorial-sovereign and national-sovereign principles, norms, and rules. The mixed system game was difficult to play. Its rules were unclear. *Territorial-sovereign norms such as territorial compensations for diplomatic favors co-existed with secessionist challenges and irridentist claims based upon ethnicity, language, or culture.* Napoleon III was expected to play the gentlemen's game, as honest broker to a brother monarch, to gain legitimacy in the eyes of dynasts. Bismarck, playing his own game, was able to ruthlessly exploit Louis Napoleon's insecurity in this regard, and change the rules at will, marching Napoleon toward ever receding goal posts.

It was, in my own view, precisely the hybrid character of the French regime, the fact that it was simultaneously an imperial, or pseudo-monarchical institutional form of collective action, and legitimated by the principle of nationality, and in full possession of a national collective identity, that rendered it so difficult for Napoleon III to successfully balance Prussian aggrandizement in Central Europe. Napoleon was an emperor so long as he and his Empire served to embody French national aspirations. The Second Empire provided an institutional form of collective action that provided a serviceable vehicle for the expression and agency of French national collective identity so long as Napoleon's goals were at a unity with the will of French national aspirations. French national aspirations willed the demise of the Vienna system which had been constructed to shackle the French people, and all the peoples of Europe, to a "legitimate" scion of the *ancien regime*. This system constituted, by design, the uncompromising nullification of the idea of the nation. Napoleon's Second Empire served, for a time, as an institutional form for the collective action of the French nation because its goals were indeed at a unity with the will of the nation.

> Napoleon's ultimate goal was to abrogate the territorial clauses of the Vienna settlement and to alter the state system on which it had been based. But he never understood that achieving his goal would also result in a unified Germany, which would forever end French aspirations to dominate Central Europe.[85]

That Napoleon's attainment of his goal of demolishing the Vienna system did entail these consequences meant that the French failure to balance the Prussian creation of the *Norddeutscher Bund* spelled the beginning of the end for the Second Empire. The Prussian aggrandizement resulting from the defeat of Austria created not only an obstacle to the advancement of specifically French national aspirations, but also an aggressive and expansive Prussian power that could muster an army four times the size of that of France.[86] By failing to "balance" this power, the Second Empire had acceded to the forging of the tool of its own destruction, as we shall briefly see.

The Franco-Prussian War and the Birth of the German Nation

Between the collapse of Napoleon's hope that he would be compensated by Prussia for its territorial gains in the northern German states, and the impending confrontation with Prussia, it had become clear that the pursuit of glory abroad under the banner of nationalism, or any other banner, would not be adequate to ensure that Napoleon could pass his Empire on to his son, Louis. The Second Empire's foreign policy had collapsed in disaster, left France friendless throughout Europe, and created an extremely powerful and aggressive neighbor to the east. Napoleon's domestic opposition included an assortment of Legitimists who sought a restoration of the Bourbons, Orleanists who were bourgeois constitutional monarchists—strong within intellectual and financial cells—and Republicans who found their strength among the teeming industrialized masses. As his opposition grew and strengthened, Napoleon found it impossible to govern as he had when the Second Empire had been declared. Then he had muzzled the press, emasculated the *corps légeslatif*, and held elections only to gauge public opinion. But the elections of 1869 had witnessed a precipitous decline in the vote for the government candidates and a half million vote rise for the Republicans, which was troubling as the Republican vote clearly constituted a vote against, not just the government, but the Empire as well.[87]

Napoleon determined to roll the dice and to venture upon maintaining the Empire by subordinating his power to that of a liberal constitution, which he had determined to grant to the French nation. Thus the "liberal empire" emerged as a rather severe consequence of the noninsularity of elite decisionmaking associated with the national-sovereign era. "Only by lifting the crown above party political strife would the Emperor be able to pass it on to his son."[88] Napoleon called to his side the liberal parliamentarian, Ollivier, to form a government, which took office on January 2, 1870. Napoleon and Ollivier then sat down to draft the constitution of the "Liberal Empire" and the reforms were put to a plebiscite vote. The reforms provided the desired effect. Seven and a half million votes were cast in favor of the Liberal Empire and only the smallest fraction of that opposed the measure.

The vote might have appeared to all but the most cynical to have assured the continuation of the Bonaparte dynasty. Louis Napoleon himself knew better. The most troubling aspect of the vote for him had been the fact that about 50,000 of his 350,000 man army had voted against the Liberal Empire.[89] It is difficult to reconstruct their motivations for this vote. It might have been simple soldierly self-protection. They might have voted explicitly against a "liberal" empire where the *corps légeslatif* would control the purse strings, rather than their emperor, with potential negative consequences for their incomes and provisions. Napoleon took is as an indication that the army had little confidence in him personally.

Napoleon had been badly shaken by the events attending the Austrian military collapse at Sadowa. According to Allan Mitchell, he introduced measures to reform the French army as early as September 1866. The reforms would vastly enhance the French state's power to conscript, and abolish or at least dramatically restrict the leaky lottery system which had in practice permitted mass draft evasion. These proposed reforms found very little domestic support. As Mitchell relates:

> Napoleon III may have been greatly stirred by Sadowa, but his people, it would appear, remained exceeding temperate in their enthusiasm for things military. Nor were the propertied classes eager to forgo the convenient procedure of "exoneration," in force since 1855, which allowed them to purchase an exemption from the draft in case one of their sons unfortunately drew a *mauvais numéro*.[90]

The Prussian system of recruitment and popular conscription appears to have been given much credit for the efficiency of the Prussian forces, in spite of the evidence we have from Eric Eyck, presented earlier, that Wilhelm and Roon had actually taken pains to limit the popularly conscripted *Landwehr* as a constituent element of the Prussian army. Prussia's mobilization procedures had provided rapid and orderly transportation of Prussian forces to the front as well, whereas French campaigns in Italy and the Crimea had demonstrated French deficiencies in both discipline and organization. Napoleon had pushed for universal conscription in order to acquire numeric parity with the forces the King of Prussia had at his command, if not for the advantages (which Wilhelm appears to have seen as a threat as much as a tool) of a highly motivated citizen army.

Unfortunately, Napoleon had been required to retain his crown and to extend the life of the Second Empire by transforming it into a Liberal Empire. The constitutional limits on his power that had taken effect with the plebescitory accession of the Liberal Empire now forced him to seek a dramatic increase in the size and capabilities of his armed forces, which were seen by the populace as a fearful tool of the Crown, when he was for the first time required to seek parliamentary approval of the budget for these forces. The French electorate feared that a more powerful French army might be employed in the cause of their oppression, or at best that it would be employed in more of the disastrous campaigns abroad that had done so much during the life of the Second Empire to isolate France so completely on the diplomatic front.[91] As Daniel Deudney has recently observed, fear of a standing army is a major impetus for insisting upon constitutional separations of authority over those forces.[92] In this case, while Napoleon retained command of them as well as the power to commit them, the *corps légeslatif* retained the power to fund them, or not. This power was soon exercised to disastrous effect for the readiness of French forces to meet their Prussian counterpart.

Napoleon had pleaded for a universal conscription arrangement that would dispense with the "exhonorations" which had ensured that the rank and file were populated with impoverished replacements for the scion of the French bourgeoisie, and even agreed to a reduction in the term of service as an inducement to grant his measure. In this way he hoped to gather into his army an additional 500,000 men to move quickly toward his goal of the 1,000,000 men that he believed would be required to meet the Prussians and their allies in any future hostilities. Even his watered-down proposals were, however, deemed "too drastic" by the increasingly self-confident *corps légeslatif*. The French parliament feared that the expense would divert too many funds away from its own agenda of domestic social reforms, feared that the formation of such a large force would invite attack, and feared that even if Napoleon would not use it against them in the future, national life would be too severely militarized at the expense of the domestic economy. It can be fairly argued that Napoleon had in the past given the French people sufficient cause to fear the growth of "his" army. As Michael Howard writes of Napoleon's policy of civil-military relations prior to the transformation of the Second Empire into the Liberal Empire:

> it [the army] remained apart from the rest of the nation, and Napoleon III deliberately kept it so, as a Praetorian Guard. "The ideal constitution," declared General Trochu, the most zealous of all military reformers, "is that which creates an army whose instincts, beliefs and habits make up a corporation distinct from the rest of the population."[93]

Thus the *corps légeslatif* had voted only 5 million of the 14 million francs that Napoleon had requested to effect the military reform.[94] To make matters worse, it cut the military budget by a further 13 million francs early in 1870,[95] just months before the Second Empire's fatal confrontation with what amounted to the combined strength of the German-speaking states of Central Europe.

In the arena of weapons modernization Napoleon had similar difficulties. After much effort he had managed to acquired a million breach-loading rifles to compete with the Prussian "needle gun," but he fell far short of obtaining a million troops to man them. The Prussians had corrected their deficit in the quality of their artillery pieces since their experience with the Austrian guns and had contracted with Krupp for new, steel, breech-loading cannon. Certain that the *corps légeslatif* would not fund modernization of his artillery, Napoleon had attempted to fund breach-loading artillery for his army from his personal funds, but the war with Prussia broke upon a French army still equipped with the old muzzle-loading artillery.[96] As the North German Confederation already had more than a million men under arms, the sum of French military reform efforts between 1866 and 1870 can be seen to have been "woefully inadequate."[97]

Moreover, at precisely this time, French domestic politics saw a resurgence in republican sentiment. The *corps légeslatif* had begun a program of long overdue domestic reforms, however modest or inadequate, designed to upgrade the economic condition of the laboring classes, and Napoleon's repeated demands for funds for military reforms could only have been seen by the working classes as insensitive to and obstructive of this purpose. The bourgeoisie had been enriched during the Second Empire, but the working classes had not. More than half of the population of Paris was living in poverty in 1870.[98] Their brief experience with the political institutions of the Liberal Empire provided them with a renewed interest in political participation, and the hope that activism and radicalism might now bring them tangible gains. The constitution of the Liberal Empire had decidedly extended the franchise of the bourgeoisie, great and small. Now even the lower economic orders had begun to strongly agitate for a stake in the nation. The voice of the *corps légeslatif* had now, again, developed into a clear voice of the will of the French nation, quite distinct from the voice of the French Emperor. In inducing Napoleon III to grant a liberal constitution in order to maintain his crown, France had again asserted its national-sovereign collective identity, however shabbily it might have been dressed (as Marx had complained) in the ragged cloak of bourgeois commercial interest.[99]

Into the glowing embers of this newly heated French domestic political environment Bismarck was to pour the gasoline of a Hohenzollern Candidature for the newly vacant Spanish throne. Eyck argues that it had been clear to Bismarck by the spring of 1870 that the southern German states were much less disposed to join the North German Confederation than they had been immediately after Sadowa, four years earlier.[100] He had worked quietly behind the scenes after an 1868 revolution had left the Spanish throne vacant, and spent £50,000, attempting to advance the candidacy of Prince Leopold, a Hohenzollern from the Catholic branch of that royal family, in spite of the strong opposition to the candidature by his sovereign, Wilhelm.

Wilhelm had opposed the candidature precisely because he had known that it would inflame French public opinion. Eyck argues that Bismarck must have known that the candidature would lead to war if pressed, as the French would see it as a provocation. Napoleon III would fear for his dynasty if he did not oppose it, and in any case "the candidature of a prince belonging to a ruling dynasty was in opposition to the principle of international practice [what Kratochwil has called, in this context, a 'tacit rule,' a 'sphere of abstention,' of the international system][101] which had evolved clearly in the nineteenth century."[102] But Bismarck, fearing that the Spanish Crown would be offered to one of the southern German princes, and thus demolish his efforts to bring these lands under Prussian rule, convinced Leopold to advance his candidature, and Wilhelm to reluctantly agree. The news of Leopold's move reached France on July 3, 1870. It was "received as a calculated slap in the face for France by Prussia. *It set France aflame.*"[103]

We can see very clearly, in the events that followed, the very pronounced transformation in the notion of state interests that national-sovereign identity produces relative to the territorial-sovereign identity of seventeenth- and eighteenth-century states. We saw in chapter 4 that the territorial-sovereign dynast and absolute monarch, Louis XIV, could not, in a fit of rage, be dissuaded from issuing orders that the port of Genoa be bombarded from a French naval squadron for refusing to offer the French ships the first salute. Now, late in the nineteenth century, we find the French Emperor, Napoleon III, working quietly behind the scenes to induce Leopold to withdraw his candidature while the *corps légeslatif*, with the enthusiastic assistance of the hot-headed Foreign Minister, Gramont, was issuing shrill and public demands to the Prussian government to back down. Aronson describes Napoleon as a "voice of sanity in a wilderness of passion . . . [while among the parliament and public] . . . [y]ears of pent-up resentment against Prussia now burst forth."[104] Napoleon's efforts bore fruit and Leopold withdrew his candidature, to the great pleasure and relief of both Napoleon and Wilhelm. The news of Leopold's sacrifice reached Paris on July 12, but as Aronson suggests, rather understating the case, "France, by now, was in no mood for peace."[105]

Ollivier, as leader of Napoleon's government, was sent to speak in the parliament to attempt to calm the deputies but:

> The truth was that instead of being relieved at the withdrawal of the candidature, a great many Frenchmen were disappointed. They had been left with a feeling of anticlimax, of having been cheated of their just revenge. . . . The cry now went up that a mere withdrawal of the candidature was not enough: Prussia, who had tried to humiliate France, must herself be humiliated. She must be forced to give a guarantee that the candidature of Prince Leopold would never again be raised. Only then would the "honor of France" be satisfied. The idea of *garanties* was quickly taken up by the deputies, the Press and the crowd. Public opinion, dangerously inflamed, would be content with nothing less.[106]

This demand, of course, constituted both the greatest madness and the greatest idiocy. But that did not prevent Gramont from issuing instructions to Benedetti, in Berlin, to approach Wilhelm to secure a guarantee that the candidature of Leopold would never again be raised. Benedetti did not wait for his appointment, but approached Wilhelm during his walk, at Ems. In response to Benedetti's demand Wilhelm politely but firmly informed Benedetti that he could not commit himself further than he had done in endorsing Leopold's withdrawal. When Benedetti had persisted, Wilhelm had politely raised his hat in salute and walked on. He sent a telegram to Bismarck that evening describing the exchange. Bismarck edited the telegram, and released the product to the press.[107] Aronson provides us with a fascinating passage describing the ruse:

> Bismarck was at dinner with Moltke and Roon when the telegram arrived. He at once recognized its potential. By a little sharpening of the already sharp tone, it could be made to seem positively insulting. It would provide him with exactly that "red rag to the Gallic bull" for

> which he was searching. By some slight but skillful editing, the King's treatment of Benedetti was made to appear distinctly high-handed. That the French Ambassador had suffered a polite but firm rebuff there could be no doubt whatsoever. The editing completed the telegram . . . was released to the Press. Copies of it were also sent to all Prussian representatives abroad.[108]

The doctored contents of the "Ems telegram" hit the French newspapers on July 14, Bastille Day in France. The document had the effect which Bismarck had desired. The French went positively mad. On the following day Gramont and Ollivier asked the Senate and the *corps légeslatif*, respectively, to vote the necessary war credits, which was done. War was now certain, and Aronson's descriptions of the reaction in Paris provide a contrast with the indifference of the European masses of previous centuries to the wars of their monarchs:

> The certainty of war was greeted with a roar of approval by the Paris crowd. For a week the city was in a state of delirium. To one observer it seemed as if the capital had been transformed into a vast lunatic asylum whose keepers had gone on a holiday. . . . The population could hardly wait for nightfall . . . to start their illuminations . . . [and cries of] . . . 'A *bas la Prusse*' . . . [and] . . . 'A *Berlin!*'[109]

They bellowed patriotic songs at the top of their lungs all night long, every night. A hysteria of patriotic unity had gripped the city.

> "The really fine thing," declared one naive witness, "is that there are no longer any party distinctions in Paris: there are neither Republicans nor Bonapartists: at the moment there are only Frenchmen." . . . in the Place de la Concorde there were more than three thousand people, who danced around the column crying "*Vive l'Empereur*!" . . . Anyone who mentioned caution was simply shouted down.[110]

Nor does nationalist fervor appear to have been entirely lacking in particularly the Prussian people. Aronson describes the Prussian Public's reaction as "less frenzied than the French . . . [but] . . . no less enthusiastic."[111] He recounts how huge crowds of people had gathered outside *Neues Palais* at Potsdam, compelling Wilhelm to show himself time and again on the balcony to acknowledge their approval. The Prussian people felt they were "embarking on a just, indeed, almost a holy war."[112] They felt certain that God was on their side and sang Lutheran hymns and *Die Wacht an Rhein* in the streets. Michael Howard's history similarly suggests that:

> The Germans greeted the coming of the war less with the excited enthusiasm displayed by the people of Paris than with a deep sense of earnestness and moral purpose. It seemed to them not merely a national but a profoundly just war, and they called with every confidence upon the God of Battles to defend their cause. Lutheran hymns mingled with patriotic songs in the celebrations. . . . Throughout North Germany swept a flame of impassioned patriotism fed by and reflected in the press. In the South enthusiasm was, as one might expect, somewhat less . . . [but] . . . the southern States had no excuse for evading their treaty obligations, even if they had wished to do anything of the sort.[113]

By September 3, when the French had been forced to capitulate at Sedan, and Napoleon had been packed off to Wilhelmshöhe as Wilhelm's prisoner, the southern German people's and especially their troops expressed as much enthusiasm for the war as had the Prussians. In spite of the nationalist fervor demonstrated by the French people and troops on July 15, Napoleon had been reduced to asking Wilhelm that he be allowed to go into captivity by way of Belgium to avoid passing through the ranks of his defeated army and potentially suffering their insults. His Empress and heir were on the run the next day and ultimately forced to seek shelter from the angry Parisian mobs in the Paris home of her American dentist.[114]

Napoleon's entire very long path to the disaster of Sedan had been lit by his need for the glow of public approval and fear that his new dynasty should not survive without it. Napoleon had stood without a single European ally, as Bismarck's machination brought him war in 1870, precisely because he had played to nationalist sentiment in France for three decades with the nationalist foreign adventures that had systematically alienated the courts of Europe. He had gone to war with Prussia realizing full well that France was utterly unprepared, because inflamed French nationalist sentiment had demanded it.

Further he had taken personal command of the French forces that had rushed eastward to meet the Prussians a Saarbrücken and Metz "despite the fact that he had only the slightest grasp of military strategy, that he was almost too ill to stand, that he was pessimistic, vacillating and exhausted" because French nationalist opinion demanded that he, as a Bonaparte, would obviously lead the French forces and restore French honor.[115] He had squandered the little time that fate had provided him to organize the disorganized military mess that he had found upon his arrival at the front with a strategically meaningless "victory" at Saarbrücken, precisely because he had feared that his apparent inactivity would not play well back in Paris.[116] When the Prussian forces had moved to cut off the Army of Châlons from its escape route to the west, Napoleon had felt that he could not retreat toward Paris with his army, which had been his only sound strategic course of action and would have dangerously stressed the German lines of communication as well, precisely because Eugenie, fearing the reaction of the Parisian mobs, had advised him it would have been a domestically disastrous move.[117] As a result of his failure to order this strategic retreat, Napoleon found himself and his army cut off and caught in the "mousetrap of Sedan," surrounded by Prussian artillery which had been ensconced on the high ground above him, and which rained down shells upon his position and troops until he had ordered the white flag of surrender to be raised.[118] The war was ineffectively continued for a time after the deposition and exile of "third Napoleon," but these events are of no consequence whatever to the purpose of the present analytic narrative.

Bismarck had been quite anxious to conclude a peace as quickly as possible after the French defeat at Sedan. Southern and northern German troops had now been blooded together and had together quite quickly, soundly, and gloriously defeated mighty France.

> Not only did he [Bismarck] want a harsh peace but he wanted a quick one. He was not in favor of a prolonged war. As far as he was concerned the campaign had achieved what he had planned it should: the bringing together of all the German States [less Austria] to fight against a common enemy. Once peace was concluded, the formal unification of Germany would not be long in following.[119]

Nor was it long in following. Sensing the popular longing for unification in the wake of Sedan, the monarchs of Württemberg, Baden, and Hesse had all expressed their willingness to sign a treaty of union with the North German Confederation by November 11 of that year. Bismarck had induced Bavaria to consent to the same by making some concessions to "Bavarian particularism" and had effectively bribed Louis II of Bavaria, who was badly in debt, to sign on in exchange for an annual sum of money.[120] In return for this sum, Louis had signed a letter prepared by Bismarck inviting Wilhelm as the King of Prussia to become a German Emperor. The Reichstag had done the same. Bismarck had been required to work hard to ensure that the events of 1849 would not be repeated and that Wilhelm would not also haughtily refuse the Crown simply because it had been offered to him by the common German people. Wilhelm accepted the Crown on the basis that it had been offered to him by the unanimous consent of the princes of Europe, and it was bestowed on him in Versailles, in the Hall of Mirrors, the symbolic holy ground of the defeated French adversary, on January 18, 1871.[121]

German national collective identity had, in Bismarck's eyes, been fleshed out with the institutional form that most suited it, and this was the imperial form. In my own view, German national collective identity could have never developed into its modern form, something very close to the form that it had developed by 1871, without the events following the Revolution of 1848. Without the experience of participatory politics, however limited that franchise might have been, that had permitted the German people within their various states to feel some stake in the policies of the governments of their monarchs, their "German" collective identity would likely have been forever subordinated to particularistic political identities developed around their particularistic relationships with their princes. Without the maintenance of that franchise and its creeping extension to ensure the participation of the people in the society and state consistent with the requirements of rampant capitalism, the people would likely have never been sufficiently politically aware for their budding self-identification as "Germans" to contain the intersubjective meanings that it did for them by this date. And, of course, certainly without their shared experience of victory[122] as Germans over a powerful French foe which had historically oriented its policy toward ensuring their continued political disunity, German national collective identity could never have crystallized (to borrow from the lexicon of Michael Mann) with the potency that it clearly did at this time.

Yet German institutional history had been, for a thousand reasons—many of these dating back to the Reformation period—both particularistic and distinctly feudal. The strength of the feudal residue in German Central Europe by 1871 was such that it would be difficult to envision German national collective identity adopting an different institutional form with which to manifest its agency to the world than that of the long lost German Empire. Germany now had its Second Reich, and Bismarck correctly observed that it suited Germany in 1871 in a fashion that would not at all suit German national collective identity today. Bismarck had written, immediately upon the promulgation of the Second Reich:

> For German patriotism to be active and effective, needs as a rule to be dependent upon a dynasty. Independent of a dynasty, it rarely comes to a rising point. . . . The German's love of the fatherland has need of a prince on whom he can concentrate his attachment. Suppose that all the German dynasties were suddenly deposed, there would then be no likelihood of German national sentiment sufficient to hold all the Germans together amid the friction of European politics.[123]

Note the manner in which this passage invokes the themes that I advanced in the theoretical development of the causal and constitutive linkages between co-constituted individual and collective identities, the legitimating principles of domestic and global social orders, and the derivative institutional forms of collective action. Durkheim's emotive identification with the "fatherland," his "organic solidarity of dissimilar individuals" is depicted here. Similarly the Habermassian, Kratochwillian, Weberian formulations of a theoretical construct oriented toward the individual's valuation of "duty" to legitimate social authority is illustrated in Bismarck's assertion of the dependence of German patriotism upon a prince. Bismarck understood intuitively that the institutional form of collective action suitable to manifest pan-German nationalism was a consequence of the particularities of co-constituted individual and pan-German national collective identity.

The historical particularities of German history had, then, ultimately proven to present a series of institutional facts that guided German national collective identity into an institutional form that is entirely consistent with our knowledge of the functioning of such facts. They provided a context in which the new game of German national-state formation took on concrete meaning.[124]

Conclusions and Theoretical Reprise

This chapter has analyzed the consequences of the development of national collective identity for the conduct of national-state security policy in the nineteenth century in the context of three critical areas of state conduct, in which realist and neorealist theory predict state security behavior that is at variance with the observed behavior of nation-states.

Structural realism argues that the condition of international anarchy imposes a requirement on each state to emulate strategically successful behavior or perish at the hands of a more powerful and successful rival. I have critiqued an extension of this structural realist argument that suggests that the rise of the mass-mobilization army was an effect of this socialization mechanism on nineteenth-century European states, and was instituted to replicate successful French strategic behavior. While the author of that argument quite responsibly limits his claims and addresses evidence that conservative European dynasts such as the Prussian King approached this innovation cautiously within their own borders, I have presented significant evidence that the Prussian monarchy and army elites were not merely cautious, but actually consciously and actively opposed efforts to expand the popular and participatory nature of Prussia's armed forces. They did so out of conviction that such forces were inimical to the legitimating principles of dynastic, territorial-sovereign domestic social order, which they represented. Prussia's territorial-sovereign collective identity did not easily accommodate the institutional structures legitimated by an emerging German national-sovereign collective identity. The Prussian elites actually resisted, to a remarkable extent, expansion of the mass mobilization army, quite irrespective of their perceptions of its benefits in enhancing the motivation and performance of the soldiery.

Both classical realism and structural neorealism predict that states will balance the attempts of powerful neighbors and adversaries to expand their territory. Yet, as has emerged in my analysis, Napoleon III was unable to take action to frustrate Bismarck's projects to unify the German states, even though French ascendancy over continental affairs was seriously endangered by the creation of the *Norddeutscher Bund* at the close of the Austro-Prussian

War. Napoleon allowed himself to be goaded by Bismarck, and the French nationalist press, into initiating a war against Prussia for which he clearly believed France to be unprepared. France fought Prussia, in 1870, for no purpose whatever consistent with an instrumentally rational definition of the interests of the French state. I have explored the impact of French domestic nationalist agitation in the origins of the Franco-Prussian War. I have demonstrated how the legitimacy of Napoleon III's reign was predicated on his policy of upholding the principle of nationality in French policy toward the Italian Peninsula, the German states of central Europe, and the Polish reaction against its partition by Russia and Prussia. I have argued that by the time Bismarck's policy of unification came to fruition, the policy of the "liberal Empire" of France was wholly at the service of the popular French conception of the principle of nationality.

In light of these observations, I argue that state interests may not be designated by the theorist with an assumption that they are static or exogenously given. The interests of societies, whatever institutional form of collective action they employ to express these interests, is demonstrated to be influenced by the self-perceptions of the society they represent. I argue that interests are a function of historically contingent societal collective identity. The structure of state interests of the Second Empire of Napoleon III, and that of Bismarck's Prussia emerge as distinctly different conceptions, derived from distinctly different notions of the nature of sovereign identity. The regime of Napoleon III, legitimated as it was by Napoleon's anti-dynastic support for the principle of nationality, led him to take decisions that were not formally rational or consistent with the rational instrumental logic that Bismarck was able to apply as Chancellor of a traditionally legitimated Prussia. Significantly Bismarck, though a confirmed monarchist, was able to employ French and pan-German national sentiment as a tool to obtain his rational-instrumental objectives. Thus a major consequence of the development of national collective identity is that it could be employed as a tool or alternately suffered as a constraint for statesmen. Variations in the structure of state identities and interests, predicated on the legitimating principles of a given regime, determined whether or not the "principle of nationality" (later followed by national-self-determination) were a constraint or a tool for statesmen who might like to pursue rational instrumental policies. Domestic nationalist ferment sometimes transforms the structure of state interests, impelling statesmen to pursue formally irrational policies. I argue that this is precisely what occurred to induce Louis Napoleon to launch the Franco-

Prussian War, which resulted in the demise of his Second Empire and in the birth of the Second German Reich.

It was precisely the hybrid nature of the "liberal Empire"; that it served neither as an appropriate institutional form of collective action to manifest monarchical territorial-sovereignty nor French popular and national sovereignty, which doomed it to extinction at the first transnational difficulty. The symbolism of earlier French national glory, latent within the imperial office and the name of Bonaparte, was cast aside like a tarnished ornament when delegitimated by defeat. Louis Napoleon's legitimation crisis came into being and passed away in a day, at Sedan. The imperial institutional form of collective action could no longer manifest French national collective identity. But it suited as a wholly appropriate institutional form to manifest the national collective identity of the newly forged Pan-German nation.

8 National Sovereignty and the New Imperialism: The Global Transmission of Bourgeois-National Identity and Culture

The truth was that only far from home could a citizen of England, Germany, or France be nothing but an Englishman or German or Frenchman. In his own country he was so entangled in economic interests or social loyalties that he felt closer to a member of his own class in a foreign country than to a man of another class in his own. Expansion gave nationalism a new lease on life and therefore as accepted as an instrument of national politics. . . . The alliance between capital and mob is to be found at the genesis of every consistently imperial policy. In some countries, particularly in Great Britain, this new alliance between the much-too-rich and the much-too-poor was and remained confined to overseas possessions.

—Hannah Arendt

. . . the Bwana shone so brightly in his uniform that we could not look upon him.

—Kapijimpanga (Solwezian Chief)

In one sense, imperialism dramatized the triumph of these [bourgeois] classes and the societies created in their image as nothing else could possibly have done.

—E.J. Hobsbawm

Take up the White Man's Burden, Send forth the best ye breed
Go bind your sons to exile, To serve your captives' need;
To wait in heavy harness, On fluttered fold and wild
Your new-caught, sullen peoples, Half-devil and half-child.

—Rudyard Kipling, 1899

From the period beginning with the close of the Franco-Prussian War in 1871, to the onset of the First World War in 1914, European nation-states expanded into the previously peripheral regions of Asia and Africa at a rate and with a purpose unprecedented in the history of European colonialism. As Hobsbawm has noted, economic and military supremacy of the capitalist nation-states of Europe over the Asian and African hinterland had at this time been unquestioned for more than a century. Europe could have partitioned the rest of the globe among its members long before it did, given its economic, technological and military supremacy.

> but no systematic attempt to translate it into formal conquest, annexation and administration had been made between the end of the eighteenth and the last quarter of the nineteenth century. Between 1880 and 1914 it was made, and most of the world outside Europe and the Americas was formally partitioned into territories under the formal rule or informal political dominance of one or another of a handful of states: mainly Great Britain, France, Germany, Italy, the Netherlands, Belgium, the USA and Japan.[1]

What amounted to a quarter of the land surface of the globe was distributed between a few states between 1876 and 1915. Great Britain's colonial possession grew, in this period by 4 million square miles, France's by 3.5 million, Germany's by more than a million square miles. Portugal added 300,000 square miles of colonial territory, and the United States and Japan 100,000 square miles each.[2] In this chapter I first explore some existing and competing explanations of the new imperialism as a point of departure. I will then develop the new imperialism from the perspective of its radically new social purpose in the transmission of the culture and social identities of the newly nationalized states of Europe, America, and Asia. I will conclude the chapter with an argument (outlined in chapter 2) regarding how the new imperialism illustrates how the sequencing of the variables in my matrix in figure 1 may, under very specific conditions, be reversed. I will argue that changes in the collective identity of specific types of societies and states result in transformation of the international system. But these systemic transformations, conversely, result in changes in the collective identities of different, but quite specific types of societies. In essence I will argue that the national collective identities of newly nationalized western societies transformed the system, but that this agency and its effect in turn transformed the collective identities of contemporarily peripheral societies.

Explaining the New Imperialism

Explanations for the onslaught of this "new imperialism," which have been offered since its inception, have varied widely in terms of the explanatory variables put forward. Some have missed it more, and some less. Woodruff Smith has pointed out that "[m]ost contemporaries of the new imperial expansion tended to view it as a result of recent economic and diplomatic changes."[3] A number of economic and diplomatic changes had indeed occurred. The rise of the new imperialism was temporally coincident with the revival of protective tariffs as a beggar-thy-neighbor tool to mitigate the effects of the economic downturn that plagued the European and especially the British economy in the later 1870s. Yet the 1840s to the early 1870s had been an era of liberal ascendancy in Britain. British policy in this period had seen a decline in enthusiasm for colonial ventures, a denigration of the eighteenth-century political economy of mercantilism, and the reign of the Manchester liberals and free traders in British financial and trade policy.[4] The liberal free-trading and anti-imperial policies of Granville's administration were never really attacked at all in the British Parliament until 1869–70, and then at the instigation of a rather small coterie of imperialist enthusiasts, only a few of whom were well-connected in parliament.[5]

Marxist economic explanations of the new imperialism have always been prolific. Lenin had been quick to argue that the new imperialism was simply a monopoly phase of capitalism in which capitalists seeking monopoly rents were dividing up the globe among themselves and would turn on one another when this had been accomplished.[6] While there was a flight of capital from Europe in this period, there was actually very little capital investment by Europeans in Africa, nor is there much evidence that the companies which did have a financial stake in Africa were very influential with their governments.[7] A larger problem with Lenin's argument is his assertion that capitalists had "invented nationalistic and strategic elements of imperialist theory in order to hoodwink public and government opinion so as to get European governments to bear the burden of securing overseas investment."[8] As I have argued throughout this work, nationalism would not have been possible without the bourgeoisie or their capitalism, but self-conscious national collective identity was not confined to the bourgeoisie, as was most dramatically evident when the working masses, even the socialists, marched in 1914.

European decisionmakers certainly faced various economic and political pressures during this period which might have contributed to the development of imperialist policies. They were hard-pressed to deal with the short-term effects of the 1873 economic downturn in Britain. Britain for the first time faced an unfavorable balance of trade, and real competition from abroad, especially from the United States and from a newly united Germany.[9] Certainly there was political agitation at home from vested overseas economic concerns. Such men had founded the Colonial Society in Great Britain with the express intent to "combat the anti-colonial sentiments expressed by many of the leading adherents of the Manchester group of economists."[10] Certainly bankers in Britain and elsewhere expressed concern that overseas investments which they had underwritten be protected by their respective national armed forces. These concerns at this time were no doubt careful to portray given overseas investments as vital to national interests, therefore to be protected at all costs.[11]

Yet Carleton Hayes suggests quite correctly that the commercial expansion during these decades does not begin to explain the political imperialism with which the capitalist nation-states of Europe (and the United States and Japan) exploded into the periphery starting with the mid-1870s. As Hayes observed in 1941:

> This [political imperialism] was inaugurated prior to any general resort to tariff protectionism in Europe, and prior also to any universal export of capital. Neither Russia nor Italy had surplus manufactures to dispose of or surplus wealth to invest; yet both engaged in the scramble for imperial domination. . . . Apparently the flag of a European nation did not have to follow its trade—or its financial investments. But once flag raising became common and competitive in Africa and in the Pacific, economic considerations spurred . . . keener competition in these regions.[12]

Michael Doyle travels some way with a systemic, economic-strategic interpretation for the European explosion into the periphery by arguing that exchange at this time was increasingly based upon an international division of labor, and that the British economy, for example, was increasingly an imperial economy.[13] He argues that after the founding of the Second Reich, the existing European balance of power had been shattered and the subsequent "multipolar national period in the center after 1871 was bound to have effects on the periphery"[14] if only by enhancing metropolitan interest in the raw materials in the periphery useful for metropolitan economic and strategic competition. Yet, as I have argued earlier, this motivation for peripheral expansion and control is more nearly consistent with a mercantilist, absolutist, territorial-sovereign structure of identities and interests, which had by this date been supplanted with a national-sovereign structure of identities and interests. Doyle stresses the limitations of a systemic interpretation of the new imperialism, even when combined with his persuasive pericentric analysis. He moves on to analyze domestic and transnational interests peculiar to each metropole, and then to an extensive and again highly persuasive analysis of the utility of the empire in helping the Tories to dominate British domestic politics in this period.[15] Yet he constrains his analysis to the political economy of the British metropole and the domestic requirements of two-party politics, and he does so without explaining "the shift to conservatism of the dissatisfied national public"[16] which played such a large role in sustaining conservative rule. He claims quite clearly that "the dispositional imperialisms of Hobson, Lenin and Schumpeter do not explain nineteenth century imperialism."[17] The present chapter is oriented toward developing and explanation of a "dispositional imperialism" that better explains the new imperialism.

What of the middle and lower bourgeoisie, and the working classes? What might have been their motivation for joining in imperialist ventures halfway across the planet? Hannah Arendt, who with Hobson credits the generation of surplus capital to a much greater extent than did Hayes as a motivation for imperialist ventures, has suggested that the nonpropertied classes were motivated by the logic of capitalist expansion which carried them along in the venture. Imperialism appeared to be the only means by which surplus capital could be exported to good effect. Imperialism, for Arendt was a product of:

> superfluous wealth . . . [and] . . . another by-product of capitalist production: the human debris that every crisis, following each period of industrial growth, eliminated permanently from producing society.

> Men who had become permanently idle were as superfluous to the community as the owners of superfluous wealth. . . . The new fact in the imperialist era is that these two superfluous forces, superfluous capital and superfluous working power, joined hands and left the country together. . . . The owners of superfluous wealth were the only men who could use the superfluous men who came from the four corners of the earth. Together they established the first paradise of parasites whose lifeblood was gold.[18]

And she quotes arch-imperialist Cecil Rhodes for a plausible economic motivation for working-class enthusiasm for imperialism that resonates with the rampant economic protectionism that became more prevalent toward the end of the century. According to Rhodes:

> The workmen find that although the Americans are exceedingly fond of them, and are just now exchanging the most brotherly sentiments with them yet are shutting out their goods. The workmen also find that Russia, France and Germany locally are doing the same, and the workmen see that if they do not look out they will have no place in the world to trade at all. And so the workmen have become Imperialist and the Liberal Party are following.[19]

Marxist and other purely economic explanations of late-nineteenth-century imperialism are too simplistic, as they overestimate the influence of commercial and investment capital upon government policy. Arendt's corrective explanation, however, also appears to overestimate explicitly economic motivations across the European socioeconomic strata in explaining the new imperialism. One major issue that these arguments miss is the cultural aggression of the new imperialism. Even in asserting that international economic competition was a motivation for imperialism, the Marxist theories of imperialism do not adequately recognize that the protectionist neomercantilism that accompanied these activities was not the absolutist mercantilism that had provided so much impetus to eighteenth-century colonialism. Neither was it in harmony with the Manchester liberalism that had guided European and specifically British foreign and trade policy throughout the earlier decades of the nineteenth century.

It was a specifically *national* imperialism. As Hobsbawm suggests, "[l]iberalism was the anarchism of the bourgeoisie and, as in revolutionary anarchism, it had no place for the state."[20] Certainly, as Marxist critics and theorists of the new imperialism have observed, capitalism had become international in both theory and practice, and had extended the operation of the market all over the globe with an international division of labor. But as Hobsbawm observes, even transnational firms wished to benefit from the stability of a national economy.[21] The enthusiasts of the new imperialism, whether they were capitalist commercial or financial concerns, or "superfluous labor," had a very prominent place for the state in their plans. The intervening decades had seen the emergence of a growing skepticism regarding the existence, or at least of the efficacy, of the "hidden hand" that the Manchester school's economists asserted would set all to rights in the global economy.

The emergence of vibrant German and American export industries in manufactured goods, the persistence of severe poverty among the industrialized working classes, and the modern necessity of engaging in the politics of participatory democracy had all provided a motivation to search for statist solutions to these problems. With the emergence of state activism in the forms of protectionist tariffs, and state-sponsored ventures abroad the "hand was becoming visible in all sorts of ways."[22] This situation was exacerbated by the growth of popular nationalism. "Not only firms but nations competed. . . . Protectionism expressed a situation of international economic competition, in part as a national popular reaction against the cosmopolitanism of Manchester economic liberalism."[23] The national-state economy was clearly emerging as an institutional consequence of the rapid escalation of popular nationalist sentiment. It would then appear odd if imperialism did not represent, in part, a similar expression.

One stark distinction between the new imperialism (national-sovereign) and the imperialism of mercantilist absolutism (territorial-sovereign) that we encountered in Chapters 4 and 5 is that the eighteenth-century variant had subordinated private economic interest to that of the state. In the late nineteenth century, private economic interest often led the state into an imperialist venture. The territorial-sovereign, mercantilist absolutist state had pursued colonialism for "reasons of state" that were bound up with the zero-sum assumptions of strategic economic policy that had been predicated on the notion of scarcity. In the late nineteenth century, some zero-sum mercantilist thinking regarding the scarcity of strategic goods remained, but as J. A.

Hobson[24] and Hannah Arendt have suggested, the economic motives for imperialist ventures were more likely to be bound up in positive-sum thinking predicated on the notion of surplus. All capitalist powers could benefit by exporting surplus goods and labor. This school of thought argued that surplus capital could find profitable investment and domestic unemployment could be reduced by the "shoveling out of paupers."[25] Nevertheless, the push for the foundation of new colonial empires certainly antedated the rise of neomercantilist economic nationalism.[26] We must look beyond purely economic explanations of the new imperialism to explain this, and to explain why imperialist policies came to be embraced across socioeconomic strata in the nation-states that propagated this aggressive policy. Not surprisingly, the explanation to both of these questions may be found within the same set of related phenomena.

Imperialism and the Transmission of Bourgeois-National Culture

The explanation stems in large measure from the simultaneous maturation and fusion of two forms of collective identity within the imperialist societies. These identities might most easily be delineated as "bourgeois" and "national." Hans Kohn, in a rarely cited tome written early in his career, begins to frame the issues for us in a couple of trenchant passages that are worth quoting at length.

> Nationalism strives to unite the members of one nation, politically and territorially, in a state organization. When that is accomplished the struggle for the possession of the earth proceeds further. The tendency towards political and economic expansion *incites the nation to extend its political and economic domination to foreign peoples* or fractions of peoples and the territory they inhabit, and in various ways to *organize their government under the suzerainty* of the expanding nation.[27]

Kohn might have suggested as well that the nation extends its *cultural* domination to foreign peoples. I will return to this point. I would pause here to note, however, that Kohn's assertion strongly indicates his belief that national collective identity is an impetus to social action at the level of international politics. Kohn goes on to assert that there is nothing fundamentally new about the new imperialism—a point I shall refute. But we should note in reading this passage that Kohn's observation of continuity in the imperialist impulse is correct insofar as he means to identify it as an expression of what Morgenthau identifies as the will-to-power. So for Kohn the new imperialism is:

> in principle . . . not different from earlier types. It, like nationalism, is *an expression of the collective egotism and love of domination of the social group which is the active political unit of the present day, namely, the nation*. Ours is an age of highly developed nationalism.[28]

What Kohn calls collective egoism, I have identified as the will-to-manifest a collective identity. Imperialist nation-states have already acted on their *will-to-manifest-identity* as a collective, in this case a nation-state. What Kohn identifies as their "love of domination," this collective will-to-power, manifests itself in the case of nationalist imperialist expansion as the desire to transmit their collective social, political and institutional culture to other societies. It is extremely important that we recognize that capitalism had by the last quarter of the nineteenth century thoroughly established what Rosenberg calls the "empire of civil society" and was thus a thoroughly bourgeois society.[29] It is just as important, as Mann suggests in proposing his "polymorphous crystallization model" that society "crystallized" as more than capitalist,[30] but explicitly as nationalist, precisely because the bourgeoisie had been required to extend the franchise and participatory government down into the lower strata of society in order to ensure their participation in the projects of the emerging bourgeois regimes. In extending the franchise, they had established the requisite preconditions for the emergence of a societal collective identity that no longer segmented the domestic political realm merely in accordance with the principle of territoriality. The principle of territoriality had served to delineate who is "us" from who is 'them" in the era of mercantilist absolutism. Segmentation of the political realm in accordance with the principle of nationality now delineated who is "us" from who is "them" by what amounted to identifiable peculiarities of regional (now "national") bourgeois culture.

As Anderson suggests, shared language, shared ethnicity, shared culture now served as the segmental delimiters of inclusion or exclusion from the nation. As the bourgeois class had indeed, just as classical Marxist theory suggests, acquired the characteristics of a ruling class by this period, it was they who defined these delimiters of inclusion or exclusion for the nation. As Gellner has suggested, language is the "minimum requirement for full citizenship . . . [in] . . . modern society. Bourgeois society had attempted to universalize literacy in its own vernacular and to create, for its own needs, a society in which "every man [is] a clerk."[31] The language, ethnicity and culture that one needed to possess to be a member of the nation were the language and/or ethnicity of the bourgeoisie. Precisely because one needed to be a member of the bourgeoisie to have access to power and resources within domestic society, bourgeois culture became an object of study and emulation by all classes within domestic society. *Bourgeois culture was national culture.*[32] Once bourgeois culture had thoroughly triumphed in domestic society, its self-confident transmission to the peripheral regions, whose peoples were ostensibly languishing in the grasp of "inferior" cultures, became a "mission" for bourgeois European society. The European bourgeoisie, triumphant on the continent, and having already replicated itself in North America, would now move to transmit the "blessings" of its culture and institutions throughout the globe with a "civilizing mission," which it somehow managed to pull off in a manner that was as aggressive as it was fatuous.

The attack on the periphery was multipronged. It was all at once military, technological, ideational, cultural, political, and institutional in nature. All of these tools of assault were experienced by the peripheral peoples as artifacts of the bourgeois nationalist culture of their respective invaders. All of them were employed quite intentionally to transform every facet of the lives and indigenous cultures of the peoples that the individual agents of imperialism—these tools of bourgeois nationalism triumphant—had encountered. The peripheral peoples "were equally at the mercy of the ships that came from abroad bringing cargoes of goods, armed men and ideas against which they were powerless, and which transformed their universes in ways which suited the invaders, whatever the sentiments of the invaded."[33]

The extent to which the new imperialism was a manifestation of national cultural aggression may be seen in the social and cultural standings of those within European imperialist societies who actively promoted imperialist expansion and those who did not. While bourgeois culture had become national culture, the commercial and financial professions within bourgeois society were by no means among the most enthusiastic advocates and promoters of imperialist expansion, as had been the case with the imperialist ventures of eighteenth-century mercantilist absolutism. Hayes insists that within the domestic political realm it was not the liberal parties "with their superabundance of industrialists and bankers," but conservative parties which agitated and stumped for imperialist expansion.[34] And "above all, it was patriotic professors and publicists regardless of political affiliation and unmindful of personal economic interest."[35] It was that segment of the bourgeoisie that had been most intimately responsible for creating a nationalist gloss for triumphant bourgeois culture which became the advocates for the global transmission of this culture abroad.[36] As Hans Kohn asserted with respect to British imperialism: "It was in her struggle with the selfish colonizing ambitions of white, Englishmen and others, in Africa and other parts of the British Empire that England's striving after reform *developed into a conscious mission*, a great trusteeship, on behalf of backward nations."[37]

But what, precisely, does "civilization" mean in this context but for the values, norms, rules, legitimating principles and social, sacral, and political institutions of the fully nationalized European bourgeoisie? When England, or France, or whoever asserted that they strove to "civilize" the peoples over whom they had extended the sovereignty of their nation, what did this "civilizing mission" entail? Eighteenth-century European imperialists had been content to exploit the raw materials and aboriginal labor of the virgin continents that they had encountered—often through the imposition of chattel slavery. As they had been pleased by these methods to fill the cargo holds of their ships with precious metals, precious spices, timbers, and all manner of exotic foodstuffs that would command a premium price in European markets, they had not paused to concern themselves with the "improvement" or "civilization" of the aborigines whose labor and lands they had so lustily exploited. Even in those few places where eighteenth-century imperialists had founded colonies of Europeans, those Europeans who were not explicitly engaged in Christian missionary activities had been content enough to leave the "heathen" natives, particularly of North America, just as "heathen" as they had found them.[38]

In the nineteenth century we find, conversely, European imperialists anxious to extend the sovereignty of their national states over remote regions of the periphery in order to ensure the abolition of indigenous slavery practices in these regions, and to thwart, for example, an internal African slave trade.[39] Here we are treated to the spectacle of the bourgeoisie of late-nineteenth-century Europe reacting in horror to the aboriginal exercise of oppressive institutions which the English (and especially French and Spanish) bourgeoisie's own ancestors had developed and encouraged a century earlier. While representatives of the eighteenth-century variant of this class had created a trade in human chattel for the purpose of ensuring a steady flow of cheaply produced raw cotton, sugar, and precious metals, nineteenth-century bourgeois culture had developed to the extent that at least chattel slavery finally offended its sensibilities. Moreover, the Christian missions were "an important adjunct to imperialism" as most were happy to call upon the military and naval protection of their home countries to protect their operations abroad, and thus many imperial "footholds" were established in reaction to aboriginal persecution of Christian missionaries.[40]

Racism, Imperialism, and Bourgeois Status Anxiety

Irrespective of whether the European bourgeoisie was now offended by the notion of chattel slavery, they were certainly not offended by the notion of white supremacy. Popular bourgeois culture had quickly reached into Darwin's ideas on natural selection and, discarding the kernel of Darwin's thought, extracted the chaff of the Victorian pseudo-science of philology and racist pseudo-scientific variants of eugenics.[41] The "scientific" status that the vulgarized Darwin had provided to racism and xenophobia supplied white, bourgeois, European society with self-confident assurance that they were naturally, racially, and culturally superior not only to all peripheral peoples and societies, but to rival European peoples as well. Racism now paraded itself more respectably within bourgeois society as "evolutionary biology." When in 1861 Du Chaillu found gorillas, previously unknown to Europeans, in the jungles of equatorial Africa, he immediately regarded the species as the "missing link" between man and his simian evolutionary ancestors.[42]

The imaginations and inflated self-images of the triumphant European bourgeoisie required no further stimulus than this to place dark-skinned Asian and African peoples at some step beneath them but some step above the newly discovered simian species on the "evolutionary scale." This vulgarization of evolutionary biology, in itself a product of triumphant, bourgeois European culture, relegitimated the tribal notion, with all of its implications for mob action against other "tribes." As the European working classes were at this time more likely to be aspirants for admission to bourgeois society than self-class-conscious proletarian socialists, they were more than happy to accept these assertions to assert their own ascendancy, at least as members of the white race that vulgarized Darwinism had declared to be "superior." Arendt reminds us that Marxist theories of imperialism have never given adequate play to the specifically racist, culturally aggressive component of European imperialism because:

> In Marxist terms the new phenomenon of the alliance between mob and capital seemed so unnatural, so obviously in conflict with the doctrine of class struggle, that the actual dangers of the Imperialist attempt—to divide mankind into master races and slave races, into higher and lower breeds, into colored peoples and white men, all of which were attempts to unify people on the basis of the mob, were completely overlooked.[43]

Neither should we overlook the impact of social Darwinism in this period on the development of a racist nationalism in Japan. The racialist, Darwinist thought of Kato Hiroyuki, then president of Tokyo University, was published in 1905 in a book that was to inspire a wave of national-racial thought in Japan, appealing to derivative pseudo-scientific theories of racial, geographical or climatic determinisms in which the Japanese race was cast as a naturally determined master race.[44] In consequence:

> A critical element within the Japanese colonial project was the assumption that differences in economic and political capacity among the peoples of East Asia were the result of natural or biological law . . . racial ideology thus offered more than a convenient explanation of contemporary international relations. It reflected a global perspective which justified that subordination and rendered it unavoidable. This perspective, founded upon the assumed inability of native populations to manage their own affairs, reaffirmed a sense of national solidarity and racial superiority among the Japanese people, regardless of their class position at home.[45]

Similarly, for the working classes, and the lower strata of the European bourgeoisie, the supposition of their inherent supremacy over their subject races carried with it enormous status advantages within colonial society as well. One major implication was that any white European arriving in, for example, African colonial society, acquired the collective social identity (and importantly, the co-constituted self-identity) of "boss." For example:

> In Africa, no white agriculturist saw himself as a peasant. White workers in the mines of Southern Africa drew upon the invented rituals of European craft unionism but they did so partly because they were rituals of exclusiveness and could be used to prevent Africans from being defined as workers.[46]

Similarly, those who would have been surely viewed as plebeian in European bourgeois society could by virtue of race alone, by taking on the mantle of white empire-builder, acquire the status of "gentleman," or "proprietor" in colonial society.

> Younger sons, well-born orphans, the sons of the clergy had experienced the "traditions" of the public school, the regiment, the university, but were not guaranteed secure advancement in British administrative hierarchies. Such men were deployed in Africa as soldiers, hunters, shop-keepers, concession-seekers, policemen, missionaries. Very often they found themselves engaged in tasks which by definition would have been menial in Britain and which only the glamour of empire-building made acceptable; the emphasis which they placed on their neo-traditional title to gentility became more intense.[47]

Thus clearly the new imperialism provided the positive benefit to European bourgeois society not so much as an outlet for superfluous capital or superfluous labor, but as *a vehicle for the alleviation of bourgeois status anxiety*, which surely amounted to the most prolific and pitiable malady of the vast majority of Europeans during this period. The importance of this bourgeois status anxiety as an impetus to political action should not be overlooked. Insofar as national collective identity was founded upon a particularistic form of bourgeois identity within domestic society, any threat to the bourgeois identity of specific individuals within society was a threat to their identity within the society of the nation-state.

While I have argued, in chapter 2, that threats to the group can be perceived as threats to individual identity and security, threats to an individual's credentials as a member of a group or society can similarly evoke an anxiety response. Insofar as imperialism ennobled the lowly and accorded bourgeois status (respectability) to those who could not otherwise attain it, it was an enormous impetus for a policy of imperialism among the lower bourgeois, and working classes. The European colonials appear to have carefully and uniformly cultivated a self-image of superiority. They regarded themselves as superior men and representatives of a superior culture and society, quite irrespective of their social or economic function within colonial society and quite irrespective of the status that function would have earned them back home. This was evidently also the case irrespective of logic or of consequences. Then as now, bourgeois status anxiety was powerful enough to conquer all of the impediments to its mitigation that reason is capable of erecting. Precisely because the retention of "an ample supply of servants"[48] was a talisman of bourgeois status, colonial aspirants to bourgeois status decided they must have them. They would have them in abundance, engaged in trivial domestic servitude, at home or abroad, irrespective of the consequences.

> Part of the self-image of the European in Africa was his prescriptive right to have black servants—at the height of the labor crisis in the South African mines, there were more black men employed in Johannesburg as domestic servants than as mine workers. . . . For most Europeans the favored image of their relationship with Africans was that of paternal master and loyal servant.[49]

In consequence, Terence Ranger argues that white colonial society witnessed a redefinition of occupations "so that it became gentlemanly to be a shopkeeper or a prospector" to address precisely this need.[50] These occupations were more profitable than attempting to grow crops and run a "landed estate," even as a "gentlemen farmers . . . drawing upon their neotraditional powers of command in order to manage [aboriginal] labor."[51] Certainly this occupational status-anxiety was no small matter. In the new bourgeois aristocracy of the late nineteenth and early twentieth centuries, gentility was conferred by money more than birth. Acquiring the financial means to buy leisure was the unmistakable mark of bourgeois gentility. Hobsbawm asserts that formal, post-secondary education was one bourgeois status symbol that money could acquire, as its "major function" could not have been utilitarian.

> What counted was the demonstration that adolescents were able to postpone earning a living. The content of education was secondary, and indeed the vocational value of the Greek and Latin on which British "public school" boys spent so much of their time, of the philosophy, letters, history and geography which filled 77 per cent of the hours in the French lycées (1890) was negligible.[52]

Similarly, Gramsci derided the bourgeois scion of the feminine gender, and abandoned himself to amusement that the bourgeois male industrialist continued to work "even if he is a millionaire, but his wife and daughters are turning, more and more, into 'luxury mammals.' "[53]

If one could not acquire the wealth necessary for idleness and dissipation, one could at least seek to acquire and announce one's bourgeois credentials by service to the empire of the bourgeois national-state of one's birth. Nearly any colonial occupation would serve this goal. Irrespective of the social class to which his occupation might have relegated him at home, any occupation that the colonial settler undertook, in this context, elevated him to the status of a full member in the bourgeois nation-state. This permitted him to effect the posture of a "civilizing" agent of his nation-state, a progressive transmitter of the national culture. In the very act of mitigating his own shallow, bourgeois status anxiety, the colonial settler became a glorious agent and servant of the nation. This was particularly true of the perennially status-anxious civil servant. As Arendt intones so effectively, near the close of the century, in Britain:

> the owning classes had become so dominant that it was almost ridiculous for a state employee to keep up the pretense of serving the nation. Division into classes left them outside the social body and forced them to form a clique of their own. . . . *In ruling foreign peoples in far away countries, they could much better pretend to be heroic servants of the nation . . . than if they had stayed at home. The colonies* were no longer simply "a vast system of outdoor relief for the upper classes."

> . . . they *were to become the very backbone of British nationalism*, which discovered in the domination of distant countries and the rule over strange peoples the only way to serve British and nothing but British interests.[54]

For the peoples on the receiving end of these imperialist ventures, in many cases no amount of service to the home country of their European masters would gain them similar status. In the case of the German colonies, while the culturally and linguistically French peoples in Alsace-Lorraine, annexed to the Second Reich in 1871, had been granted legal German citizenship, this franchise was certainly not to be granted to the native African denizens of the late-arriving extra-European German Empire. A German authority on constitutional law, writing in 1909, affirmed that the natives were "subjects (*Untertanen*)" of the German Empire, and only Europeans could be "imperial citizens (*Reichsangehörige*)."[55] Lacking the status of imperial citizens, they lacked freedom of movement, among many other very rudimentary freedoms attaining to the citizenship franchise. It should be evident at this point in my analysis that racist, bourgeois, national-social Darwinism was the first legitimating principle of the new imperialism, for European, American, and Asian imperialists alike.

The Transmission of Bourgeois-National Culture

Significantly, and in contrast to eighteenth-century colonialism, nineteenth-century imperialists were careful to instill in their colonial subjects the notion of their subjection not only to the nation-state which their white (in the European case) rulers represented, but to the values, culture, and institutions that nation-state manifested. Ranger has argued that there were typically three phases in the course of African exposure to what he calls "European invented traditions"[56] which appear to me to correspond to what I would suggest were at least three phases in the transmission of European culture to peripheral societies. These may be rendered roughly and sequentially as the military phase, the missionary phase, and the bureaucratic phase.[57]

The military phase was the first in which the utter subordination of indigenous peoples and cultures to those of the imperial metropole was emphasized. Once established by brute force and effective demonstration of the superiority of European military technology, this military culture (but not the technology) was transmitted to the conquered aboriginal society. The reasons the military culture could be transmitted, so long as the technology remained in European hands, is well illustrated in this rhyme: .

> Whatever happens we have got
> the Maxim Gun, and they have not.[58]

This pattern appears to have been to be as true of French imperialism as of British imperialism, and as true of British imperialism in India as in Africa. While French colonial policy considered theoretical relationships between the colonies and the metropole ranging from subjection to autonomy to assimilation and association,[59] nearly all of these relationships either began or ended with peripheral subjection, which was rarely accomplished peaceably. Michael Doyle's distinctions between tribal peripheries and formal empires and patrimonial peripheries and informal empires are useful,[60] but as he also notes, they all tended to end in formal control of the periphery by bourgeois-nationalist imperial metropoles.

Significantly, the transmission of European culture and institutions followed upon the acceptance of the conquest by the aboriginal society. The French recruited young Africans from an early age to consider a military career, and regularized aboriginal troops rather quickly. The British would later move to regularize their own African regiments. Ranger notes that the contemporary Professor George Sheppison, had observed: "the narrowness of the line between the civilian and the military [in British colonial society] . . . It was through its forces as much as its missions that European culture was brought to the indigenous inhabitants of British Central Africa."[61]

In India, which had been under British rule for a longer period, military subjection of India had been sure and swift. Britain had acquired all of France's Indian colonial possessions a century before, as a consequence of France's defeat in the Seven Years' War. Britain was therefore slow to equip and regularize Indian troops. For a good part of the nineteenth century, British rule featured numerous festivals and parades, normally with a properly intimidating display of British force, while "Indians participated marginally in the parades, as servants or as audiences for the public parts of the celebrations."[62]

During the missionary phase, natives, subdued by force and habituated to servitude through its continuous display, were socialized not only into the sacral institutions and ecclesiology of the cultures of their conquerors, but also educated, through the activities of mission schools, to become participants in the administration of their own subordination. It was self-evident to the Europeans that an integral part of their "civilizing" mission required the conversion of the "heathen" and their instruction in the rudiments of bourgeois morality. As Hobsbawm and Doyle have both suggested, the didactic function of the mission schools succeeded more often in socializing the aboriginal peoples than in converting them to Christianity.[63] In India conversion was actively discouraged by colonial authorities, and in the Islamic regions it was quite impractical in any event. Certainly the missionaries were often at cross purposes with the secular colonial authorities, and generally intervened on the side of their newly gathered flocks. But:

> if Christianity insisted on the equality of souls, it underlined the inequality of bodies—even of clerical bodies. It was something done by whites for natives, and paid for by whites. And though it multiplied native believers, at least half the clergy remained white. As for a colored bishop, it would require a powerful microscope to detect one anywhere between 1880 and 1914.[64]

The educational function of missionary schools prepared the groundwork for the administrative-bureaucratic phase in the transmission of European culture to peripheral societies. A large number of Africans educated in these schools were subsequently drafted into the lower ranks of the colonial bureaucracy. African clergymen were recruited and trained, and "African clerks came to value the rubber stamp and the row of pens in the breast pocket."[65] Even more significantly, according to Terence Ranger, it was in the discipline of the missionary school where the sub-Saharan African was socialized into the distinctly bourgeois, European concept of industrial time. Upon their encounter with this regimen, even the notion of time was to take on a new meaning to the peripheral peoples.

> Embedded in the neo-traditions of governance and subordination there were very clear-cut requirements for the observance of industrial

> time and work discipline—the neatly, even frantically prescribed segments of the schoolboys' day at Budo; the drill square as the source and symbol of discipline and punctuality.[66]

Having been socialized into European culture, the bureaucratic phase followed. The peripheral schoolboy was to educated in the language of his colonial master, according to a curriculum devised by his colonial master, within a strict schedule laid out by, and in the time of his colonial master, to prepare him for service in the military, bureaucratic, ecclesiastical and administrative institutions of his colonial master. The culture of his colonial master was to become the schoolboy's culture. Most importantly he was to be socialized into the political culture of his colonial master. The master's ruler would be the schoolboy's ruler, and it was desperately important to the nineteenth-century imperialist that the schoolboy not only accept this rule, but also that he embrace it—that he participate in it, willingly and enthusiastically. To this end the nineteenth-century imperialists first went about replicating their institutions, separate and quite unequal, all over their peripheral realms. Thus, the "College of Arms in Calcutta was to be the Indian equivalent of the British College of Arms in London, which would in effect establish and order a 'peerage' for India."[67] In sub-Saharan Africa:

> They began socializing Africans into one or another readily available European neo-traditional modes of conduct—the historical literature is full of Africans proud of having mastered the business of being a member of a regiment or having learnt how to be an effective practitioner of the ritual of nineteenth century Anglicanism.[68]

But even the transmission of bureaucratic-administrative culture and institutions on the periphery did not, in itself, ensure the remaking of the periphery in the image of the bourgeois-nationalist society that had invaded it. Importantly, and not surprisingly—if I have not failed utterly in highlighting the major threads of the arguments of this work—the imperialists felt the need to *legitimate* not only to themselves, but also to their colonial subjects, their peripheral rule. Their "civilizing mission" could serve as an adequate *legitimating principle* for their actions for themselves, and for domestic political consumption back home in the bourgeois-nationalist European metropole; but something much grander was required to put the stamp of legitimacy on the new imperialism in the eyes of their colonial subjects. The imperialists "felt the need for a shared ideology of Empire which could embrace whites and blacks alike, dignify the practicalities of collaboration and justify white rule."[69] This was to emerge as the ideology of imperial monarchy. It was the incessant subject of pedagogic discourse from the inception of the German colonies in the mid-1880s to their transfer in 1918, and for much longer in the British colonies. It was so effective in the British colonies that during World War II Britain was capable of calling on troops from as far away from as India, South Africa, Australia, and Singapore to assist in the defense of some threatened and far-flung corner of the Empire.[70]

A major opportunity appeared to further the development of the ideology of imperial monarchy when Queen Victoria expressed the desire to acquire the title of Empress of India. There can be little doubt that Disraeli saw an additional benefit: the Queen's new title constituted a warning against external European designs on the British interest in India and to indicate to Russia in particular that " 'it was the unanimous determination of the people of this country to retain our connection with the Indian empire.' "[71] Yet we should not surmise that the primary purpose of this move was diplomatic and oriented toward impressing European opinion of Britain's imperial resolve. Cohn, who has studied the records of the parliamentary debate over the Royal Titles Act of 1876, which awarded the imperial title to Victoria, argues that:

> at the base of the Conservative defense of the bill was the idea that Indians were a different kind of people from the British. The Indians were more susceptible to high-sounding phrases, and would be better ruled by appeal to their Oriental imaginations, as "they attach enormous value to very slight distinctions."[72]

Lytton, who served at that time as Viceroy of India, sought to underscore this ideology of imperial monarchy by numerous machinations, not the least of which was the gathering and pageantry of an imperial assemblage, for which he had ordered banners for the Indian princes and chiefs, designed "shield-shaped in the European mode. The crests were also European with the heraldic devices derived from the history of a particular [Indian] royal house."[73] All was designed to encourage a self-identification of the Indian nobility with their newly proclaimed Empress and to foster "the redefinition of the relationship between the ruler and the ruled."[74] Sadly, this endeavor was mounted with the most derisive intent on the part of the British authorities in charge of it. The reliance on pageantry and symbolism to earn the self-identification of the once-proud Indian nobility with the British Crown was an act of studied condescension, as is evidenced by Lytton's revolting explanation that "the further East you go, the greater becomes the importance of a bit of bunting."[75]

Nor were the employment of symbols of monarchy, pageantry, and ceremony to be less patronizingly relied upon in awing and cowing the native British subjects of British sub-Saharan Africa. The monarchy was carefully spoken of in quasi-sacral terms by secular and Anglican Church administrators alike, presenting "to African audiences a king who was almost divine; omnipotent, omniscient, and omnipresent."[76] The royal message to the Sotho, transmitted to them directly in 1910, is a sterling indicator of the paternal relationship between the colonial natives and the British Crown that the ideology of imperial monarchy had attempted to encourage. It is difficult to imagine, given the progress of participatory democracy in Europe by this date, the contempt for the native inhabitants of Sotho that must have encouraged Edward to address them with the condescending tripe that follows:

> When a child is in trouble he will go to his father, and his father after hearing all about the matter will decide what must be done. Then the child must trust and obey his father, for he is but one of a large family and his father has had great experience in settling the troubles of his older children and is able to judge what is best not only for the young child but . . . for the whole family . . . The Basuto nation is a very young child among the many people of the British Empire.[77]

In the German Colonies, this paternalistic relationship was extended to the frequent employment of corporal punishment against African natives, something that the British to their credit, condescending as they might have been, appear to have employed relatively rarely.[78] "Paternalistic" corporal punishment seems to have become quite fashionable in the German colonies by 1907, as we read of the complaint of Colonial Secretary Bernhard Dernburg, reporting from Dar es Salaam, that " 'nearly every white man walks around with a whip . . . and almost every white man indulges in striking any black man he chooses to.' "[79] Neither should it surprise us that the racial paternalism that animated British and German imperial ideology found its counterpart in the ideology of Japanese imperialism. Michael Wiener has recently argued that:

> the principle of *naichi enchōshugi* (extension of the homeland) implied that both the spatial and psychological boundaries of the nation could be expanded to incorporate all populations within the empire. At the same time, the existence of a family state, presided over by the father / emperor, provided further impetus for the Japanization of colonial peoples . . . the replacement of indigenous institutions and culture by Japanese forms of behavior. . . . The relationship between the colonizer and the colonized was likened to that between the parent and child. In nurturing the progress of its client states, Japan was responsible for ensuring that subject populations assumed their proper place in a well defined racial hierarchy.[80]

And it must be admitted that Japan had learned the value of imperialist aggression from the United States. While the Japanese had not likely experienced racial brutalization at the hands of the Americans, it is clear enough that their encounter with Perry's fleet a mere generation before Japan began to launch its own imperialist ventures had left a quite significant impression upon the Japanese. They had learned from the United States, at the least, the benefits of commercial imperialism, and of forcibly opening up an area previously closed to commercial, or more overt forms of exploitation. As a recent analyst suggests, in this context, "[i]t may be that the United States's [*sic*] most enduring export has been a new world order based on the principles of liberal capitalism."[81] This is not at all to suggest that the United States was in any way exonerated from the role of "paternal" brutalizer of native peoples. Clearly, not only had a large portion of the American economy been dependent upon the maintenance of the institution of black, chattel slavery through the middle of the nineteenth century, but the American development of a continental nation-state had been dependent upon a policy, conscious or otherwise, of genocide against aboriginal peoples.[82] Recent analysis even suggests that the Jim Crow legal structure was essential in solidifying American national identity well into the twentieth century, and even into the lifetime of the present author.[83]

Peripheral Nationalisms: Agents and Objects of Systemic Transformation

The effects on the new imperialism on the periphery were cataclysmic and permanent. To borrow the lexicon of Michael Mann, they were ideological, economic, military, and political at a minimum. Every form of social power at the command of the imperialist states was harnessed to thoroughly penetrate and transform peripheral society, economy, ideas, and self-perceptions. As noted earlier, the imperial experience had transformed even the notion of time for the peripheral peoples. It is important to break, for a moment, from the historical analysis to demonstrate that the sequencing of the variables introduced back in the third chapter of this work may, *under specific conditions*, be reversed. Reversing this sequence helps to explain why the impact of imperialism on the periphery led, in the twentieth century, to the development of national collective identity in the peripheral societies that developed after the experience of European, or Japanese, or American social and economic imperialism. It is crucially important to note that this sequence may be reversed *only under specific conditions*, which I will shortly specify. The reader should not infer that the sequencing of the variables is irrelevant or haphazard. Changes in the collective identity of *specific types of societies* result in systemic transformation. Change in the system induced by these societies, conversely, results in changes in the collective identity of societies of a specifically different nature than systemic agent societies.

First, the discussion above emphasizes my earlier assertion that the development of national collective identity has both international and domestic (systemic and unit level, in neorealist parlance) sources. We now have examples of two distinct, and mirror-image sequences of changes in the variables in Figure 1 (chapter 2) available to us to illustrate this assertion. As in the case of the European nation-states that instigated the new imperialism, national collective identity can develop from a very large number of domestic sources of that identity, and then provide a new legitimating principle for a domestic social order.[84] The new legitimating principles then require a new institutional form[85]—leading to a new global social order and "system" when aggregated with those of societies which have achieved a similar collective identity by their own path. Conversely, national collective identity can develop in response to what might amount to a structural condition of the privileging of a specific institutional form of collective action, and therefore, of specific legitimating principles of that institutional form. This is what happened to the peripheral societies upon suffering the experience of Western imperialism. Again, in shorthand, and with reference to figure 1:

Sequence 1:

{Δ collective identity → Δ legitimating principles → Δ institutions → Δ domestic & international norms/rules/principles → Δ system}.

or, conversely, under different circumstances,

Sequence 2:

{Δ system → Δ domestic & international norms/rules/principles → Δ institutions →

Δ legitimating principles → Δ collective identity}

In sequence 1, changes in the collective identity of *agents* of systemic transformation transform the international system. European territorial-sovereign states, for example, developed national collective identity and transformed the system from the Westphalian, territorial-sovereign system to the present national-sovereign system. In sequence 2, the collective identity of the *objects* of systemic transformation is transformed by changes in the system. In neorealist parlance they are "socialized" by the system made manifest by the agents of the system's construction. This is indeed, again, where the distribution of capabilities[86] in the system so central to Kenneth Waltz's view of systemic change is useful. This is also where it becomes clear that culture and ideological resources are capabilities, which dominant rational choice theories of international relations would tend to deny.

The sequencing of this transformational logic, for a given society that is en route to a change in collective identity, depends strongly upon whether that society is experiencing transformations in domestic relations (irrespective of whether the source of this transformation is exogenous to that society) and whether that society is in a position to make its agency felt throughout international society. The second of these criteria is, of course, fertile ground for bringing the structural variables of classical and neorealism into the analysis, such as the distribution of capabilities across the system, with the caveat that we must expand what counts as a capability to include, at a minimum, cultural and ideational resources.

Societies that experience rapid and/or far-reaching transformations in domestic relations, and that are well positioned to exert influence on other societies, tend to follow Sequence 1. Chapters 3–8 were designed to illustrate this as effectively as possible. They constitute *agents* of systemic transformation. Societies that are domestically socially conservative or stagnant tend to reproduce their social structure and institutions domestically and, to the extent that they are in a position to exert influence on other societies, to reproduce international systemic structure as well. The societies of the peripheral peoples prior to their encounter with the new imperialism constituted precisely such societies, in comparison with the dynamic and aggressive societies that would become their colonial masters. If these domestically socially conservative societies are poorly positioned to exert influence on other societies, they tend to follow Sequence 2. They become *objects* of systemic transformation. The agency of those who follow Sequence 1 creates a systemic transformation, whose influential norms and rules the target society cannot avoid, when forced into interaction with them. To the extent that the norms and rules of the international system privilege an institutional form at variance with the institutional form of collective action of the target society, the latter experiences powerful incentives to replicate the privileged institutional forms, their legitimating principles, and associated collective identities. These traditional societies find themselves under siege by the agency of the system transforming societies, irrespective of the form these traditions take. This is so precisely because the legitimating principles of the traditional social orders are challenged when their institutional forms cannot replicate the success of the institutions of the system-transforming societies. In both of these sequences, societies encounter the transience of institutional facts. In the first sequence societies are *impelled to create* new institutions. In the second sequence they are *required to adopt* new institutions.

The success of aggressive, Western, bourgeois-nationalist culture, norms, practices and institutions created new institutions for previously peripheral societies. The agency of the imperialist nation-states consciously transformed peripheral societies and remade them in their own image. It was precisely because the successful, imperialist actors were nationalist, as well as imperialist, as well as bourgeois societies, that they purposefully transformed peripheral societies. Toward the end of the colonial experience, and during and after the wave of decolonization that was to follow the Second World War, the peripheral peoples had begun to learn to develop national collective identity as a final lesson under the tutelage of their colonial masters. According to Kohn: "The nationalism of the Eastern [peripheral] peoples has been organized under European influence, and the social changes caused by European penetration have supplied its new dominant class."[87]

The literature on third world and post colonial nationalisms is vast, and their discussion, as well as the discussion of competing theories of their origins is outside of the scope of the present work. We can catch a glimpse of the impetus and consequences of these nationalisms in this insightful passage by Theodore Von Laue, describing the task of the third world nationalist leaders who have generally been constrained to attempt to create "westernized" societies in aboriginal dress as a salve to "national" pride:

> Western ascendancy was so complete that it left only one rational response: abject imitation as a condition of survival and self-affirmation. . . . For the sake of feeding, housing, transporting, educating, and employing the world's populations, "Westernization" is now pressed forward by non-Westerners themselves. Culturally neutralized, it has become "modernization" or simply "development," the common goal of all peoples and governments no matter how handicapped in achieving it.[88]

Yet we should recognize that nationalism has taken on different meanings to different peoples historically, and resulted in different practices, with interesting consequences.[89]

Imperialism and Nationalism: National-Sovereign Status Competition

Thus far this analysis has focused on explaining the impetus for and the effects of the transmission of bourgeois-nationalist culture to the peripheral peoples in large measure from the perspective of explanations of why individuals or significant social groupings within the polities of the imperialist nation-states were motivated to replicate their societies and culture abroad. I will now proceed to link their "bourgeois" imperialism more closely to their "national" imperialism. In doing so I hope to more fully emphasize the systemic agency and transnational consequences of their novel social identities. While capitalists, aspirants to bourgeois status, adventurers, fortune seekers, racists, missionaries, and status-anxious petty bureaucrats and petty bourgeoisie all had individual and class-collective motivations to participate in imperialist ventures, the flag did follow them. National-state governments that supported and abetted late-nineteenth and early-twentieth-century imperialist ventures were rewarded with popular acclaim at home, and competed with other national-state governments in doing so. The new imperialism was a collective enterprise, however disparate might have been the personal motivations of its individual propagators.

Early arguments in favor of French imperialism flowed in 1874 from the pen of French political economist Paul LeRoy-Beaulieu, and for German Imperialism from the historian Heinrich von Treitschke, each arguing in imperative, "either / or" form for their respective imperialisms. These arguments took the form that "either" France / Germany (fill in the blank) would become an imperial power "or" they would become a third or fourth rate world power.[90] These geostrategic oriented arguments may well have abounded in the academy, and may have been played back to the public through the mouthpiece of public officials, but it is as difficult to make a case that the impetus for the new imperialism was diplomatic or geostrategic as it is to make the case that the motive was primarily economic.

Michael Doyle provides us with an admirable critique of what he considers to be largely "pericentric" and largely "metrocentric" theories of the impetus behind the new imperialism, and argues persuasively that such formulations miss a geostrategic element that he feels must have impelled European statesmen to compete for colonial territory in the periphery. Yet he tends to reduce competing European peripheral claims to what he calls "predictable effects of multipolar, non-collective competition in the periphery."[91] This focus on the economic and strategic logic ignores the cultural and ideational impetus to European bourgeois-nationalist expansion and most importantly ignores the novel social purposes of late-nineteenth and early-twentieth-century imperialism. Doyle agrees that multipolar competition alone does not explain the new imperialism as it "should have led to incentives for containing Germany [on the continent]."[92] He emphasizes the mastery of Bismarck's policy of creating competing constellations of diplomatic concentration, each with an axis in Berlin, in diverting European attention toward the periphery. Yet it is difficult to simultaneously argue that Bismarck consciously attempted to divert European attention to the periphery—an argument which is likely correct—and that there was a serious geostrategic rationale for European competition in the periphery. Bismarck clearly did not see any pressing geostrategic requirement for German peripheral expansion. Popular nationalist pressure, and pressure from specific capital ventures, not geostrategy, led European governments into the imperial scramble. He emphasizes, as evidence, the move to formal rule over the periphery as necessary for the requirements of multipower status competition.[93] Doyle's arguments are well constructed, tightly reasoned, and entirely plausible. Yet they miss the fact that formal rule over peripheral peoples was also increasingly necessary to thoroughly and irresistibly socialize peripheral peoples into the prevailing metropolitan, bourgeois-nationalist culture and institutions. Formal rule was also increasingly a requirement of the novel social purpose of the new imperialism; the reproduction of bourgeois-national culture and institutions abroad.

We cannot escape the conclusion that the new imperialism was a collective expression of expansion. Having become a national community, the societies of the imperialist states then projected that collective personality to the world around them. Von Laue captures the issue succinctly, though, perhaps he overdraws the argument somewhat. Collectivities, like individuals, project themselves into their external environment, hoping not only to control it, but to transform it.

> In order to make the most of their lives individuals assert themselves, *radiating their personalities into their environment.* Heads of families want more progeny, more land, more trade, more influence. The *ambition to prevail and enlarge one's identity becomes collectivized,* growing in scale with the size of the community. It becomes part of its religion, its essence, omnipresent, all-powerful God mightier than all other gods. What, in short, holds together all societies, religions, and cultures down to the core of individual wills is a *pervasive faith in the practical and metaphysical superiority of the common bonds: in pursuit of community people need to universalize their ways to the limit or else community falls apart for lack of common conviction.*[94]

No truncated, purely "third image" logic could lead us to this understanding.[95] The national community's domestic requirements for social cohesion generate an aggressive (culturally, economically, politically, and militarily) response to the environment external to the national community. The external environment becomes friendly, palatable, "tolerable"[96] only inasmuch as it reflects the culture, norms, rules, and principles of the national community back toward that community. If rival national communities, reflecting different national cultures, appear to threaten to project their own collective personalities into the environment, this may appear to a different national community to be a form of a threat.

Nationalism had arisen in response to both internal and external threats to this notion of community. Bourgeois society was domestically, highly socially atomized in this period. Extended networks of kinship had become defunct in helping people to manage their lives, and survive in the rapidly changing economy. In such an environment, the citizen had need for the "imaginary [*sic*] community of 'the nation' . . . [to] . . . fill this void . . . [while] . . . the state . . . needed to make the nation . . . [as] . . . a counterweight to those who appealed to loyalties other than state loyalty . . . above all to class."[97] Nationalism had provided a solution to the socially centrifugal forces of the emerging "crisis of bourgeois liberalism" that had developed as a bourgeois response to the anxiety and xenophobia attending competition for jobs with foreign migrants. Neotraditionalism and nationalism had emerged as a socially conservative reaction against social atomization in this context. Rather than squandering their hard-won (largely imaginary) bourgeois social status on a proletarian socialist venture—the other possible outcome this crisis—the middle and lower bourgeoisie had opted for xenophobic, neotraditional reaction against the migrants. It is worth noting that this option does not appear to have lost its popularity. In present-day Europe and North America, particularly in France, Germany, and the United States, it appears that the lower and middle economic strata of society are reacting to the economic insecurity attending the movement of productive capital to lower wage markets by xenophobic reaction against migrants and foreigners rather than by reacting and legislating against capital mobility, which is a much more plausible source of their economic insecurity.

Bourgeois timidity had foreclosed the "solution" of proletarian revolution. Rightist and ultra-rightist, racist, culturally aggressive nationalism became a natural palliative to this crisis. Bourgeois identity had been salvaged, and emerged as distinctly nationalist.[98] This is the aggressive social identity, manifest in the potent institutional form of the national state, that had then proceeded to descend upon the peripheral peoples. As with imperialism, support for nationalism had its social rewards for status-anxious aspirants to bourgeois status. As Hobsbawm suggests, echoing my earlier citation of Hannah Arendt:

> For this widening body of middle strata, nationalism also had a wider and less instrumental appeal. It provided them with a collective iden-

> tity as the 'true defenders" of the nation which eluded them as a class, or as aspirants to the full bourgeois status they so much coveted. Patriotism compensated for social inferiority. . . . In Britain, as the [First World] war was to show, even clerks and salesmen in the service of the nation could become officers and—in the brutally frank terminology of the British upper class—"temporary gentlemen."[99]

But bourgeois status had been accorded to the clerk-imperialist precisely because *imperialism came to be viewed as national competition* with other Western societies. As Carleton Hayes has argued, the sequence of the march of European imperialism after 1870 had entailed (1) "pleas for colonies on the ground of national prestige" (2) "getting them" (3) "disarming critics by economic argument" and finally (4) "carrying this into effect and relating the results to the neo-mercantilism of tariff protection and social legislation at home."[100] Significantly, as Cecil Rhodes had quipped, governments "followed" popular pressures for imperialist ventures rather than leading them. One can quickly understand why a racist capitalist would welcome national support for imperial expansion. Contra Doyle, it is more difficult to find objective geostrategic rationale for doing so.

No less a "realist" than Bismarck had seen no practical value in acquiring colonies that would have made it an attractive policy from the perspective of an objective *Realpolitik* calculus. When approached in the 1870s regarding the question of acquiring colonies for Germany to match those being snapped up by the French and British and others Bismarck had simply pointed to the map of Europe and quipped that "[h]ere is Russia and here is France and here we are in the middle. That is my map of Africa."[101] Bismarck's policy later changed in response to popular national pressure[102], diplomatic maneuvering as the colonial issue was employed in an attempt by Bismarck to forge an entente with France,[103] and from the "desire to secure new markets and raw materials."[104] The German case was, relative to that of Britain and France, indeed a rather "marginal" colonialism. There is no reason to doubt, of course, that Bismarck's attentions was clearly focused on European affairs. Moreover, Bismarck at this time still enjoyed an insularity in his decisionmaking that Granville or Disraeli in Britain, or Jules Ferry in France, could only envy. Yet ultimately the same Bismarck that had wittily insisted that his map of Africa was to be found in Europe in the 1870s sat at table at the Berlin Conference from November 1884 to February 1885, and carved up the globe with fourteen other powers.[105]

Where in the eighteenth century the acquisition of colonies had been a status symbol of territorial sovereigns, in the late nineteenth century they had become *an ornament to the greatness of peoples*, of self-aware, self-identified national communities. Statesmen who wished to garner public support did not deny their polities, which constituted these national communities, the objects of their vanity. Imperialist conquest of other societies papered over remaining differences in bourgeois, domestic society. The spectacle of watching the agents of the national community conquer other societies, and replicate the national community abroad reified the national community, and remanded real social cleavages to the status of mere quibbles among brothers. As Woodruff Smith suggests, an imperialist policy:

> seemed the ideal way to link together disparate interests and social groups and to create broad public support. The elements of an imperialist ideology were . . . cemented with the *popular identification of colonies with national self-esteem*. A highly emotional imperialist ideology could perhaps *overcome seemingly irreconcilable class and interest differences by emphasizing shared images of national greatness and shared fears of dangers to that greatness*. Such images could also hide the many internal contradictions that an ideology appealing to so many different groups and interests was bound to contain.[106]

Thus for western societies, the new imperialism had, in the terms of Weberian sociology, a social control function. Upon discovering this, western governments never ceased to exploit every opportunity to manipulate public opinion to cement the social cohesion that a policy of imperialism had helped to accomplish by all possible means, vehicles and media.[107] The new imperialism was more significant for its impact on the societies that were the *objects* of the social agency, and *subjects* of the rule, of the newly nationalized states of the West than for its impact on relations between Western states. Yet the Western competition for colonies after 1870 was very much an expression of this national-collective identity. In this context I will give the last word to the historian Carleton Hayes.

> Basically the new imperialism was a nationalistic phenomenon. It followed hard upon the national wars which created an all-powerful Ger-

> many and a united Italy, which carried Russia within sight of Constantinople, and which left England fearful and France eclipsed. It expressed a resulting psychological reaction, an ardent desire to retain or recover national prestige. France sought compensation for European loss in overseas gain. England would offset her European isolation by enlarging and glorifying the British Empire. Russia, halted in the Balkans [by Austria-Hungary], would turn anew to Asia, and before long Germany and Italy would show the world that the prestige they had won by might inside Europe they were entitled to enhance by imperial exploits outside.[108]

When the periphery no longer served as an adequate forum for the national-sovereign competition for Western societies and states that it once had, a more suitable forum was found. The colonial periphery, in many ways, served as a venue for a late-nineteenth century "cold war" among national-sovereign, principally European states. As economic, military, political, and importantly, cultural tensions between these societies escalated very early in the twentieth century, this cold war was to heat up, as will be discussed in the next chapter.

Conclusions and Theoretical Reprise

The chapter illustrates that the new imperialism was a mass phenomenon that is inexplicable without recourse to analysis of the social collective identities of the European masses that perpetrated it on peripheral peoples. The acquisition of bourgeois status was the key to full bourgeois-national citizenship in this period and generally impossible without it. Bourgeois status anxiety could be mitigated, and bourgeois status attained, through peripheral colonial service as an agent of the "nation." Bourgeois culture, in its local, European manifestation, largely constituted national culture. Mass self-identification with these bourgeois-national cultures was axiomatic when we consider the requirements of attaining bourgeois status to enjoy even limited social mobility in class-conscious, Victorian society. Co-constituted, bourgeois-national self-identity and collective identity were then purposefully transmitted to peripheral peoples. The social purposes of this new imperialism differed radically, in this regard, from the commercial, mercantilist, quasi-strategic ventures of earlier absolutist, territorial-sovereign colonialisms. Collectivities, like individuals, project themselves into their external environment hoping not simply to control, but to transform it.

The sequencing of my theoretical model was illustrated to also work in reverse order for peripheral peoples who found themselves to be *objects* rather than agents of systemic transformation. After their colonial subjection, which transformed the social and institutional universes of peripheral peoples, third world leaders of newly decolonized peripheral states engaged in active and self-conscious "nation-building" projects. They had been left in control of administrative institutions that generally constituted fully functional territorially contiguous states. National collective identity then either developed in response to *ressentiment* induced by colonial oppression, or more often was consciously cultivated by the "official nationalism" of newly aboriginally administered states.

9 "Over-The-Top" and "Over There": Status Contests Among National-Sovereigns

How I long for the Great War! It will sweep Europe like a broom, it will make kings jump like coffee beans on the roaster.

—Hillaire Belloc

If the Monarchy is doomed to perish, let it at least perish decorously. —Emperor Franz Joseph

A thick mist blurred everything that morning . . . It was cold and drizzling; suddenly a Boche patrol appeared out of the mist ahead . . . hands in pockets . . . smoking cigarettes. Dumbstruck, our men hesitated for a moment. That was when the Boche n.c.o. suggested in a mournful voice, "Sad war, gentlemen! Sad war!" Then they disappeared back into the mist.

—La Saucisse, [French trench-newspaper] June 1916

If I should die, think only this of me:
That there's some corner of a foreign field
That is for ever England. There shall be
in that rich earth a richer dust concealed —Rupert Brooke

So much has been written about the origins, conduct, and effects of the First World War that the theorist attempting to approach this event from a fresh perspective may easily be daunted by the scope of the literature and may despair of the prospect of saying anything original or new about the matter whatever. From the beginning of the war, let alone from its end, historians and social scientists of various stripes and schools have continuously debated what appear to constitute the conflict's pertinent issues and have staked out well-marked claims to explanatory virtuosity regarding its origins.

One comes away from prolonged exposure to this literature impressed by several salient features of this debate that I will take as a pertinent starting point to my discussion of the contribution of national-sovereign identity in explaining the conflict. First, I am impressed by the general agreement among historians regarding the proximate causes of the war. The sequence of events beginning with the assassination of the Austrian Archduke in Sarajevo in June of 1914, to the initiation of hostilities by all major European Powers by the second week in August 1914 is well documented, well debated and fairly well agreed upon. Most historians have apparently found agreement concerning why each actor took the decisions they did in this tragic sequence of errors, misperceptions, and miscalculations. Second, I am impressed by the general agreement among many social scientists and historians regarding the "structural causes"[1] of the war. The array of conflicting rational, geopolitical, strategic, and other "realist interests"[2] experienced by the relevant actors has been well developed in the literature. The conflicts among these interests have been explored. Those who regard the war as a result of classic, Great Power rivalry, have found no difficulty in tracing the history of these rivalries or in finding examples of "Great Power interests" which were being threatened in the years leading up to the war. I will discuss these accounts in detail later in this chapter.

Third, I am struck by the general lack of agreement among historians and social scientists who have contributed to this quite substantial literature regarding whether the proximate causes or "structural causes" were more contributing (or determining, dependent upon the epistemological perspective of the analyst) in generating the conflict. Fourth, and more importantly, I am struck by the fact that the debate continues so strongly, even among those investigating these events from the analytic perspective of "realist interests," regarding whether proximate (microrealist) or structural (macrorealist)[3] causes were more important in generating the conflict. This debate continues, to my reading, in the context of an almost universal, stunned, and awed consensus among most analysts of the period that the effects of the war were so wildly out of proportion to, at the least, both the proximate causes of the war, and the declared war aims. As Kissinger has recently observed: "There was not a single specific Russian demand on Germany or a single German demand on Russia which merited a local war, much less a general one." War broke out "because nationalistic politics in each country made them afraid to challenge their military establishments."[4]

The gulf between intentions and consequences, between war aims and effects, is so vast that scholars must continue to question whether they have understood the nature of the conflict at all, quite irrespective of the many volumes devoted to the topic that already weigh down the library shelves. The Treaty of Versailles was not concluded until millions lay dead, the Austro-Hungarian Empire was dismantled geographically as well as politically, and three major European dynasties—the Hapsburg, Hohenzollern and Romanov—had vanished.[5] Additionally, in another view, "a world organization of supranational functions was created . . . [the League of Nations] . . . [t]he colonial era came to a close . . . [m]onarchy as an institution of real authority received a death blow while democracy and socialism made giant advances."[6] Why should a war that many maintain began as just another Great Power struggle for European hegemony have been so physically, mortally, and politically destructive with such socially and institutionally creative consequences? The map of Europe was remade at the war's termination, a natural enough *Aussenpolitik* consequence of so momentous a struggle. Yet the principles by which the map was remade, though certainly and obviously influenced by the "realist interests" of the victorious Great Power architects of the peace, were generally predicated on the what was then the relatively novel principle of national self-determination. The post-First World War map of Europe was the most substantial *institutionalization* of the new, system-legitimating principle of national self-determination achievable at that time, and is a monument to the strength of the new principle.

The close of the war also placed upon the world two institutions whose nature had not previously been encountered. The first of these was Soviet Russia—a gargantuan experiment in Marxist, proletarian socialism. The creation of the Soviet Union constituted the most substantial *institutionalization* of class identity then achievable. It was a manifestation of class identity of continental proportions that moved quickly to encompass the polyglot peoples of the old Czarist Empire within a theoretically unique form of *working class sovereignty*—the dictatorship of the proletariat.[7] Why should such an institutional form spring from the war-torn soils that had for so many centuries nurtured so well the reactionary roots of Czarist autocracy? Why this particular manifestation of *Innenpolitik*, so out of step with the second historically unique institution to be built on the political ground that had been leveled so thoroughly by the war—the first comprehensive, international institution of multilateralism, the League of Nations? Wilson's League of Nations had been envisioned as a multilateral peacekeeping forum for the resolution of the disputes that would inevitably arise from the world of nationally self-determining, national sovereigns that he had envisioned. How could Lenin's worker's state—founded on Marxist notions of class consciousness, for which national divisions were anathema, and for which national consciousness constituted "false-consciousness"—find sustenance in the same climate as a Europe reconstituted in accordance with national-sovereign principles?

I will argue that a large measure of the answer to this and related puzzles lies in the evidence I will present that *both national collective identity and class collective identity* were stimulated and developed in the years leading up to the war, and brought to a crisis by it. National-identity commitments generally served as a stronger impetus to social action than class-identity commitments in this context. As others have observed, "the socialists marched." National identity and class identity had, in the domestic political arena, developed simultaneously throughout the long nineteenth century, but had developed differentially within various "national" institutional contexts in Europe. In the terminology of Michael Mann, the state had "crystallized" as both capitalist and nationalist nearly everywhere. Variations in domestic institutional arrangements, however, resulted in variations in the franchises of the citizenry of relevant Great Power actors, with attendant variations in the depth of popular nationalist sentiment among them. Where the political franchise was relatively restricted, the popular internalization of the notion of bourgeois-national political citizenship that was so instrumental in the development of popular nationalism was relatively retarded, as in autocratic Russia, and the Austro-Hungarian Empire. Germany proved an important exception to this tendency, for reasons that will be developed later. The significance of these observations is that internal domestic political arrangements (or regime type, if we prefer) constituted an institutional fact[8] that helped to structure popular, competing identity commitments within a "national" context. The legitimating principles of domestic social orders that were institutionalized in regimes, and that most severely limited bourgeois-national political citizenship, were unable to survive the legitimation crisis that accompanied defeat in war[9] and the attendant popular privation.[10] Survival was particularly difficult subsequent to the mass mobilization of these societies[11] for modern "total warfare."

As will shortly become clear, co-constituted individual and collective identity was not monolithically "national" identity on the eve of the First World War. Class- and national-identity commitments coexisted and competed with one another in different segments of European populaces. Tensions between classes, which we might expect to be socially centrifugal, proved to be socially integral when the fear and hostility induced by increasing economic and social status anxiety in the lower and middle bourgeoisie was transferred to peoples whose "otherness" was defined by their ethnic, linguistic, and cultural attributes rather than by their socioeconomic class.

Nation and Class: The Issue of Middle-Class Nationalism and the Bourgeois-Nationalist Milieu

In the last chapter I hope to have established my proposition that the competitive imperialist behavior of European (and American and Asian) nation-states in the late nineteenth century constituted a bourgeois-nationalist status competition in the periphery. For quite a long time, emerging European nation-states apparently satiated their appetite to manifest their national collective social identity to the world by transmitting the bourgeois-nationalist culture that encapsulated much of that identity to the periphery. The Social Darwinism that had provided the intellectual figleaf for the cultural aggression and racist condescension that had characterized the new imperialism soon found expression in a wholly European context, however. These expressions were both ethnic (racial) and cultural. When fellow Europeans could be viewed through the eyes of Social Darwinism, European Great Power politics could take on an entirely different dimension, particularly when considering actions taken by other European Powers, such as the German drive for naval parity with Great Britain, that could be interpreted as a challenge to existing power arrangements.

Eric Hobsbawm has recently argued that the period between the close of the Franco-Prussian War and the close of the First World War, saw the transformation of nationalism from the more diffuse, cultural-national affinities ("Mazzini nationalism") that had served as the impetus for the German and Italian national-state-building projects to a more potent, neotraditional, rightist nationalism. In the period between 1880 and 1914, the principle of national self determination was evolving into a right to sovereign territorial independence for any group laying claim to nationhood. Ethnicity and language had become the criterion for putting forward claims to independent national-statehood, and the period witnessed a sharp move to the right of both nation and flag.[12]

Nationalist movements were now to be found in regions where they had not previously been seen. This was to become an enormous, and ultimately insurmountable problem for the polyglot Hapsburg Empire, which had been driven to the exigency of a "dual-monarchy" arrangement with the increasingly rebellious Magyar peoples, who constituted the most significant non-German minority governed increasingly ineffectively from Vienna. Racially virulent, ethno-linguistic nationalisms had developed in this period in response to both social and political changes that were transforming the lives of all European peoples after 1870. Socially, nationalism developed as a reaction to the insecurities and anxieties attending industrialization, urbanization, and mass migration. Politically, these economically and status-anxious peoples were becoming politically active in an era characterized by the "citizen-mobilizing" state, the rise of mass politics (with the creep of democratization), and the increasing nationalization of language attending the rise of administrative vernaculars.[13] The relentless penetration of the state into society, particularly through the exposure of the masses of the citizenry to the institutions of the army, and of public schools, had brought the official (high-culture)[14] vernacular into universal usage.

As the official vernacular became the language of the bourgeoisie, of administration and of the state, and the vehicle for the transmission of secondary education, Hobsbawm argues that the middle strata of society became fragmented in accordance with its proficiency in adopting the official vernacular. This enhanced the insecurity of the lower bourgeoisie, which adopted the official vernacular less proficiently. Xenophobic, neotraditional nationalism became attractive to them, as national identity developed in reaction to liberalism, capitalism, Jews and migrant workers, and other sources of lower-bourgeois economic and social status insecurity. In this view, chauvinism compensated, at the level of individual and class psychology, for the insecurity attending rapid social and economic change, and petty bourgeois downward mobility.[15] According to Hobsbawm: ". . . identification with the state was essential to the nationalist petty-bourgeoisie and lesser middle classes. If they had no state as yet, national independence would give them the position they felt they deserved . . . nationalism gave them the social identity that proletarians got from their class movement."[16]

While Hobsbawm provides us with a plausible explanation for the origins of the phenomena of middle-class nationalism in particular, and popular nationalism in general, his account has been subjected to scrutiny and criticism. I assert that Europe approached the First World War strongly under the influence of a bourgeois, hypernationalist milieu that permeated society and enhanced its proclivity for a violent confrontation to settle competing nationalist status claims. This environment also exacerbated the scope and destructiveness, thus the ultimate social and political consequences of the war. It is worthwhile to pause briefly and examine the debate regarding the social composition and breadth of the promoters of this nationalist sentiment in order to more fully comprehend the significance of the interplay of overlapping national and class self-identifications during this period. I will attempt to demonstrate later in the chapter how the interplay between these overlapping identity commitments help to illuminate the debate regarding whether macrorealist, *Aussenpolitik* factors, or microrealist, *Innenpolitik* issues were more pertinent to explaining the events attending the origins, conduct, and consequences of the First World War.

Mann's work suggests that virulent national collective identity was by no means uniformly in evidence throughout the middle classes. Yet in criticizing Hobsbawm's analysis, he appears to support the argument that the lurch toward the right by the middle strata of the European bourgeoisie in this period, and their consistent tendency to ally themselves with capital and the state, is a consequence of what I have earlier referred to as bourgeois timidity. Middle-class conservatism, he argues, may be explained with reference to the middle strata bourgeoisie's "integration into capitalist investment channels . . . [and] . . . desire to distinguish themselves in consumption, culture, and qualifications from workers."[17] Mann's verdict on the significance of this class as agents of social change and historical transformation is roughly similar in tone to Greenfeld's judgment that the French bourgeoisie inherited rather than made the French Revolution as they were "a middling sort of people, smart enough to recognize a good opportunity."[18] Mann all but dismisses them when he intones that "[i]f the state were merely capitalist, without other significant crystallizations, the middle class might bore the historian."[19] The analytically significant component of Mann's argument is his division of the middle strata of the bourgeois into four distinct substrata. Each of these substrata exhibited different levels and behavioral manifestations of national-identity commitments. In Mann's taxonomy, the middle bourgeoisie may be subdivided into petty bourgeoisie (shopkeepers, small-business proprietors etc.), corporate careerists, bureaucratic careerists and professionals.[20]

There had indeed developed an important domestic alliance—particularly in the multiparty democracies such as Great Britain, France, and the United States—between capital and their middle-bourgeois staffs. This alliance helped to avoid major class upheavals through the extension of political citizenship to these middle strata. Mann observes that the virulently nationalist element of the middle class, that I argue contributed so tragically to the bourgeois-nationalist milieu that enveloped Europe as it approached 1914 came predominantly from the substrata of the state careerist (bureaucrats, state employees, public school teachers) and from the most highly educated elements among the corporate careerists and professionals.[21]

Middle-class nationalism was, then, a distinctly "statist nationalism"[22] and drawn from self-identifications of elements of the middle-bourgeois with the national-state. The state careerists drew their bourgeois status, so essential to self-esteem and social respectability in a thoroughly bourgeois society, from their function in service to the bourgeois-national state, and from no other source. The most highly educated segments of the corporate careerist and professional strata, even in relatively authoritarian Germany and Austria, had been thoroughly imbued with the nationalist thought parceled out in the process of acquiring a university education.[23] Neither were university students in the multiparty democracies spared an infusion of nationalist indoctrination in the course of their studies. According to one study, the number of undergraduates in residence at the Oxford examination schools fell from 3,097 at the onset of hostilities in the summer of 1914 to 1,387 by October, as young men (the "lost generation") left Oxford in waves for the trenches. This resident population had fallen to 369 by 1918.[24] Mann and Howard agree that the more highly educated one was, the more virulently nationalist one was likely to be.[25]

Thus nationalism was not everywhere middle-bourgeois. Just as the middle-bourgeoisies were not uniformly virulently nationalist within a domestic setting, there were also important variations among middle-bourgeois nationalisms in various national settings. Mann argues that middle-class nationalism was very hard to find in the United States during this period.[26] Of course, unlike the German case, the American middle-bourgeois strata had no real cause to fear American proletarians.[27] Karl Polanyi's account of the fictional nature of the functioning of the "hidden hand" of the "self-regulating market" in the context of the American nineteenth century goes a long way toward explaining the absence of this class conflict here.[28] What Polanyi refers to as "free land," "free labor" and "free money" in America, so long as the frontier remained open and immigration remained unrestricted, had obviated the bourgeois timidity that reminded the status-anxious German and Austrian middle-bourgeois strata to remain loyal, socially conservative servants of capital and of the state. The middle-bourgeoisie could hardly have been said to exist in quasi-feudal, rural, and autocratic Russia, and was more likely to have been populated by semiliterate, *kulak*[29] rural proprietors than servants or staffs of urban, industrialized capital concerns in any case.

It was in Austria, and particularly in Germany, that the bourgeois status anxiety of the middle-bourgeoisie was adequate for the practice of "social imperialism" policies by the state. Much more than elsewhere, class and national identity "cross-cut" one another. The national-state loyalty of the nationalist segments of the middle-strata bourgeois class was a necessary prop to the maintenance of the bourgeois identity and respectability, with which their functions in service to the national-state alone provided them. Specifically the German regime was able to practice "divide and rule" domestic politics by playing on the bourgeois status anxiety of all of the middle strata.[30] The German government "brought the middle class to the edges of the state in order to keep labor [especially the socialists and social democrats] and ethnic minorities well outside it."[31]

The emerging definition of German citizenship in this period had fully enfranchised some and disenfranchised others. In the Wilhelmine period, the citizenship laws were reformed to deal with the specific problems that the old citizenship law, based upon Prussian law, had created, in an era of rampant ethno-linguistic nationalism. Under the older laws, the *Auslandsdeutsche*—Germans living abroad, having emigrated to America or the German colonies—automatically lost their citizenship if they did not return to Germany to reside there within ten years of emigrating abroad. This rankled the burgeoning German nationalist pressure groups, particularly the Pan-German League, the German Colonial Society, and the German School Association, which put enormous popular pressure on the relatively insulated monarchic German government for revision of this stipulation. Neither had it been acceptable to German nationalists that under the Prussian-based legal citizenship code that ethnic Germans who had emigrated from Germany to potentially forfeit their German citizenship could be replaced by *Volksfremde*—foreigners of non-German ethnicity—as citizens. Thus German citizenship law changed in 1913 to predicate German citizenship explicitly on German ethnicity, in order to ensure that *Reichesdeutsche* (citizens of the Reich) were also *Volksdeutsche* (ethnic Germans).[32] In a move that appeared clearly designed to appease specifically nationalist sentiment, the new Wilhelmine citizenship law "made citizenship more accessible to emigrants permanently settled outside, and less accessible to immigrants permanently settled inside, the Reich."[33]

French nationalism had also "migrated to the right" in this period.[34] By the last decade of the nineteenth century the French conception of nationality had in practice if not in theory narrowed from a broader "state-centered and assimilationist" view to a "ethnocultural counteridiom."[35] In practice this appeared to exclude Jews. France struggled madly with the issue of French nationality for a decade during the Dreyfus Affair. The issue at stake here was whether the French nation could bear the blow to the prestige of the French Army that would attend the revelation that an innocent officer of Jewish extraction had been interred for life on Devil's Island on the basis of evidence manufactured against him by the French army.[36] This revelation was ultimately professed in turn by the journalist Émile Zola and then by French Army Colonel Georges Picquart, at the cost of significant personal sacrifice at the hands of the French nation in return for their effort. That the issue of Dreyfus's innocence or guilt so polarized the French nation for so many years, that taking a stand in favor of his innocence was for so many an insult to the Army and thus the nation, indicates that in these years of right-leaning nationalism many minority citizens of France had but a tenuous hold on their citizenship. The issue of Austro-Hungarian citizenship was increasingly problematic as centrifugal nationalist pressures for ethnolinguistic nationalist self-determination mounted inside the Dual Empire.[37] Thousands of lives were lost in nationalist and anti-imperialist struggles against the Hapsburg masters in this period. The Hapsburg monarchy lurched from crisis to crisis in this period in a continuous search for a means by which an ancient, territorial-sovereign dynasty could continue to rule over a vast assortment of peoples and cultures who were increasingly self-aware as particularistic ethno-linguistic nationals. The Empire was progressively becoming too great a dinosaur to survive the full dawn of the national-sovereign era. It was dead even before it was aware of its own demise. It is undeniable that Vienna's insistence upon desperate reaction against this centrifugal nationalism, to the very end, both hastened that end and served as a proximate cause of the war.

As is well known, the assassin's bullet that felled the Austrian Arch-Duke in Sarajevo was an instrument of Serbian nationalism. This Serbian nationalism had been alive even at the formation of the Dual Empire between

Austria and Hungary in 1867 when the Serbian prince was juridically the vassal of the Turkish Sultan, and Serbia already languished under the rule of the Ottoman Empire that was so soon to precede the Hapsburg Empire into collapse.[38] I have perused few issues in the literature on the proximate causes of the war upon which I have found more agreement than that Austro-Hungarian insistence on punishing Serbia was one of the most critical proximate causes of the war. The court at Vienna had been simply desperate to make an example of Serbia, lest more nationalist uprisings be encouraged in the Empire, and quite irrespective of the highly conciliatory Serb response to the impossibly drafted ultimatum. Thus one of the most spectacular consequences of the continued coexistence of national-collective identity, and territorial-sovereign institutional structures was an event that served as a trigger for a global war. The perceived requirements for the confederal state of territorial-sovereign Hapsburg Austria to punish subject, centrifugally nationalist Serbia provided the spark that would ignite a generational holocaust and ultimately demolish the continental institutional manifestations of the territorial-sovereign form. But before turning to and testing the microrealist and macrorealist accounts, it is important to pause and illustrate how domestic, *Innenpolitik*, nationalist pressures contributed to, among other things, the policies that became the *Aussenpolitik* grievances that macrorealist and structural realist theories suggest were the "structural causes" of the war.

Nationalist Pressure Groups and the Old Regime's Insecurities: Wilhelm II as Germany's Napoleon III

The historiography of the First World War, to the extent that it concerns itself with assigning responsibility for the initiation of hostilities, generally recognizes that there was plenty of blame to go around but pays special attention to the issue of German nationalism and what is seen to be a particularly aggressive German foreign policy in the years leading up to the war. The work of Fritz Fischer has been particularly influential in this regard.[39] Among theorists of international relations, Stephen Van Evera's 1986 game theoretic evaluation of the events leading up to the war concludes by drawing upon the title of Fischer's most influential work by suggesting that "World War I was a *war of illusions*, caused by the misperceptions that afflicted contemporary European societies . . . misperceptions were the taproot of the war."[40] Many of these "illusions" and "misperceptions" were generated by what must be acknowledged to be the extraordinarily aggressive and consistently threatening German policy and behavior during the reign of Wilhelm II after his dismissal of Bismarck as Chancellor in 1890.[41] The latter event had its origins in Wilhelm's obvious resentment under Bismarck's tutelage from the time of his succession to the imperial throne in 1888.[42]

The sources of this aggressive foreign policy, according to realist accounts, are to be found alternatively in Germany's "fear of encirclement" by the other Great Powers in the European system, or strangely conversely, in Germany's insistence upon challenging British hegemony. In the latter sort of account, Germany is a rising star on the European scene whose rate of economic growth (fungibly translatable into military power) outstrips that of all rivals, including the reigning but declining hegemon, Great Britain.[43] Other important realist accounts treat Germany's behavior as a more generically directed attempt to alter "the balance of power," if not to replace the reigning hegemon.[44] These are, of course, all largely structural arguments. Even those which deal with the issue of nationalism as an aggravating factor, such as Morgenthau's work, pay inadequate attention to the interplay between popular national collective identity and elite decisionmaking procedures. As I will shortly argue, even elites that were still nominally afforded the luxury of a relatively insulated decisionmaking process, in the era of popular nationalism, found that *Innenpolitik*, popular nationalist pressures oriented them toward policy moves and decisions that could appear bellicose and threatening to other powers, who were generally subject to similar pressures.

One source of this pressure, particularly important in the German context, were the patriotic societies, the *Nationale Verbände*—voluntary associations that functioned as nationalist pressure groups and actively sought to sway public opinion, through the publication of pamphlets and propaganda, and thus influence the press and national decisionmaking centers to consider their particularistic policy goals.

> these associations included the Colonial Society (1882; consolidated 1887), the Pan-German League (1891), the Society of the Eastern Marches (1894), the Navy League (1898), the Imperial League against Social Democracy (1904), and the Army League (1912). By the Eve of the First World War, the patriotic societies could muster impressive membership totals: the Colonial Society (42,000), the Pan-German

League (18,000), the Imperial League against Social Democracy (221,000), the Navy League (331,000), and the Army League (90,000).[45]

Historical evaluation of the social composition of these nationalist pressure groups, and their effectiveness in impacting Imperial German policy, has yielded interesting debates regarding the assertions of some social historians that Imperial Germany had been able to practice a domestic policy of *Sammlungspolitik*. This has been argued to have been a form of social imperialism, by which the Prussian, Junker elites had been able to keep the masses in check by identifying domestic proponents of socialism, social democracy, and even milder forms of liberal reformism as *Reichsfeinde*, or enemies of the Reich. This was ostensibly accomplished by identifying the military with the Crown and state, and with the *Vaterland*. If *Sammlungspolitik* was practiced successfully by the German government this would tend to support the view that nationalism was a tool for statesmen that enabled them to accomplish foreign policy objectives determined by rationally calculated status interests. It would not support the contrary position, that policies which reflected the will of the people as a national collectivity were placed on the foreign policy agenda of statesmen anxious to maintain their position and popularity by satisfying that national-sovereign will with their *Aussenpolitik* policy prescriptions.

Geoff Eley's work on the social composition of the German right, and on the Navy League, has made the contrary argument.[46] Eley argues that these German *Nationale Verbände* were "self-mobilized, popular nationalist association[s]"[47] dominated by the petty-bourgeoisie, and quite critical of the government, which would indicate that class conflict was too antipathetic within German society to be fobbed off by a transparent *Sammlungspolitik* ploy by the government. These associations were in no way subject to elite manipulation in this view, but rather were hotbeds of "radical nationalism." They were a "constructive ideological assault on the old order, its parliamentary practices and forms of legitimacy."[48] They became "mobilizers of a new kind of patriotic and political movement, independent of government control."[49]

Coetzee's data, however, support quite effectively Michael Mann's arguments regarding the character of middle-class nationalism in this period. Note that 75 percent of the membership of the League during the war period

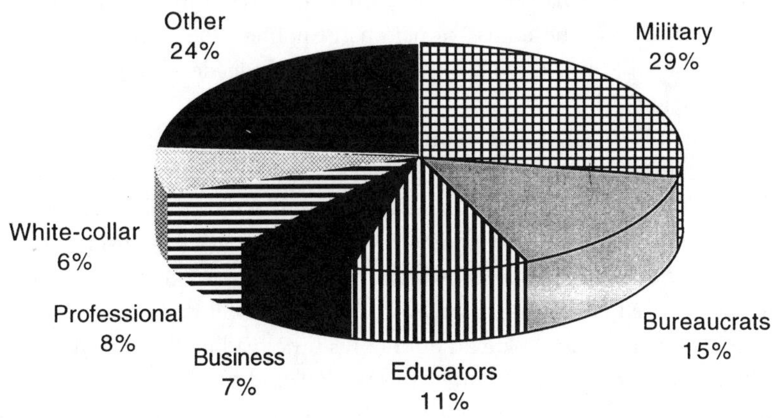

FIGURE 4 Social Composition of German Army League 1914–18[50]

consisted of members of the bourgeois classes. Of the members in the 24 percent category marked "other" in figure 4, 2.4 percent were landed elites, 0.6 percent were nonacademic intellectuals, 1.9 percent were clergyman, 5 percent were innkeepers, 1.5 percent were doctors, and 3.8 percent were women. Only 1 percent were artisans, only 1.1 percent were workers, 0.3 percent were retired and the occupational status of 7.1 percent was unknown.[51] Thus we can see that we can place 75 percent of the membership within those substrata of the middle-bourgeoisie that Mann suggests were statist nationalists—people who owed their bourgeois status to their functions and positions in the national state, or who were highly educated professional or business people who had been subjected to the virulently nationalist content of a university education. The underrepresentation of "innkeepers" or shopkeepers or artisans indicates that at least the German Army League was not a petty-bourgeois association. Mann argues that similar data provided by Roger Chickering and Geoff Eley—regarding the social composition of the Navy League, the Pan-German League, and the Society of the Eastern Marches—provide results that appear to be quite similar to those that I have derived from Coetzee's work on the German Army League.[52]

The importance of this issue is that it helps us to assess the social composition of the nationalist groups that actively sought to become opinion leaders in Wilhelmine German society. Coetzee argues that "By mobilizing the opinions of German citizens, in particular those of the middle classes, in order to redirect the course of nationalist politics, the Army League activists intended to prove themselves more effective leaders than Germany's ruling bureaucrats."[53]

Due, if only in part, to the efforts of these *Nationale Verbände*, one outlet of opinion formation that certainly had an effect on the attitudes and policies of Wilhelm II, was the press. The German press had became increasingly nationalistic, jingoistic, and critical of what it perceived as governmental failure to establish a *Weltpolitik* which would gain Germany the respect on the world stage that it had earned by its accomplishments since unification. Wilhelm spent an inordinate amount of his time reading through and marginally annotating press clippings. Bismarck would have regarded this as a vain, idle, and quixotic way in which the bearer of the imperial crown of the German Empire should spend his time. But Wilhelm had dismissed Bismarck, and had become convinced that he could best gain insight into the likely policy movements of any nation with which Germany maintained diplomatic relations by reading its press.

Wilhelm was convinced of the power of mass opinion, perhaps by the ruinous impact that a poor opinion of his parents, Friedrich and Victoria, which had been strongly reflected over the years in the German press, had delivered to his own families' life and happiness.[54] It is interesting to contemplate the significance of Wilhelm's respect for the power of popular opinion when we consider that he, aside from Nicholas II, might otherwise be thought of as the most insulated decisionmaker to take part in the Great War—if we are to judge the matter by internal institutional arrangements.

Clearly Franz Joseph in Vienna was aware that his decisionmaking must at least take into account internal centrifugal nationalist opinion. Nicholas had demonstrated little more understanding of the domestic difficulties that his autocratic decisionmaking procedures had caused him than had his father, Alexander III, before him.[55] Wilhelm regarded any statement critical of him, his government, or policies in the domestic or international press to be a matter of first importance. His concern for what he perceived to be the bellicose tone of the British press is evident as early as 1903 in his marginal annotation of a newspaper account of a British-Portuguese diplomatic engagement. British King "Edward's statement at a banquet given by the king of Portugal, '*Je ne veux pas la guerre . . . c'est la paix que je désire*,' prompted Wilhelm to write; '*Mais la* Times!' referring to the influential and Germanophobic British paper."[56]

No less a realist than Henry Kissinger has paused in his writings to note the sensitivity of Wilhelm to mass opinion, particularly as expressed in the press, and especially those expressions of mass opinion that issued forth from the opinion leadership of nationalist pressure groups. Kissinger writes in his recent book that:

> the German public was demanding an ever more assertive foreign policy . . . it was the new industrial managerial and the growing professional classes that provided the nucleus of nationalist agitation. . . . As autocratic as Germany was, its leaders were extremely sensitive to public opinion and heavily influenced by nationalistic pressure groups. These groups saw diplomacy and international relations almost as if they were sporting events, always pushing the government to a harder line, more territorial expansion, more colonies, a stronger army, or a larger navy.[57]

Yet as Jervis has already pointed out,[58] none of these "assertive" policies could be viewed without alarm by the government of Great Britain, among other powers. Incremental enhancements in the power of an already powerful Germany, even if designed to enhance German defensive capabilities, or simply to appease the jingoistic mob at home, could be viewed as an offensive threat to the security of Germany's neighbors. British opinion certainly could not be persuaded that Germany's crash program to build a powerful blue-water navy was a defensive measure.

The theoretical and empirical ground regarding the "security dilemma" that these policies generated has been well trod upon. I am more than happy to acknowledge Robert Jervis's important contribution to our understanding of these issues. What interests me here are two propositions. The first is the extent to which the security dilemma, so well described by Jervis, was exacerbated by the hypernationalist milieu in which these policies were formulated and executed. The second is the extent to which these policies, generated as they were, at least in part, by the pressure of the national-sovereign voice of the German people, were formally irrational and executed by a government which recognized them as formally irrational.[59] The latter issue, if it can be demonstrated, is particularly significant for what it says about the radical reduction of the insularity of elite decisionmaking in the nationalist era. To the extent that Wilhelm formulated an aggressive foreign policy, while aware of the risks that he was running, in order to appease the nationalist press and mass nationalist opinion, he emerges as the German version of Napoleon III.[60]

It is hardly difficult to argue that the hypernationalist environment in which Wilhelmine foreign policy was formulated was conducive to envisioning any expansion of a potential adversary's national military or economic power as a potentially mortal threat. The promulgation of faddish Social Darwinism, which had laced the already combustible nationalist ideologies of the day with the even more incendiary proposition of national, cultural, or racial survival, had ensured that this would be the case. The patriotic societies had nearly uniformly preached the inevitability and desirability of war as "an indispensable factor of culture, in which a true civilized nation finds the highest expression . . . a biological necessity of the first importance."[61]

In this view, any future war would be a *Krieg ums Dasein*, a *Vernichtungskrieg*,[62] a "natural" and "healthy," almost biological function. Those elements of German society which denigrated this view, especially socialists and pacifists, were condemned by the nationalist pressure groups as "decadent classes who used peace as a 'weapon of domination' to protect their interests."[63] We can express little surprise that to the extent that this crude Social-Darwinist thought was influential in Germany and in European society at large in the early twentieth century, the First World War would consequently constitute a "total war" between mobilized, national-sovereign societies. Industrial society was thoroughly organized and mobilized to provide the masses of armaments and material required to sustain a global conflict between armies numbering in the millions. Even the liberal Third Republic was to introduce a new and intrusive conscription measure in preparation for the coming conflict.[64] Industrial mobilization proceeded in the teeth of quite divisive class conflict providing unprecedented firepower. British artillery delivered 1.7 million shells on German positions in eight days at the opening of the summer 1916 Somme offensive, and 4.2 million shells in the fourteen days preceding the summer 1917 Passchendaele offensive.[65]

German opinion, in the years leading up the war, had been particularly nationally charged as the German people had taken justifiable pride in their collective accomplishments since unification. They hoped and expected, and then later demanded, to see these accomplishments acknowledged by the rest of European society, and were thrilled to discern any indication of this recognition in their reading of the fruits of Wilhelmine diplomacy. Wilhelm had been quite responsive to these demands and it is not surprising that German society registered the world's treatment of Wilhelm as the world's treatment of Germany.

This proclivity of the German people to live vicariously, as it were, through the *Aussenpolitik* of Wilhelm and the German nation is both causally significant for the conduct of prewar German foreign policy, and inexplicable without reference to the constitutive linkages between individual and collective identity in my earlier theoretical development. Durkheim's insights regarding the "organic solidarity of dissimilar individuals" develops demonstrable social agency in this context.[66] It is here that Druckman's observations, gleaned from his analysis of the literature on in-group biases, regarding the criticality of collective identification of the self with the group for individual self-esteem, become so analytically cogent.[67]

As Kohut notes in a passage that resonates perfectly with my assertions regarding collective identity formation and collective societal goals:

> In an age of nationalism people define themselves to a greater or lesser degree in terms of the nation to which they belong. Thus a nation's defeat or victory may be experienced with a sense of personal humiliation or exhilaration by its citizens even though that defeat or victory does not affect them directly. Defining themselves as part of that collective identity called Germany, Germans were emotionally invested in their country's fortunes and invested in the personal symbol of that collective identity. In an age of nationalism, in other words, Wilhelm II was experienced by his subjects as an extension of themselves.[68]

Unlike the hapless Napoleon III, Wilhelm could claim dynastic legitimacy and a legacy of illustrious Hohenzollern forbears stretching back in popular patriotic memory to Friedrich the Great, the conqueror of Austrian Silesia in the early eighteenth century. Kohut's biographical account of Wilhelm's relationship with his subjects leaves little doubt, however, that Wilhelm sensed quite correctly that if he wished to reign in the nationalist era—particularly at the dawn of the twentieth century, that "his position and power depended upon popular support."[69] As German nationalist opinion continued to develop, Wilhelm had increasingly found his personal popularity to be hostage to his capacity to satisfy this opinion. To the extent that this was true, Wilhelm found himself in a very similar position to that which had caused Napoleon III to take such consistently disastrous decisions in the interests of appeasing public and nationalist opinion.

The notion of interest expressed by the national-sovereign, the people of the German Empire, could emerge as significantly different than the notion of interest that we might expect a territorial-sovereign, rational, insulated decisionmaker to pursue. An effective strategy for Wilhelm to practice, in this context, was to pursue policies that allowed him to tap into the emotional energy that the German people had invested in the German nation, and in him as the personal symbol of the nation. Wilhelm thus often practiced *Gefühlspolitik*, the politics of feeling, rather than *Realpolitik*, with often disastrous results for German relations with other European powers. This was the case, for example, when Wilhelm had sent a telegram in 1896 to South African President Krüger, to offer congratulations upon a Boer victory over British forces. Publication of the telegram boosted Wilhelm's stock in Germany, and inflamed British opinion to very ill effect.[70] Kissinger has recently argued that the publication of Wilhelm's congratulatory note to Krüger "undermined [Wilhelm's] option for a British alliance for the rest of the century."[71] But the response to the Krüger telegram in Germany was distinctly pleasurable. The German liberal daily *Allgemeine Zeitung*, had intoned appreciatively that "Nothing that the government has done for years . . . has given as complete satisfaction . . . It is written from the soul of the German people."[72] However desirous they might have been of returning to a Bismarckian policy of *Realpolitik*, and however often they might try to steer Wilhelm back to it, the Old Regime statesmen surrounding Wilhelm were aware of the difficulties. As Wilhelm's Chancellor, Bethmann-Hollweg, had remarked shortly after the publication of the Krüger telegram, and the concomitant uproar, "[t]he threat of war in our times lies . . . in the internal politics of those countries in which a weak government is confronted by a strong nationalist movement."[73]

Thus it may be argued that nationalist opinion, and Wilhelm's dependence upon it for the popularity of his personal reign and political regime, increasingly drove an aggressive German foreign policy posture that had begun to appear quite threatening to Germany's neighbors. Kohut has argued that these dynamics were at work in the Kaiser's shift to a policy of *Weltpolitik*, in the German colonial expansion, in the 1897 German occupation of Kiaochow, Wilhelm's 1899 Samoan treaty, his extreme reaction to the 1900 Boxer Rebellion in China, and his "conduct in the Moroccan crises 1905 and 1911."[74] Bethmann-Hollweg indicated that he understood very well how the interplay between German nationalist sentiment at home, and Wilhelm's reliance upon basking in the glow of that sentiment, caused Wilhelm to pursue policies that were alarming to Europe, without providing a *Realpolitik* benefit to Germany. Bethmann-Hollweg described Wilhelm's foreign policy in 1913 in the following, clearly disgusted, terms. "Challenge everybody, put yourself in everybody's path and actually weaken no one in this fashion. Reason: aimlessness, the need for little prestige successes and solicitude for every current of public [nationalist] opinion."[75]

Wilhelm's naval policy, oriented toward the development of a blue-water German navy capable of challenging British naval supremacy is the best example of a policy that played to adoring crowds at home in Germany, and caused Britain and others to feel fundamentally threatened by Germany. Regardless of the benefit Germany derived from such a naval buildup, it "was *kaiserliche*: it embodied monarchical-imperial power."[76]

These observations tend to support those analysts who argue that the Wilhelmine policies of naval expansion and *Weltpolitik* indicate a policy of social imperialism at the level of *Innenpolitik*. Kohut acknowledges that "the Kaiser, Bülow, and [Admiral] Tirpitz all hoped that the naval construction and *Weltpolitik* would have an integrative [domestic] effect."[77] Yet he goes on to argue persuasively that this policy was more effective in this regard than Wilhelm and his Old Regime colleagues might have hoped.

> Within short order, however, the government found itself attacked for being too moderate, too modest, too Anglophile. At that point, rather than attempting to stir up nationalist and imperialist sentiment, the government found itself trying to damp that sentiment down. The attempt to manipulate the public had failed. Like the sorcerer's apprentice, the leaders of the Reich found themselves overwhelmed by forces they had called forth and could not control.[78]

Social Identities in the Critique of Realist Theories of the Great War

I want to conclude this chapter with some observations that I hope will serve in the way of correctives to some of the more rigid structural realist explanations of the First World War, and with some observations regarding its revolutionary consequences for the subsequent patterns of politics in the international system. Structural realist accounts of the Great War, whether written by historians, sociologists, or political scientists, tend to view the war as quite nearly a pure product of great-power rivalry. Such analysis tends to focus on the primacy of *Aussenpolitik* and of *Realpolitik*. State policies, decisions, and actions follow neatly from the responses of statesmen to changes in the relative position of international actors in these accounts.

It is far from my purpose to argue that there were no structural factors—including those stemming from changes in the relative positions of, for example, Germany and Great Britain—which contributed to the generation of the conflict. Clearly Great Britain was suffering relative economic decline with respect to both Germany and the United States and was suffering relative military decline with respect to unified Germany, particularly after Germany embarked on its aggressive naval program.[79] Certainly the demise of the Ottoman Empire, after a lingering illness, left a vacuum in the Balkans and elsewhere in Southeastern Europe in which Austrian and Russian territorial-geopolitical interests were bound to clash. Certainly German concern over an ambitious Russian modernization program, particularly Russian modernization of its rail system, provided an inducement for Germany to fight Russia sooner rather than later if Berlin were truly committed to the notion of the inevitability of such a conflict. Certainly European alliance formation in this period had polarized the continent militarily, particularly subsequent to the Russo-French *Entente Cordiale* of 1891, and even more severely after Britain joined the *Entente*. There can be little doubt that this confronted Germany with the prospect of a two-front war, thrust Germany into closer alignment with Austria-Hungary, and enhanced the security penalties for failing to support an ally in even the most reasonable of demands. These issues, and all the rest of the structural and positional issues that are so well developed in the familiar, structural realist lore regarding the sources of the First World War are, in my view, salient and significant sources of the conflict. I will not quarrel in this respect.

I will, however, quarrel with the attendant accounts of the reasons that these issues were as salient as they were, and with the notion that the conflict was an "unavoidable" consequence of these structural features of the contemporary international system. One of the major reasons these factors were such salient sources of conflict is that the quixotic social identities of particularly Central European elites "tended to reinforce realist behavior among statesmen."[80] The "Old Regime" component of the social identity of these statesmen induced them to think reflexively in terms of an old regime conception of the pursuit of national interest that was still distinctly territorial. As Mann observes, in the thinking of these Old Regime statesmen—though they were now in the service of increasingly national-sovereign rather than territorial-sovereign regimes—national "status" and "honor" were still bound up with the anachronistically territorial conceptions of nineteenth-century geopolitics. This residual territoriality was reinforced by the retention of the territorially bounded state as an institutional form of collective action, even while the latter was in the process of becoming the nation-state. In the lexicon of Mann, national status and honor (as opposed to dynastic status and honor) were to be defended territorially because " '[w]e' are defined territorially as the members of a state, not of localities, regions, or transnational collectivities."[81]

These Old Regime statesmen were not themselves nationalist but were "pro-capitalist, monarchist, militarist," particularly in Central Europe, but "nationalism pressured them without and within."[82] When the Austro-Serbian crisis came in the summer of 1914, a combination of nationalist pressure and Old Regime misperceptions generated a spiral of posturing that resulted in mobilization. Austria felt it had to punish Serbia or face unending centrifugal nationalist violence and agitation the regime in Vienna could not survive. Germany felt it had to back Austria or lose a valuable ally, and face withering criticism from the nationalists at home. Russia felt it had to at least partially mobilize or face continued bullying from Germany, which in any case preferred to fight Russia prior to further Russian modernization. France could not afford to tarry in mobilizing with the memories of Sedan still fresh in the popular mind. Britain could not tolerate German occupation of Belgium and Belgian ports near the channel, particularly in light of the German naval expansion.

As Mann observed, contra Morgenthau, the war was by no means an "inevitable" consequence of geopolitical shifts in relative position or of balances of power. It is not clear than any party to the conflict regarded the war as a rational means of "reordering the system." The war was not fought for either material or ideational reasons.[83] Mann argues persuasively that the pressures of popular nationalism, continuously expanded in this period by the aggressive, middle-bourgeois, statist nationalists, created the environment in which statesmen were impelled to go to war for formally irrational reasons. He provides an amusing but helpful illustration.

> the nation can be represented as that cartoonist's delight, the late nineteenth-century anarchist's bomb, a black, pudding-shaped ball with a protruding fuse. The fuse is composed of the statist nationalists; the combustible material is composed of the full citizens, whose shallow aggressive [nationalist] pressure endures long enough to cause the explosion, which is the enormous power of the military state hurling outward the jagged fragments, coercively disciplined workers and peasants. The fuse needed igniting, however.[84]

The fuse was surely ignited in Sarajevo in June of 1914.

One of the most significant aspects of Mann's quite original development of the sources of the First World War is his observation that the most intense nationalist pressure came from the middle-bourgeois statist-nationalists (those middle-bourgeoisie who owed their bourgeois societal status to their statist functions in society). Much of European society, among the "full citizens," those fully enfranchised, were "shallow" nationalists. They responded to nationalist messages, identified with nationalist goals, and possessed national collective identity, but were not as fully committed to this identity as the statist nationalists. They were committed, unequally, to "multiple identities"[85] which imbued them with identity commitments that diluted the salience of the social action that stemmed from the more undiluted national identity commitments of the statist-nationalists, and from what Eley calls the radical nationalists.

Carleton Hayes is correct that the First World War "turned out to be a supremely nationalistic war . . . [and that] . . . [a]s soon as war was declared, both masses and classes rallied to the support of their respective governments"[86], and that nationalism was, perhaps, both the "cause and result of World War I."[87] Yet it is not the case that public enthusiasm for the war was universal or instantaneous. In a recent study of the French reaction to the mobilization of August 1914, it appears that the initial news of the mobilization in the French countryside and provincial towns was met more often with expressions of surprise, consternation, graveness and sadness than with enthusiasm.[88] However, "[b]y the time the soldiers departed [for the front], those who responded negatively to mobilization had become a minority."[89] A caustic remark by David Lloyd George suggests that the same pattern of response was observed among the mobilizing populace of Great Britain, when he suggested that " '[t]he War had leaped into popularity between Sunday and Monday' "[90] as war was declared across Europe.

As Mann suggests, and as we should at this juncture have no difficulty in understanding or explaining, there was very little working-class nationalism or peasant nationalism to be found in Europe at this date precisely because these classes were still largely socially and economically disenfranchised. They had not been accorded the full citizenship that is so important to the generation of national collective identity. They "did not usually identify strongly . . . with the nation-state . . . [b]ecause it was not their state."[91] The bourgeoisie, particularly the state-dependent substrata of the middle-bourgeoisie, had found the institutional form of collective action which permitted them to express their own social agency, and manifest it to the world. "[T]he state was *theirs*. Because it symbolized their imagined community, they might more easily identify with its 'greatness,' 'honor,' and geopolitical interests. As the state had become the nation-state, sacred reasons of state might become sacred national interests."[92]

The working and peasant classes were not able to acquire an institutional form of collective actions that could serve as a vehicle for the expression of their particular structure of identities and interests in 1914. These classes might have been quite aware of their class identity and interests at this time, but the social agency that these identity commitments might have expressed or propagated was encumbered by an institutional obstacle. The horizons of working-class social identity were, in 1914, severely circumscribed by the institutional structures of the national-state. The levers by which these institutional structures might be manipulated were already firmly in the hands of the domestic bourgeoisie. This is still the case. Only in Soviet Russia, in 1917, were the working classes to find an institutional form of collective action that was at all capable of serving as a vehicle for the encapsulation of their class-based form of social agency. Even here, the scope of their agency was to be limited by the stubborn failure of the national-statist institutional structures of the rest of capitalist international society to crumble under the persistent pressure of class antagonism. In fact, the capitalist national state was, in Mann's lexicon, to "crystallize" as even more intensely nationalist in the intervening years between the First World War and the next, but this is a topic for another book.

I conclude this section by signaling broad agreement with Mann's analysis. European society on the eve of the First World war was infused with national collective identity, and thus quite combustible, but was not uniformly aggressively nationalist due to the persistence of class antagonisms. As Mann argues trenchantly, "[n]ational identity was now deeply rooted in both intensive and extensive social practices, but aggressive nationalism was not."[93] Aggressive nationalism was to later become much more broadly experienced within European (and non-European society), but was not so broad nor uniform in 1914.

Still, we are left not only with the fact that "the socialists marched," but also with the fact that once enlisted in the struggle the men who fought in the trenches for four devastating years did go "over the top" into withering fire with unprecedented loss of life. The American doughboys and Canadian denizens of the "dominion" did go "over there" to fight and often to die in a struggle removed from their land and lives by a vast ocean. We must be impressed by how far removed these battles were from the eighteenth-century conflicts that I have described earlier in this work. Long gone from the order of battle were the ranks of noncommissioned officers, equipped with spontoons, and charged with the duty of executing on the spot the foreign mercenary infantryman who might be tempted to break ranks and desert as the battle lines formed. How far had warfare traveled into haze of formal irrationality! In contrast to the attitude of the Whig oligarchy during the Seven Years' War of the territorial-sovereign era, in the nationalist era, dying for one's country became not only conceivable, but a duty. How can we hope to understand the motivations that impelled men to propel themselves out of entrenched positions and into a probable violent death? The severe dangers of the early-twentieth-century battlefield were unprecedented and thoroughly horrific. The following passage from a French trench newspaper relates quite graphically the experience of going "over the top."

> At the prescribed hour the officers gave us the usual little pep-talk, with last instructions, and then inquired if we were ready. At our response in the affirmative, there was a moment's silence and contemplation, and then suddenly the shout "Advance." We were in the second jumping-off line. *Without hesitation* officers and men jumped up on to the parapet and ran to the front line to take the place of friends who were already close to the Boche lines. We hardly stopped before we heard the cry again, "Advance!" We scrambled over the next parapet and ran forward after the first wave, shouting whatever came into our heads. . . . The guns were crackling away ahead of us, the machine-guns spitting out their ribbons of death. Tack, tack, tack, tack. We caught up with our friends but—to our horror—we met a barbed wire

> barrier that was still intact and more than 30 meters deep. And all this time the enemy machine guns went on . . . while we could see our friends on our left, falling, covering the ground with their blue uniforms, red with blood where they were hit.[94]

Audoin-Rouzeau provides us with the root of an explanation for how these dangers and hardship were born, overwhelmingly by men whose class origins might signify that they would not be strongly responsive to nationalist pressures, or strongly motivated by nationalist sentiment. He does so in a fashion that brings to mind Max Weber's observation[95] that compliance with the injunctions of a legitimate social authority is taken on as a sense of "duty." No search for motives consistent with our understanding of individual rationality is required, as the individual "values absolutely" those of the legitimate social order with which he is complying. Audoin-Rouzeau describes the feeling of shame that the soldiery suffered upon losing some ground to which they had previously formed attachment as it had been gained at high loss of life. He argues that "[t]o this attachment should be linked the instinctive reflex of defense of 'one's own.' "[96] Defense of one's countrymen had become a "moral obligation" in a way it had never been in the past. It is expressed eloquently by one soldier-turned-trench-journalist:

> We fought because we could not do otherwise. . . . We were forced to make war and to fight by all the social ties which bind us: by the dependence and the subjection in which the individual exists in relation to the State within modern societies; by the thousand threads which attach him to the soil, to the very atmosphere of his land, and which form the morally binding attitudes more powerful than any physical shackles.[97]

Thus the national-sovereign social order had acquired a legitimacy which impelled a conception of a moral duty to defend it in the soldiery. This appears to have been the case even in those elements of the soldiery that had benefited least from a social order which had crystallized, as Mann would have it, as capitalist, statist, militarist, and nationalist all at once. When the guns had finally fallen silent, the experience of national identity had been much more thoroughly infused in the international and domestic social orders of the participants in the war than at the beginning. The legitimating principle of the global social order had changed thoroughly. The last vestiges of the old regime territorial-sovereign order had been swept away, as had the monarchs and institutions of that order. The map of Europe was redrawn to recreate the continent according to a scheme in which nationality and territoriality were co-extensive. The principle of national self-determination would henceforth serve as the basis for the legitimate claim to sovereignty.[98]

Conclusions and Theoretical Reprise

The chapter has illustrated the profound consequences of the resolution of competing European class and national-identity commitments in favor of national collective identity. Regime types were depicted as institutional facts which helped to structure competing identity commitments within a national context. The demolition of residual, territorial-sovereign, monarchical institutions at the close of the war is of elementary theoretical significance. Their demise punctuates my assertion that regimes legitimated by principles that most severely limited the bourgeois-national citizenship that has become constitutive of a national-sovereign polity were unable to survive the legitimation crisis that accompanied defeat in war.

The chapter explored competing explanations for the victory of popular and middle-class nationalism without which mass mobilizations of European national economies for total war would not have been possible. As Hobsbawm suggests, xenophobic, neotraditional nationalism emerges as a reaction to liberalism and the socially corrosive artifacts of industrial revolution capitalism. Chauvinistic collective identity emerges as compensation for insecurity and dislocation, fostering self-identification with the national state where available and a compensating stateless imagined community where unavailable. But analysis of Coatzee's studies of German *Nationale Verbände* corroborates Michael Mann's assertion of an uneven distribution of nationalist sentiment with the middle classes. Most vociferous in their nationalist sentiment were the "statist nationalists" whose self-identification with the nation was strengthened by the fact that they drew their self-esteem and bourgeois social respectability from service to the bourgeois national-state. In this sense, the increasingly eudomonic function of the national-state was axiomatic for them.

The chapter has also shown how domestic nationalist grievances and pressures contributed fundamentally to the macrorealist, *Aussenpolitik* policies, particularly in Germany, that were major proximate causes of the Great War. Domestic nationalist pressures fueled "old regime insecurities," punctuating the radical reduction of the insularity of elite decisionmaking in the national-sovereign era, and exacerbating the "security dilemma" associated with internal balancing with a hypernationalist milieu. The resultant, bellicose German foreign policies were formally irrational and it appears that they were recognized to be so by Wilhelm and his government even as they put them into execution. In this sense, Wilhelm II emerges as a German variant of Napoleon III, similarly dooming his government and throne as the Hohenzollern dynasty was similarly delegitimated when it proved incapable, through humiliating defeat in war, of providing a serviceable vehicle for the expression of German national identity.

The defeat of the regimes of the dynasties exposed a glaring discontinuity between residual dynastic, territorial-sovereign institutional forms of collective action among elites, and proliferating national-sovereign structures of identities and interests among the peoples. This gap had been papered over by nationalist martial tunes, uniforms, bunting, and military brocade until 1917–1918. But when war exhaustion and defeat had silenced the bands, tattered the uniforms, soiled the bunting, and pulled off the epaulettes, the map of Europe was redrawn in accordance with a more mature manifestation of national-self-determination of peoples. I now move to conclude this book with a more contemporary example of the mismatch between emergent and prevailing social identities and incongruent and defunct institutional forms of collective action.

Part IV

Conclusions and Implications

10 The Helpless Colossus: The Politics of Identity and Hopeful Nondeterminism

"Est' obichai na rusi, nochiu slushat' bi-bi-si"
(There is a custom in Russia, at night to listen to BBC)
—Moscow jingle, *Rossiiskaia Gazeta*

Reduced to its essence, political power is based on both moral authority and physical force. One group of people can not tell another group what to do without having both recognized norms for legitimacy and recognizable means for enforcement.
—James H. Billington

Neither "objective" in the sense of existing outside the constituent practices of its members and opponents, nor completely "subjective" in the sense of existing only when perceived to exist by members or opponents, a nationality or social class is here understood to be both socially and discursively constituted.
—Ronald Grigor Suny

To travel hopefully is a better thing than to arrive.
—Robert Louis Stevenson

I will conclude with the analysis of two puzzles that provide some interesting contrasts and tests for the scope of application of a theoretical framework predicated on changes in societal collective identity. The first of these puzzles also constitutes an anomalous case for the thrust of late-nineteenth and early-twentieth-century collective identity formation. Western Europe's political institutions (institutional forms of collective action) had in general clearly been reconstituted after the First World War, and its borders redrawn, to service national collective identity and the new system legitimating principle of national self-determination that Wilson had helped to enshrine in the Paris peace. Russia and the East, however, had rejected bourgeois-nationalism in favor of its mirror image, proletarian-internationalism, as a domestic legitimating principle which the Soviets argued and believed was to become the legitimate organizing principle for the next (post-bourgeois-nationalist) phase of human history. The first puzzle regards why bourgeois-nationalist collective identity and institutions prevailed in the West, and proletarian-internationalist identity and institutions prevailed in the East. The question is important because the legitimating principles of the Union of Soviet Socialist Republics constituted an alternative principle for the legitimation and organization of both the domestic and international social orders for most of the twentieth century. As such, Soviet Russia constituted an implicit challenge to the international order no less significant than had the legitimating principles of the domestic order of Revolutionary France in the late eighteenth and early nineteenth centuries.

This challenge had not arisen as quickly or as earnestly following the Russian Revolution as it had in the case in the French case, in part because the Russian Revolution occurred in an economically and militarily exhausted Russia. As structural realists might correctly suggest in this context, Soviet Russia lacked the "capabilities" to carry the revolution beyond its borders. Yet the challenge to the bourgeois-nationalist order emerged in full force by the close of the Second World War. This war, I would argue, had constituted a communitarian-nationalist[1] (Germany-Italy-Japan) challenge to the liberal, bourgeois-nationalist (France-Great Britain-United States) order that had emerged between the wars. The events between 1917 and 1945 are too complex to be analyzed as consequences of the politics of identity within the pages of this volume, and are deserving of a book-length treatment in themselves. I shall have to leave the bulk of this discussion for another book. But the importance of the question of the emergence, by 1947, of a proletarian-internationalist challenge to the bourgeois-nationalist legitimating principle of national self-determination is adequately illustrated by the fact that by this date "one third of the human race . . . found itself living under communist regimes."[2] These proletarian-internationalist regimes were to contend the future evolution of the international system with their bourgeois-nationalist adversaries rigorously enough for the conflict to dominate international systemic discourse for the next four decades following the postwar freeze. The history of international relations for much of the twentieth century is the history of cold war between competing visions of domestic and global social order.

The second puzzle is the question of why proletarian-internationalist identity and institutions suddenly collapsed in the late twentieth century. I hope to persuade the reader that if we analyze the demise of the Soviet Union in this context, and within an analytic framework oriented toward the politics of identity, the fragmentation of the USSR and the demise of the cold war are explainable *post-facto*, even if they were only a very limited sense predictable. It was at the least something we might have anticipated as a conceivable outcome of changing Soviet societal self-identification. The importance for international relations theory of resolving this puzzle is self-evident. The demise of the cold war was an event so momentous that no competent theory of international relations should have failed to predict it. Yet all of them did.[3]

Serfdom, Class Identity and the Czarist Imperial Legacy

Let me deal briefly with the first puzzle, which is, in essence: why did not the collapse of Czarist autocracy with the abdication of the Romanov dynasty, in 1917, result in the replacement of the imperial monarchy with a series of bourgeois republics organized along ethnic or national lines, as had been the case in the West? Certainly part of this question is relatively easy to answer. Russia had withdrawn from the war late in 1917 when the Bolsheviks had turned out the provisional Kerensky government, whose major error had been that it had seemed quite anxious to continue to conduct the war.[4] Lenin and the Bolsheviks had offered the exhausted Russian people bread, land, and peace and they had at least delivered the peace. As a consequence of this withdrawal, with Russian soldiers deserting the trenches in droves, the Bolsheviks were forced to sign the harsh and putative Treaty of Brest-Ltovsk. This peace was signed quite irrespective of Leon Trotsky's assertion that as proletarian internationalists, a Soviet foreign policy was a contradiction in terms, and that in his new capacity as Commissar for Foreign Affairs he would "issue a few revolutionary proclamations to the peoples of the world and then shut up shop."[5]

But the fact that Nicholas II had allied himself with France and Great Britain had proved providential for the new Soviet government. The Czar's former allies sat down in Paris and carved up the territory of Russia's former enemies along rough ethnic boundaries, with significant exceptions dictated by Britain and France for strategic considerations to the considerable consternation of Woodrow Wilson.[6] The Hohenzollern, and especially the Hapsburg (Austro-Hungarian, dual) empire was apportioned by the victorious powers meeting in Paris for ethnic-nationalist foxes, who snapped up these portions and established their own national bourgeois republics. Hungary was cut loose from Austria, the southern Slavs in the Balkans were bound up in an independent Yugoslavia, the independence of Poland was reestablished, an enlarged and independent Romania was established, along with a Czecho-Slovak republic. While the new Soviet regime had forfeited a seat at the victor's table, as well as Czarist possessions in the Baltics and Poland, by abandoning the allies of the Czar it had chosen to retain another component of the Czarist legacy and this was the multiethnic character of the Russian Empire. As with many East European states, the Soviet Union was never a "national-state" from the beginning of its life to the end.

One question that may be asked is why did the Eastern peoples who had populated this empire, and particularly the intellectuals among them, accede to a proletarian-internationalist solution to the collapse of the economy and of legitimate political authority in the First World War? Perhaps a better one, however is why did the disparate peoples of the empire fail to use this collapse to emancipate themselves from Russian rule and establish their own national states? This is a question that is somewhat distinct from that of why the Marxist Bolsheviks prevailed, rather than social revolutionaries or some other group. One cannot answer the question of why the non-Russian peoples did not break loose from the new empire of the Russian Bolsheviks simply by observing that the Bolsheviks possessed the military capabilities to prevent their departure. These capabilities were thin. And perhaps because they did not have this capability, Lenin insisted from the beginning upon the right of national republics to secede from the union.[7] Stalin and Bukharin, along with most of the non-Russian communists, opposed this policy—obviously with some success, as the civil war in Soviet Russia, following for several years upon the heels of the Bolshevik Revolution, took the form at various times of abortive national revolutions on the Russian periphery.

But the Soviet government prevailed in these conflicts, quite irrespective of its own quite limited military and economic capabilities, and irrespective of the fact that Soviet Russia was invaded at times by expeditionary forces of other powers who were lending support to various secessionist national movements in the hopes of strangling, or at least crippling, the new proletarian-internationalist regime whose very existence implicitly challenged the newly declared legitimating principles of the bourgeois-nationalist global order. The reader will not be surprised to learn that I recommend looking for the answers to the reasons that the revolution in Russia was not bourgeois-nationalist, and that non-Russian nationalists in the Russian periphery were unable to rouse their people to emancipate themselves from Russian rule after 1917, in the *constitution of the collective identity commitments of these societies at this time.*

First, the late persistence of quasi-feudal modes of social organization in the Czarist Russian empire had left the vast majority of people in the position of agrarian peasantry. The Russian Empire in the second decade of the twentieth century had been highly underdeveloped both industrially and commercially relative to Western Europe and thus had contained a small and marginal bourgeoisie. Bourgeois culture in Russia had not developed as the basis for national culture as it had in the West. Russia had more often borrowed from the bourgeois-nationalist cultures of others than it had sought to transmit an indigenous bourgeois-nationalist culture abroad. Unlike the European "new imperialism," Russian imperialism had been driven by the dynamics of state-building and considerations of security.[8] Serfdom, which had bound the peasants legally to the land, had not been abolished until the 1860s. Peasant life under these conditions had ever been collective and dominated by a long ingrained attitude or equality of condition and right to subsistence—a "moral economy."[9] The prevalence and significance of the "leveling" ethic of the Russian peasantry is indicative of a predisposition on the part of these peoples to the message of social equality inherent in the rhetoric of contemporary Bolshevism. This ethic is illustrated in a somewhat amusing and popular, if unflattering, Russian anecdote told to Hedrick Smith in the Soviet Union in the late 1980s. According to the anecdote:

> God comes to a lucky Russian peasant one day and offers him any wish in the world. The peasant is excited and starts dreaming his fantasies. "Just remember," God says, "whatever you choose, I will do twice as much for your neighbor as I do for you." The peasant is stumped because he can not bear to think of his neighbor being so

> much better off than he is, no matter how well off he becomes. Finally he is struck by an idea and he tells God, "Strike out one of my eyes and take both the eyes of my neighbor."[10]

Additionally, the peoples of the Czarist empire had been subjected to intensive and persistent administrative (and legal) Russification, engendered by bureaucratic absolutism, an instrumental self-Russification, or coercive cultural and linguistic Russification, as had been the case with the suppression of the Ukrainian language.[11] Administrative and cultural homogenization over a few generations mitigates distinctive national and ethnic self-identifications. Czarist imperialism had resulted in trans-societal integration in other respects as well, in the creation of an all-Russian market, in disrupting the isolation of village life, and in blurring kinship distinctions as these ties became less significant for assuring subsistence with the advance of imperial economic integration.[12] Yet the nature of Czarist imperial administration had entailed a "complex meshing of social and ethnic grievances in situations where class and ethnicity reinforced individual and collective positions in the hierarchy of power and powerlessness."[13]

For all of these reasons, class antagonisms and grievances were, in many locations, felt more powerfully than ethnic antagonisms. The Bolsheviks promised (irrespective of what they delivered) to address both forms of social grievance. They promised regional autonomy to constituent ethnic republics, but more importantly they promised land to the peasantry. Many a peasant who only weakly identified himself as a Ukrainian, or a Belorussian,[14] could still quite firmly identify himself as a peasant. As Suny suggests: "Almost everywhere the nationalist movements were either strengthened or fatally weakened by the nature of their class base . . . [w]here social, particularly agrarian reform was delayed or neglected, ethnic political aspirations alone did not prove strong enough to sustain nationalist intellectuals in power."[15]

The paramount form of societal collective identity of many of the peoples in the Russian periphery at this time was in no sense ethnically or nationally based at the level of the masses. Intellectuals are always another matter. Ultimately, the answer to the question of why the Soviet Union did not fragment into nationalist pieces when the Bolsheviks had freed the non-Russian peoples from Czarist imperialism, and was yet too weak to replace it with Soviet imperialism, was that in many areas "class based socialist movements were far more potent than political nationalism. Socialism as presented by the dominant intellectual elite answered the grievances of both social and ethnic inferiority and promised a social-political solution to the dual oppression."[16]

Matters were to change in the intervening years between the consolidation of Soviet power within the boundaries of the old Czarist Empire,[17] and the implosion of the Soviet Empire in 1991. The proletarian-internationalist institutions of the superstate gave way to what appeared to outside observers to constitute a rapid and spontaneous regeneration of bourgeois-nationalist movements, both within the Russian Federation, and what now again lies on the Russian periphery. As I shall shortly argue, neither can this event be explained without arguments drawn from the analysis of the politics of identity.

The Demise of Proletarian-Internationalist Identity and Institutions

Throughout the Soviet era, the power of the Leninist machine and the totalitarian control that it exercised over society had simplified interest calculations of citizens of the Soviet Union, both in the Russian Federation and in the constituent republics. National identity in the constituent republics had been subordinated to class identity or "Soviet" identity as a matter of state policy. No effort had been spared by the regime to create *novo homo Sovieticus*. The regime had proscribed and exalted a Soviet, working-class morality.[18] The story of the terror that the Soviet regime had employed under Stalin to thoroughly atomize Soviet society and ensure utter command and control of society, and its application to the purposes of the regime, has been well told.[19] But with the death of Stalin in 1953, Soviet society began to "de-Stalinize" and a nascent civil society to reemerge.[20] While the regime retained tight controls over the press, society was no longer so terrorized that domestic critics and opponents of the regime would not chance finding an outlet for their views in a burgeoning *samizdat*, underground press.[21]

The literature of Western academics on conditions within the USSR had been so strongly dominated through the 1960s by this discourse on the totalitarian aspects of the Soviet regime that the Western mind had become acclimated to the monolithic view of Soviet society that the regime had in fact wished to project. Western liberal thought focused on dissidence within

Soviet society as a confrontation between Soviet totalitarians and Soviet liberals more than between the Soviet government and nationalist movements. Both forms of confrontation were salient. Yet the USSR collapsed in no small measure due to declarations of the independence of ethnic national-states which had previously been half-recognized by the West only as constituent republics of the monolith.

The national states that separated from the Union of Soviet Socialist Republics were in large measure "formed" during the Soviet era. In doing so, they ultimately made nonsense of the notion of a Union of Soviet Socialist Republics.[22] But it is important to note that they did not suddenly and spontaneously become aware of a latent national sentiment that had remained dormant in the subconsciousness of the constituent nationalities. The nationalist discourses that were translated into political action at the end of the Gorbachev years were formed during the long decades of Soviet rule, and in response to nationalist interpretation of the conditions of that rule. Ronald Suny has recently argued persuasively that these nationalist discourses depicted Soviet repression in many forms, forced Russification, imposed modernization, the suppression of nationalist traditions, and the destruction of village life. These discourses obscure the extent to which communist rule contributed to the continued process of "nation building."[23] The regime had actively promoted the linguistic and institutional-administrative[24] bases employed by nationalist activists in the development of national collective identity. The regime had done much to foster peripheral resentments against the Russian center during the Stalinist period of crash industrialization.[25] Ethnic interests had been mercilessly subordinated to the requirements of economic efficiency during the collectivization of agriculture as well.[26] Ethnicity had been territorialized administratively,[27] and ethnicity had been institutionalized as ethnic administrative centers in the constituent republics, which had acquired their own governmental and cultural institutions over the years.

But the terror had not eradicated traditional kinship forms of association in the Russian periphery. As Suny reminds us, "[s]ocialization still takes place in the family."[28] These kinship networks adapted Soviet economic institutions to their own purposes for the distribution of patronage and power, and more nearly represented corrupt, regional ethnic mafias (as they still do in the post-Soviet era) than the parochial administrative organs of a transcontinental proletarian-internationalist state.[29] The corruption and organization of Soviet society into regional and ethnic syndicates limits in a very substantial manner the extent to which post-Stalinist Soviet society can really be described as an emerging "civil-society."[30] These organizations were so successful in resisting efforts from the center to reform them during the Brezhnev years that Moscow had dispatched career KGB officers Geidar Aliev and Eduard Shevardnadze to Azerbaijan and Georgia respectively to reform them, with little success.[31] The Soviet state had not been able to dispense with the primacy of primary social relations as a guide to social action. People continued to choose their own associations and objects of loyalty. "Favors done or received are the operative currency of both social and political relations. So powerful are the obligations to one's relatives and friends that the shame incurred by nonfulfillment was, for many . . . much more serious than the penalties imposed by law."[32]

All of these factors served as the bases for nascent developments of national mobilization within the Soviet Union. Suny recounts how the stirrings of nationalist sentiment showed up early in Georgia and Armenia. It appeared in Tbilisi in 1956, during an essentially nationalist protest by students against the removal of a monument to their Georgian, Stalin, in which dozens were killed. It appeared in Armenia in 1965 during an unofficial demonstration to mark the fiftieth anniversary of genocide against Armenians by Kemalist Turks. It appeared in Tbilisi again in 1978 when students demonstrated against a government plan to change the an article in Georgian constitution which declaring Georgian to be the state language of the republic.[33] Nationalist protest was also frequent in the Baltics and Western Ukraine. Suny argues persuasively that all of these disturbances provide evidence that a "growing disillusionment in society with the goals and the competence of Soviet leaders was increasingly expressed . . . in the idiom of nationalism." Proletarian-internationalist identity was already on the wane as the crisis of the command economy of the worker's state deepened throughout the Brezhnev "years of stagnation."

Upon Brezhnev's death in November 1982 the Soviet regime set upon an essentially pseudo-Stalinist path of reform. They set out to whip up the performance of the Soviet economy through ultimately fruitless attempts to impose more strict labor discipline, at first in the corrupt and recalcitrant Caucasus, and then throughout the Soviet Union under the successive chairmanships of Yuri Andropov and Konstantin Chernenko.[34] When Mikhail Gorbachev came to power with Chernenko's death in March of 1985, he had initially inclined toward the model of the authoritarian disciplinarian of his predecessors, emphasizing work discipline, excoriating alcoholism and absenteeism in the workplace, and consolidating ministries. Even when he had settled on a course of real reform, he had behaved very much like a Leninist. He had employed Leninist tactics in constructing his program, appointing young professionals as a counterweight to the bureaucracy, constructing a vague policy slogan (*perestroika*), created a "super-presidency" to gather power into his own hands.[35] He began with the mission that had consumed Andropov and Chernenko, to break the power of the local and regional mafias that had captured the administrative apparatus of the state and the Communist Party. The ethnic, increasingly national state functionaries and party officials in the constituent republics had translated their positions into what at this point constituted more than generically bureaucratic resistance to reform. They were more than corrupt bureaucrats, and unfortunately for Gorbachev, "[c]orruption and nationalism grew hand in hand, limiting the Kremlin's writ in the borderlands."[36] When this "*perestroika*-from-below" was contained by continued resistance from the national *apparatchiki*, Gorbachev had begun the democratization process that he needed to loosen the press and invite the criticism of the *apparatchiki* that he needed to pressure them to reform.

The policy of *glasnost* that Gorbachev prescribed to correct his powerlessness in the Russian periphery itself began the process by which the institutions through which he exercised power, the Soviet state and especially the Communist Party of the Soviet Union (CPSU), were to become delegitimated in a very short period of time. As Suny frames the issue:

> Faith in the socialist project had long since eroded among educated people, but the subversive power of the new criticism undermined what was left of the authority and influence of the party apparatus. *Glasnost* eliminated within a few years the privileged position of Marxism-Leninism, and the rewriting of Soviet history moved back in time beyond the permitted critique of Stalinism into a fundamental rereading of Lenin's revolution.[37]

This internal relaxation of the terms of domestic political discourse, coupled with a relaxation of Soviet foreign policy toward both the West and toward Soviet client states in Eastern Europe, had given heart to political entrepreneurs in the constituent republics who wished to present their coethnics with an alternative model of their futures than the reformed, federative socialist commonwealth that Gorbachev had begun moving toward. Significantly, in the international arena, Gorbachev had begun to signal a shift in the zero-sum conception of Russian *interests* to which the West had grown accustomed. He had signaled a desire for a "partial convergence" with Western political and economic institutions, which was later to be expressed much more dramatically and emphatically in the Yeltsin government of Russia.[38]

Gorbachev had also effectively renounced the Brezhnev doctrine which had insisted that the Soviet Union would forcibly ensure the socialist character of their client and satellite states in Eastern Europe. This change in policy also signified a shift in the familiar conception of Russian interests by indicating that the USSR's relations with Eastern European states would be constituted on more equal terms.[39] When it had become clear that Moscow would not intervene, Eastern European peoples brought down communist regimes in Prague, East Berlin, Budapest, Warsaw, and Bucharest with a pace that left the watching world speechless. The failure of the command economy had long been evident to the citizens of these countries. Attempts by the Hungarians in 1956 and the Czechoslovaks in 1968 to throw off these regimes had been crushed by Soviet tanks. The Soviets had hanged Imre Nagy, the Hungarian leader who had supported the Budapest uprising, and his colleagues in 1958, and a decade later had exiled Alexander Dubcek, who had initiated the reforms that led to the Prague spring and its aftermath, to a menial position in forestry.

The Marxist regimes that retained power after these uprisings were seen by many denizens of these countries as oppressive organs of Soviet imperialism imposed on their nations. National collective identity had continued to persist, sullen and shackled. I was able to observe a vibrant Hungarian nationalism, which cannot have arisen recently, when I visited Budapest in June of 1996. I observed that Imre Nagy is now revered as a Hungarian patriot, and I was able to visit a monument that has been erected to him at the site at which he has recently been reburied at Kossuth Lajos tér, near the Hungarian Parliament building in central Pest. While thousands of people pass by this busy street corner every day, I noted on the day that I visited that there are always a dozen or so people standing at the site of the monument, hat in hands, contemplating the site in respectful silence. Not far from this site, at the intersections of Balassi utca and Szalay utca,[40] stands a building pocked and scarred with hundreds of rounds of Russian ammunition; an unintended monument to the Red Army's 1956 visit to Budapest.

It is difficult to observe these monuments without realizing that the 1956 uprising and the 1989 revolutions in Budapest were in large measure Hungarian national uprisings.

While all these national liberation movements were brewing in Eastern Europe, Gorbachev had faced the visible manifestations of surging national identity within the borders of the Soviet Union. Having abandoned the Brezhnev doctrine, and a credible threat to use force to prop up communist regimes in Eastern Europe, Gorbachev could not control events there, and the pace at which communist power was demolished in Eastern Europe in the late 1980s demonstrates this was well understood in Eastern Europe at the time, if not in the West. What was less well understood, even within the USSR, was the extent to which Gorbachev's policy of *glasnost* had generated the conditions under which more open political discourse had encouraged a reformulation of the structure of identities and interests in the constituent republics of the Russian periphery. The first flashpoint of this reformulation came in Karabagh, an ethnic Armenian enclave in Azerbaijan, when the Armenian denizens began a series of demonstrations for union with Armenia in mid-February of 1988. The Azerbaijanis responded with riots on the 28th and 29th resulting in thirty-one fatalities and hundreds of injuries and Gorbachev suddenly found himself mediating a bloody nationalist dispute within the Soviet Union over territory.[41] By the beginning of 1990 the Azerbaijanis were holding mass rallies in favor of separation from the USSR and Azerbaijani extremist nationalists were massacring ethnic Armenians in Baku. Gorbachev had responded by dispatching troops to both Karabagh and Baku, resulting in the deaths of hundreds of Azerbaijanis who were crushed as armored columns rolled over manned barricades.[42] Soviet troops had similarly crushed huge demonstrations in Tiblisi which had called for Georgian independence, but these actions had been critically excoriated in the press that Gorbachev's own policies had liberalized. Any coercive action Gorbachev would attempt to take from then on to forcibly maintain the territorial integrity of the USSR from secessionist movements would not be tolerated by the liberalized press. This had "made it nearly impossible for the Kremlin to use armed force again against the burgeoning nationalist movements."[43]

Matters were not improved by the political maneuvering that Gorbachev had to conduct to contend for power even within the Russian Federation with Boris Yeltsin, after his election as Chair of the Supreme Soviet of the Russian Federation. Each of these men had employed centrifugal nationalist tendencies within the USSR as political tools to undermine one another's power. Gorbachev had employed this tactic, during their 1990 power struggle, to encourage the nationalist sentiments of Yeltsin's clients in the non-Russian ethnic autonomies of the Russian Federation. Yeltsin's government is clearly still dealing with the consequences of this ethnic nationalism as the bloody war in Chechnya ground on irrespective of the cease-fire which Yeltsin had, perhaps, arranged in order to survive the 1996 elections in Russia. Yeltsin had encouraged centrifugal nationalist tendencies in the Baltic states of Latvia, Lithuania, and Estonia in order to weaken Gorbachev's Soviet power base.[44]

By the end of 1990 all of the union republics and most of the autonomous republics were moving toward declaring themselves sovereign or in other cases as independent states. If Gorbachev were to maintain his commitment to democratization and eschew maintenance of the Soviet Union by force, which would have cost him his "last shred of legitimacy," he was forced to negotiate with the union republics on a more equal footing.[45] The Russian Federation had declared itself sovereign, and all union republics had been offered the opportunity to assess whether their interests were better served by mapping a course independent of federation with Gorbachev's USSR. Lithuania responded to Vytautas Landbergis's calls for civil disobedience and Lithuanian independence with upheaval, Gorbachev's last attempt to suppress a secessionist movement militarily ended with a "demonstration of the limited value of bayonets" and he was reduced to complaining about the illegality of opposition tactics.[46] Lithuania declared independence in March 1990.

By April 23, 1991 Gorbachev was compelled to draft a new union treaty with Yeltsin and the leaders of eight other republics at a dacha at Novo-Ogarevo, which would reduce the Soviet center to an executive that would depend upon the revenues of the republics to sustain itself. Gorbachev then left for vacation in the Crimea and his absence from Moscow in the days before the union treaty was to be signed on August 21 precipitated the putsch that shredded the last remnants of the legitimacy of the army, the KGB, and the CPSU. Billington described this putsch as a shift from the "struggle for legitimacy" between the organs of the Marxist-Leninist Soviet state, to a "struggle for power" in Moscow. The institutions of proletarian internationalism had lost the "struggle for legitimacy," and they knew it, as evidenced by Billington's observation that the documents drafted by the junta that led the putsch to justify their actions to the public did not suggest that they were defending communism or socialism, but simply that they were combating chaos.[47] In Gramscian terms, the putsch leaders had lost the "war of position" and had gambled on a "war of maneuver"[48] to prevent the signing of a new union treaty that would have transformed the Soviet Union into a loose confederation of effectively sovereign states. They lost both wars, and Gorbachev was retrieved from his Crimean captivity. Billington suggests, however, that Gorbachev also lost his war to maintain a USSR in a looser, collaborative, reformist configuration, when he demonstrated during his address to the crowd which had gathered to greet him at Vnukovo Airport near Moscow, that he did not realize he had returned to a different country. As Gorbachev addressed the crowd "he soon lost them with his lawyerly manner, his self-justifying tone, and his assumption that the Communist Party as such would not be implicated . . . [and he continued to address them with] . . . formulaic languages about 'stages in the development of *perestroika*.' "[49] The identity of the people that Gorbachev addressed had been thoroughly transformed by the experience of defending their rights as a democratic society in the face of mortal threat. Gorbachev's address was oriented toward a people who no longer existed. When he had made it sufficiently clear that he did not understand this, his address was interrupted with "whistles of derision" and "calls to turn off his loudspeaker."[50] It was turned off.

The putsch had capped the crisis of legitimacy of the proletarian-internationalist institutions of the USSR. The societal self-identity that had emerged from the tumultuous years between 1985 and 1991 was in a limited sense bourgeois (democratic, liberal, and willing to hitch its fate to the fortunes that market reforms might bring) and in a fundamental sense nationalist, particularly in the constituent republics and ethnic autonomies. Little remained for Gorbachev to do by the close of 1991 beyond acknowledging the fact that *societal self-identity in the Soviet Union had been transformed, that the changed structure of identities had transformed the structure of societal interests, and to bow to these changes by transforming domestic institutions into forms of collective action that were capable of allowing society to express the identity it had declared.*

Gorbachev resigned as General Secretary of the CPSU on August 24 and ordered the confiscation of all CPSU property in his capacity as President.[51] The Congress of People's Deputies then dissolved itself and a maelstrom of independence declarations followed from the constituent republics.[52] Yeltsin, Kravchuk, and Shushkevich, as Presidents of the independent states of Russia, Ukraine, and Belarus, announced the dissolution of the USSR and their union in the Commonwealth of Independent States on December 8. When the Central Asian states, Armenia, Azerbaijan, and Moldova agreed to join, Gorbachev bowed to the *fait accompli* and resigned as President of the USSR on the 25th. The proletarian-internationalist colossus had ceased to exist and had been replaced by more than a dozen genuinely national-states. A socialist superpower had collapsed, in full possession of enough military capability to devastate every capitalist nation on the planet. The policies of Gorbachev's administration had loosened nationalist and liberal forms of societal self-identification on a proletarian-internationalist reformulation of the Eurasian empire of the Czars. Unfortunately for Gorbachev and the Soviet Union: "Nation and democracy both proved to be subversive to empire, for neither would tolerate the supranational relationship of superordination and subordination dictated by the imperial system."[53]

The significance of the collapse of the Soviet Union and the attendant demise of the cold war for international relations theory has been adequately stated by others. I will give the last word on this subject to Rey Koslowski and Friedrich Kratochwil, who have written the classic constructivist formulation of the argument.

> Fundamental change of the international system occurs when actors, through their practices, change the rules and norms constitutive of international interaction. Moreover, reproduction of the practice of international actors . . . depends on the reproduction of practices of domestic actors . . . Therefore, fundamental changes in international politics occur when beliefs and identities of domestic actors are altered thereby also altering the rules and norms that are constitutive of their political practices.[54]

Implications for Future Research

The present study has focused on the emergence and resurgence of national collective identity as the basis of an empirically distinct international system, a global social order, in the nineteenth and twentieth centuries. Simultaneously, the post-cold war globalization of political and economic liberalism has caused other scholars of international relations to examine neoliberal assertions that a "new world order," founded upon global democratization and a common global market, is at hand. As Barber has recently suggested, the forces of nationalist and religious particularism, and of liberal and consumer globalism, have both emerged to lay claim to shape a world that has been freed of a bipolar war of ideology.[55] As he suggests, the victory of either might have negative consequences for notions of civil society or democratic governance at the levels of both domestic and international society. I propose expanding a constructivist research agenda to encompass a study of the politics of identity to explore the causal significance of variations in the emerging, post-cold war forms of societal collective identity among states—from nationalistic particularism to liberal globalism—for the future organization of the international system. We should proceed rather from the proposition, which I have already elaborated in this book, that the notion of state interests varies with variations in societal self-identification. These variations have produced, and continue to produce, significant consequences for the behaviors of states, and for the evolution of social identities within the modern nation-state.

Analyses of the integrative processes of globalization have focused on the dangers to the national-state, and the classical notion of interests that ostensibly impel its action. In a recent, influential issue of *Daedalus*, analysts proceed with generally exogenous assumptions regarding the interests of states in the wake of the resurgence of the globalization of economic liberalism. They assert that in the teeth of these forces, the state is "diminished," "defective," "insecure."[56] The "real-state" is "waning."[57] All of these assertions beg the following question. If the "real-state," or "national-state," with exogenously and classically conceived interests is succumbing to the forces of the globalization of liberalism, then *whose* interests are prevailing, and how will the world be organized when (or perhaps we should ask "if") the globalization of liberalism proceeds to transform national-states around the globe? What impact does this process have on societal self-identification? Are the societies that conceive of themselves as nations facing inducements by the forces of global liberalism to abandon national identity for new forms of social identities, with implications for global social order and global governance?

In examining these issues we should continue to treat societal collective identity as an independent variable. The emergence of post-national social identities arising from the globalization of liberalism—social identities that we must identify—should similarly entail consequences for the institutional forms of collective action by which, I argue, new social identities manifest themselves in social action. My work on the implications of the politics of identity to date has been largely historical. The research agenda that I propose, however, focuses strongly on the implications of the politics of identity as response to globalization processes in the twentieth century, with particular emphasis on the implications of emerging national and economic societal collective identities in the post-cold war period and for the future.

A small part of this agenda is also historical, and is oriented toward uncovering the manner in which the economic and security relations of the twentieth century, and the mass movements that have characterized them, have been so strongly structured by the politics of identity as a response to an earlier manifestation of the globalization of liberalism. This earlier manifestation constituted the industrial revolution and I argue that the history of the twentieth century has been structured by societal responses, in the form of transformations in social identity commitments, to the global depression which marked the culmination of the industrial revolution. In this context we should, in part, mine what promises to constitute some of the richest empirical veins for explaining societal and international responses to "globalization processes" with insights drawn from a theoretical approach centered on the politics of identity. Not a few of these veins will surely be found under the crust of the history of the interwar period between 1918 and 1939. This is the period in which not only European, but also Asian and American national states developed their strongest, most far-reaching and nationalist responses to global economic crisis and its attendant domestic upheavals.

The state crystallized quite firmly as the national-state in this period. The emergence of national-collective identity in the nineteenth century had demanded the replacement of the laissez-faire state with the eudomonic (welfare) state in response to global domestic economic distress. The responses of the national, eudomonic state ranged from Keynsian countercyclical stimulus in the United States and Great Britain, to National Socialism and Fascism in Germany and Italy, to Imperial fascist militarism in Japan. These phenomena and their security implications will be explained with reference to transformations in societal collective identity.[58]

These investigations should focus in part upon the economic component of the notion of societal security and state security. In the heyday of popular nationalism no form of government that did not diligently seek to provide for the economic well-being of its people was capable of surviving the social upheaval attending the spectacle of the "world in depression."[59] The competitive currency devaluations that each national-state practiced to mitigate the consequences of the depression for its populace, the redefinition of political citizenship attending the rise of National Socialism and fascism in Europe, the New Deal in the United States, and the emergence of Tokyo as a militaristic, imperialist metropole in the Pacific,[60] may all be evaluated as differing responses to the demands of nationally self-aware peoples for redefinition of their interests. Each of the nationally self-aware states that engaged one another in the calamity of the Second World War did so in pursuit of different notions of the security interests of their societies and the nation-states that manifested the agency of these societies to the world. Each entered the war with the firm conviction that these security interests could be obtained only by a successful prosecution of the war, although many of these societal collective identities were as thoroughly demolished in the course of the war as were the states these identities had legitimated.

The larger part of this research agenda, however, should seek to elucidate, through a theoretical focus on the politics of identity, key trends in national and international organization that has emerged in the wake of the demise of Cold War bipolarity. We should investigate the "new nationalism" which has emerged in the context of the demise of the Soviet Union and the postwar order of Cold War and strategic bipolarity. In the former USSR and former Marxist states of Eastern Europe, proletarian internationalist and Soviet collective identity have given way to social collective identities which are arguably capitalist and democratic, but decidedly nationalist in character. While the security interests of the new Russian, Chechnyan, Serb, Croat, and Bosnian national identities have apparently required violent ethnic conflict in order to realize new national collective societal goals, the security interests of many other new national-states have not. An analytic approach centered on the politics of identity explains these events by appending the list of strategically significant consequences of the nationalization of state actors with the emergence of secessionist and irredentist challenges to the existing international order.[61] These secessionist and irredentist movements have created conditions under which members of multilateral security institutions such as NATO have been forced to reconceptualize their own security identities and interests, as they have been called upon to restore order to areas that have been destabilized by these movements.[62] These events portend significant changes in the structure of civil-military relations, as the armed forces of national-states are deployed for purposes that fail to conform to traditional notions of the security interests of national-states, but may well conform to those of the post-national-sovereign state identities that may be emerging in the industrialized West.[63]

We should examine these phenomena as a response to social and economic transformation in comparative analysis with a similar xenophobic response, in Europe and elsewhere, to the globalizing social and economic dislocation of the great industrial revolution near the end of the nineteenth century. Thus, while I assert the forms of national and global institutions to be dependent on the independent variable of social identities, I reaffirm that social identities do vary in response to globalizing, transnational forces.

In contrast to this response, we should examine the strongly integrative social identities that are emerging in the West—particularly in the United States and Western Europe—as quite different responses to the globalization of liberalism. If, as I claim, the institutional forms of collective action change with changes in social identities, we should be able to discover, and critically and comparatively analyze, for example, transnational European social identity commitments which impel the institutional form of the emerging European Union. We should be able to discover, and critically and comparatively analyze, particularistic national identity commitments in Central and Eastern Europe and the Former Soviet Union that helped to shatter proletarian internationalist identity commitments and the creation of national-states to manifest these emerging social identities.

These investigations should then continue with focus on the issue that we must clarify, according to my theoretical assertions, to provide us with the outlines of the future structure of global governance. While the question is necessarily generalized in the context of this short discussion, it essentially emerges as follows. If nationalist and religious particularism, and social and economic liberal transnationalism are both emerging as societal responses to the globalization processes of the late twentieth century which is likely to prevail? If the pattern of the late nineteenth century is not repeated, and ethnic and economic nationalism does not again rally social identities to construct socially insulating institutions against the atomizing forces of globalization, into what form will the institutional outlines of the post-national-statist world crystallize? Our social identities could be bound up with institutional forms of collective action that replace the national-state with transnational economic blocs, or with corporate feudalism, or a contemporarily unimagined institutional form. If my theoretical focus is fruitful, we must address the question of the transformation of international institutional forms by rigorous analysis of the changing social identities that mold institutions to their service.

Conclusion: International Change and Hopeful Nondeterminism

I will certainly have failed to accomplish my objective with this work if I have not persuaded the reader that the politics of identity cannot be neglected in the study of the historical development of the international system, or in the study of its contemporary development. Note that I employ the term historical "development" rather than, for example, "evolution." I do so because it is not my purpose to argue that the international system evolves as a progressive outgrowth of social interaction among a rational or enlightened human species. I have not developed an evolutionary theory of human progress. I do not argue that the Kantian "enlightenment project" of global pacification and progress is in the process of being realized by rational man—infinitely perfectible through the expansion of human reason.[64] I have not argued, with the liberals, that human history has terminated in the triumph of democracy and the blessings of the self-regulating market.[65] There have always been limits to the level of human misery and deprivation that the many can suffer to reify a liberal paradise for the few.[66] The effect of the globalization of liberalism on human well-being has by no means been uniformly sanguine.[67] While resistance to this project has experienced difficulty in acquiring a globally coherent voice,[68] it is by no means clear that the left will not ultimately marshal an alternative program.[69] History is unlikely to "end" in accordance with the expectations of adherents of liberal Hegelianism and bourgeois eschatology, just as it failed to end in accordance with the expectations of Marxist Hegelianism and proletarian eschatology. The resurgence of post-cold-war nationalisms and their potentially brutal expressions would tend to preclude this. Ideologies such as liberalism and Marxism do not "triumph" or "end history." They simply spawn eschatologies among their true believers, and persist in dominating public discourse in the regions where they legitimate rule until changes in social collective identities render them inoperable, and expose their eschatologies as infantile.

I have argued instead that the rules of the game, and not a few of the objectives of international relations have changed with variations in socially constructed conceptions of sovereignty. My outlook for the future development of the international system is neither the optimism of the Marxists and the liberals, nor the pessimism of the realists. What emerges from constructivist theory is an admonishment that the future of human social interaction and of relations between societies is in the hands of those of us now living. We are less impelled to international conflict by "anarchy" than by our will-to-manifest-identity. As Wendt has argued so effectively, "anarchy is what states make of it."[70] As Onuf has argued, we live in a "world of our making."[71] As Ferguson and Mansbach remind us, we construct and reconstruct new "polities."[72] Our collective interests change with our collective identities. We construct the domestic and global social orders that provide the structural context of our relations. We possess social agency that may enable us to organize its future quite differently. I would leave the reader only with a caveat. We can organize that future as a dystopia as easily as we can construct a utopia. We have seen these dystopias arise from severe applications of both national and class identity in the twentieth century. We may see them arise from the severe applications of liberal or illiberal ideology in the twenty-first century.

Our social agency levies upon us the burden of responsibility for that future. If we lacked social agency *qua* social collectivities, we might well fall back upon arguments that the international political realm is an "amoral" rather than an "immoral" realm.[73] If we own up to the system-transforming capacity of our social agency, we must also own the consequences of the decisions we make in executing that agency. What we call ourselves says a lot about us. Our societal self-identifications segment the political realm. When we formulate them we include some and exclude others. This is as true of transnational collective identities as of national collective identity. We cannot formulate an argument regarding who we are without at least implying an argument about who we are not. If I am a Pole, then I am not a Czech. If I am a proletarian, then I am not bourgeois. If I am a denizen of Christendom, then I am not a Muslim. If I am a *conquistador*, then I am not a "savage." If I am a liberal then I am not a socialist. We can see in these examples that historically we seem compelled to segment political space. We must define what is "inside" and what is "outside" this space. Liberalism is no guard against social closure if it results in the "secession of the rich,"[74] which entails designating the "other" through economic rather than ethnic criteria. This segmentation, however it is allocated, unfortunately appears to help us to avoid the ethical consequences of our social action with respect to that which is, and those who are, "outside" this space.[75]

A collective identity that is wholly inclusive appears difficult to achieve, but does appear needed if we are to avoid segmenting the political realm in a manner that enables intersocietal conflict by defining those "outside" our collective identity schemas as "other." We can arguably catch a glimpse of what a wholly inclusive collective identity would look like when we ponder the identity that the ecologists have constructed for each of us—denizens of spaceship earth. Certainly we can agree that none of us are "outside" the solution set that must be worked to keep the planet habitable for all of us. Only those who would deny the problem would find themselves "outside."

History in the view of constructivist social theory is, in no small part, the history of human agency. Institutional forms of social organization are adapted to the needs of social collectivities which transform these as they transform their own societal collective self-identifications. The "interests" and motivations of those societies change with these changing self-identifications. If this is so—and I have argued that it is so—then history is neither cyclical nor progressive, and practitioners of international relations are neither necessarily rushing toward catastrophe nor toward global cooperation and passivity. History will go where the changes that we effect in global social orders lead it. We are doomed to repeat nothing, yet neither is there a utopian, eschatological goal or place toward which we are all heading. The evolutionary perspective of a constructivist theory centered on the politics of identity is that of hopeful nondeterminism. We may hope that the direction of human social agency will improve the nature of interaction between societies, though we may not necessarily expect such a sanguine outcome.

Notes

1. *International Relations Without Nations?*

1. See Benedict Anderson, *Imagined Communities: Reflections on the Origins and Spread of Nationalism* (London: Verso, 1983).
2. An example of this type of theorizing is found in Kenneth N. Waltz, *Theory of International Politics* (New York: Random House, 1979).
3. For a description of the difficulties of dominant theories of international relations in contending with nationalist phenomenology see Yosef Lapid and Friedrich Kratochwil, "The Taming of the Shrew? Neorealist Appropriations and Theorizations of Nationalism," Presented at the 35th ISA Annual Convention, Washington, D.C., March 1994. For an updated version of this argument see Yosef Lapid and Friedrich Kratochwil. "Revisiting the 'National': Toward an Identity Agenda in Neorealism?" in Yosef Lapid and Friedrich Kratochwil (eds.), *The Return of Culture and Identity in IR Theory* (Boulder: Lynne Reinner, 1995), pp. 105–26.
4. An important debate on the extent to which the state apparatus possesses, and is empowered to express, autonomous interests is ongoing in the comparative politics literature. For the strongest elaboration of the neo-statist view see Theda Skocpol, *States and Social Revolutions: A Comparative Analysis of France, Russia, and China* (New York: Cambridge University Press, 1979), Theda Skocpol, "Bringing the State Back In: Strategies of Analysis in Current Research" in Evans, Rueschemeyer and Skocpol (eds.), *Bringing the State Back In* (Cambridge: Cambridge University Press, Cambridge, 1985), pp. 3–37, and Stephen D. Krasner, "Approaches to the State: Alternative Conceptions and Historical Dynamics" *Comparative Politics* 16 (2) (1984): 233–46. Critical reviews of the

neo-statist perspective may be found in Gabriel Almond, "The Return to the State" *American Political Science Review* 82 (3) (1988): 853–74, J. L. Himmelstein, and Micheal Kimmel, "Review Essay: States and Social Revolutions: The Limits and Implications of Skocpol's Structural Mode" *American Journal of Sociology* 86 (5) (1981): 1145–54. and Timothy Mitchell, "The Limits of the State: Beyond Statist Approaches and Their Critics," *American Political Science Review* 85 (1) (1991): 77–96.

5. Raymond Aron, *Peace and War: A Theory of International Relations* (New York: Praeger, 1966), p. 285.
6. Michael Mann, *The Sources of Social Power, Vol. II: The Rise of Classes and Nation-States, 1760–1914,* (New York: Cambridge University Press, 1993), p. 74.
7. I will employ the theoretical construct of the "structure of identities and interests" throughout this work. Wendt is the author of this concept. See Alexander Wendt, "Anarchy is What States Make of It: The Social Construction of Power Politics," *International Organization* 46 (2) (1992): 391–425.
8. William Bloom has expressed this as follows. "Nation-building requires that the mass of individuals make an identification with the nation-state this requires: 1) that the individual actually experiences the state and 2) that this experience is such as to evoke identification." See William Bloom, *Personal Identity, National Identity and International Relations* (Cambridge: Cambridge University Press, 1990), p. 61.
9. Waltz, *Theory of International Politics*, p. 168.
10. See Robert Gilpin, *War and Change in World Politics* (Cambridge: Cambridge University Press, 1981).
11. See Robert Gilpin, *The Political Economy of International Relations* (Princeton: Princeton University Press, 1987).
12. Anthony D. Smith, "The Problem of National Identity: Ancient, Medieval and Modern?," *Ethnic and Racial Studies* 17 (3) (July 1994): 381
13. Lapid and Kratochwil have made this observation. Lapid and Kratochwil, "The Taming of the Shrew?" For examples of the appropriative strategy criticized by Lapid and Kratochwil, see John Mearsheimer, "Back to the Future," *International Security* 15 (1) (1990): 5–56, and Barry R. Posen, "Nationalism, the Mass Army, and Military Power" *International Security* 18 (2) (1993): 80–124.
14. Ibid.
15. Ibid. p. 12.
16. Richard Little, "Rethinking System Continuity and Transformation," in Barry Buzan, Richard Little and Charles Jones, *The Logic of Anarchy* (New York: Columbia University Press, 1993), p. 87.
17. See Robert Gilpin, *War and Change in World Politics*, and A. F. K. Organski

and Jacek Kugler. *The War Ledger* (Chicago: University of Chicago Press, 1980).

18. For a development of the notion of institutional facts and their role in structuring action, see Friedrich Kratochwil, "Regimes, Interpretation and the 'Science' of Politics: A Reappraisal." *Millennium* 17 (2) (1988): 263–84. For a new and more general development of the significance of institutional facts in social life, see John R. Searle, *The Construction of Social Reality* (New York: Free Press, 1995). See especially pp. 79–126.
19. Lapid and Kratochwil, "Revisiting the 'National'," p. 119.
20. Frederick Frey illuminates how ubiquitous this problem is for analysis in all of the social sciences in "The Problem of Actor Designation in Political Analysis" *Comparative Politics* 17 (2) (1985): 127–52.
21. Waltz, *Theory of International Politics*, p. 79.
22. This would appear to be the case so long as Waltz's other two definitional elements of systemic structure are addressed in the system under study. The ordering principle of the system must be "anarchic" and there must be no "functional differentiation" among the interacting units.
23. Frey, "The Problem of Actor Designation in Political Analysis," p. 142.
24. Nevertheless, for samples of early and influential criticism in this vein, see the following articles, collected in Robert O. Keohane (ed.), *Neorealism and its Critics* (New York: Columbia University Press 1986). See, for example, John Gerard Ruggie, "Continuity and Transformation in the World Polity: Toward a Neorealist Synthesis," pp. 131–57; Robert O. Keohane, "Theory of World Politics: Structural Realism and Beyond," pp. 158–203; Robert W. Cox, "Social Forces, States and World Orders: Beyond International Relations Theory," pp. 204–54; and Richard K. Ashley, "The Poverty of Neorealism," pp. 255–300.
25. See Little, "Rethinking System Continuity and Transformation," in Buzan et. al. *Logic of Anarchy*.
26. Frey, "The Problem of Actor Designation in Political Analysis," p. 131.
27. Ibid. p. 132.
28. Ibid. p. 136. The emphasis is mine.
29. Helen Milner, "The Assumption of Anarchy in International Relations Theory: A Critique, *Review of International Studies* 17 (1991): 67–85.
30. Paul Schroeder, "Historical Reality vs. Neo-realist Theory," *International Security* 19 (1) (1994): 108–48.
31. Hans J. Morgenthau, *Politics Among Nations: The Struggle for Power and Peace* (4th ed.) (New York: Knopf, 1967), p. 5.
32. Martin Griffiths, *Realism, Idealism and International Politics: A Reinterpretation* (London: Routledge, 1992), p. 63.
33. Morgenthau, *Politics Among Nations*, p. 241 ff.

34. Ibid. p. 242 ff.
35. See, for example, Hedley Bull, *The Anarchical Society: A Study of Order in World Politics* (New York: Columbia University Press, 1977). A very useful comparison of the theoretical constructs of the American and British academies within the large umbrella of the realist tradition of international relations scholarship is found in Barry Buzan, "From International System to International Society: Structural Realism and Regime Theory Meet the English School," *International Organization* 47 (3) (1993): 327–52.
36. In addition to the works of Bull cited earlier see especially Hedley Bull and Adam Watson (eds.) *The Expansion of International Society* (Oxford: Clarendon Press, 1984); James Mayall. *Nationalism and International Society* (Cambridge: Cambridge University Press, 1990); Adam Watson, *The Evolution of International Society: A Comparative Historical Analysis* (London: Routledge, 1992); Martin Wight, *Systems of States* (Leicester: Leicester University Press, 1977). In addition to Buzan's 1993 essay, an elaboration of the distinctive contributions of the English school may be found in Peter Wilson, "The English School of International Relations: A Reply to Sheila Grader," *Review of International Studies* 15 (January 1989): 49–58.
37. Morgenthau, *Politics Among Nations*, p. 243.
38. Ibid. p. 244.
39. Hoffmann, "Commentary: Theory as a set of answers" in Stanley Hoffman (ed.), *Contemporary Theory in International Relations* (Englewood Cliffs, N.J.: Prentice-Hall, 1960), p. 35.
40. Kratochwil, "On the Notion of 'Interest' in International Relations" *International Organization* 36 (1) (1982): 21 ff.
41. See Eric Eyck, *Bismarck and the German Empire* (New York: Norton, 1968).
42. Kratochwil, "On the Notion of 'Interest' in International Relations," pp. 21–22.
43. Griffiths writes, "it is Morgenthau's power monism and unidimensional view of international politics that is really the basis for his reification of political man, an idealist distortion of real man." See Griffiths, *Realism and Idealism in International Politics*, p. 67.
44. I have recently provided elsewhere an explanation and illustration of the positional consequences of the ability to impose one's moral vision on others. See Rodney Bruce Hall, "Moral Authority as a Power Resource," *International Organization* 51 (4) (1997): 591–622
45. Justin Rosenberg, *The Empire of Civil Society: A Critique of the Realist Theory of International Relations* (London: Verso, 1994), p. 36. The emphasis is in the original.
46. Jürgen Habermas, "Citizenship and National Identity: Some Reflections on the Future of Europe," in Ronald Beiner (ed.) *Theorizing Citizenship* (Albany: SUNY Press, 1995), p. 258.

47. Yael Tamir, *Liberal Nationalism* (Princeton: Princeton University Press, 1993), p. 20.
48. The notion of "societal security" appears to be one such societal consensus principle offered recently. See Ole Waever, "Societal Security: The Concept" in Waever et. al., *Identity, Migration and the New Security Agenda in Europe* (New York: St. Martin's Press, 1993), chapter 2.
49. Rosenberg, *The Empire of Civil Society*, p. 30.
50. Ibid., p. 124.
51. See Micheal Walzer, "The Civil Society Argument," in Ronald Beiner (ed.), *Theorizing Citizenship* (Albany: SUNY Press, 1995), pp. 153–74. For a different argument see Charles Tilly (ed.), "Reflections on the History of European State-Making," in Charles Tilly (ed.), *The Formation of National States in Western Europe* (Princeton: Princeton University Press, 1975), pp. 3–84.
52. Rosenberg, *The Empire of Civil Society*, p. 125.
53. See Isser Woloch, *The New Regime: Transformations of the French Civic Order, 1789–1820* (New York: Norton, 1994). See especially chapter 8, "The Rise and Fall of Revolutionary *Bienfaisance*."
54. Michael Mann, *The Sources of Social Power Volume II*, p. 69.
55. See Hendrik Spruyt, *The Sovereign State and Its Competitors: An Analysis of Systems Change* (Princeton: Princeton University Press, 1994) pp. 178–79. For a briefer statement of Spruyt's institutional selection argument, see Hendrik Spruyt, "Institutional Selection in International Relations," *International Organization* 48 (4) (1994): 527–57.
56. , 2:Mann, *The Sources of Social Power* Volume II, p. 31.
57. Ibid. pp. 31—32.

2. Social Identities and Social Systems

1. Little cites this assertion by Nicholas Onuf in Buzan, et. al., *Logic of Anarchy*, p. 103. See Nicholas Greenwood Onuf, *World of Our Making* (Columbia, S.C.: University of South Carolina Press, 1989), especially pp. 35–65. For a comprehensive view of new approaches see Hayward R. Alker, *Rediscoveries and Reformulations: Humanistic Methodologies for International Studies* (Cambridge: Cambridge University Press, 1996). See also Chris Brown, *International Relations Theory: New Normative Approaches* (New York: Columbia University Press, 1993).
2. Alexander Wendt, "The Agent-Structure Problem in International Relations Theory," *International Organization* 41 (3) (1987), p. 359.
3. See Conrad Black, "Canada's Continuing Identity Crisis," *Foreign Affairs* 74 (2) (1995): 99–115.
4. Ontologies are "the substantive entities and configurations the theory postu-

lates." They provide the "concrete referents of an explanatory discourse" and consist of "the real-world structures (things, entities) and processes posited by the theory and invoked in the theory's explanations." See David Dessler, "What is at Stake in the Agent-Structure Debate?," *International Organization* 43 (Summer 1989): 444–45.

5. This is Anderson's explanation for postcolonial nationalism in the third world. See Benedict Anderson, *Imagined Communities*, pp. 139–40.
6. The definition of principles employed in theories of international regimes is wholly applicable here. Stephen Krasner defines principles as "beliefs of fact, causation and rectitude." It is specifically beliefs about the "rectitude" of authority that interest us in the present argument. See Stephen D. Krasner, "Structural Causes and Regime Consequences," in Stephen D. Krasner (ed.), *International Regimes* (Ithaca: Cornell University Press, 1983), pp. 1–21. Krasner's definition of principles in the context of international regimes is found on p. 2.
7. Gellner argues that an educated "clerisy" provides a high culture through which legitimate social governance is effected, and through which the technical requirements of centralized social organization are derived. When the literacy and high culture of the clerisy is secularized and ultimately universally held, societal self-identification, in essence, derives from this culture that now pervades the entire society. "That is the secret of nationalism." Gellner, *Nations and Nationalism* (Ithaca: Cornell University Press, 1983), pp. 9–18. Gellner is quoted here on p. 18.
8. Friedrich Kratochwil, *Rules, Norms, and Decisions: On the Conditions of Practical and Legal Reasoning in International Relations and Domestic Affairs* (Cambridge: Cambridge University Press, 1989), p. 126 ff. Emile Durkheim, *Sociology and Philosophy*. Translated by D. F. Pocock. With an introduction by J.G. Peristiany (New York: Free Press, 1953).
9. William Bloom, *Personal Identity, National Identity and International Relations*, pp. 14 ff.
10. Ibid. p. 15.
11. This is Waltz's development of the term and of the concept of socialization in the context of international interaction. In this view, in the international arena, socialization functions only as a structural constraint on the behavior of international actors. See Waltz, *Theory of International Politics*, pp. 74–77.
12. See, for example, Erik H. Erikson, *Identity: Youth and Crisis* (New York: Norton, 1968).
13. For persuasive examples of this literature, see W. R. Bion, *Experiences in Groups* (New York: Basic Books, 1959), Vamik D. Volkan, *Cyprus-War and Adaptation: A Psychoanalytic History of Two Ethnic Groups in Conflict* (Charlottesville: University Press of Virginia, 1979); Vamik D. Volkan, *The Need to Have Enemies and Allies* (Northvale: Jason Aronson, 1988); and the Group for the Ad-

vancement of Psychiatry, Report no. 123, *Us and Them, The Psychology of Ethnonationalism* (New York: Brunner/Mazel, 1987).

14. Daniel Druckman, "Nationalism, Patriotism, and Group Loyalty: A Social Psychological Perspective," *Mershon International Studies Review* (Supplement to the International Studies Quarterly) 38, Supplement 1 (April 1994): 49–50. The emphasis is mine.
15. Friedrich Kratochwil, *Rules, Norms, and Decisions*, pp. 116–17.
16. Max Weber, *The Theory of Social and Economic Organization*, Translated by A.M. Henderson and Talcott Parsons, Edited with an Introduction by Talcott Parsons (London: Collier-Macmillan, 1964), p. 124. Emphasis in the original.
17. Friedrich Kratochwil, *Rules, Norms, and Decisions*, p. 124.
18. Milner, "The Assumption of Anarchy," p. 74.
19. These social ordering principles are not to be confused with Waltz's systemic "ordering principle" of anarchy.
20. Bloom, *Personal Identity, National Identity and International Relations*, p. 47.
21. Ibid. pp. 47–48.
22. Jürgen Habermas, *Legitimation Crisis* (Boston: Beacon Press, 1975), pp. 3–4. Also quoted in William Bloom, Personal Identity, National Identity and International Relations, p. 48. The emphasis is mine.
23. Friedrich Kratochwil, "Regimes, Interpretation and the 'Science' of Politics: A Reappraisal," pp. 270–72.
24. For the role of social change, especially rapid social change, in evoking mass societal transformation in conceptions of legitimate social order see William Kornhauser, *The Politics of Mass Society* (New York: Free Press, 1959). For a related discussion in the context of developing societies see Samuel P. Huntington, *Political Order in Changing Societies* (New Haven: Yale University Press, 1968). See especially chapters 1–3.
25. See, for example, Adam B. Ulam, *The Bolsheviks: The Intellectual, Personal and Political History of the Triumph of Communism in Russia* (New York: Collier Books, 1965).
26. See, for example, Benjamin S. Lambeth, "Russia's Wounded Military," *Foreign Affairs* 74 (2) (1995): 86–98.
27. For novel attempts to explain these transformations with a theoretical framework outside the realist tradition see Rey Koslowski and Friedrich Kratochwil, "Understanding Change in International Politics: the Soviet Empire's Demise and the International System," *International Organization* 48 (2) (1994): 215–47, and Timur Kuran, "Now Out of Never: The Element of Surprise in the Eastern European Revolution of 1989," *World Politics* 44 (1) (1991): 7–48.
28. Skocpol, *States and Social Revolutions*, p. 4. The emphasis is mine.
29. Ibid. p. 5.
30. Ibid. pp. 4–5.

31. This assertion stands in opposition to the assertions of Waltz that an international system may be described fully by designating systemic structure, units, and interaction between these units. Waltz, *Theory of International Politics*, p. 79.
32. Kratochwil, *Rules, Norms and Decisions*, p. 69.
33. Waltz, *Theory of International Politics*, pp. 74–7 and pp. 127–28.
34. See Walker Connor, "The Nation and its Myth," *International Journal of Comparative Sociology* 33 (1992): 48–57.
35. Robert Jackson argues that postcolonial states in the third world have retained state-structures and juridical sovereignty left them by departing Europeans for precisely this reason. See Robert Jackson, "Quasi-states, Dual Regimes, and Neoclassical Theory: International Jurisprudence and the Third World," *International Organization* 41 (4) (1987): 519–50.
36. Waltz's discussion of structure as a causal agency may be found in Waltz, *Theory of International Politics*, pp. 73–74.

3. *Identities and Social Orders*

1. See, for example, Gerald Strauss, "The Reformation and its Public in the Age of Orthodoxy" in R. Po-Chia Hsia (ed.) *The German People and the Reformation*. (Ithaca: Cornell University Press 1988), pp. 194–215.
2. For an interesting discussion of the level of social penetration of the sixteenth-century state in Germany see Gerald Strauss, *Luther's House of Learning: Indoctrination of the Young in the German Reformation* (Baltimore: Johns Hopkins University Press, 1978). Strauss provides a fascinating discussion of the elaborate measures taken by Protestant German princes to ensure that the reformed faith was being taught and internalized in the far reaches of their realms . This involved visitations by an entourage of clerics and state officials, elaborate examinations of parochial clerics and catechists, and the transcriptions and archiving of highly detailed protocols of the examinations. See especially chapters 8, 9 and 12.
3. E. J. Hobsbawm, *Nations and Nationalism Since 1780: Programme, Myth, Reality*, Second Edition (Cambridge: Cambridge University Press, 1990), p. 57.
4. See, for example, the first chapter of A. G. Dickens, *The German Nation and Martin Luther* (London: Edward Arnold, 1974). Chapter 1, entitled "Nationalism and Anticlericalism: Prophecy and Piety," is studded, quite anachronistically, with references to sixteenth-century "nationalism."
5. Gerald Strauss, *Manifestations of Discontent in Germany on the Eve of the Reformation* (Bloomington: Indiana University Press, 1971). The book contains a wealth of primary source documents of the period, in English translation.
6. Edward Hallett Carr, *Nationalism and After* (London: Macmillan, 1945), p. 2.

7. Even in the medieval period from the inception of the Carolingian Empire (800 A.D.) to the late medieval period when Strayer suggests that the outlines of the modern territorial state could be clearly discerned (circa 1300 A.D.), the institution of kingship increasingly had become secularized, and its legitimacy separated from the legitimating principles provided by the political theology of the Church. See Ernst Kantorowicz, *The King's Two Bodies: A Study in Medieval Political Theology* (Princeton: Princeton University Press, 1957). Kantorowicz provides a monumental study of how the particulars of the political theology of divine ordination changed significantly, between the tenth and early sixteenth centuries, with respect to the specific qualities the king's anointing was thought to have conferred upon him. The sacrality of the anointed king was significantly downgraded over the centuries from what Kantorowicz has referred to as an early "Christ-centered kingship," to a "law-centered" kingship, to a "man-centered" kingship. See especially chapters 3, 4, and 8. See also my "Moral Authority as a Power Resource." Strayer's argument regarding the origins and appearance of the modern state is found in Joseph Strayer, *On the Medieval Origins of the Modern State* (Princeton: Princeton University Press, 1970).
8. See, for example, R. N. Swanson, *Church and Society in Late Medieval England* (Oxford: Basil Blackwell, 1989).
9. Georges Duby, *The Three Orders: Feudal Society Imagined*, Arthur Goldhammer (trans.) (Chicago: University of Chicago Press, 1986), see chapter 1.
10. Robert L. Reynolds, *Europe Emerges: Transition Toward an Industrial World-Wide Society 600–1750* (Madison: University of Wisconsin Press, 1961), pp. 403–19.
11. For valuable discussions of the importance of literacy in the early modern state, see Ronald J. Deibert, "Typographica: The Medium and the Medieval to Modern Transformation," *Review of International Studies* 22 (1996): 29–56. For a more highly developed version of these arguments see Ronald J. Deibert, *Parchment, Printing, and Hypermedia: Communication in World Order Transformation* (New York: Columbia University Press, 1997). For the importance of literacy in the promulgation of the Reformation, see: E. J. Baskerville, "John Ponet in Exile: A Ponet Letter to John Bale," *Journal of Ecclesiastical History* 37 (3) (1986): 442–47; Mariam U. Chrisman, "Printing and the Evolution of Lay Culture in Strasbourg: 1480–1599" in R. Po-Chia Hsia (ed.), *The German People and the Reformation* (Ithaca: Cornell University Press, 1988), pp. 74–101; Carole Levin, *Propaganda in the English Reformation: Heroic and Villainous Images of King John*, (Lewistown, NY: The Edwin Mellen Press, 1988); Nancy L. Roelker, "The Impact of the Reformation Era on Communication and Propaganda," in Laswell, Lerener and Speier (eds.), *Propaganda and Communication in World History, II* (Honolulu: University of Hawaii Press, 1980),

pp. 41–84; Helga Robinson-Hammerstein, "Luther and the Laity," In Helga Robinson-Hammerstein (ed.), *The Transmission of Ideas in the Lutheran Reformation* (Dublin: Irish Academic Press, 1989), pp. 11–46; and Robert W. Scribner, *For the Sake of Simple Folk: Popular Propaganda for the German Reformation* (Cambridge: Cambridge University Press, 1981).

12. For a study of the French case during the transition from the Valois to the Bourbon, and the causes and consequences of the French civil wars of religion, see Emannuel Le Roy Ladurie, *The Royal French State 1460–1610*, Juliet Vale (trans.) (London: Blackwell, 1994). See especially chapters 4–11.
13. Greengrass argues that early on in the Augsburg system: "Edicts of toleration presented a principle which it was difficult for French monarchs to be seen to concede openly. They were Most Christian Kings, and the traditions, rituals and ceremonies of their office were closely linked to the beliefs and practices of the Catholic Church. Edicts of toleration were difficult, but not impossible, to justify [but] [t]here was already the example of the famous Interim settlement in the Holy Roman Empire in 1548, modified and eventually accepted as the pacification of Augsburg of 1555. The 'permitting' of another religion could be presented as necessary to the state's survival. The verb '*permettre*' (as in the 'permitting' of a privilege) was much more acceptable that the verb '*tolérer*', which still carried overtones of the kind of dangerous license which would lead inevitably to atheism and libertinism, fears of which were often voiced by contemporaries during the civil wars." Mark Greengrass, *The French Reformation* (Oxford: Basil Blackwell, 1987), p. 69.
14. A very tidy summary of the events leading up to the Thirty Years War may be found in Andreas Osiander, *The States System of Europe, 1640–1990: Peacemaking and the Conditions of International Stability*, (Oxford: Clarendon Press, 1994), pp. 16–17.
15. Le Roy Ladurie, *The Royal French State 1460–1610*, pp. 232–40 and p. 298.
16. Ibid. p. 284.
17. England proved a significant exception. Her early self-identification as a "Protestant nation" had early and significant consequences for her domestic institutional formation, with significant and sanguine consequences for the early emergence of capitalist production relations as well as national self-identification. See Liah Greenfeld, *Nationalism: Five Roads to Modernity* (Cambridge: Harvard University Press, 1992). See Chapter 1, "God's Firstborn: England."
18. For studies of the impact of rapid social change in the Anabaptist movement see R. Po-Chia Hsia, "Munster and the Anabaptists," in R. Po-Chia Hsia (ed.). *The German People and the Reformation* (Ithaca: Cornell University Press, 1988), pp. 51–69, and Norman Cohn, *The Pursuit of the Millennium: Revolutionary Millenarians and Mystical Anarchists of the Middle Ages*, Revised and Expanded Edition (New York: Oxford University Press, 1970), pp. 252–80. For

the impact of rapid social change on the Lutheran Reformation, particularly in an urban context, see Robert Scribner, "Ritual and Reformation" in R. Po-Chia Hsia (ed.), pp. 122–44, and Hans-Christoph Rublach "Martin Luther and the Urban Social Experience" in Helga Robinson-Hammerstein (ed.), *The Transmission of Ideas in the Lutheran Reformation*, pp. 65–82.

19. For the "top-down" character of the English Reformation, see J. J. Scarisbrick, *The Reformation and the English People* (Oxford: Basil Blackwell, 1984).
20. Kalevi J. Holsti, *Peace and War: Armed Conflicts and International Order 1648–1989* (Cambridge: Cambridge University Press, 1991). See Table 3.1, pp. 48–49.
21. See Table 3.2 in Ibid., p. 49.
22. Osiander, *The States System of Europe*, 1640–1990, pp. 77–89.
23. Ibid. pp. 87–88.
24. Evan Luard, *War in International Society: A Study in International Sociology* (New Haven: Yale University Press, 1987), p. 346.
25. Ibid. p. 348.
26. Ibid. pp. 348–50.
27. Ibid. p. 351.
28. John Gerard Ruggie. "Territoriality and Beyond: Problematizing Modernity in International Relations," *International Organization* 47 (1) (1993): 163.
29. Isser Woloch, *Eighteenth-Century Europe: Tradition and Progress 1715–1789* (New York: Norton, 1982), pp. 51–52.
30. Jeremy Black, *Eighteenth Century Europe 1700–1789* (New York: St. Martin's Press, 1990), pp. 315–21.
31. It is interesting to note that in Napoleonic France, where noble privilege saw a normative resurgence during the Empire that followed the Jacobin and Thermidorian republics, and that proceeded the Bourbon Restoration, the bourgeoisie in France returned to their pre-Revolutionary pattern of evasion of military service. Isser Woloch's recent study of post-Revolutionary French society indicates that the urban bourgeoisie obtained bogus medical deferments and hired replacements during the Napoleonic conscription at rates much higher than other segments of society. Woloch, *The New Regime*, pp. 383–87.
32. Spruyt, *The Sovereign State and Its Competitors*, p. 178.
33. Ibid. pp. 178–79.
34. Luard, *War in International Society*, p. 352.
35. While the literature on international regimes is vast, the best introduction to the topic may be found in Stephen D. Krasner (ed.). *International Regimes*.
36. Kratochwil, *Rules Norms and Decisions*, pp. 61–64.
37. Luard, *War in International Society*, pp. 352–53.
38. Schroeder, "Historical Reality vs. Neo-realist Theory." Schroeder begins this argument on p. 124.

39. Ibid. p. 125.
40. Osiander, *The States System of Europe*, pp. 110–20.
41. See, for example, the wartime letters of Washington in Henry Steele Commager and Richard B. Morris (eds.). *The Spirit of Seventy-Six: The Story of the American Revolution as Told by Participants* (New York: Bonanza Books, 1983).
42. See Carl L. Becker, *The Heavenly City of the Eighteenth-Century Philosophers* (New Haven: Yale University Press, 1932), and Alisdair MacIntyre, *After Virtue: A Study in Moral Theory* (Notre Dame, Indiana: University of Notre Dame Press, 1984). Especially Chapters 4–5.
43. Tamir, *Liberal Nationalism*, pp. 18–19.
44. Ibid. p. 20.
45. See Douglass C. North, *Structure and Change in Economic History* (New York: Norton, 1981).
46. E. J. Hobsbawm, *The Age of Capital:1848–1875* (New York: Scribner's, 1975), p. 29.
47. Mann, *The Sources of Social Power, II*, pp. 125–26.
48. Mann, *The Sources of Social Power, II*, p. 161. See also Catherine Drinker Bowen, *Miracle at Philadelphia: The Story of the Constitutional Convention* (Boston: Little, Brown, 1966), pp. 69–72 and pp. 139–40.
49. Liah Greenfeld questions the assertions of analysts of Marxian heritage such as Barrington Moore that the French Revolution should be regarded as a bourgeois revolution, as its intellectual heritage was a French Enlightenment that was in significant measure a product of aristocratic reaction to absolutism. Rather than seeing them as intellectual agents of the revolution, she argues that the French bourgeoisie "consisted of a middling sort of people, smart enough to recognize a good opportunity. The elite forged and armed the middle classes with weapons it had not much use for itself. The French national identity was of a mixed heritage. The chief reason for the adoption of the idea of the nation in France was the fact that this French elite in the eighteenth century was in a state of crisis, and the idea of national patriotism offered a means of resolving it." Greenfeld, *Nationalism: Five Roads to Modernity*, p. 186.
50. Mann, *The Sources of Social Power, II*, p. 170.
51. Ibid. p. 171.
52. For a description of the war debt and the crisis of confidence that resulted from subsequent inability of the French crown to manage it see James C. Riley, *The Seven Years War and the Old Regime in France: The Economic and Financial Toll* (Princeton: Princeton University Press, 1986) See especially chapters 6 and 7.
53. Mann, *The Sources of Social Power, II*, p. 221.
54. Ibid. p. 222.
55. Hobsbawm, *Nations and Nationalism Since 1780*, p. 118.

56. Mann, *The Sources of Social Power, II*, p. 225 .
57. Rogers Brubaker, *Citizenship and Nationhood in France and Germany* (Cambridge: Harvard University Press, 1992), pp. 31–34.
58. Ibid. p. 28.
59. Little, "Rethinking System Continuity and Transformation."

4. Raison d'Etat and Territorial Sovereignty

1. Evan Luard, *The Balance of Power: The System of International Relations, 1648–1815* (New York: St. Martin's Press, 1992) pp. 101–3. Quotation of Frederick William of Prussia taken from p. 103.
2. Woloch, *Eighteenth-Century Europe*, p. 4.
3. Ibid. pp. 61–63.
4. A worthwhile description of, for example, the relationship of the French peasantry to *seigneur* and state may be found in Barrington Moore, *The Social Origins of Dictatorship and Democracy* (Boston: Beacon Press, 1966), pp. 70–101.
5. Woloch, *Eighteenth-Century Europe*, p .9.
6. Ibid. pp. 71–72.
7. Ibid. pp. 79–81.
8. Ibid. p. 82.
9. Ibid. p. 92.
10. A significant debate has emerged in the historical literature on absolutism in recent years regarding the extent to which the rule of even the French monarchy was unchallenged in all its aspects. Significantly, however, the bulk of this skepticism regarding "how absolute was it?" is directed toward the sixteenth and seventeenth centuries, not the eighteenth century by which time centralization of the state and power in the hands of the monarchy had been well consolidated. For examples of the revisionist literature on absolutism see, for example, David Parker, "Sovereignty, Absolutism and the Function of the Law in Seventeenth-Century France," *Past and Present*, No. 122 (February 1989): 36–74; Phyllis K. Leffler, "French Historians and the Challenge to Louis XIV's Absolutism," *French Historical Studies* 14 (1) (1985): 1–22. For the English case see John Miller, "The Potential for 'Absolutism' in Later Stuart England," *History: The Journal of the Historical Association* 69 (226) (1984): 187–207. For a debate, see J. Russell Major, "The Revolt of 1620: A Study of the Rise of Fidelity," *French Historical Studies* 14 (3) (1986): 391–407; Sharon Kettering, "Patronage and Politics During the Fronde," *French Historical Studies* 14 (3) (1986): 409–41; and Ellery Schalk, "Clientage, Elites, and Absolutism in Seventeenth-Century France," *French Historical Studies* 14 (3) (1986): 442–46.
11. Woloch, *Eighteenth-Century Europe*, p .92.

12. Greenfeld, *Nationalism: Five Roads to Modernity*, p. 138.
13. R. R. Palmer, "Frederick the Great, Guibert, Bülow: From Dynastic to National War," in Edward Mead Earle (ed.), *Makers of Modern Strategy: Military Thought From Machiavelli to Hitler* (Princeton: Princeton University Press, 1973), p. 54.
14. Woloch, *Eighteenth-Century Europe*, pp. 89–90.
15. Ibid. pp. 86–87.
16. Palmer, "Frederick the Great," p. 50.
17. Ibid. The emphasis is mine.
18. Woloch, *Eighteenth-Century Europe*, pp. 95–98.
19. Ibid. pp. 101–2.
20. Rosenberg, *The Empire of Civil Society*, p. 125.
21. See G.M Trevelyan, *The English Revolution 1688–1689* (New York: Oxford University Press, 1965). pp. 70–92.
22. Jeremy Black. "Chatham Revisited," *History Today* 41 (August 1991): 34–39.
23. Woloch, *Eighteenth-Century Europe*, pp. 30–31.
24. Ibid. p. 33.
25. England had become adept at systematically marginalizing Catholics in particular. The government of James I had even created a national holiday to be celebrated on November 5, long used to reproach Catholics, in commemoration of a "gunpowder plot" by Guy Fawkes and a band of Catholic radicals to destroy parliament and James's government on that date in 1605. See David Cressy, "National Memory in Early Modern England," in John R. Gillis (ed.), *Commemorations: The Politics of National Identity* (Princeton: Princeton University Press, 1994), pp. 61–73. For a discussion of the popular equation of English Catholicism with Jacobinism in this era, see Geoffrey Holmes and Daniel Szechi, *The Age of Oligarchy: Pre-industrial Britain 1722–1783* (London: Longmans, 1993). See Chapter 6, pp. 89–100.
26. Woloch, *Eighteenth-Century Europe*, pp. 33–34.
27. H.T. Dickinson, "Whiggism in the Eighteenth Century," in John Cannon (ed.), *The Whig Ascendancy: Colloquies on Hanoverian England* (New York: St. Martin's Press 1981), pp. 28–50. See especially pp. 29–36.
28. Greenfeld, *Nationalism: Five Roads to Modernity*, See Chapter 1, "God's First Born: England."
29. Ibid.
30. Luard, *The Balance of Power*, pp. 104–5.
31. Ruggie, "Territoriality and Beyond," p. 162.
32. From the Latin, "treaties are to be observed."
33. Friedrich Meinecke, *Machieavellism: The Doctrine of Raison d'Etat and Its Place in Modern History* (Boudler: Westview Press, 1984), p. 1.
34. Quoted in Luard, *The Balance of Power*, pp. 111–12.

35. Ibid. p. 112.
36. Ibid. pp. 113–15.
37. Ibid. p. 117.
38. John H. Herz. "Rise and Demise of the Territorial State," *World Politics* 9 (4) (1957): 478–79.
39. Ibid. pp. 116–26.
40. For the importance of consensual knowledge in fostering shared understandings in international interaction see Kratochwil, *Rules, Norms and Decisions*, p. 60 ff.
41. Luard, *The Balance of Power*, p. 127.
42. Osiander, *The States System of Europe*, pp. 120–47.
43. Ruggie. "Territoriality and Beyond," pp. 164–65.
44. Luard, *The Balance of Power*, pp. 305–7.
45. Ibid. pp. 308–16.
46. See Mlada Bukovansky, "American Identity and Neutral Rights From Independence to the War of 1812," *International Organization* 51 (2) (1997): 209–43.
47. Luard, *The Balance of Power*, pp. 316–21.
48. Ibid. p. 321.
49. Ibid. pp. 323–34.
50. Joseph A. Schumpeter, *Imperialism and Social Classes*, Henz Norden (trans.) Paul M. Sweezy (ed.) (New York: Augustus M. Kelley, 1951), p. 82.
51. Luard, *The Balance of Power*, p. 129.
52. Ibid. p. 131.
53. Ibid. p. 132.
54. Ibid. pp. 134–36.
55. Ibid. pp. 136–42.
56. Ibid. p. 137.
57. Paul Kennedy, *The Rise and Fall of the Great Powers: Economic Change and Military Conflict from 1500 to 2000* (New York: Random House, 1987), p. 73. For a very fine discussion of alliance politics during this era see Luard, *The Balance of Power*, pp. 256–80.
58. Ruggie, "Territoriality and Beyond," pp. 148–52.
59. James Mayall. *Nationalism and International Society*, p. 72.
60. Edward Mead Earle, "Adam Smith, Alexander Hamilton, Friedrich List: The Economic Foundation of Military Power," in Edward Mead Earle (ed.), *Makers of Modern Strategy: Military Thought From Machiavelli to Hitler* (Princeton: Princeton University Press, 1973), p. 118.
61. Mayall, *Nationalism and International Society*, p. 72.
62. Woloch, *Eighteenth Century Europe*, pp. 124–25.
63. Luard, *The Balance of Power*, p. 226.
64. Woloch, *Eighteenth Century Europe*, p. 128.

65. Luard, *The Balance of Power*, p. 228.
66. Ibid. p. 227.
67. Darrett B. Rutman. "The Virginia Company and Its Military Regime," in Darrett B. Rutman (ed.), *The Old Dominion: Essays for Thomas Perkins Abernethy* (Charlottesville: University Press of Virginia, 1964), pp. 1–20.
68. Luard, *The Balance of Power*, pp. 228–29.
69. Ibid. p. 229.
70. Lawrence A. Harper. "The Effect of the Navigation Acts on the Thirteen Colonies," in Richard B. Morris (ed.), *The Era of the American Revolution: Studies Inscribed to Evarts Boutell Greene* (New York: Columbia University Press, 1939), pp. 38–39.
71. Earle, "Adam Smith, Alexander Hamilton, Friedrich List," pp. 118–19.
72. Adam Smith, *An Inquiry into the Nature and Causes of the Wealth of Nations: Vols. I and II*, R. H. Campbell and A. S. Skinner (eds.), (Indianapolis: Liberty Press, 1981). See especially Book IV, "On Systems of Political Oeconomy," pp. 428–688.
73. See, for example, David A. Baldwin, *Economic Statecraft* (Princeton: Princeton University Press, 1985).
74. See Albert O. Hirschman, *National Power and the Structure of Foreign Trade* (Berkeley: University of California Press, 1945), pp. 29–40.
75. Martin Staniland, *What is Political Economy? A Study of Social Theory and Underdevelopment* (New Haven: Yale University Press, 1985), p. 106.
76. We should not pass by the issue of chattel slavery in the eighteenth century with a blithe phrase. There would have scarcely been a French colonial empire at all without millions of slaves to work the sugar plantations. Of course the British colonial cotton production relied on slaves, as did Spanish mining and other concerns. Of a total of 9.3 million Africans enslaved, 6 million were enslaved in the eighteenth century. Mortality was high on tropical plantations, and in transit from Africa. Mortality in passage from Africa averaged 11% during the height of the slave trade, due to shipboard "packing" schemes. See Woloch, *Eighteenth Century Europe*, pp. 131–34.
77. Luard, *The Balance of Power*, pp. 232–36.
78. Herz, "The Rise and Demise of the Territorial State," pp. 478–79.
79. Luard, *The Balance of Power*, p. 174.
80. Herz, "The Rise and Demise of the Territorial State," p. 479. The emphasis is Herz's.
81. Luard, *The Balance of Power*, pp. 175–76.
82. Ibid. pp. 184–95.
83. Ibid. p. 198.
84. A particularly thorough account of the impact of colonial wars on indigenous

peoples may be found in Francis Jennings, *Empire of Fortune: Crowns, Colonies and Tribes in the Seven Years War in America* (New York: Norton, 1988).

85. Rosenberg, *The Empire of Civil Society*, p. 120.
86. Ibid. p. 118.
87. Ibid. p. 121. The emphasis is mine.
88. See Antonio Gramsci, *Selections from the Prison Notebooks*, Q. Hoare and G. N. Smith (eds. & trans.) (New York: International Publishers, 1971), pp. 52–120.
89. Michael Doyle, *Empires* (Ithaca: Cornell University Press, 1986), p. 110.

5. Territorial-Sovereign Identity and the Seven Years' War

1. Earlier in this work I have sometimes referred to "England" rather than "Great Britain" or "Britain." In the remainder of this work I will generally be referring to events that occurred after the union of England with Scotland, from which time it is more appropriate to speak of "Britain," rather than "England." As this naming convention changed in history, it will now also change in my analytic narrative.
2. Kennedy, *The Rise and Fall of the Great Powers*, p. 77.
3. I have presented graphically data taken from Homes & Szechi, *The Age of Oligarchy*, See Table L.1:"Industrial output, exports and home consumption in England and Wales, 1700–1785," p. 388.
4. Also a graphical representation of data taken from Homes & Szechi, *The Age of Oligarchy*, See Table I.2:"The armed forces and the cost of war, 1689–1783," p. 374.
5. Kennedy, *The Rise and Fall of the Great Powers*, p. 76.
6. Ibid. p. 78.
7. Ibid. p. 79.
8. Ibid.
9. Riley, *The Seven Years War and the Old Regime in France*, p. 56.
10. Kennedy, *The Rise and Fall of the Great Powers*, pp. 82–83.
11. Ibid. p. 84.
12. Riley, *The Seven Years War and the Old Regime in France*, p. 90.
13. Ibid. p. 91. For a study of the post-war consequences of the massive French debt, see the following reprint of the 1944 Columbia University Press study of Paul H. Beik, A *Judgment of the Old Regime: Being a survey by the Parlement of Province of French economic and fiscal politics at the close of the Seven Years War (New York: 1967).*
14. Kennedy, *The Rise and Fall of the Great Powers*, pp. 80–81.
15. Woloch, *Eighteenth Century Europe*, p. 85.

16. See Carl William Eldon, *England's Subsidy Policy Towards the Continent During the Seven Years' War*, Ph. D. Dissertation: University of Pennsylvania, Philadelphia, 1938.
17. See, for example, Julian S. Corbett, *England in the Seven Years' War: A Study in Combined Strategy, Vol. 1*, AMS Press reprint of Longmans, Green and Co., London, 1918, Reprinted 1973 by AMS Press, New York, pp. 112–15, and Homes & Szechi, *The Age of Oligarchy*, pp. 252–57.
18. Corbett, *England in the Seven Years' War*, p. 14.
19. Ibid. p. 15. Note that the Duke of Newcastle headed the government of George II at the start of the Seven Year's War in a position very much like the modern office of Prime Minister, which did not yet then exist.
20. Ibid. p. 24.
21. See Daniel J. O'Neil, "Enclave Nation-Building: The Irish Experience," *Journal of Ethnic Studies* 15 (3) (Fall 1987): 1–25.
22. See Kohn, *The Idea of Nationalism: A Study of its Origins and Background*, (New York: Collier Books, 1967), pp. 263–325, and Greenfeld, *Nationalism*, pp. 399–491.
23. See, for example, Woloch, *Eighteenth Century Europe*, p. 41.
24. Karl Schweizer, "The Seven Years' War: A System Perspective," in Jeremy Black (ed.), *The Origins of War in Early Modern Europe* (Edinburgh: John Donald, 1987), p. 242.
25. Ibid. p. 255, fn 4.
26. Eldon, *England's Subsidy Policy* , p. 11.
27. Corbett, *England and the Seven Years' War, Vol. I*, p. 23.
28. Kennedy, *The Rise and Fall of the Great Powers*, pp. 111–13.
29. Eldon, *England's Subsidy Policy* , See the appendix, "Table II - Subsidy Payments," p. 160.
30. Ibid. p. 18.
31. Ibid. p. 20.
32. For an extended critique of the Waltzian version of structure in this context see Schroeder, "Historical Reality vs. Neo-realist Theory." Schroeder points out that states in this period indeed "specialized" functionally within the system in many ways at odds with the assumptions of the structural realist account.
33. Ibid. p. 14.
34. Ibid. p. 47.
35. Ibid. pp. 51–52.
36. Ibid. pp. 53–54.
37. Kennedy, *The Rise and Fall of the Great Powers*, p. 113.
38. Eldon, *England's Subsidy Policy* , pp. 55–57.
39. Ibid. p. 58.
40. Ibid. p. 61.

41. Ibid. p. 62.
42. Ibid. p. 71.
43. It is interesting to consider the extent to which the French Wars of Religion of the sixteenth century had promoted this conflict among the dynastic sovereigns. Decades of the sixteenth century had, for France, been filled with the calamity of several Wars of Religion. The long-term peace and toleration they hoped would follow were ended by the treacherous actions of the crown in sponsoring the assassination of Protestant notables gathered for a wedding in the royal household (in the 1572 St. Bartholomew Massacre). The religious wars were renewed. At their end, the death of the last Valois king left the Bourbon, Calvinist prince, Henri de Navarre, in line as the leading contender for the French crown under Salic law. Henri's accession as Henry IV was followed in short order by his reconversion to Catholicism (essential if he expected to reign securely over a country that was still overwhelmingly Catholic). His reign did make a full French religious reconciliation possible, however, and official state intolerance of Protestantism finally ended with the promulgation of the 1598 Edict of Nantes. The conflict, and its termination at the accession of a man of pragmatic religious conduct, set a pattern of French pragmatism on the matter of alignment in accordance with confessional factors. See Greengrass, *The French Reformation*, and Le Roy Ladurie, *The Royal French State: 1440–1610*.
44. Eldon, *England's Subsidy Policy*, pp. 73–78.
45. Schwiezer, "The Seven Years' War: A System Perspective," p. 242.
46. Dickinson, "Whiggism in the Eighteenth Century," p. 43.
47. Eldon, *England's Subsidy Policy* , p. 100.
48. Black, "Chatham Revisited," p. 38.
49. Eldon, *England's Subsidy Policy*, p. 101.
50. Ibid. p. 103.
51. Ibid. p. 118.
52. Schweizer, "The Seven Years War, A System Perspective," p. 248.
53. It is equally problematic, contra Marx, to speak of the "objective interests" of a socioeconomic class, and for similar reasons, but this is a topic for another book.
54. Aron, *Peace and War*, p. 285.
55. Eldon, *England's Subsidy Policy*, pp. 131–32.
56. Ibid. pp. 137–39.
57. Ibid. p. 140.
58. Ibid. p. 143.
59. Kennedy, *The Rise and Fall of the Great Powers*, p. 114.
60. Corbett, *England and the Seven Years' War, Vol. II*, Corbett provides the English language text of the treaty in the appendix to his second volume, pp. 377–90.

61. Kennedy, *The Rise and Fall of the Great Powers*, p. 114.
62. Ibid. See his comments on p. 98.
63. Eldon, *England's Subsidy Policy*, p. 160.

6. The Emergence of National-Sovereign Identity: Revolutionary Nationalism and Reaction

1. See E.J. Hobsbawm, *The Age of Revolution* (London: Weidenfeld and Nicholson, 1962).
2. I rely upon the work of Liah Greenfeld for much of this discussion. See Greenfeld, *Nationalism: Five Roads to Modernity*, pp. 145–88.
3. Ibid. pp. 148–49.
4. Ibid. p. 175. Note that both Rousseau and his cultured, aristocratic patrons had much to draw upon from classical Greek philosophy as a source of inspiration for their vehement loathing of the "vulgar rich." Consider, for example, just a brief sample of the argument for the philosopher-king from Plato's Republic, in response to a query by the trusty Adeimantus: "you spoke as astonished that philosophers are not held in honor by their country . . . it would be far more astonishing if they were . . . he is right in calling the best sort of philosophers useless to the public; but for that he must rather blame those who make no use of them. It is not in the natural course of things for the pilot to beg the crew to take his orders, any more than for the wise to wait on the doorsteps of the rich; the author of that epigram was mistaken. What is natural is that the sick man, whether rich or poor, should wait at the door of the physician, and that all who need to be governed should seek out the man who can govern them; it is not for him to beg them to accept his rule, if there is really any help in him." *The Republic of Plato*, F. M. Cornford (trans.) (Oxford: Oxford University Press, 1945), p. 196.
5. For a most useful and readable scholarly edition of this work, see Alan Ritter and Julia Conaway Bondanella (eds.), *Rousseau's Political Writings*, J.C. Bondanella (trans.) (New York: Norton, 1988). Rousseau's essay "On Social Contract or Principles of Political Right" is found on pp. 83–173. Rousseau ultimately dispenses with the notion of aristocracy, either by birth or merit, in his sixth chapter "On Monarchy," pp. 128–32.
6. Greenfeld, *Nationalism: Five Roads to Modernity*, p. 178.
7. Ibid. p. 15.
8. All quotations from these two sentences are found in Habermas, *Legitimation Crisis*, pp. 3–4.
9. Greenfeld, *Nationalism: Five Roads to Modernity*, p. 16. Emphasis in the original.

10. Ibid. pp. 16–17. Emphasis in the original.
11. A wonderful source of some of this material is Claude Manceron, *The Age of the French Revolution, Volume Two: The Wind From America 1778–81* (New York: Simon and Schuster, 1989). See especially pp. 76–84.
12. Greenfeld, *Nationalism: Five Roads to Modernity*, p. 180.
13. Ibid. p. 186.
14. Ibid. p. 185.
15. Ibid.
16. See Moore, *Social Origins of Dictatorship and Democracy*, pp. 40–110, and Alexis de Tocqueville, *The Old Regime and the French Revolution* (New York: Doubleday, 1955).
17. Skocpol, *States and Social Revolutions*, pp. 174–80.
18. In Mann's historical sociology, the causally significant sources of social power are ideological, economic, military, and political (thus IEMP). See Mann, *The Sources of Social Power, Vol. II*, pp. 1–22.
19. Ibid. p. 167. The emphasis is mine.
20. Douglass Johnson, "The Making of the French Nation," in Mikulas Teich and Roy Porter (eds.), *The National Question in Europe in Historical Context* (Cambridge: Cambridge University Press, 1993), pp. 47–48.
21. See William H. Sewell Jr., "Ideologies and Social Revolutions: Reflections on the French Case," in Theda Skocpol, *Social Revolutions in the Modern World* (Cambridge: Cambridge University Press, 1994), pp. 169–98. See especially Woloch, *The New Regime*, p. 13. Woloch appears to take Eugen Weber to task (see Woloch's fn. 2) for overstating the extent to which French nation-building was incomplete until the Third Republic; the major argument of Weber's book. See Eugen Weber, *Peasants Into Frenchmen: The Modernization of Rural France 1870–1914* (Stanford: Stanford University Press, 1976.)
22. Paul Schroeder, *The Transformation of European Politics 1763–1848* (Oxford: Clarendon Press, 1994), p. 67.
23. Ibid. pp. 70–71.
24. Ibid. pp. 71–72.
25. Ibid. p. 72.
26. For a brief and useful discussion of most of these issues see Mayall, *Nationalism and International Society*, pp. 52–53.
27. Charles Tilly, "National Self-Determination as a Problem for All of Us," *Daedalus*, 122 (3) (1993), p. 29.
28. Kratochwil, *Rules, Norms and Decisions*, p. 69.
29. Charles Tilly, "National Self-Determination as a Problem for All of Us," p. 29.
30. Schroeder, *The Transformation of European Politics*, p. 73.
31. Ibid. p. 94.
32. Ibid. p. 96.

33. Ibid.
34. Stephen M. Walt, *Revolution and War* (Ithaca: Cornell University Press, 1996), pp. 62–74.
35. Ibid. p. 73.
36. James J. Sheehan, *German History 1770–1866* (Oxford: Clarendon Press, 1989), p. 222.
37. Ibid. p. 223.
38. Woloch, *The New Regime*, p. 383.
39. Ibid.
40. Posen, "Nationalism, the Mass Army, and Military Power," pp. 92–93.
41. Mann, *The Sources of Social Power, II*, p. 272.
42. Ibid. p. 95. Here Posen quotes from John A. Lynn, *The Bayonets of the Republic: Motivation and Tactics in the Army of Revolutionary France, 1791–94* (Urbana: University of Illinois Press, 1984), p. 283.
43. Posen, "Nationalism, the Mass Army, and Military Power," p. 81.
44. Ibid.
45. Ibid. Posen cites these arguments of Greenfeld in fn 13 and fn 48 of his article, pp. 86 and 96 respectively.
46. Ibid. p. 86.
47. Ibid. p. 87.
48. Waltz, *Theory of International Politics*, pp. 74–77.
49. See Schroeder's important argument in Schroeder, *The Transformation of European Politics*, pp. 445–516. See also Paul W. Schroeder, "The Vienna System: What Made it Work?" Presented at the 36th Annual Convention of the International Studies Association, Chicago, February 25, 1995, p. 12.
50. Woloch, *The New Regime*, p. 420. Note that in addition to his own primary source research, and his previous work on this topic, Woloch relies upon the work of Alan Forrest and J. P. Bertaud in his development of his arguments regarding the limits of even republican and nationalist conscription. See also I. L. Woloch, "Napoleonic Conscription: State Power and Civil Society," *Past and Present*, 111 (May 1986): 101–29; Alan Forrest, *Conscripts and Deserters: The Army and French Society During the Revolution and Empire* (Oxford: Oxford University Press, 1989); J. P. Bertraud, *The Army of the French Revolution: From Citizen-Soldiers to Instrument of Power* (Princeton: Princeton University Press, 1988).
51. Woloch, *The New Regime*, p. 424.
52. Mann, *The Sources of Social Power, II*, p. 242.
53. Ibid. p. 243.
54. Ibid.
55. Sheehan, *German History*, p. 386. Sheehan's references to Arndt and Jahn refer to the contemporary popularizers of German nationalism Ernst Moritz Arndt

and Turnvater Jahn. The former was a polemicist and poet, inspired in large measure by hatred of the French and the latter ran a consortium of gymnasiums which drilled young men in rigorous paramilitary exercises, complete with paramilitary uniforms, and in pan-German nationalism. See Greenfeld, *Nationalism: Five Roads to Modernity*, pp. 360–78. See also Louis Snyder, *German Nationalism: The Tragedy of a People, Extremism Contra Liberalism in Modern German History* (Harrisburg: Telegraph Press, 1953). A comprehensive study of Arndt is found in Alfred G. Pundt, *Arndt and the Nationalist Awakening in Germany* (New York: AMS, 1968).

56. Hagen Schulze, *The Course of German Nationalism: From Frederick the Great to Bismarck, 1763–1867* (Cambridge: Cambridge University Press, 1991), pp. 75–76.
57. Robert Jervis, "From Balance to Concert: A Study of International Security Cooperation," in Kenneth A. Oye (ed.), *Cooperation Under Anarchy* (Princeton: Princeton University Press, 1986), p. 59. The most extensive developments of the application of the prisoner's dilemma game to international relations theory may be found in Thomas C. Schelling, *The Strategy of Conflict* (Oxford: Oxford University Press, 1963) and Robert Axelrod, *The Evolution of Cooperation* (New York: Basic Books, 1984).
58. Morgenthau, *Politics Among Nations*, pp. 210–15.
59. Henry Kissinger, *Diplomacy* (New York: Simon and Schuster, 1994), p. 79.
60. Ibid. pp. 79–80. The emphasis is mine.
61. Osiander, *The States System of Europe, 1640–1990*, p. 190.
62. Ibid. p. 211.
63. Kissinger, *Diplomacy*, p. 84.
64. Osiander, *The States System of Europe, 1640–1990*, p. 221.
65. Kissinger, *Diplomacy*, p. 83.
66. Ibid. p. 85.
67. Ibid. pp. 84–85.
68. Osiander, *The States System of Europe, 1640–1990*, p. 222.
69. Sheehan, *German History*, p. 458.
70. Ibid. p. 485.
71. Ibid. pp. 487–92. Quotation is found on p. 491.
72. Ibid.
73. Ibid. pp. 502–3.
74. See Timothy J. McKeown, "Hegemonic Stability Theory and Nineteenth Century Tariff Levels in Europe," *International Organization* 37 (1) (1983): 73–91.
75. Ibid. p. 473
76. Ibid. pp. 474–75. Quotation is found on p. 475.
77. Ibid. pp. 481–83.
78. Ibid. p. 505.

79. Ibid. pp. 505–6.
80. Posen, "Nationalism, the Mass Army, and Military Power," pp. 95–99.
81. Sheehan, *German History*, p. 507.
82. Posen, "Nationalism, the Mass Army, and Military Power," p. 103.
83. Sheehan, *German History*, p. 508.
84. Ibid.
85. Mann, *The Sources of Social Power, II*, pp. 120–29.
86. Ibid. p. 124.
87. Ibid. p. 125.
88. Ibid. p. 214. Again, for Mann, the sources of social power are ideological, economic, military and political, thus his IEMP model.
89. Sheehan, *German History*, p. 588.
90. Ibid. p. 589.
91. Mann, *The Sources of Social Power, II*, p. 221.
92. Ibid.
93. Sheehan, *German History*, pp. 599–600.
94. Ibid. pp. 628–29.
95. Ibid. p. 633.
96. Ibid. pp. 635–37. Quotation is found on p. 637.
97. Schulze, *The Course of German Nationalism*, p. 68.
98. Heinrich August Winkler, "Nationalism and Nation-State in Germany," in M. Teich and R. Porter (eds.), *The National Question in Europe in Historical Context* (Cambridge: Cambridge University Press, 1993), p. 182.
99. Sheehan, *German History*, p. 660.
100. Ibid. pp. 663–64.
101. For lucid and detailed accounts of these events of March 1848 see Schulze, *The Course of German Nationalism*, pp. 3–32, Sheehan, *German History*, pp. 657–69, and Eyck, *Bismarck and the German Empire*, pp. 20–30.
102. Mann, *The Sources of Social Power, II*, p. 339.
103. Sheehan, *German History*, p. 669.
104. Ibid. pp. 670–72.

7. Use and Misuse of the Principle of Nationality

1. Eyck, *Bismarck and the German Empire*, p. 21.
2. Sheehan, *German History*, p. 673.
3. Ibid. p. 680.
4. Ibid. p. 681.
5. Eyck, *Bismarck and the German Empire*, p. 27.
6. Ibid. p. 28. As Eyck describes the arrangement, "[t]he richest men, who paid a third of the taxes, came in the first class. The second class contained the men

of moderate means, who paid the second third. All the rest, the overwhelming majority of the voters, belonged to the third class. Every class had to vote indirectly for *Wahlmänner* (electors) who had to elect the deputy. In this way the first two classes always outvoted the third class, which was practically without any representation."

7. Sheehan, *German History*, p. 704.
8. Ibid. p. 710.
9. Theo Aronson, *The Fall of the Third Napoleon* (Indianapolis: Bobbs-Merrill, 1970), p. 15.
10. Significantly, the inconstancy of the French form of government was utilized by Bismarck, after the French defeat at Sedan that ended the Franco-Prussian War, to justify the imposition of a harsh peace on France. The French general Wimpffen had attempted to convince Bismarck that such a harsh peace would result in "unending strife" between France and Prussia and that Prussian generosity would, conversely, earn the gratitude of France. Bismarck responded scornfully, according to Aronson: "The gratitude of the people, he [Bismarck] said, was nothing more than 'a myth.' 'It is possible to meet with the gratitude of a sovereign, sometimes even from a ruling family,' he claimed, 'and it occasionally happens that you may implicitly rely on such gratitude. But you must never count on a nation's gratitude. Were the French like other peoples; if they honored and respected their institutions; if their sovereigns followed one another regularly on the throne—if all these things were so, why then we might have faith in the gratitude of the Emperor and his son, and estimate its worth. But during the last eighty years governments in France have been so unstable and so numerous; they have changed so rapidly, so curiously, so contrary to all expectation, that one can rely on nothing in your country. Consequently it would be madness, it would be building on sand, for any government to base any hopes on the friendship of a French sovereign.' How could he be sure, asked Bismarck, that a revolution might not tomorrow topple the Empire?" Ibid. pp. 175–76.
11. Ibid. p. 15.
12. Kissinger, *Diplomacy*, p. 105.
13. Ibid. p. 106.
14. Aronson, *The Fall of the Third Napoleon*, p. 15.
15. Kissinger, *Diplomacy*, p. 107
16. Ibid.
17. Sheehan, *German History*, p. 865.
18. Eyck, *Bismarck and the German Empire*, pp. 102–3.
19. See, for example, Woloch's treatment of the anticlerical nature of French domestic educational policy during the First Republic and much of the First Empire. See Woloch, *The New Regime*, pp. 173–236.

20. Aronson, *The Fall of the Third Napoleon*, pp. 20–21.
21. Ibid. p. 55.
22. Ibid. p. 56.
23. Ibid. p. 17.
24. Eyck, *Bismarck and the German Empire*, p. 48.
25. Ibid.
26. Ibid.
27. Ibid. p. 49.
28. Sheehan, *German History*, p. 877.
29. Ibid.
30. Ibid.
31. Ibid. The emphasis is mine.
32. Eyck, *Bismarck and the German Empire*, p. 71.
33. Kissinger, *Diplomacy*, p. 122.
34. See especially Eyck's account of Bismarck's domestic divide and rule tactics in this context in Eyck, *Bismarck and the German Empire*, pp. 195–215.
35. Mann, *The Sources of Social Power, II*, pp. 330–31.
36. Doyle, *Empires*, pp. 92–97.
37. Mann, *The Sources of Social Power, II*, p. 331.
38. Sheehan, *German History*, p. 856.
39. Eyck, *Bismarck and the German Empire*, pp. 77–78.
40. Ibid. p. 81.
41. Ibid.
42. Sheehan, *German History*, p. 890.
43. Ibid.
44. Eyck, *Bismarck and the German Empire*, p. 64.
45. Sheehan, *German History*, p. 891.
46. Kissinger, *Diplomacy*, p. 128.
47. Ibid.
48. Ibid. p. 129. Kissinger is citing Bismarck's *Werke*, here. The cited passage was written in March 1858.
49. Eyck, *Bismarck and the German Empire*, p. 90.
50. Ibid. pp. 92–94.
51. Ibid. p. 100.
52. Ibid. p. 106.
53. Ibid. pp. 107–10.
54. Sheehan, *German History*, p. 900.
55. Eyck, *Bismarck and the German Empire*, p. 115.
56. Ibid.
57. Kissinger, *Diplomacy*, pp. 124–25. Kissinger's quotations of the exchange between Gerlach and Bismarck are taken from p. 125.

58. Ibid. p. 85.
59. Eyck, *Bismarck and the German Empire*, p. 116.
60. Sheehan, *German History*, pp. 902–3.
61. Eyck, *Bismarck and the German Empire*, p. 128.
62. As Eyck's narrative suggests, Bismarck had likely been hoping to ensure the acquisition of other German lands, and had been concerned about the impression that the Prussian terms for Austria might create among the Great Powers of Europe, and the Confederation. Consider this passage from Ibid. pp. 132–33: "Bismarck wrote to his wife [from Nikolsburg]: 'If we do not exaggerate our demands and do not believe that we have conquered the world, we shall get a peace worth the efforts we have made. But we—that means, of course, the King—are as easily intoxicated as we are depressed, and I have the thankless task of pouring water into his wine and bringing home the truth that we do not live alone in Europe, but with three neighbors [surely an allusion to France, Austria and Russia].' These are the thoughts and words of a real statesman. But [t]he King fought for his idea with his accustomed stubbornness. It was at Nikolsburg that this struggle between the King and his Minister was fought out with the utmost bitterness. 'Bismarck yesterday wept in my presence about the hard things that the King said to him,' wrote the Crown Prince in his diary."
63. Ibid. pp. 132–33.
64. For the balancing expectations of classical realist scholarship see Morgenthau, *Politics Among Nations*, Chapters 11–14, pp. 161–215; Gilpin, *War and Change in World Politics*, Chapters 4–5, pp. 156–210; Edward Hallett Carr, *The Twenty Years' Crisis, 1919–1939: An Introduction to the Study of International Relations*, 2nd ed. (New York: Harper and Row, 1964), pp. 102–46; Organski and Kugler, *The War Ledger*, pp. 13–62. Neorealist expectations of balancing activity among states are best described in Waltz, *Theory of International Politics*, pp. 102–28 and the "expected utility" model presented in Bruce Bueno de Mesquita, *The War Trap*, (New Haven: Yale University Press, 1981).
65. Waltz, *Theory of International Politics*, p. 121.
66. Kissinger, *Diplomacy*, p. 107.
67. Ibid. p. 114.
68. Ibid. p. 107.
69. Kratochwil, "Regimes, Interpretation and the 'Science' of Politics: A Reappraisal," pp. 270–72.
70. For a discussion of the problem of irredentism to the stability of international order see Mayall, *Nationalism and International Society*, pp. 57–61.
71. Kissinger, *Diplomacy*, p. 108.
72. Ibid. p. 109.
73. Sheehan, *German History*, p. 893.
74. Kissinger, *Diplomacy*, p. 114.

75. See Eyck, *Bismarck and the German Empire*, p. 129. Aronson also writes of the state of Napoleon's health in this period that "Never really strong, he had been suffering increasingly from pains in the bladder during the last few years. Although his doctors had once diagnosed a stone, no treatment had been carried out, and the discomfort experienced by the Emperor during subsequent ministrations had made him ever more loath to be examined. His nature, moreover, was of a type that prefers a quick alleviation of the symptoms to a treatment of the cause. As a result his pain became worse. This in turn sapped his energy, clouded his brain and weakened his resolve. His tendency to evade, to procrastinate, to drift with the tide, became more pronounced as the years went by. At council meetings, he was often in a state of drugged and hopeless apathy." Aronson, *The Fall of the Third Napoleon*, p. 28.
76. This was Prince Richard von Metternich (1829–1895), the Austrian Ambassador to France and at the time, and son of the famous framer of the Vienna settlement of the Napoleonic wars, Clemens von Metternich (1773–1859).
77. Paul Schroeder in a recent paper has noted that while Napoleon's wife and Empress was an ardent admirer of the Hapsburg monarchy, she advocated a policy of pushing defeated Austria into sterner opposition of Prussia between Austria's defeat at the hands of Prussia in 1866, and France's defeat at the hands of the same in 1870, quite "heedless of Austria's needs and limitations." See Paul Schroeder, "A Pointless and Enduring Rivalry: France and the Habsburg Monarchy, 1715–1918." Delivered at the 1995 annual meeting of the American Political Science Association, Chicago, September 2, 1995. p. 15.
78. Eyck, *Bismarck and the German Empire*, p. 128.
79. Ibid. p. 117.
80. Eyck, *Bismarck and the German Empire*, p. 136.
81. Ibid. p. 156.
82. Kissinger, *Diplomacy*, p. 115.
83. Eyck, *Bismarck and the German Empire*, p. 129.
84. Ibid. p. 130.
85. Kissinger, *Diplomacy*, p. 107.
86. According to Eyck, having cowed the Southern German states by his annexation of most of those in the north, Bismarck had been careful to obtain alliances, stipulated in secret treaties, with nearly all of these states to the effect that they would put their forces at the disposal, and under the command of the King of Prussia in the event of a future Prussian war with, particularly, France. See Eyck, *Bismarck and the German Empire*, p. 136. As a consequence, according to Howard, the Prussian army had at its disposal as many as 1,200,000 men compared to 288,000 Frenchmen under arms at the end of 1866. See Michael Howard, *The Franco-Prussian War: The German Invasion of France*, 1870–1871, (New York: Collier Books, 1969), p. 29.

87. Aronson, *The Fall of the Third Napoleon*, pp. 42–44.
88. Ibid. p. 45.
89. Ibid. p. 49.
90. Allan Mitchell, *Victors and Vanquished: The German Influence on Army and Church in France after 1870* (Chapel Hill: University of North Carolina Press, 1984), pp. 5–6. Note that the attitude of the French bourgeoisie with respect to military service for their sons appears to be one of the most constant features of the French political landscape between the birth of the First Republic and the demise of the Second Empire. Recall, for example, how Isser Woloch's recent study of post-Revolutionary French society indicates that the urban bourgeoisie obtained bogus medical deferments and hired replacements during the Napoleonic conscription at rates much higher than other segments of society during the campaigns of the first Napoleon. (See Woloch, *The New Regime*, pp. 383–87.) This is curious, as the bourgeois classes in France had been among the most consistently nationalistic and bellicose during this period. They had acceded to the martial tone of Napoleon III's regime and its replacement, according to the caustic observation of Karl Marx, of "*Liberté, Egalité, Fraternité*" with "Cavalry, Infantry, Artillery" (See Aronson, *The Fall of the Third Napoleon*, p. 49.) Yet they did not themselves appear to have much of a taste for the fighting.
91. Aronson, *The Fall of the Third Napoleon*, p. 51.
92. Daniel H. Deudney, "The Philadelphia System" *International Organization* 49 (2) (1995): 203.
93. Howard, *The Franco-Prussian War*, p. 15.
94. Aronson, *The Fall of the Third Napoleon*, p. 52.
95. Ibid. p. 53.
96. Ibid.
97. Ibid. p. 54.
98. Ibid. p. 60.
99. For a small sample of Marx's prolific criticism of the French bourgeoisie during the Second Empire of Napoleon III, see Karl Marx "[Excerpts from] The Civil War in France," with Introduction by Friedrich Engles, in Lewis S. Feurer (ed.). *Marx and Engels: Basic Writings on Politics and Philosophy* (New York: Doubleday, 1959), pp. 349–91. For a sample of Marx's explicit criticisms of Napoleon III and the Second Empire's coup against the Second Republic in this context see Karl Marx, "[Excerpts from] The Eighteenth Brumaire of Louis Napoleon," Ibid. pp. 318–48. The reader is cautioned that this second essay's historical subject matter terminates with the events of the year 1852.
100. Eyck, *Bismarck and the German Empire*, p. 162.
101. Kratochwil, *Rules, Norms, and Decisions*, pp. 81–88. Kratochwil argues that over time tacit understandings develop regarding spheres of influence and

spheres of abstention in which powers agree not to interfere in the affairs of states bordering, or claimed within the sphere of influence, of a powerful potential antagonist. In the context of the Hohenzollern Candidature, the consequences of the War of Spanish Succession in the early eighteenth century had resulted in a tacit rule that the Hapsburg dynasty would not again advance the candidature of a Hapsburg prince for the Spanish throne while the Hapsburg dynasty ruled the Austrian Empire. The Hohenzollern Candidature violated that tacit rule so long as the Hohenzollern family ruled powerful Prussia and the North German Confederation and potentially compromised France's security in light of Spain's geostrategic position to the south and west of France.

102. Eyck, *Bismarck and the German Empire*, p. 170.
103. Aronson, *The Fall of the Third Napoleon*, p. 81. The emphasis is mine.
104. Ibid.
105. Ibid. pp. 82–83. The passage quoted is found on p. 83.
106. Ibid. p. 83.
107. Ibid. p. 84. Also see Eyck, *Bismarck and the German Empire*, pp. 169–71.
108. Aronson, *The Fall of the Third Napoleon*, p. 84.
109. Ibid. p. 85.
110. Ibid. p. 86.
111. Ibid. p. 100.
112. Ibid.
113. Howard, *The Franco-Prussian War*, pp. 59–60.
114. Aronson, *The Fall of the Third Napoleon*, p. 178–79.
115. Ibid. p. 89.
116. Ibid. p. 105.
117. Ibid. pp. 138–39.
118. The classic account of the entrapment of the Army of Châlons and the bombardment and surrender of Sedan is found in Howard, *The Franco-Prussian War*, pp. 183–223. Also see Aronson, *The Fall of the Third Napoleon*, pp. 227–61.
119. Aronson, *The Fall of the Third Napoleon*, p. 176.
120. Eyck, *Bismarck and the German Empire*, pp. 178–79.
121. Ibid. pp. 181–82.
122. Note that shared victory over a common foe conforms to the essence of the creation what Anderson calls "shared history" in his multivariate definition of nationalism. With a shared experience of battle against the French, the integrated German states of Central Europe now added shared history to their shared language and culture as pillars of their "imagined [pan-German, national] community." This shared memory allowed them to begin a shared forgetting of their internecine conflictual past. See Anderson, *Imagined Communities*, pp. 187–203.

123. Ibid. pp. 183–84.
124. Friedrich Kratochwil, "Regimes, Interpretation and the 'Science' of Politics," p. 271.

8. *National Sovereignty and the New Imperialism: The Global Transmission of Bourgeois-National Identity and Culture*

1. Eric J. Hobsbawm, *The Age of Empire: 1875–1914* (New York: Vintage Books, 1987), p. 57.
2. Ibid. p. 59.
3. Woodruff D. Smith, *European Imperialism in the Nineteenth and Twentieth Centuries* (Chicago: Nelson-Hall, 1982), p. 75
4. See Carleton J.H. Hayes, A *Generation of Materialism, 1871–1900* (New York: Harper, 1941), p. 216.
5. See C. C. Eldridge, *England's Mission: The Imperial Idea in the Age of Gladstone and Disraeli 1868–1880* (London: Macmillan, 1973). See especially Chapter 3, pp. 52–91, and chapter 4, pp. 93–119.
6. See Anthony Brewer, *Marxist Theories of Imperialism: A Critical Survey* (2nd Edition) (London: Routledge, 1990), pp. 116–23. For crucial excerpts of Lenin's influential pamphlet see V. I. Lenin, "The Highest Stage of Capitalism" in Harrison M. Wright (ed.), *The New Imperialism: An Analysis of Late-Nineteenth-Century Expansion* (Lexington, MA: D.C. Heath, 1976), pp. 44–59.
7. Smith, *European Imperialism in the Nineteenth and Twentieth Centuries*, p. 78.
8. Ibid. p. 77.
9. Ibid. p. 89.
10. Eldridge, *England's Mission*, pp. 95–97.
11. Smith, *European Imperialism in the Nineteenth and Twentieth Centuries*, pp. 91–92.
12. Hayes, A *Generation of Materialism*, p. 219.
13. Doyle, *Empires*, p. 258.
14. Ibid. p. 246.
15. Ibid. pp. 257–96.
16. Ibid. p. 283.
17. Ibid. p. 339.
18. Hannah Arendt, *The Origins of Totalitarianism* (New York: Harcourt, Brace 1951), pp. 150–51.
19. Rhodes is quoted in Ibid. p. 151.
20. Hobsbawm, *The Age of Empire*, p. 40.
21. Ibid. pp. 41–42.
22. Ibid. p. 54.

23. Ibid. p. 42.
24. J. A. Hobson, "Imperialism: A Study," in Harrison M. Wright (ed.), *The New Imperialism*, pp. 5–44.
25. Klaus Knorr reminds us that this term originated in Britain at the end of the Napoleonic wars when the demobilization of large numbers of British soldiers generated a labor surplus in Britain, with the attendant miseries. This thinking is more consistent with the Malthusian critique of liberal political economy [see Thomas Malthus, *An Essay on the Principle of Population* (London: Penguin, 1970)], than with the Marxian critique, or with the popular nationalist pressure that generated protectionist and imperialist policies in the late nineteenth century. (See Klaus E. Knorr, *British Colonial Theories 1570–1850* (Toronto: University of Toronto Press, 1944). See especially portions of Chapter 9, "Emigration and Colonization 1815–1850," pp. 269–300).
26. Hayes, A *Generation of Materialism*, p. 220.
27. Hans Kohn, *Nationalism and Imperialism in the Hither East*, Margaret M. Green (trans.) (London: Routledge, 1932), p. 49. The emphasis is mine.
28. Ibid. p. 50. The emphasis is mine. My interpretation of Kohn's assertion of behavioral continuity in the new imperialism stems in part from his elaboration of this on page 51, where he asserts, as would Morgenthau, that "[t]he common exercise of power is the fundamental and essential object of political activity."
29. For Rosenberg, the "empire of civil society" is the "condition of social relations mediated through things rather than through personalized relations of domination." This is the dramatic innovation that makes possible the shift from empire to the state as a basis for political authority in the modern era in his argument. See Rosenberg, *The Empire of Civil Society*, p. 155. It is interesting that in the case of the new imperialism, which entailed both the economic exploitation and cultural and political subjection of indigenous societies, that social relations between imperialist and aborigine were mediated through both "things" and through "personalized relations of domination."
30. Mann, *The Sources of Social Power, II*, p. 69. For an extended development of Mann's "polymorphous crystallization model" of social power by which he aims to explain the form in which states "crystallize" in terms of power and institutional structures, see Ibid. Chapter 3, "A Theory of the Modern State," pp. 44–91.
31. See Ernest Gellner's essay "Nationalism" in Ernest A. Gellner, *Thought and Change* (London: Weidenfeld and Nicholson, 1964), pp. 158–69.
32. In a later book Gellner refines his 1964 argument and argues that nationalisms are based upon education-dependent "high cultures," which are protected by their own state. These culture come to be seen as repositories of political legitimacy. Nationalism is seen as "societal self-worship" in this view. See Gellner, *Nations and Nationalism*, pp. 48–62. I would emphasize that Gellner does not, as I do, explicitly identify this "high culture" as bourgeois culture.

33. Hobsbawm, *The Age of Empire*, p. 20.
34. Hayes, A *Generation of Materialism*, p. 220.
35. Ibid.
36. For numerous treatments of the importance of intellectuals in the invention, propagation and transmission of nationalist ideology and nationalist culture in various contexts see, for example, Karl W. Deutsch, *Nationalism and Social Communication: An Inquiry Into the Foundations of Nationality* (2nd ed.) (Cambridge: M.I.T. Press, 1966); Gellner's essay "Nationalism" in Ernest A. Gellner, *Thought and Change*, pp. 158–69; E. J. Hobsbawm, "Mass-Producing Traditions: Europe, 1870–1914" in Eric Hobsbawm and Terence Ranger (eds.), *The Invention of Tradition* (Cambridge: Cambridge University Press, 1983), pp. 263–307; Hans Kohn, *The Idea of Nationalism*, pp. 329–31; Tom Nairn, *The Break-up of Britain: Crisis and Neo-Nationalism* (2nd ed.) (London: New Left Books, 1977), pp. 332–41; Anthony D. Smith, *The Ethnic Revival* (Cambridge: Cambridge University Press, 1991), pp. 90–104; Anthony D. Smith, "The Origins of Nations," *Ethnic and Racial Studies* 12 (3) (1989): 349–56; Max Weber, "The Nation," in *From Max Weber: Essays in Sociology*, H. H. Gerth and C. Wright-Mills (trans. and ed.) (London: Routledge, 1948), pp. 171–9: among many other authors in a vast literature.
37. Kohn, *Nationalism and Imperialism in the Hither East*, p. 59. The emphasis is mine.
38. Spanish and French Catholic missionary activities in Central and South America and what had been French North America prior to the Seven Years' War are significant exceptions to this rule.
39. Smith, *European Imperialism in the Nineteenth and Twentieth Centuries*, p. 93. For a description of the political pressures brought to bear, and the operations of such groups as the British Anti-Slavery Society and the Aborigines Protection Society see Eldridge, *England's Mission*, pp. 149–67.
40. Hayes, A *Generation of Materialism*, pp. 223–24. See also Doyle, *Empires*, pp. 170–71.
41. Hobsbawm, *The Age of Empire*, pp. 252–58.
42. Hayes, A *Generation of Materialism*, p. 224.
43. Arendt, *The Origins of Totalitarianism*, p. 152.
44. Michael Weiner, "Discourses of Race, Nation and Empire in pre-1945 Japan," *Ethnic and Racial Studies* 18 (3) (1995): 446–48.
45. Ibid. p. 451.
46. Terence Ranger, "The Invention of Tradition in Colonial Africa," in Eric Hobsbawm and Terence Ranger (eds.), *The Invention of Tradition* (Cambridge: Cambridge University Press, 1983), pp. 211.
47. Ibid. p. 215.
48. Hobsbawm, *The Age of Empire*, p. 165.
49. Ibid. p. 221.

50. Ibid. p. 218.
51. Ibid.
52. Hobsbawm, *The Age of Empire*, p. 174.
53. Gramsci, *Selections from the Prison Notebooks*, p. 306.
54. Arendt, *The Origins of Totalitarianism*, p. 154. Arendt quotes James Mill in this passage. The emphasis is mine.
55. Helmuth Stoecker, "The Position of Africans in the German Colonies," in Arthur J. Knoll and Lewis H. Gann (eds.) *Germans in the Tropics: Essays in German Colonial History* (Westport: Greenwood Press, 1987), p. 123.
56. Ranger, "The Invention of Tradition in Colonial Africa," p. 226.
57. Ibid. p. 227. Note that Ranger refers to these phases as "neo-traditions" and he is primarily interested in the "invention of traditions" as much as their subsequent transmission to peripheral societies.
58. Hillaire Belloc (London, 1898), quoted in Hobsbawm, *The Age of Empire*, p. 20.
59. Stephen H. Roberts, *The History of French Colonial Policy 1870–1925* (London: Frank Cass, 1963), pp. 64–65.
60. Doyle, *Empires*, 163–229.
61. Ranger, "The Invention of Tradition in Colonial Africa," p. 224.
62. Bernard S. Cohn, "Representing Authority in Victorian India," in Hobsbawm and Ranger (eds.), *The Invention of Tradition*, p. 178.
63. Hobsbawm, *The Age of Empire*, p. 76. Doyle, *Empires*, pp. 170–71.
64. Ibid. p. 71.
65. Ranger, "The Invention of Tradition in Colonial Africa," p. 226.
66. Ibid. p. 228.
67. Cohn, "Representing Authority in Victorian India," p. 190.
68. Ranger, "The Invention of Tradition in Colonial Africa," p. 227.
69. Ibid. p. 229.
70. Churchillian imperial rhetoric and mobilization orders ring out in telegrams and dispatches throughout his six-volume history of the Second World War, but see especially Winston S. Churchill, *The Hinge of Fate* (Boston: Houghton-Mifflin, 1950), especially pp. 3–59, and 416–17, Winston S. Churchill, *Closing the Ring*, 1951, especially pp. 687–8, and Winston S. Churchill, *Triumph and Tragedy*, 1953.
71. See Eldridge, *England's Mission*, p. 213, and Cohn, "Representing Authority in Victorian India," p. 184.
72. Cohn, "Representing Authority in Victorian India," p. 184.
73. Ibid. p. 191.
74. Ibid.
75. Ibid. p. 192.
76. Ranger, "The Invention of Tradition in Colonial Africa" pp. 230–31.

77. Edward is quoted in Ibid., p. 231.
78. See the complaint of the German acting governor of Togo, in 1904, contrasting this situation with that of the natives under the control of the British in the nearby Gold Coast Colony in Stoecker, "The Position of Africans in the German Colonies," p. 124.
79. Ibid. p. 125.
80. Weiner, "Race, Nation and Empire in pre-1945 Japan," pp. 452–53.
81. William Earl Weeks, "American Nationalism, American Imperialism: An Interpretation of United States Political Economy, 1789–1861," *Journal of the Early Republic* 14 (Winter 1994): 490.
82. See, for example, the classic account by Dee Alexander Brown, *Bury My Heart at Wounded Knee: An Indian History of the American West* (New York: Holt, 1970).
83. See Anthony W. Marx, "Race-Making and the Nation-State," *World Politics* 48 (2) (1996): 180–208.
84. Most recently this principle is "national self-determination."
85. The nation-state.
86. Waltz, *Theory of International Politics*, pp. 97–99.
87. Kohn, *Nationalism and Imperialism in the Hither East*, p. 60.
88. Theodore H. Von Laue, *The World Revolution of Westernization: The Twentieth Century in Global Perspective* (Oxford: Oxford University Press, 1987), p. 4.
89. See, for example, Barnett's argument regarding the case of pan-Arab nationalism in Michael N. Barnett, "Sovereignty, Nationalism and Regional Order in the Arab States System," *International Organization* 49 (3) (1995): 479–510.
90. Hayes, *A Generation of Materialism*, pp. 221–22.
91. Doyle, *Empires*, p. 251.
92. Ibid. p. 252.
93. Ibid. pp. 252–56.
94. Von Laue, *The World Revolution of Westernization*, p. 18. The emphasis is mine.
95. For synopsis of the value of "third image" theoretical analysis of political systems see Waltz, *Man the State and War: A Theoretical Analysis* (New York: Columbia University Press, 1959), pp. 159–86.
96. For a discussion of nationalist imperialist aggression as a problem of "intolerance" see Carleton J. H. Hayes, *Nationalism: A Religion* (New York: Macmillan, 1960), pp. 97–115.
97. Hobsbawm, *The Age of Empire*, pp. 148–49.
98. Hobsbawm, *The Age of Empire*, pp. 152–60.
99. Ibid. pp. 160–61.
100. Hayes, *A Generation of Materialism*, p. 223.
101. Kissinger, *Diplomacy*, p. 146.

102. Ibid. For a study of the activities and social composition of the domestic German enthusiasts for colonial ventures in this period see Richard Pierard, "The German Colonial Society," in Knoll and Gann (eds.), *Germans in the Tropics*, pp. 19–37.
103. See this diplomatic argument in A. J. P. Taylor, *Germany's First Bid for Colonies:1884–1885: A Move in Bismarck's European Policy* (New York: MacMillan, 1967).
104. Lewis H. Gann, "Marginal Colonialism: The German Case," in Knoll and Gann (eds.) *Germans in the Tropics*, p. 5.
105. Hayes, A *Generation of Materialism*, pp. 232–34.
106. Smith, *European Imperialism in the Nineteenth and Twentieth Centuries*, p. 96.
107. A fascinating study of the manipulation of British public opinion in support of a policy of imperialism, over many decades is found in John M. MacKenzie, *Propaganda and Empire: The Manipulation of British Public Opinion, 1880–1960* (Manchester: Manchester University Press, 1984). See also Gary S. Messinger, *British Propaganda and the State in the First World War* (Manchester: Manchester University Press, 1992).
108. Hayes, A *Generation of Materialism*, pp. 220.

9. "Over-the-Top" and "Over There": Status Contests Among National-Sovereigns

1. This is the terminology of structural realism. The extent to which political structures may be considered a "cause" of war is, of course, still an issue of contention.
2. This is Michael Mann's phrase. Mann employs the terms as a shorthand for the standard explanatory repertoire and the tendency of realism and theories of rational choice to focus on the "geopolitical interests" of states, guided by the assumptions that (1) states have rationally determinable geopolitical "interests," (2) these interests persistently conflict and (3) war is a normal, rational means of securing the ends suggested by these interests. I will occasionally avail myself of Mann's shorthand for the sake of convenience in this chapter. See Mann, *The Sources of Social Power, II*, p. 743.
3. The parenthetic phrases are also Mann's lexicon.
4. Kissinger, *Diplomacy*, p. 205.
5. Ibid. p. 217.
6. Bernadotte E. Schmitt and Harold C. Vedeler, *The World in the Crucible: 1914–1919* (New York: Harper, 1988), p. xv.
7. Kautsky develops the notion of working-class sovereignty within a proletarian dictatorship in a work completed shortly after the Bolshevik Revolution in Russia. See Karl Kautsky, *The Dictatorship of the Proletariat* (with introduction by

John Kautsky). Reprint of the 1919 National Labour Press edition (Westport: Greenwood, 1981). See especially chapter 5, pp. 42–58.

8. The reader is again referred to Kratochwil's treatment of the functioning of institutional facts in Kratochwil, "Regimes, Interpretation and the 'Science' of Politics," pp. 263–84.
9. An example of what William Kornhauser refers to as "discontinuities in authority." Kornhauser, *The Politics of Mass Society*, p. 129.
10. Or "discontinuities in society." Ibid. p. 159.
11. Or "discontinuities in community." Ibid. p. 143.
12. Hobsbawm, *Nations and Nationalism Since 1780*, p. 101. For Hobsbawm's extended discussion of the rise of ethno-linguistic nationalisms see especially pp. 101–11. Note that another important scholar of nationalism, Elie Kedourie, appears to disagree with this last contention. Kedourie views the emergence of nationalism in terms of a youth movement, and a reaction by youth against the traditionalism of their parents, and argues that it is "a misunderstanding to ask whether nationalism is politics of the right of the left. It is neither. Left and right are concepts which arose in the course of struggle between aristocracy, middle class and working class in European countries in the nineteenth and twentieth centuries, and are unintelligible apart from this particular history." Elie Kedourie, *Nationalism* (2nd ed) (London: Hutchinson, 1966). See pp. 89–90. Quote is from p. 89.
13. Hobsbawm, *Nations and Nationalism Since 1780*, pp. 109–10.
14. This is Gellner's lexicon. See Gellner, *Nations and Nationalism*, pp. 29–38.
15. Ibid. pp. 115–21.
16. Ibid. p. 122.
17. Mann, *The Sources of Social Power, II*, p. 575.
18. Greenfeld, *Nationalism: Five Roads to Modernity*, p. 186.
19. Mann, *The Sources of Social Power, II*, p. 575.
20. Ibid. p. 589.
21. Ibid.
22. Ibid. p. 588.
23. See, for example, John Haag, "Students at the University of Vienna in the First World War," *Central European History* 17 (4) (December 1984): 299–309, and Konrad H. Jarausch, "German Students in the First World War," *Central European History* 17 (4) (December 1984): 310–29.
24. See Michael Howard, "Europe on the Eve of the First World War," in R. J. W. Evans and Martmut Pogge von Strandmann (eds.), *The Coming of the First World War* (Oxford: Clarendon Press, 1988), pp. 1–18. Note that Howard attributes this effect to the content of the education, rather than official propaganda. He argues, on p. 15, that the general enthusiasm for the call to arms was due to: "Nationalistically oriented public education; military service which,

however unwelcome and tedious, bred a sense of cohesion and national identity; continuing habits of social deference: all this helps explain, at a deeper level than does the strident propaganda of the popular press, why the population of Europe responded so readily to the call when it came."

25. See Ibid. p. 18, and Mann, *The Sources of Social Power, II*, p. 578.
26. Ibid. p. 579.
27. Ibid. p. 577.
28. See Karl Polanyi, *The Great Transformation: The Political and Economic Origins of our Time* (Boston: Beacon Press, 1944).
29. The term "*kulak*" translates from the Russian as "fist" as was long employed by the Russian peasantry as an imprecation of resentment against the wealthier agricultural proprietors of peasant origins who employed the peasantry at unfavorable wages. The liquidation of *kulak* power became the goal of the Stalinist collectivization of agriculture in the bid to build "socialism in one country" See Robert C. Tucker, *Stalin as a Revolutionary 1879–1929*, especially chapter 10. See also Robert C. Tucker, *Stalin in Power: The Revolution from Above, 1928–1941* (New York: Norton, 1990), pp. 139–81. For a general study of "dekulakization" in the context of the class conflict leading to Russian and Ukrainian agricultural collectivization see Robert Conquest, *The Harvest of Sorrow: Soviet Collectivization and the Terror-Famine* (New York: Oxford University Press, 1986). See especially Chapter 6.
30. This appears to be a viable strategy to the present day. U.S. domestic politics has long witnessed political parties to be effectively employing this strategy in electoral politics by creating "wedge issues" to divide the electorate, break up voting blocks, and impede the formation of oppositional coalitions.
31. Mann, *The Sources of Social Power, II*, p. 584.
32. Brubaker, *Citizenship and Nationhood in France and Germany*, pp. 114–19.
33. Ibid. p. 119.
34. Ibid. p. 11.
35. Ibid. pp. 12–13.
36. A rather brief but excellent and accessible account of the Dreyfuss Affair may be found in Barbara W. Tuchman, *The Proud Tower: A Portrait of the World Before the War: 1890–1914* (New York: Macmillan, 1966). See Chapter 4.
37. An outstanding account of these pressures is provided in Robert A. Kann, *A History of the Habsburgh Empire 1526–1918*, University of California Press, Berkeley, 1974. See pages 406–67.
38. See Ian Armour, "The Roots of Sarajevo: Austria-Hungary and Serbia, 1867–81," *History Today* 38 (August 1988): 12–19. The piece nicely summarizes the origins of Serb nationalism under the Ottomans.
39. See especially Fritz Fischer, *Germany's Aims in the First World War* (New York:

Norton, 1967); Fritz Fischer, *World Power or Decline: The Controversy Over Germany's Aims in the First World War* (trans. L. L. Farrar, Robert Kimber and Rita Kimber) (New York: Norton, 1974); and Fritz Fischer, *War of Illusions: German Policies from 1911 to 1914* (trans. Marian Jackson) (New York: Norton, 1975).

40. See Stephen Van Evera, "Why Cooperation Failed in 1914," in Kenneth A. Oye (ed.), *Cooperation Under Anarchy* (Princeton: Princeton University Press, 1985), p. 116. The emphasis is mine.
41. See Eyck's particularly poignant account of this event in Eyck, *Bismarck and the German Empire.*
42. For an extraordinary account of the sequential successions of 1887 and 1888 see J. Alden Nichols, *The Year of the Three Kaisers: Bismarck and the German Succession, 1887–88* (Urbana: University of Illinois Press, 1987).
43. Three important examples of this sort of account that spring to mind are Robert *Gilpin's War and Change in World Politics*, A. F. K. Organski and Jacek Kugler's *The War Ledger*, and Paul Kennedy's, *The Rise and Fall of the Great Powers.*
44. Here the most prominent examples are Hans J. Morgenthau's, *Politics Among Nations*, and Henry Kissinger's *Diplomacy*.
45. Marilyn Shevin Coetzee, *The German Army League: Popular Nationalism in Wilhelmine Germany* (New York: Oxford University Press, 1990), p. 4.
46. See Geoff Eley, *Reshaping the German Right: Radical Nationalism and Political Change after Bismarck* (New Haven: Yale University Press, 1980), and Geoff Eley, "Reshaping the Right: Radical Nationalism and the German Navy League, 1898–1908," *Historical Journal* 21 (1978): 327–54.
47. Coetzee, *The German Army League*, p. 7.
48. Ibid. p. 8.
49. Ibid. p. 9.
50. Graphical representation of data taken from Ibid., "Table 6. Rank and File According to Region," p. 90. Data presented in the figure are rounded to the nearest whole percentile.
51. Ibid.
52. Mann, *The Sources of Social Power, II*, pp. 587–58. The sources cited by Mann are Roger Chickering, *Imperial Germany and a World Without War* (Princeton: Princeton University Press, 1975), Roger Chickering, *We Men Who Feel Most German: A Cultural Study of the Pan-German League, 1886–1914* (London: Allen & Unwin, 1984), and Eley, *Reshaping the German Right.*
53. Coetzee, *The German Army League*, p. 121.
54. See Thomas A. Kohut, *Wilhelm II and the Germans: A Study in Leadership* (New York: Oxford University Press, 1991). See especially chapters 1 and 6.
55. An excellent account of Russian domestic difficulties in this context is Adam

B. Ulam, *Russia's Failed Revolutions: From the Decembrists to the Dissidents* (London: Weidenfeld & Nicholson, 1981).

56. Kohut, *Wilhelm II and the Germans*, p. 130. Edward's statement is rendered as "I don't want war. it's peace that I desire." Wilhelm scribbles "But the [London] *Times*!" The translations are mine.
57. Kissinger, *Diplomacy*, p. 184.
58. Robert Jervis, "Cooperation Under the Security Dilemma," *World Politics* 30 (2) (1978): 167–214.
59. Mann suggests that the First World War was formally irrational as it could not achieve its stated goals. See Mann, *The Sources of Social Power*, 2: 755–56.
60. I refer the reader back to Chapter 7.
61. Coetzee, *The German Army League*, p. 52. Here Coetzee is quoting from an article entitled "*Krieg und Völkerfrieden*" (which I translate as "War and a Peaceable People") from the German Army League's journal, *Die Wehr*.
62. These phrases are rendered as "war of survival" and "fight to the finish" respectively. See Ibid., p. 52. The translations are Coetzee's. I would note that *Vernichtungskrieg* could alternatively be rendered "war of extermination."
63. Ibid. Coetzee cites articles from *Dei Wehr* entitled "*Das Volk und sein Treiber*" (1913) and "*Wehrmacht und Volskraft*" (1912). In English these are rendered as "The People and their Oppressors" and "The Armed Forces and National Vigor." The translations are mine.
64. See Gerd Krumeich, *Armaments and Politics in France of the Eve of the First World War: The Introduction of Three-Year Conscription 1913–14*, Stephen Coll (trans.) (Warwickshire and Dover: Berg, 1984).
65. See, for example, Ian F. W. Beckett, "Total War," in C. Emsley, A. Marwick and W. Simpson (eds.), *War, Peace and Social Change in Twentieth Century Europe* (Philadelphia; Open University Press, 1989), pp. 31–32.
66. Durkheim, *Sociology and Philosophy*.
67. Druckman, "Nationalism, Patriotism, and Group Loyalty."
68. Kohut, *Wilhelm II and the Germans*, p. 163.
69. Ibid. p. 131.
70. Ibid. p. 140.
71. Kissinger, *Diplomacy*, p. 184.
72. Ibid. p. 185. Kissinger quotes from the January 5, 1896 issue of *Allgemeine Zeitung*.
73. Ibid. p. 184.
74. Kohut, *Wilhelm II and the Germans*, p. 177.
75. Kissinger, *Diplomacy*, p. 208.
76. Kohut, *Wilhelm II and the Germans*, p. 184.
77. Ibid. p. 195.

78. Ibid. p. 196.
79. Note that it has been recently argued that both British economic and military decline could have been avoided by the abandonment of British liberal ideology in the area of international trade issues, and by the initiation of appropriate policies to stem these losses. See John Robert Ferris, *Men, Money, and Diplomacy: The Evolution of British Strategic Foreign Policy, 1919–1926,* (Ithaca: Cornell University Press, 1989). See also Aaron L. Friedberg, *The Weary Titan: Britain and the Experience of Relative Decline, 1895–1905* (Princeton: Princeton University Press, 1988) For a different view see Kennedy, *The Rise and Fall of the Great Powers*, pp. 194–274.
80. Mann, *The Sources of Social Power, II*, p. 744.
81. Ibid. p. 746.
82. Ibid. p. 760.
83. Ibid. pp. 751–52.
84. Ibid. p. 734.
85. For a brief discussion of "multiple identities" and overlapping social identities as guides to social action see Smith, *National Identity*, pp. 3–18.
86. Hayes, *Nationalism: A Religion*, p. 122.
87. Ibid. This phrase is part of the title of Hayes' ninth chapter.
88. See Jean-Jacques Becker, "That's the Death Knell of Our Boys" in Patrick Fridenson (ed.), *The French Home Front: 1914–1918* (Providence and Oxford: Berg, 1992), pp. 17–36.
89. Ibid. p. 31.
90. Lloyd George is quoted in Mann, *The Sources of Social Power, II*, p. 767.
91. Ibid. p. 782.
92. Ibid. p. 786. Emphasis in the original.
93. Ibid.
94. Stéphane Audoin-Rouzeau, *Men at War 1914–1918: National Sentiment and Trench Journalism in France during the First World War* (trans. Helen McPhail) (Providence and Oxford: Berg, 1992), p. 70. Audoin-Rouzeau quotes here from the trench newspaper *L'Echo de tranchées-ville,* October 28, 1915. The emphasis is mine.
95. See the extended quote of Weber in Chapter 2 of this work, under the subheading "Legitimating Principles."
96. Audoin-Rouzeau, *Men at War 1914–1918*, p. 180.
97. Ibid. p. 181. Audoin-Rouzeau quotes here from the trench newspaper *Le Tordboyau,* August 1917.
98. For development of this point see J. Samuel Barkin and Bruce Cronin, "The State and the Nation: Changing Norms and the Rules of Sovereignty in International Relations," *International Organization* 48 (1) (1994): 199–22. For a

masterful account of the Paris Peace Conference and the forging of this legitimating principle in the course of the negotiations see Osiander, *The States System of Europe*, pp. 248–315.

10. The Helpless Colossus

1. Tamir, *Liberal Nationalism*, pp. 18–20.
2. E.J. Hobsbawm, *The Age of Extremes: A History of the World, 1914–1991*, Vintage Books (New York: Random House, 1996).
3. See John Lewis Gaddis, "International Relations Theory and the End of the Cold War," *International Security* 17, No. 3 (Winter 1992/93): 5–58 and Friedrich Kratochwil, "The Embarrassment of Changes: Neo-realism and the Science of Realpolitik Without Politics," *Review of International Studies* 19 (1993): 63–80.
4. See Bruce Lincoln, *Passage Through Armageddon: The Russians in War and Revolution 1914–1918* (New York: Simon and Schuster, 1986), pp. 397–425.
5. See Robert Wistrich, *Trotsky: Fate of a Revolutionary* (Briarcliff Manor, NY: Stein and Day, 1979), p. 100 ff.
6. Arthur S. Link, *Wilson the Diplomatist: A Look at His Major Foreign Policies*, The Albert Shaw Lectures on Diplomatic History, 1956. (Baltimore: Johns Hopkins University Press, 1957) pp. 114–17.
7. For a discussion of Lenin's view of self-determination in the Soviet context see Richard Pipes, *The Formation of the Soviet Union: Communism and Nationalism 1917–1923*, Revised edition (Cambridge: Harvard University Press, 1964), pp. 41–49.
8. See Ronald Grigor Suny, *The Revenge of the Past: Nationalism, Revolution, and the Collapse of the Soviet Union* (Stanford: Stanford University Press, 1993), p. 24.
9. This ethic is not inconsistent with the peasant ethic that Scott has described in his explanation of peasant affinity for, for example, the Viet Cong in colonial French-Indochina. See James C. Scott, *The Moral Economy of the Peasant: Rebellion and Subsistence in Southeast Asia* (New Haven: Yale University Press, 1976).
10. Hedrick Smith, *The New Russians* (New York: Random House, 1990), p. 204.
11. Suny, *The Revenge of the Past*, p. 25.
12. Ibid. p. 28.
13. Ibid. p. 29.
14. The persistent weakness of Belorussian national identity is even now limiting the new state of Belorus's policy autonomy with respect to Russia relative to, for example, that of Ukraine. See, for example, John Edwin Mroz and Oleksandr Pavliuk, "Ukraine: Europe's Linchpin," *Foreign Affairs* 75 (3) (1996):

52–62. For another view see Jan Zaprudnik, "Development of Belarusian National Identity and Its Influence on Belarus's Foreign Policy Orientation," in Roman Szporluk (ed.), *National Identity and Ethnicity in Russia and the New States of Eurasia* (Armonk: M. E. Sharpe, 1994), pp. 129–49.

15. Suny, *The Revenge of the Past*, p. 79.
16. Ibid. p. 81. This was not true in other areas, such as Armenia, where political nationalism prevailed.
17. But for Finland and Poland, which were never recovered, but were to become satellites after World War II.
18. See Mark D. Steinberg, "Vanguard Workers and the Morality of Class," in Lewis H, Siegelbaum and Ronald Grigor Suny (eds.), *Making Workers Soviet: Power, Class and Identity* (Ithaca: Cornell University Press, 1994), pp. 66–84, and Victoria E. Bonnell, "The Iconography of the Worker in Soviet Political Art," in Ibid., pp. 341–75.
19. See, for example, Robert Conquest, *The Harvest of Sorrow: Soviet Collectivization and the Terror Famine*; Robert Conquest, *The Great Terror: A Reassessment* (New York: Oxford University Press, 1990); Robert Daniels (ed.), *The Stalin Revolution: Foundations of Soviet Totalitarianism* (Lexington, MA: D. C. Heath, 1972); Isaac Deutscher, *Stalin: A Political Biography* (2nd ed.) (New York: Oxford University Press, 1968); Aleksandr Solzhenitsyn, *The GULAG Archipelago 1918–1956: An Experiment in Literary Investigation* (New York: Harper, 1973); Robert C. Tucker, *Stalin in Power: The Revolution From Above, 1928–1941*.
20. See, for example, Robert C. Tucker, *The Soviet Political Mind: Stalinism and Post-Stalin Change* (rev. ed.) (New York: Norton, 1971), and Frederick S. Starr, "Soviet Union: A Civil Society," *Foreign Policy*, No. 70. (Spring 1988): pp. 26–41.
21. A collection of such material is found in George Saunders (ed.), *Samizdat: Voices of the Soviet Oppostition* (New York: Pathfinder, 1974).
22. For an important related neoinstitutionalist argument see Rogers Brubaker, "Nationhood and the National Question in the Soviet Union and its Successor States: An Institutionalist Account," in Rogers Brubaker, *Nationalism Reframed: Nationhood and the National Question in the New Europe* (Cambridge: Cambridge University Press, 1996), pp. 23–54.
23. Suny, *The Revenge of the Past*, p. 101.
24. Brubaker, "Nationhood and the National Question in the Soviet Union and its Successor States."
25. Suny, *The Revenge of the Past*, pp. 106–7.
26. Conquest, *The Harvest of Sorrow*.
27. Suny, *The Revenge of the Past*, pp. 110–11.
28. Ibid., p. 114.

29. For a sobering account of the power of post-Soviet era organized crime in Russia, see Stephen Handelman, *Comrade Criminal: Russia's New Mafiya* (New Haven: Yale University Press, 1995).
30. For an early argument that a civil society was emerging in the USSR), see Frederick S. Starr, "Soviet Union: A Civil Society."
31. Suny, *The Revenge of the Past*, p. 119.
32. Ibid., p. 120.
33. Ibid., pp. 122–23.
34. See Timothy J. Colton, *The Dilemma of Reform in the Soviet Union*, Revised and expanded edition (New York: Council on Foreign Relations, 1986).
35. James H. Billington, *Russia Transformed: Breakthrough to Hope* (New York: Free Press, 1992), p. 27.
36. Suny, *The Revenge of the Past*, p. 130.
37. Ibid. p. 140.
38. Karen Dawisha and Bruce Parrott, *Russia and the New States of Eurasia: The Politics of Upheaval* (Cambridge: Cambridge University Press, 1994), p. 60.
39. Rey Koslowski and Friedrich Kratochwil, "Understanding Change in International Politics," pp. 238–39.
40. The word "*utca*" is Magyar for "street."
41. Suny, *The Revenge of the Past*, pp. 133–34.
42. Ibid. p. 137.
43. Ibid. p. 141.
44. Dawisha and Parrott, *Russia and the New States of Eurasia*, p. 67.
45. Suny, *The Revenge of the Past*, pp. 142.
46. Ibid. pp. 148–49.
47. Billington, *Russia Transformed*, p. 29.
48. Gramsci, *Selections from the Prison Notebooks*, pp. 52–120.
49. Billington, *Russia Transformed*, pp. 68–69.
50. Ibid. p. 69.
51. Ibid. p. 81.
52. Suny, *The Revenge of the Past*, p. 153.
53. Ibid. p. 131.
54. Koslowski and Kratochwil, "Understanding Change in International Politics," p. 216.
55. Benjamin Barber, *Jihad vs. McWorld: How Globalism and Tribalism Are Reshaping the World* (New York: Ballantine, 1996).
56. See the essays by Vincent Cable, Susan Strange and Stephen J. Del Rosso Jr. in "What Future for the State?, *Daedalus* 124 (2) (Spring 1994).
57. See Daniel Deudney, "Nuclear Weapons and the Waning of the Real-State," Ibid., pp. 209–29.
58. For a very recent collection of essays dealing with some of these issues from a

constructivist approach see Thomas J. Biersteker and Cynthia Weber (eds.), *State Sovereignty as a Social Construct* (Cambridge: Cambridge University Press, 1996).

59. For a description of the political economy of this era which has become important in the context of neorealist scholarship, see Charles Kindleberger, *The World in Depression, 1929–1939* (Berkeley: University of California Press, 1986).
60. For a development of the notion of the imperial metropole see Michael Doyle, *Empires.*
61. For recent identity based arguments in the Balkan case see Franke Wilmer, "Identity, Culture and Historicity: The Social Construction of Identity in the Balkans," *World Affairs* 60 (1) (Summer 1997): 3–16 and Mariia Nikoleava Todorova, *Imagining the Balkans* (New York: Oxford University Press, 1997).
62. A significant glimpse at this debate may be found in the following recent arguments. See Charles G. Boy, "Making Peace with the Guilty," *Foreign Affairs* 74 (5) (1995): 22–38; Arthur Schlesinger, Jr., "Back to the Womb?," *Foreign Affairs* 74 (4) (1995): 2–8; Misha Glenny, "Heading Off War in the Southern Balkans," *Foreign Affairs* 74 (3) (1995): 98–108; and Richard Holbrooke, "America, A European Power," *Foreign Affairs* 74 (2) (1995): 38–51.
63. See, for example, the following recent contributions. G. John Ikenberry, "Funk de Siècle: Impasses of Western Industrial Society at Century's End," *Millennium: Journal of International Relations* 24 (1) (1995): 113–26. Vincent Cable, "The Diminished Nation-State: A Study in the Loss of Economic Power," *Daedalus* 124 (2) (Spring 1995): 23–53. Jürgen Habermas, "Citizenship and National Identity: Some Reflections on the Future of Europe."
64. See Immanuel Kant, "Perpetual Peace: A Philosophical Sketch" in Hans Reiss (ed.), *Kant: Political Writings* (trans. H. B. Nisbet), Second Enlarged Edition (Cambridge: Cambridge University Press, 1991), pp. 93–130.
65. See Francis Fukuyama, "The End of History?," *The National Interest*, No. 16 (Summer 1989), pp. 3–18.
66. Tony Judt, "The Social Question *Redivivus*," *Foreign Affairs* 76 (5) (1997): 95–117.
67. See, for example, the collection of essays in James H. Mittleman (ed.), *Globalization: Critical Reflections* (Boulder: Lynne Rienner, 1997).
68. For the reasons for these difficulties see Cecelia Lynch, "Social Movements and the Problem of 'Globalization'," *Alternatives*, 23 (2) April–June (1998): 149–73.
69. See, for example, R. Burbach, O. Núñez and B. Kagarlitsky, *Globalization and its Discontents: The Rise of Postmodern Socialisms* (London and Chicago: Pluto Press, 1997).
70. Alexander Wendt, "Anarchy is What States Make of It."

71. Onuf, *World of Our Making.*
72. Yale H. Ferguson and Richard W. Mansbach, *Polities: Authority, Identity, and Change* (Columbia: University of South Carolina Press, 1996).
73. Richard Ashley criticizes structural realism and neorealism for a tendency to assert that the international political realm is "amoral" in the most severe terms in Ashley, "The Poverty of Neorealism." Gilpin refutes Ashley's argument in Robert Gilpin, "The Richness of the Tradition of Political Realism," in Robert O. Keohane (ed.), *Neorealism and Its Critics* (New York: Columbia University Press, 1986), pp. 301–21.
74. For a discussion of the current "politics of secession" see Robert B. Reich, *The Work of Nations: Preparing Ourselves for 21st Century Capitalism* (New York: Vintage Books, 1992).
75. Walker suggests that segmentation by the principle of state sovereignty, for example, provides these convenient ethical blinders in the contemporary international system. See R. B. J. Walker, *Inside / Outside: International Relations as Political Theory* (Cambridge: Cambridge University Press, 1993), p. 67.

Bibliography

Alker, Hayward. *Rediscoveries and Reformulations: Humanistic Methodologies for International Studies*. Cambridge: Cambridge University Press, 1996.

Almond, Gabriel. "The Return to the State." *American Political Science Review* 82 (3) (1988): 853–74.

Anderson, Benedict. *Imagined Communities: Reflections on the Origins and Spread of Nationalism*. London: Verso, 1983.

Arendt, Hannah. *The Origins of Totalitarianism*. New York: Harcourt, 1951.

Armour, Ian D. "The Roots of Sarajevo: Austria-Hungary and Serbia, 1867–81." *History Today* 38 (August 1988): 12–19.

Aron, Raymond. *Peace and War: A Theory of International Relations*. New York: Praeger, 1966.

Aronson, Theo. *The Fall of the Third Napoleon*. Indianapolis: Bobbs-Merrill, 1970.

Ashley, Richard K. "The Poverty of Neorealism." In Robert O. Keohane (ed.). *Neorealism and its Critics*. New York: Columbia University Press, 1986, pp. 255–300.

Audoin-Rouzeau, Stéphane. *Men at War 1914–1918: National Sentiment and Trench Journalism in France during the First World War*. (trans. Helen McPhail) Providence and Oxford: Berg, 1992.

Axelrod, Robert. *The Evolution of Cooperation*. New York: Basic Books, 1984.

Baldwin, David A. *Economic Statecraft*. Princeton: Princeton University Press, 1985.

Barber, Benjamin. *Jihad vs. McWorld: How Globalism and Tribalism are Reshaping the World*. New York: Ballantine, 1996.

Barkin, J. Samuel and Bruce Cronin. "The State and the Nation: Changing Norms and the Rules of Sovereignty in International Relations." *International Organization* 48 (1) (1994): 107–30.

Barnett, Michael N. "Sovereignty, Nationalism and Regional Order in the Arab States System." *International Organization* 49 (3) (1995): 479–510.

Baskerville, E.J. "John Ponet in Exile: A Ponet Letter to John Bale." *Journal of Ecclesiastical History* 37 (3) (1986): 442–47.

Becker, Carl L. *The Heavenly City of the Eighteenth-Century Philosophers*. New Haven: Yale University Press, 1932.

Becker, Jean-Jacques. "That's the Death Knell of Our Boys" in Patrick Fridenson (ed.), *The French Home Front: 1914–1918*. Providence and Oxford: Berg, 1992, pp. 17–36.

Beckett, Ian F. W. "Total War." In C. Emsley, A. Marwick and W. Simpson (eds.), *War, Peace and Social Change in Twentieth Century Europe*. Philadelphia: Open University Press, 1989, pp. 26–44.

Beik, Paul H. *A Judgment of the Old Regime: Being a Survey by the Parlement of Provence of French Economic and Fiscal Politics at the Close of the Seven Years War*. New York: AMS, 1967.

Bertraud, J. P. *The Army of the French Revolution: From Citizen-Soldiers to Instrument of Power*. Princeton: Princeton University Press, 1988.

Biersteker, Thomas J. and Cynthia Weber (eds.). *State Sovereignty as a Social Construct*. Cambridge: Cambridge University Press, 1990.

Billington, James H. *Russia Transformed: Breakthrough to Hope*. New York: Free Press, 1992.

Bion, W. R. *Experiences in Groups*. New York: Basic Books, 1959.

Black, Conrad. "Canada's Continuing Identity Crisis." *Foreign Affairs* 74 (2) (1995): 99–115.

Black, Jeremy (ed.). *The Origins of War in Early Modern Europe*. Edinburgh: John Donald, 1987.

Black, Jeremy. *Eighteenth Century Europe 1700–1789*. New York: St. Martin's Press, 1990.

Black, Jeremy. "Chatham Revisited." *History Today* 41 (August 1991): 34–39.

Bloom, William. *Personal Identity, National Identity and International Relations*. Cambridge: Cambridge University Press, 1990.

Bonnell, Victoria E. "The Iconography of the Worker in Soviet Political Art" in Lewis H. Siegelbaum and Ronald Grigor Suny (eds.), *Making Workers Soviet: Power, Class and Identity*. Ithaca: Cornell University Press, 1994, pp. 341–75.

Bowen, Catherine Drinker. *Miracle at Philadelphia: The Story of the Constitutional Convention, May to September 1787*. Boston: Little, Brown, 1966.

Boy, Charles G. "Making Peace with the Guilty." *Foreign Affairs* 74 (5) (1995): 22–38.

Brewer, Anthony *Marxist Theories of Imperialism: A Critical Survey*. (2nd ed.) London: Routledge, 1990.

Brown, Chris. *International Relations Theory: New Normative Approaches*. New York: Columbia University Press, 1993.

Brown, Dee Alexander. *Bury My Heart at Wounded Knee: An Indian History of the American West*. New York: Holt, 1970.

Brubaker, Rogers. "Nationhood and the National Question in the Soviet Union and its Successor States: An Institutionalist Account." In Rogers Brubaker, *Nationalism Reframed: Nationhood and the National Question in the New Europe*. Cambridge: Cambridge University Press, 1996, pp. 23–54.

Brubaker, Rogers. *Citizenship and Nationhood in France and Germany*. Cambridge: Harvard University Press, 1992.

Bueno de Mesquita, Bruce. *The War Trap*. New Haven: Yale University Press, 1981.

Bukovansky, Mlada. "American Identity and Neutral Rights From Independence to the War of 1812." *International Organization* 51 (2) (1997): 209–43.

Bull, Hedley. *The Anarchical Society: A Study of Order in World Politics*. New York: Columbia University Press, 1977.

Bull, Hedley and Adam Watson (eds.) *The Expansion of International Society*. Oxford: Clarendon Press, 1984.

Burbach R., O. Núñez and B. Kagarlitsky, *Globalization and its Discontents: The Rise of Postmodern Socialisms*. London and Chicago: Pluto Press, 1997.

Buzan, Barry, Richard Little and Charles Jones. *The Logic of Anarchy*. New York: Columbia University Press, 1993.

Buzan, Barry. "From International System to International Society: Structural Realism and Regime Theory Meet the English School." *International Organization* 47 (3) (1993): 327–52.

Cable, Vincent. "The Diminished Nation-State: A Study in the Loss of Economic Power." *Daedalus* 124 (2) (Spring 1995): 23–53.

Cannon, John (ed.). *The Whig Ascendancy: Colloquies on Hanoverian England*. New York: St. Martin's, 1981.

Carr, Edward Hallett. *Nationalism and After*. London: Macmillan, 1945.

Carr, Edward Hallett. *The Twenty Years' Crisis, 1919–1939: An Introduction to the Study of International Relations* (2nd ed.) New York: Harper, 1964.

Chickering, Roger. *Imperial Germany and a World Without War*. Princeton: Princeton University Press, 1975.

Chickering, Roger. *We Men Who Feel Most German: A Cultural Study of the Pan-German League, 1886–1914*. London: Allen & Unwin, 1984.

Chrisman, Mariam U. "Printing and the Evolution of Lay Culture in Strasbourg: 1480- 1599" in R. Po-Chia Hsia (ed.). *The German People and the Reformation*. Ithaca: Cornell University Press, 1988, pp. 74–101.

Churchill, Winston S. *The Hinge of Fate*. Boston: Houghton Mifflin, 1950.

Churchill, Winston S. *Closing the Ring*. Boston: Houghton Mifflin, 1951.

Churchill, Winston S. *Triumph and Tragedy*. Boston: Houghton Mifflin, 1953.

Coetzee, Marilyn Shevin, *The German Army League: Popular Nationalism in Wilhelmine Germany*. New York: Oxford University Press, 1990.

Cohn, Bernard S. "Representing Authority in Victorian India." In Eric Hobsbawm and Terence Ranger (eds.), *The Invention of Tradition*. Cambridge: Cambridge University Press, 1983, pp. 165–209.

Cohn, Norman. *The Pursuit of the Millennium: Revolutionary Millenarians and Mystical Anarchists of the Middle Ages* (rev. ed., expanded). New York: Oxford University Press, 1970.

Colton, Timothy J. *The Dilemma of Reform in the Soviet Union* (rev. ed., expanded) New York: Council on Foreign Relations, 1986.

Commager, Henry Steele and Richard B. Morris (eds). *The Spirit of Seventy-Six: The Story of the American Revolution as Told by Participants*. New York: Bonanza Books, 1983.

Conner, Walker. "The Nation and its Myth" *International Journal of Comparative Sociology* 33 (1992): 48–57.

Conquest, Robert. *The Harvest of Sorrow: Soviet Collectivization and the Terror-Famine*. New York: Oxford University Press, 1986.

Conquest, Robert. *The Great Terror: A Reassessment*. New York: Oxford University Press, 1990.

Corbett, Julian S. *England in the Seven Years' War: A Study in Combined Strategy*, 2 vols. London: Longmans, Green, 1918. Reprint: New York: AMS Press, 1973.

Cox, Robert W. "Social Forces, States and World Orders: Beyond International Relations Theory." In Robert O. Keohane (ed.). *Neorealism and its Critics*. New York: Columbia University Press, 1986, pp. 204–54.

Cressy, David. "National Memory in Early Modern England." In John R. Gillis (ed.), *Commemorations: The Politics of National Identity*. Princeton: Princeton University Press, 1994, pp. 61–73.

Daniels, Robert V. (ed.), *The Stalin Revolution: Foundations of Soviet Totalitarianism*. Lexington: D. C. Heath. 1972.

Dawisha, Karen and Bruce Parrott. *Russia and the New States of Eurasia: The Politics of Upheaval*. Cambridge: Cambridge University Press, 1994.

Deibert, Ronald J. "Typographica: The Medium and the Medieval-to-Modern Transformation." *Review of International Studies* (22) (1996): 29–56.

Deibert, Ronald J. *Parchment, Printing, and Hypermedia: Communication in World Order Transformation*. New York: Columbia University Press, 1997.

Dessler, David, "What is at Stake in the Agent-Structure Debate?" *International Organization* 43 (Summer 1989): 441–74.

Deudney, Daniel H. "The Philadelphia System." *International Organization* 49 (2) (1995): 191–228.

Deudney, Daniel. "Nuclear Weapons and the Waning of the Real-State." *Daedalus* 124 (2) (Spring 1994): 209–29.

Deutsch, Karl W. *Nationalism and Social Communication: An Inquiry Into the Foundations of Nationality* (2nd ed.) Cambridge: MIT Press, 1966.

Deutscher, Isaac. *Stalin: A Political Biography* (2nd ed.) New York: Oxford University Press, 1968.

Druckman, Daniel. "Nationalism, Patriotism, and Group Loyalty: A Social Psychological Perspective." *Mershon International Studies Review*. (Supplement to the *International Studies Quarterly*) 38, Supplement 1 (April 1994): 43–66.

Dickens, A.G. *The German Nation and Martin Luther*. London: Edward Arnold, 1974.

Dickinson, H. T. "Whiggism in the Eighteenth Century." In John Cannon (ed.). *The Whig Ascendancy: Coloquies on Hanoverian England*. New York: St. Martin's Press, 1981, pp. 28–50.

Doyle, Michael. *Empires*. Ithaca: Cornell University Press, 1986.

Duby, Georges. *The Three Orders: Feudal Society Imagined*. trans. (Arthur Goldhammer), Chicago: University of Chicago Press, 1980.

Durkheim, Emile. *Sociology and Philosophy*. Trans. (D.F. Pocock). New York: Free Press, 1953.

Earle, Edward Mead. "Adam Smith, Alexander Hamilton, Friedrich List: The Economic Foundation of Military Power." In Edward Mead Earle (ed.), *Makers of Modern Strategy: Military Thought From Machiavelli to Hitler*. Princeton: Princeton University Press, 1973, pp. 117–54.

Eldon, Carl William. *England's Subsidy Policy Towards the Continent During the Seven Years' War*. Ph. D. Dissertation: University of Pennsylvania, Philadelphia, 1938.

Eldridge, C. C. *England's Mission: The Imperial Idea in the Age of Gladstone and Disraeli 1868–1880*. London: Macmillan, 1973.

Eley, Geoff. "Reshaping the Right: Radical Nationalism and the German Navy League, 1898–1908." *Historical Journal* (21) (1978): 327–54.

Eley, Geoff. *Reshaping the German Right: Radical Nationalism and Political Change after Bismarck*. New Haven: Yale University Press, 1980.

Emsley, Clive., A. Marwick and W. Simpson (eds.), *War, Peace and Social Change in Twentieth Century Europe*. Philadelphia: Open University Press, 1989.

Erikson, Erik H. *Identity: Youth and Crisis*. New York: Norton, 1968.

Evans, R.J.W. and Martmut Pogge von Strandmann, *The Coming of the First World War*. Oxford: Clarendon Press, 1988.

Eyck, Eric. *Bismarck and the German Empire*. New York: Norton, 1968.

Ferguson, Yale H. and Richard W. Mansbach. *Politics: Authority, Identities and Change*. Columbia, S.C.: University of South Carolina Press, 1996.

Ferris, John Robert. *Men, Money, and Diplomacy: The Evolution of British Strategic Foreign Policy, 1919–1926*. Ithaca: Cornell University Press, 1989.

Fischer, Fritz. *Germany's Aims in the First World War*. New York: Norton, 1967.

Fischer, Fritz. *World Power or Decline: The Controversy Over Germany's Aims in the First World War*. (trans. L. L. Farrar, Robert Kimber and Rita Kimber), New York: Norton, 1974.

Fischer, Fritz. *War of Illusions: German Policies from 1911 to 1914*. (trans. Marian Jackson) New York: Norton, 1975.

Forrest, Alan. *Conscripts and Deserters: The Army and French Society During the Revolution and Empire*. Oxford: Oxford University Press, 1989.

Frey, Frederick. "The Problem of Actor Designation in Political Analysis" *Comparative Politics* 17 (2) (1985).

Fridenson, Patrick (ed.). *The French Home Front: 1914–1918*. Providence and Oxford: Berg, 1992.

Friedberg, Aaron L. *The Weary Titan: Britain and the Experience of Relative Decline, 1895–1905*. Princeton: Princeton University Press, 1988.

Fukuyama, Francis. "The End of History?" *The National Interest*. No. 16 (Summer 1989): 3–18.

Gaddis, John Lewis. "International Relations Theory and the End of the Cold War." *International Security* 17 (3) (Winter 1992/93): 5–58.

Gann, Lewis H. "Marginal Colonialism: The German Case." In Arthur J. Knoll and Lewis H. Gann (eds.) *Germans in the Tropics: Essays in German Colonial History*. Westport: Greenwood, 1987, pp. 1–18.

Gellner, Ernest. *Thought and Change*. London: Weidenfeld and Nicholson, 1964.

Gellner, Ernest. *Nations and Nationalism*. Ithaca: Cornell University Press, 1983.

Gillis, John R. (ed.), *Commemorations: The Politics of National Identity*. Princeton: Princeton University Press, 1994.

Gilpin, Robert. *War and Change in World Politics*. Cambridge: Cambridge University Press, 1981.

Gilpin, Robert. "The Richness of the Tradition of Political Realism." In Robert O. Keohane (ed.), *Neorealism and Its Critics*. New York: Columbia University Press, 1986, pp. 301–21.

Gilpin, Robert. *The Political Economy of International Relations*. Princeton: Princeton University Press, 1987.

Glenny, Misha. "Heading Off War in the Southern Balkans." *Foreign Affairs* 74 (3) (1995): 98–108.

Gordon, Michael R. "Domestic Conflict and the Origins of the First World War: the British and the German Cases." In C. Emsley, A. Marwick and W. Simpson (eds.), *War, Peace and Social Change in Twentieth Century Europe*. Philadelphia: Open University Press, 1989, pp. 89–101.

Gramsci, Antonio. *Selections from the Prison Notebooks*. Q. Hoare and G. N. Smith (eds. & trans.) New York: International Publishers, 1971.

Greenfeld, Liah. *Nationalism: Five Roads to Modernity*. Cambridge: Harvard University Press, 1992.

Greengrass, Mark. *The French Reformation*. Oxford: Basil Blackwell, 1987.

Griffiths, Martin. *Realism, Idealism and International Politics: A Reinterpretation*. London: Routledge, 1992.

Group for the Advancement of Psychiatry, Report no. 123, *Us and Them, The Psychology of Ethnonationalism*. New York: Brunner/Mazel, 1987.

Haag, John. "Students at the University of Vienna in the First World War." *Central European History* 17 (4) (1984): 299–309.

Habermas, Jürgen. *Legitimation Crisis*. Thomas McCarthy (trans.), Boston: Beacon, 1975

Habermas, Jürgen. "Citizenship and National Identity: Some Reflections on the Future of Europe." In Ronald Beiner (ed.) *Theorizing Citizenship*. Albany: SUNY Press, 1995, pp. 255–282.

Hall, Rodney Bruce and Friedrich V. Kratochwil, "Medieval Tales: Neorealist 'Science' and the Abuse of History." *International Organization* 47 (3): 479–91.

Hall, Rodney Bruce. "Moral Authority as a Power Resource." *International Organization* 51 (4) (1997): 591–622.

Handelman, Stephen. *Comrade Criminal: Russia's New Mafiya*. New Haven: Yale University Press, 1995.

Harper, Lawrence A. "The Effect of the Navigation Acts on the Thirteen Colonies." In Richard B. Morris (ed.), *The Era of the American Revolution: Studies Inscribed to Evarts Boutell Greene*. New York: Columbia University Press, 1939, pp. 3–39.

Hayes, Carleton J. H. A *Generation of Materialism, 1871–1900*. New York: Harper, 1941.

Hayes, Carleton J. H. *Nationalism: A Religion*. New York: Macmillan, 1960.

Herz, John H. "Rise and Demise of the Territorial State." *World Politics* 9 (4) (1957): 473–93.

Himmelstein, J. L. and Micheal Kimmel, "Review Essay: States and Social Revolutions: The Limits and Implications of Skocpol's Structural Model." *American Journal of Sociology* 86 (5) (1981): 1145–54.

Hischman, Albert O. *National Power and the Structure of Foreign Trade*. Berkeley: University of California Press, 1945.

Hobsbawm, E.J. *The Age of Revolution*. London: Weidenfeld and Nicholson, 1962.

Hobsbawm, E.J. *The Age of Capital: 1848–1875*. New York: Scribner's, 1975.

Hobsbawm, E.J. and Terence Ranger (eds.), *The Invention of Tradition*. Cambridge: Cambridge University Press, 1983.

Hobsbawm, E.J. "Mass-Producing Traditions: Europe, 1870–1914" in Eric Hobsbawm and Terence Ranger (eds.), *The Invention of Tradition*. Cambridge: Cambridge University Press, 1983, pp. 263–307.

Hobsbawm, E.J. *The Age of Empire: 1875–1914*. New York: Random House, 1987.

Hobsbawm, E.J. *Nations and Nationalism Since 1780: Programme, Myth, Reality* (2nd ed.) Cambridge: Cambridge University Press, 1990.

Hobsbawm, E.J. *The Age of Extremes: A History of the World, 1914–1991*. New York: Random House, 1996.

Hobson, J.A. "Imperialism: A Study." In Harrison M. Wright (ed.), *The New Impe-*

rialism: Analysis of Late-Nineteenth-Century Expansion (2nd ed.) Lexington, MA: D.C. Heath, 1976, pp. 5–44.

Hoffman, Stanley (ed.) *Contemporary Theory in International Relations*. Englewood Cliffs, N.J.: Prentice-Hall, 1960.

Holbrooke, Richard. "America, A European Power." *Foreign Affairs* 74 (2) (1995): 38–51.

Holmes, Geoffrey and Daniel Szechi, *The Age of Oligarchy: Pre-industrial Britain 1722- 1783*. London: Longmans, 1993.

Holsti, Kalevi J. *Peace and War: Armed Conflicts and International Order 1648–1989*. Cambridge: Cambridge University Press, 1991.

Howard, Michael. *The Franco-Prussian War: The German Invasion of France, 1870–1871*. New York: Collier Books, 1969.

Howard, Michael. "Europe on the Eve of the First World War." In R. J. W. Evans and Martmut Pogge von Strandmann, *The Coming of the First World War*. Oxford: Clarendon Press, 1988, pp. 1–18.

Hsia, R. Po-Chia. "Munster and the Anabaptists." In R. Po-Chia Hsia (ed.). *The German People and the Reformation*. Ithaca: Cornell University Press, 1988, pp. 51–69.

Huntington, Samuel P. *Political Order in Changing Societies*. New Haven: Yale University Press, 1968.

Ikenberry, G. John. "Funk de Siècle: Impasses of Western Industrial Society at Century's End." *Millennium: Journal of International Relations* 24 (1) (1995): 113-26.

Jackson, Robert. "Quasi-states, Dual Regimes, and Neoclassical Theory: International Jurisprudence and the Third World." *International Organization* 41. No. 4, (1987): 519–50.

Jarausch, Konrad H. "German Students in the First World War." *Central European History* 17 (4) December (1984): 310–29.

Jennings, Francis. *Empire of Fortune: Crowns, Colonies and Tribes in the Seven Years' War in America*. New York: Norton, 1988.

Jervis, Robert. "Cooperation Under the Security Dilemma" *World Politics*. 1978, pp. 167–214.

Jervis, Robert. "From Balance to Concert: A Study of International Security Cooperation." In Kenneth A. Oye (ed.), *Cooperation Under Anarchy*. Princeton: Princeton University Press, 1986, pp. 58–79.

Johnson, Douglass. "The Making of the French Nation." In Mikulas Teich and Roy Porter (eds.), *The National Question in Europe in Historical Context*. Cambridge: Cambridge University Press, 1993, pp. 35–62.

Judt, Tony. "The Social Question Redivivus." *Foreign Affairs* 76 (5) (1997): 95–117.

Kann, Robert A. A *History of the Habsburg Empire 1526–1918*. Berkeley: University of California Press, 1974.

Kant, Immanuel. "Perpetual Peace: A Philosophical Sketch" in Hans Reiss (ed.), *Kant: Political Writings* (trans. H. B. Nisbet) (2nd ed., enlarged) Cambridge: Cambridge University Press, 1991, pp. 93–130.

Kantorowicz, Ernst. *The King's Two Bodies: A Study in Medieval Political Theology*. Princeton: Princeton University Press, 1957.

Kautsky, Karl. *The Dictatorship of the Proletariat*, National Labour Press: 1919. Reprint: Westport: Greenwood, 1981.

Kedourie, Elie. *Nationalism* (2nd ed.). London: Hutchinson, 1966.

Kennedy, Paul (ed). *The War Plans of the Great Powers, 1880–1914*. London: Allen & Unwin, 1979.

Kennedy, Paul. *The Rise and Fall of the Great Powers: Economic Change and Military Conflict From 1500–2000*. New York: Random House, 1987.

Keohane, Robert O. "Theory of World Politics: Structural Realism and Beyond" in Robert O. Keohane (ed.). *Neorealism and its Critics*. New York: Columbia University Press, 1986, pp. 158–203.

Kettering, Sharon. "Patronage and Politics During the Fronde." *French Historical Studies* 14 (3) (1986): 409–41.

Kindleberger, Charles. *The World in Depression, 1929–1939*. Berkeley: University of California Press, 1986.

Kissinger, Henry. *Diplomacy*. New York: Simon and Schuster, 1994.

Knoll, Arthur J. and Lewis H. Gann (eds.). *Germans in the Tropics: Essays in German Colonial History*. Westport: Greenwood, 1987.

Knorr, Klaus E. *British Colonial Theories 1570–1850*. Toronto: University of Toronto Press, 1944.

Kohn, Hans. *Nationalism and Imperialism in the Hither East*. Margeret M. Green (trans.), London: Routledge, 1932.

Kohn, Hans. *The Idea of Nationalism: A Study of its Origins and Background*. New York: Collier Books, 1967.

Kohut, Thomas A. *Wilhelm II and the Germans: A Study in Leadership*. New York: Oxford University Press, 1991.

Kornhauser, William. *The Politics of Mass Society*. New York: Free Press, 1959.

Koslowski, Rey and Friedrich V. Kratochwil, "Understanding Change in International Politics: the Soviet Empire's Demise and the International System." *International Organization* 48 (2) (1994): 215–47.

Krasner, Stephen D. (ed.). *International Regimes*. Ithaca: Cornell University Press, 1983.

Krasner, Stephen D. "Approaches to the State: Alternative Conceptions and Historical Dynamics." *Comparative Politics* 16 (2) (1984): 233–46.

Kratochwil, Friedrich. "On the Notion of 'Interest' in International Relations." *International Organization* 36 (1) (1982): 1–30.

Kratochwil, Friedrich. "Regimes, Interpretation and the 'Science' of Politics: A Reappraisal." *Millennium: Journal of International Relations* 17 (2) (1988): 263–84.

Kratochwil, Friedrich V. *Rules, Norms, and Decisions: On the Conditions of Practical and Legal Reasoning in International Relations and Domestic Affairs.* Cambridge: Cambridge University Press, 1989.

Kratochwil, Friedrich. "The Embarrassment of Changes: Neo-realism and the Science of Realpolitik Without Politics." *Review of International Studies* (19) (1993): 63–80.

Krumeich, Gerd. *Armaments and Politics in France of the Eve of the First World War: The Introduction of Three-Year Conscription 1913–14.* (trans. Stephen Coll) Warwickshire and Dover: Berg, 1984.

Kuran, Timur. "Now Out of Never: The Element of Surprise in the Eastern European Revolution of 1989." *World Politics* 44 (1) (1991): 7–48.

Lambeth, Benjamin S. "Russia's Wounded Military." *Foreign Affairs* 74 (2) 1995, pp. 86–98.

Lapid, Yosef, and Friedrich Kratochwil. "The Taming of the Shrew? Neorealist Appropriations and Theorizations of Nationalism" March 1994. Presented at the 35th ISA Annual Convention, Washington, D.C.

Lapid, Yosef, and Friedrich Kratochwil. "Revisiting the 'National': Toward an Identity Agenda in Neorealism?" in Yosef Lapid and Friedrich Kratochwil (eds.), *The Return of Culture and Identity in IR Theory*. Boulder, CO: Lynne Reinner, 1995, pp. 105–26.

Leffler, Phyllis K. "French Historians and the Challenge to Louis XIV's Absolutism." *French Historical Studies* 14 (1) (1985): 1–22.

Lenin, V.I. *Imperialism: The Highest Stage of Capitalism.* (new, revised translation), New York: International Publishers, 1939.

Lenin, V.I. "The Highest Stage of Capitalism" in Harrison M. Wright (ed.), *The New Imperialism: Analysis of Late-Nineteenth-Century Expansion* (2nd ed.), Lexington, MA: D.C. Heath, 1976, pp. 44–59.

Le Roy Ladurie, Emannuel. *The Royal French State 1460–1610* , Juliet Vale (trans.) London: Blackwell, 1994.

Levin, Carole. *Propaganda in the English Reformation: Heroic and Villainous Images of King John.* Lewistown, NY: The Edwin Mellen Press, 1988.

Lincoln, Bruce. *Passage Through Armageddon:* The Russians in War and Revolution 1914–1918. New York: Simon and Schuster, 1986.

Link, Arthur S. *Wilson the Diplomatist: A Look at His Major Foreign Policies.* The Albert Shaw Lectures on Diplomatic History, 1956. Baltimore: Johns Hopkins University Press, 1957.

Luard, Evan. *War in International Society: A Study in International Sociology.* New Haven: Yale University Press, 1987.

Luard, Evan. *The Balance of Power: The System of International Relations, 1648–1815.* New York: St. Martin's Press, 1992.

Lynch, Cecelia. "Social Movements and the Problem of 'Globalization.' " *Alternatives* 23 (2) (April–June 1998): 149–73.

Lynn, John A. *The Bayonets of the Republic: Motivation and Tactics in the Army of Revolutionary France, 1791–94*. Urbana: University of Illinois Press, 1984.

MacIntyre, Alisdair. *After Virtue: A Study in Moral Theory*. Notre Dame, Indiana: University of Notre Dame Press, 1984.

MacKenzie, John M., *Propaganda and Empire: The Manipulation of British Public Opinion, 1880–1960*. Manchester: Manchester University Press, 1984.

Major, J. Russell. "The Revolt of 1620: A Study of the Rise of Fidelity." *French Historical Studies* 14 (3) (1986): 391–407.

Malthus, Thomas. *An Essay on the Principle of Population*. (Introduction by Anthony Flew) London: Penguin, 1970.

Manceron, Claude. *The Age of the French Revolution, Volume Two: The Wind From America 1778–81*. New York: Simon and Schuster, 1989.

Mann, Michael. *The Sources of Social Power, Volume II: The Rise of Classes and Nation-States, 1760–1914*. Cambridge: Cambridge University Press, 1993.

Manning, C. A. W. *The Nature of International Society*. London: London School of Economics, 1962.

Marx, Anthony W. "Race-Making and the Nation-State." *World Politics* 48 (2) 1996, pp. 180–208.

Marx, Karl. "[Excerpts from] The Eighteenth Brumaire of Louis Napoleon." In Lewis S. Feurer (ed.). *Marx and Engels: Basic Writings on Politics and Philosophy*. New York: Doubleday, 1959, pp. 318–48.

Marx, Karl. "[Excerpts from] The Civil War in France." with Introduction by Friedrich Engels, in Lewis S. Feurer (ed.). *Marx and Engels: Basic Writings on Politics and Philosophy*. New York: Doubleday, 1959, pp. 349–91

Mayall, James. *Nationalism and International Society*. Cambridge: Cambridge University Press, 1990.

McKeown, Timothy J. "Hegemonic Stability Theory and Nineteenth Century Tariff Levels in Europe." *International Organization* 37 (1) (1983): 73–91.

Mearsheimer, John. "Back to the Future." *International Security* 15 (1) (1990): 5–56.

Meinecke, Friedrich. *Machieavellism: The Doctrine of Raison d'Etat and Its Place in Modern History*. Boulder, CO: Westview, 1984.

Messinger, Gary S. *British Propaganda and the State in the First World War*. Manchester: Manchester University Press, 1992.

Miller, John. "The Potential for 'Absolutism' in Later Stuart England." *History: The Journal of the Historical Association* 69 (226), 1984, pp. 187–207.

Milner, Helen. "The Assumption of Anarchy in International Relations Theory: A Critique." *Review of International Studies* (17) (1991): 67–85.

Mitchell, Allan. *Victors and Vanquished: The German Influence on Army and Church in France after 1870*. Chapel Hill: University of North Carolina Press, 1984.

Mitchell, Timothy. "The Limits of the State: Beyond Statist Approaches and Their Critics." *American Political Science Review* 85 (1) (1991): 77–96.

Mittleman, James H. (ed.) *Globalization: Critical Reflections*. Boulder, CO: Lynne Reinner, 1997.

Moore, Barrington. *The Social Origins of Dictatorship and Democracy*. Boston: Beacon, 1966.

Morgenthau, Hans J. *Scientific Man Versus Power Politics*. Chicago: University of Chicago Press, 1946.

Morgenthau, Hans J. *Politics Among Nations: The Struggle for Power and Peace* (fourth ed.), New York: Knopf, 1967, Chapters 11–14, pp. 161–215.

Morris Richard B. (ed.). *The Era of the American Revolution: Studies Inscribed to Evarts Boutell Greene*. New York: Columbia University Press, 1939.

Mroz John Edwin, and Oleksandr Pavliuk. "Ukraine: Europe's Linchpin." *Foreign Affairs* 75 (3) (1996): 52–62.

Nairn, Tom. *The Break-up of Britain: Crisis and Neo-Nationalism* (2nd ed.), London: New Left Books, 1977.

Nichols, J. Alden. *The Year of the Three Kaisers: Bismarck and the German Succession, 1887–88*. Urbana: University of Illinois Press, 1987.

North, Douglass C. *Structure and Change in Economic History*. New York: Norton, 1981.

O'Neil, Daniel J. "Enclave Nation-Building: The Irish Experience." *Journal of Ethnic Studies* Vol. 15 (3) (Fall 1987): 1–25.

Onuf, Nicholas Greenwood. *World of Our Making: Rules and Rule in Social Theory and International Relations*. Columbia, S.C.: University of South Carolina Press, 1989.

Organski, A. F. K. and Jacek Kugler. *The War Ledger*. Chicago: University of Chicago Press, 1980.

Osiander, Andreas. *The States System of Europe, 1640–1990: Peacemaking and the Conditions of International Stability*. Oxford: Clarendon Press, 1994.

Oye (ed.), Kenneth A. *Cooperation Under Anarchy*. Princeton: Princeton University Press, 1986.

Palmer, R. R. "Frederick the Great, Guibert, Bülow: From Dynastic to National War." In Edward Mead Earle (ed.), *Makers of Modern Strategy: Military Thought From Machiavelli to Hitler*. Princeton: Princeton University Press, 1973, pp. 49–76.

Parker, David. "Sovereignty, Absolutism and the Function of the Law in Seventeenth-Century France." *Past and Present*. No. 122 (February 1989): 36–74.

Pierard, Richard V. "The German Colonial Society." In Arthur J. Knoll and Lewis H. Gann (eds.) *Germans in the Tropics: Essays in German Colonial History*. Westport: Greenwood, 1987, pp. 19–37.

Richard Pipes, *The Formation of the Soviet Union: Communism and Nationalism 1917- 1923*. Revised edition, Cambridge: Harvard University Press, 1964.

Plato, *The Republic of Plato*. Cornford, F. M. (trans.), Oxford: Oxford University Press: 1945.

Polanyi, Karl. *The Great Transformation: The Political and Economic Origins of our Time*. Boston: Beacon, 1944.

Posen, Barry R. "Nationalism, the Mass Army, and Military Power" *International Security* 18 (2) (1993): 80–124.

Pundt, Alfred G. *Arndt and the Nationalist Awakening in Germany*. New York: AMS Press, 1968.

Ranger, Terence. "The Invention of Tradition in Colonial Africa." In Eric Hobsbawm and Terence Ranger (eds.), *The Invention of Tradition*. Cambridge: Cambridge University Press, 1983, pp. 211–62.

Reich, Robert B. *The Work of Nations: Preparing Ourselves for 21st Century Capitalism*. New York: Vintage, 1992.

Reynolds, Robert L. *Europe Emerges: Transition Toward an Industrial World-Wide Society 600–1750*. Madison: University of Wisconsin Press, 1961.

Riley, James C. *The Seven Years' War and the Old Regime in France: The Economic and Financial Toll*. Princeton: Princeton University Press, 1986.

Roberts, Stephen H. *The History of French Colonial Policy 1870–1925*. London: Frank Cass, 1963.

Robinson-Hammerstein, Helga. "Luther and the Laity." In Helga Robinson-Hammerstein (ed.), *The Transmission of Ideas in the Lutheran Reformation*. Dublin: Irish Academic Press, 1989, pp. 11–46.

Roelker, Nancy L. "The Impact of the Reformation Era on Communication and Propaganda." In Laswell, Lerener and Speier (eds.), *Propaganda and Communication in World History, II*. Honolulu: University of Hawaii Press, 1980, pp. 41–84.

Rosenberg, Justin. *The Empire of Civil Society: A Critique of the Realist Theory of International Relations*. London: Verso, 1994.

Rousseau, Jean Jacques, "On Social Contract or Principles of Political Right" in Alan Ritter and Julia Conaway Bondanella (eds.) , *Rousseau's Political Writings*. J. C. Bondanella (trans.), New York: Norton, 1988, pp. 83–173.

Rublach, Hans-Christoph. "Martin Luther and the Urban Social Experience." In Helga Robinson-Hammerstein (ed.), *The Transmission of Ideas in the Lutheran Reformation*, pp. 65–82.

Ruggie, John Gerard. "Continuity and Transformation in the World Polity: Toward a Neorealist Synthesis." In Robert O. Keohane (ed.). *Neorealism and its Critics*. New York: Columbia University Press, 1986, pp. 131–57.

Ruggie, John Gerard. "Territoriality and Beyond: Problematizing Modernity in International Relations." *International Organization* 47 (1) (1993): 139–74.

Rutman, Darrett B. "The Virginia Company and Its Military Regime." In Darrett B. Rutman (ed.). *The Old Dominion: Essays for Thomas Perkins Abernethy*. Charlottesville: University Press of Virginia, 1964, pp. 1–20.

Saunders, George (ed.). *Samizdat: Voices of the Soviet Oppostition*. New York: Pathfinder Press, 1974.

Scarisbrick, J.J. *The Reformation and the English People*. Oxford: Blackwell, 1984.

Schalk, Ellery. "Clientage, Elites, and Absolutism in Seventeenth-Century France." *French Historical Studies* 14 (3) (1986): 442–46.

Schelling, Thomas C. *The Strategy of Conflict*. Oxford: Oxford University Press, 1963.

Schlesinger, Arthur Jr., "Back to the Womb?" *Foreign Affairs* 74 (4) (1995): 2–8.

Schmitt, Bernadotte E. and Harold C. Vedeler, *The World in the Crucible: 1914–1919*. New York: Harper, 1988.

Schroeder, Paul. "A Pointless and Enduring Rivalry: France and the Habsburg Monarchy, 1715–1918." Prepared for delivery at the 1995 annual meeting of the American Political Science Association, Chicago, September 2, 1995.

Schroeder, Paul. *The Transformation of European Politics 1763–1848*. Oxford: Clarendon Press, 1994.

Schroeder, Paul. "Historical Reality vs. Neo-realist Theory." *International Security* 19 (1) (1994): 108–48.

Schulze, Hagen. *The Course of German Nationalism: From Frederick the Great to Bismarck, 1763–1867*. Cambridge: Cambridge University Press, 1991.

Schweizer, Karl. "The Seven Years' War: A System Perspective." In Jeremy Black (ed.), *The Origins of War in Early Modern Europe*. Edinburgh: John Donald, 1987, pp. 242–60.

Schumpeter, Joseph A. *Imperialism and Social Classes*. Henz Norden (trans.) New York: Augustus M. Kelley, 1951.

Scott, James C. *The Moral Economy of the Peasant: Rebellion and Subsistence in Southeast Asia*. New Haven: Yale University Press, 1976.

Scribner, Robert W. *For the Sake of Simple Folk: Popular Propaganda for the German Reformation*. Cambridge: Cambridge University Press, 1981.

Scribner, Robert. "Ritual and Reformation" in R. Po-Chia Hsia (ed.), *The German People and the Reformation*. Ithaca: Cornell University Press, 1988, pp. 122–44.

Searle, John R. *The Construction of Social Reality*. New York: Free Press, 1995.

Sewell, William H. Jr., "Ideologies and Social Revolutions: Reflections on the French Case." In Theda Skocpol, *Social Revolutions in the Modern World*. Cambridge: Cambridge University Press, 1994, pp. 169–98.

Sheehan, James J. *German History 1770–1866*. Oxford: Clarendon Press, 1989.

Siegelbaum, Lewis H. and Ronald Grigor Suny (eds.), *Making Workers Soviet: Power, Class and Identity*. Ithaca: Cornell University Press, 1994.

Skocpol, Theda. *States and Social Revolutions: A Comparative Analysis of France, Russia, and China*. Cambridge: Cambridge University Press, 1979.

Skocpol, Theda. "Bringing the State Back In: Strategies of Analysis in Current Research" in Evans, Reuschmeyer and Skocpol (eds.) *Bringing the State Back In*. Cambridge: Cambridge University Press, 1985, pp. 3–37.

Skocpol, Theda. *Social Revolutions in the Modern World*. Cambridge: Cambridge University Press, 1994.

Smith, Adam. *An Inquiry into the Nature and Causes of the Wealth of Nations: Vols. I and II*. R. H. Campbell and A. S. Skinner (eds.), Indianapolis: Liberty Press, 1981.

Smith, Anthony D. "The Origins of Nations." *Ethnic and Racial Studies* 12 (3) (1989): 349–56.

Smith, Anthony D. *The Ethnic Revival*. Cambridge: Cambridge University Press, 1991.

Smith, Anthony D. *National Identity*. Reno: University of Nevada Press, 1991.

Smith, Anthony D. "The Problem of National Identity: Ancient, Medieval and Modern?" *Ethnic and Racial Studies* 17 (3) July (1994): 375–99.

Smith, Hedrick. *The New Russians*. New York: Random House, 1990.

Smith, Woodruff D. *European Imperialism in the Nineteenth and Twentieth Centuries*. Chicago: Nelson-Hall, 1982.

Snyder, Louis. *German Nationalism: The Tragedy of a People, Extremism Contra Liberalism in Modern German History*. Harrisburg: Telegraph Press, 1953.

Solzhenitsyn, Aleksandr. *The GULAG Archipelago 1918–1956: An Experiment in Literary Investigation*. New York: Harper, 1973.

Spruyt, Hendrik . *The Sovereign State and Its Competitors: An Analysis of Systems Change*. Princeton: Princeton University Press, 1994.

Spruyt, Hendrik . "Institutional Selection in International Relations." *International Organization* 48 (4) (1994): 527–57.

Staniland, Martin. *What is Political Economy? A Study of Social Theory and Underdevelopment*. New Haven: Yale University Press, 1985.

Starr, Frederick S. "Soviet Union: A Civil Society." *Foreign Policy*. No. 70 (Spring 1988): 26–41.

Steinberg, Mark D. "Vanguard Workers and the Morality of Class." In Lewis H. Siegelbaum and Ronald Grigor Suny (eds.), *Making Workers Soviet: Power, Class and Identity*. Ithaca: Cornell University Press, 1994, pp. 66–84.

Stoecker, Helmuth. "The Position of Africans in the German Colonies." In Arthur J. Knoll and Lewis H. Gann (eds.) *Germans in the Tropics: Essays in German Colonial History*. Westport: Greenwood, 1987, pp. 119–30.

Strauss, Gerald. *Manifestations of Discontent in Germany on the Eve of the Reformation*. Bloomington: Indiana University Press, 1971.

Strauss, Gerald. *Luther's House of Learning: Indoctrination of the Young in the German Reformation*. Baltimore: Johns Hopkins University Press, 1978.

Strauss, Gerald. "The Reformation and its Public in the Age of Orthodoxy" in R. Po-Chia Hsia (ed.) *The German People and the Reformation*. Ithaca: Cornell University Press, 1988, pp. 194–215.

Strayer, Joseph. *On the Medieval Origins of the Modern State*. Princeton: Princeton University Press, 1970.

Suny, Ronald Grigor. *The Revenge of the Past: Nationalism, Revolution, and the Collapse of the Soviet Union*. Stanford: Stanford University Press, 1993.

Swanson, R. N. *Church and Society in Late Medieval England*. Oxford: Blackwell, 1989.

Sweet, David. "The Domestic Scene: Parliament and People." In Peter H. Liddle (ed.), *Home Fires and Foreign Fields: British Social and Military Experience in the First World War*. London: Brassey's Defence Publishers, 1985, pp. 9–20.

Szporluk, Roman (ed.). *National Identity and Ethnicity in Russia and the New States of Eurasia*. Armonk: M. E. Sharpe, 1994.

Tamir, Yael. *Liberal Nationalism*. Princeton: Princeton University Press, 1993.

Taylor, A.J.P. *Germany's First Bid for Colonies 1884–1885: A Move in Bismarck's European Policy*. New York: Macmillan, 1967.

Teich, Mikulas and Roy Porter (eds.). *The National Question in Europe in Historical Context*. Cambridge: Cambridge University Press, 1993.

Tilly, Charles. "Reflections on the History of European State-Making." In Charles Tilly (ed.). *The Formation of National States in Western Europe*. Princeton: Princeton University Press, 1975, pp. 3–84.

Tilly, Charles. "National Self-Determination as a Problem for All of Us." *Daedalus*. 122 (3) (1993): 29–35.

Tocqueville, Alexis de. *The Old Regime and the French Revolution*. New York: Doubleday, 1955.

Todorova, Maria Nikoleava. *Imagining the Balkans*. New York: Oxford University Press, 1997.

Trevelyan, G.M. *The English Revolution 1688–1689*. New York: Oxford University Press, 1965.

Tuchman, Barbara W. *The Proud Tower: A Portrait of the World Before the War: 1890–1914*. New York: Macmillan, 1966.

Tucker, Robert C. *The Soviet Political Mind: Stalinism and Post-Stalin Change*. Revised edition, New York: Norton, 1971.

Tucker, Robert C. *Stalin as a Revolutionary 1879–1929*. New York: Norton, 1973.

Tucker, Robert C. *Stalin in Power: The Revolution from Above, 1928–1941*. New York: Norton, 1990.

Ulam, Adam B. *The Bolsheviks: The Intellectual, Personal and Political History of the Triumph of Communism in Russia*. New York: Collier Books, 1965.

Ulam, Adam B. *Russia's Failed Revolutions: From the Decembrists to the Dissidents*. London: Weidenfeld & Nicholson, 1981.

Van Evera, Stephen. "Why Cooperation Failed in 1914." In Kenneth A. Oye (ed.), *Cooperation Under Anarchy*. Princeton: Princeton University Press, 1985, pp. 80-117.

Volkan, Vamik D. *Cyprus-War and Adaptation: A Psychoanalytic History of Two Ethnic Groups in Conflict*. Charlottesville: University Press of Virginia, 1979.

Volkan, Vamik D. *The Need to Have Enemies and Allies*. Northvale: Jason Aronson, 1988.

Von Laue, Theodore H. *The World Revolution of Westernization: The Twentieth Century in Global Perspective*. Oxford: Oxford University Press, 1987.

Waever, Ole. Barry Buzan, Morten Kelstrup and Pierre Lamaitre, *Identity, Migration and the New Security Agenda in Europe*. New York: St. Martin's Press, 1993.

Walker, R. B. J. *Inside / Outside: International Relations as Political Theory*. Cambridge: Cambridge University Press, 1993.

Walt, Stephen M. *Revoution and War*. Ithaca: Cornell University Press, 1996.

Waltz, Kenneth N. *Man the State and War: A Theoretical Analysis*. New York: Columbia University Press, 1959.

Waltz, Kenneth N. *Theory of International Politics*. New York: Random House, 1979.

Walzer, Micheal. "The Civil Society Argument." In Ronald Beiner (ed.), *Theorizing Citizenship*. Albany: SUNY Press, 1995, pp. 153–74.

Watson, Adam. *The Evolution of International Society: A Comparative Historical Analysis*. London: Routledge, 1992.

Weber, Eugen. *Peasants Into Frenchmen: The Modernization of Rural France 1870–1914*. Stanford: Stanford University Press, 1976.

Weber, Max. "The Nation." In *From Max Weber: Essays in Sociology*. H. H. Gerth and C. Wright-Mills (trans. and ed.), London: Routledge 1948, pp. 171–79.

Weber, Max. *The Theory of Social and Economic Organization*. Translated by A. M. Henderson and Talcott Parsons, Edited with an Introduction by Talcott Parsons, London: Collier-Macmillan, 1964.

Weeks, William Earl. "American Nationalism, American Imperialism: An Interpretation of United States Political Economy, 1789–1861." *Journal of the Early Republic* 14 (Winter 1994): 485–95.

Weiner, Michael. "Discourses of Race, Nation and Empire in pre-1945 Japan." *Ethnic and Racial Studies* 18 (3) (1995): 433–56.

Wendt, Alexander, "The Agent-Structure Problem in International Relations Theory." *International Organization* 41 (3) (1987): 335–70.

Wendt, Alexander. "Anarchy is What States Make of It: The Social Construction of Power Politics." *International Organization* 46. No. 2., (1992): 391–425.

Wight, Martin. *Systems of States*. Leicester: Leicester University Press, 1977.

Wilmer, Franke. "Identity, Culture and Historicity: The Social Construction of identity in the Balkans." *World Affairs* 160 (1) (Summer 1997): 3–16.

Wilson, Peter. "The English School of International Relations: A Reply to Sheila Grader." *Review of International Studies* 15, January (1989): 49–58.

Winkler, Heinrich August. "Nationalism and Nation-State in Germany." In M. Teich and R. Porter (eds.), *The National Question in Europe in Historical Context*. Cambridge: Cambridge University Press, 1993, pp. 181–95.

Wistrich, Robert. *Trotsky: Fate of a Revolutionary*. Briarcliff Manor, NY: Stein and Day, 1979.

Woloch, Isser. *Eighteenth-Century Europe: Tradition and Progress 1715–1789*. New York: Norton, 1982.

Woloch, Isser. "Napoleonic Conscription: State Power and Civil Society." *Past and Present* 111 (May 1986): 101–29.

Woloch, Isser. *The New Regime: Transformations of the French Civic Order, 1789–1820*. New York: Norton, 1994.

Wright, Harrison M. (ed.), *The New Imperialism: Analysis of Late-Nineteenth-Century Expansion* (2nd ed.), Lexington, MA: D.C. Heath, 1976.

Zaprudnik, Jan. "Development of Belarusian National Identity and Its Influence on Belarus's Foreign Policy Orientation." In Roman Szporluk (ed.), *National Identity and Ethnicity in Russia and the New States of Eurasia*. Armonk, NY: M. E. Sharpe, 1994, pp. 129–49.

Index

Index by Alan Greenberg